Vernon Gregson, editor

The Desires
of the Human Heart

An Introduction to the
Theology of Bernard Lonergan

paulist press *new york/mahwah*

To Frederick E. Crowe, S.J.
priest, scholar, educator

Library of Congress Cataloging-in-Publication Data

The Desires of the human heart : an introduction to the theology of
  Bernard Lonergan / edited by Vernon Gregson.
     p.   cm.
  Includes bibliographies and index.
  ISBN 0-8091-3002-5 (pbk.) : $12.95
     1. Lonergan, Bernard J.F.   2. Catholic Church—Doctrines—
History—20th century.   3. Theology, Doctrinal—History—20th
century.   I. Gregson, Vernon.
BX4705.L7133D47 1988
230'.2'0924—dc19   88-18768
                                                                                          CIP

Published by Paulist Press
997 Macarthur Boulevard
Mahwah, New Jersey 07430

Printed and bound in the
United States of America

Contents

Vernon Gregson

Preface

Bernard Lonergan is widely regarded as one of the premier Catholic theologians of our time. The range of his interests, the depth of his analyses, and the integrative power of his understanding have given him an influence on Catholic theology comparable only to that of Karl Rahner. But despite his acknowledged importance and influence on a whole generation of Catholic theologians, his work, in large part, has not been easily accessible even to the broadly educated reader and to university and seminary students.

The aim of this collaborative work is to try to bridge that gap by making his key insights on theological method and on specific theological issues more widely available. Theological method has come a long way from the time when it was an obscure sub-issue, of interest only to professional theologians. Today method, both in theology and in all other disciplines, is seen as a crucial issue. Our deeper historical awareness of the shifts in cultural contexts throughout the centuries and our experience of the fruitfulness in the development of the sciences have significantly influenced that change.

These advances have made obvious that only with the appropriate method used conscientiously can we have any confidence in our own or others' conclusions. For instance, we are now aware that method structures our entire knowing and creative processes: from what we focus on in the first place, to how we move from there to our understandings and our results.

Lonergan's genius in his exploration of method is his recognition, and his capacity to help us recognize, that method is not something obscure and extrinsic to ourselves. Rather, method is precisely ourselves at our spontaneous, inquiring, and choosing best as we sift the data and the meanings of the past in order to face the issues of the present so that we may create the future.

In the course of this study, method will be seen to be identical with the deep structure of our desires: our desires to understand and to know, our desires to respond to and to create value. "When the classicist notion of culture prevails, theology is conceived as a permanent achievement, and then one discourses on its nature. When culture is conceived empirically [and historically], theology is known as an ongoing process, and one writes on its method."[1]

In a word, Lonergan's work on method explores the unfolding of our desires and, as well, the obstacles to that unfolding and our liberation from those obstacles. These inquiries into our desires, their structure, and their vicissitudes, lead Lonergan to seek the meaning and process of personal authenticity and to investigate the transformative power of religious, moral, and intellectual conversions in our lives.

Further, these inquiries lead him to explore how our authenticity is involved in our decisions to accept and/or to change our religious and secular traditions and to investigate the diversity of our traditions themselves. In this age of ever vaster accumulations of knowledge, is there an underlying unity in our desire to know or only ultimate fragmentation either in the way we know or in what we know? Are then the fields of faith, the humanities, the sciences, and everyday life finally unifiable or finally disparate?

All of these issues of faith, knowledge, and life deeply concerned Lonergan and permeate his work. On them he unfailingly sheds new light. But perhaps Lonergan's greatest contribution is the challenge he presents to us not only to know ourselves and come into possession of ourselves in a new way, but also for us to take responsible action from that new perspective.

In writing this book, the authors, following Lonergan, hope to lead you to seek your own deeper self-understanding and the expansion of your capacity to choose wisely and well. Lonergan's work can illuminate your desires and can also challenge your heart. To forward that goal, the authors, in addition, hope that their work will lead you to seek direct contact with Lonergan's own writings. His works can further aid you on your own quest, as they have aided the authors of this book on ours.

As is widely recognized, Lonergan generally sought to influence theology not directly, but through those who influence theology, namely other theologians. As a consequence, Lonergan's philosophical and theological books and articles are often, but certainly not exclusively, written in a technical, even though lively, style. This introduction to his method and to his theology will hopefully prepare you to be able to appreciate the power and insightfulness of his works directly.

Lonergan's principal works include two major studies retrieving Thomas Aquinas' insights on Grace[2] and on Word,[3] significant Latin scholastic works on the Incarnate Word[4] and on the Trinity,[5] a massive work on human understanding,[6] his ground-breaking study on theological method,[7] and three volumes of insightful and expansive occasional essays.[8] These writings reveal Lonergan's profound grasp of the richness contained in our western philosophical and theological traditions as well as his openness to other traditions. They also reveal his equally profound commitment to transpose and to broaden the received traditions in the light of the turn to the human subject characteristic of modern thought. This present book is structured to present to the reader key insights and perspectives contained in these major writings.

There are some scholars of Lonergan's thought who make a sharp distinction between Lonergan's early theological works, written in the then current seminary style, and his later work, principally on theological method. Lonergan sometimes suggests that distinction himself. The authors of this book, however, although recognizing a significant shift in Lonergan's style and definite advances and even transformations in perspective over the course of his writings, discover a common focus on understanding and a common concern with the exploration of the range of human subjectivity throughout his work. This book, therefore, will point out but will not sharply delineate his early from his later writings, except as it is important in specific instances.

The various contributors to the book write in their own styles throughout. No effort has been made to homogenize the various personal perspectives on Lonergan's thought which the authors individually have come to. This approach seemed most appropriate in a work focusing on subjectivity and aiming at evoking the reader's own subjectivity. It likewise seemed appropriate, since this approach mirrors the respect Lonergan always showed to those who integrated his work into their own theologies in their own unique ways. The authors do, however, both individually and communally aim at accuracy, clarity, and readability.

A brief summary reflection on the contents of this work might be helpful.

The Introduction to the book, "Lonergan: An Appreciation," explores some of the principal values and perspectives which motivated Lonergan's work and which make it of continuing significance. The interplay between tradition and modernity—how one discovers tradition, evaluates it, and brings it to meet the circumstances of the present—is one of those pervasive concerns of Lonergan.

Related to that concern is Lonergan's desire to ground in authenticity the conditions for a community that avoids becoming either "a solid right that is determined to live in a world that no longer exists" or "a scattered left, captivated by now this, now that new development." He saw that "what will count is a perhaps not numerous center, big enough to be at home in both the old and the new, painstaking enough to work out one by one the transitions to be made, strong enough to refuse half measures and insist on complete solutions even though it has to wait."[9] It is this long-range point of view which is the third principal perspective that the Introduction treats. Lonergan was willing to do the arduous intellectual homework needed to go all the way. He seeks to explore the dynamics of progress, decline, and healing as they work themselves out in our individual and communal human decisions in history.

In the first five chapters of this book the focus is on Lonergan's increasingly significant *Method in Theology*. These chapters, although complete in themselves, are also intended to be useful as an introduction to that text.

The first three chapters, "The Desire To Know: Intellectual Conversion," "The Desire for Authenticity: Conscience and Moral Conversion," and "The Desire for Transcendence: Religious Conversion," focus on Lonergan's retrieval of major dimensions of our reality as human persons: our capacity to know, our power to value, and our openness to transcendence. These three chapters present Lonergan's basic foundational stance on knowledge, ethics, and religion. And they present that stance through a critical analysis of the structure and range of our subjectivity.

Chapters four and five, "Theological Method and Theological Collaboration I," and "Theological Method and Theological Collaboration II," build on the first three chapters and develop their implications for theological work. They present the structure and indicate, through examples, the significance of Lonergan's work on theological method.

More precisely, these two chapters focus on how theologians and other religious believers can understand the classic religious texts of the past and bring those understandings to bear on the changed context of the present. The chapters reveal the common set of interlocking questions which our minds raise as we seek to move from received texts to new interpretations and applications. These chapters likewise address the similarities and differences of the method of theologians to the methods of those working in the other humanities and in the natural sciences. Are we one type of knower and doer or many?

Chapter six, "Philosophy, Theology and God," presents and discusses many of Lonergan's key original perspectives, developed in *Insight,* on the questions of the existence of God and of the intelligibility of our universe. This chapter discusses as well the process of emergent probability which operates in our world. What does our desire to know and our experience of knowing reveal about the type of universe in which we live and about the range of what we can know? This chapter also ties these significant philosophical questions into Lonergan's theological perspective.

The remaining chapters of the book, chapters seven through fourteen, present Lonergan's major contributions to core themes of Christian theology: Trinity, Grace, Christ, Redemption, Church, Sacraments, Social Ethics. These chapters reveal Lonergan's immense respect for tradition. He takes tradition so seriously that he brings to it the new challenges which come from modern historical and philosophical perspectives. In the process he vigorously advances a mutually enriching and purifying dialogue between what we have received and what we are challenged to by our present existence.

Neither Lonergan nor the authors would consider that his specific theological insights flow necessarily from his understanding of method. Method is a framework for creativity and choice, not a system for deducing conclusions. Others employing their own Christian religious reflection might achieve other theological understandings. Those from other world religions, beginning with other classic texts, would surely express their understandings in a different way, even in those instances in which their understandings are similar or complementary to Christian understandings.

There is a universality, however, to the basic religious issues which Lonergan explores through Christian mysteries and symbols: the experienced graciousness of the transcendent, the fragmentation and alienation in the human condition, how the transcendent's graciousness heals, the role of the beloved community in fostering and embodying that healing. These theological understandings of our human condition and our relationship to the transcendent, which Lonergan comes to, are profound and challenging in their own right. They reveal the mind and heart of a great Christian theologian. But they likewise prepare Christian theology for dialogue with other world religions by their reflection on our basic human condition, what ails it, and how it may be healed.

Chapter seven, "A Note on Scholasticism" is precisely that, a brief explanation of the context and characteristics of the scholasticism in which Lonergan often taught and wrote in his years as a professor at the Gregorian University in Rome. This background is necessary to appreciate, in particular, the next two chapters on the Trinity and grace. The material contained in these next chapters was originally written by Lonergan in the then current scholastic context, even though their content often burst the presuppositions of that context.

Chapter eight, "Three Persons—One God," presents Lonergan's exposition and exploration of this central Christian mystery. As always, Lonergan aims at understanding. Because of this he places particular emphasis on the "sendings," on the Son and Spirit in their relationship to us. He likewise develops and applies a profound psychological analogy of the Trinity.

Chapter nine, "Grace," addresses the key experiential reality of the transformative character of God's action in our lives. Perhaps nowhere more than on this question is the complementary character of Lonergan's early, middle, and later work more evident. "Operative Grace" is the actual transformation of our willingness, our conversion, our falling in love with God. It is "the love of God . . . poured forth in our hearts by the Holy Spirit who is given to us" of which Paul speaks in Romans 5:5.

Chapter ten, "Jesus, the Son of God," presents Lonergan's understanding of the Council of Chalcedon's doctrine of the two natures of Jesus the Christ and Lonergan's transposition of that affirmation into a contemporary context. What does Chalcedon mean when one shifts from speaking of substance, nature, and will to identity, subject and consciousness? Lonergan, the conservative theologian, and Lonergan, the theologian of subjectivity, merge in this theological understanding of Jesus as Son of God.

Chapter eleven, "Redemption," focuses on the Christian mystery of the death and resurrection of Jesus. Lonergan shows how the punitive view of God requiring the death of Jesus as retribution for our sins is a perversion of the meaning of this event. Rather, Jesus by his death reveals to us the only way to overcome the evils of this world, namely, to transform them, as he was called to do, by incorporating them into a greater good, by self-sacrificing love. The cross of Jesus not only models this for us, but affectively challenges and empowers us to respond by self-sacrificing love to the evils of our world.

Chapter twelve, "The Church," continues the theme of the last chapter by understanding the church as a redemptive community in the context of world history. The history of our world is a history of progress when attentiveness, intelligence, reasonableness, and responsibility reign, and a history of decline when through the operation of our own biases they do not. The church is envisaged by Lonergan as a self-constituting community with a redemptive historical function to play in overcoming the evils of our world by self-sacrificing love.

Chapter thirteen, "The Sacraments: Symbols Which Redirect Our Desires," treats of the fundamental role that images and symbols play in our experience. It also explores how these images and symbols lead us toward or away from religious mystery and how they can redirect and reconstruct our social experience. Finally this chapter explores how Lonergan's understanding of the symbolic and social function of the sacraments can contribute to a more comprehensive contemporary theology of the sacraments.

The last essay, chapter fourteen, "The Social and Political Dimensions of Lonergan's Theology," integrates many of the most significant insights and themes of Lonergan's philosophical and theological work and reveals their social intent and impact. The desires of the human heart to experience, to understand, to judge, to decide, and to love are deeply interior, but they are not by that fact either solitary or privatizing. Quite the contrary, they form the very foundation for our union with and our cooperation with others. "Deep cries out to deep." Our shared experiencing, understanding, judging, deciding, and loving are the base of community.

This last chapter explores, in sum, the character of our human community, the many obstacles we put in its way, and the need for self-sacrificing love to heal our suffering human community. This discussion of the social and political dimensions of Lonergan's theology has been placed at the end because this chapter makes fully explicit the intention of Lonergan's work, an intention which has been at least implicit throughout. Lonergan's whole theological enterprise has been directed to illuminating the structure of human progress and of human decline and to challenging us, through the rich transformative power of religious mysteries, to choose to become cooperators with God in the healing of the human condition.

For the editor of this work, the power and value of Lonergan's theology lie in the following: the depth to which his theology sheds light on the emergent development of our universe; the depth to which it illuminates our power to act through the unfolding structure of our human consciousness; the depth to which it unveils the tenacious structure of our biases; and the depth to which it reveals the power of incarnate meaning (for Christians, the Christ) to heal and to liberate our energies for cooperation with one another and with Transcendent Mystery to reverse and redirect what can seem at times the almost inexorable undertow of decline.

Completing this work provides an occasion for remembrance and for gratitude. I am deeply appreciative to Rev. Kevin Lynch, publisher at Paulist Press, for first suggesting this book and for his encouragement throughout. Mr. Douglas Fisher, my editor at Paulist Press, has shown extraordinary cooperation, helpfulness, and patience with the long process of bringing this work from conception to realization. My co-authors, of course, have my special gratitude for their eagerness to take up this task of writing an introduction of Lonergan's method and theology, for the splendid quality of their contributions, and, not least, for their long-suffering tolerance of me during the process.

I am grateful as well to Loyola University in New Orleans, which has been most eager to help on this project. The Faculty Research Development Fund has supported this work by providing the funds for my visiting the Lonergan Research Institute in Toronto and by financing the preparation of the Index. To Mr. John Baker, I am most appreciative for his careful work in preparation of the Index, and to Mr. Mitchell Moss and Ms. Joan Schaefer for their critical reading of the original manuscript. Invaluable assistance has been given to me throughout the stages of this project by Mrs. Carol Cortazzo, departmental secretary extraordinaire.

My co-authors and I are dedicating this work to Rev. Frederick E. Crowe, S.J., long-time colleague, companion, and friend of Father Lonergan, and now professor emeritus of Regis College and director of the Lonergan Research Institute. He has been unfailingly supportive of each of our research efforts on Lonergan's thought and has been a pioneer in recognizing the value of Lonergan's work and in making it available for the ages. We congratulate him on the appearance, as we go to press, of *Collection*, the first of a projected twenty volume edition of *The Collected Works of Bernard Lonergan*, to be published by the University of Toronto Press.

NOTES

[1] Bernard Lonergan, *Method in Theology* (New York: Herder and Herder, 1972,) p. xi.

[2] Bernard Lonergan, *Grace and Freedom: Operative Grace in the Thought of St. Thomas Aquinas*, ed. J. Patout Burns (New York: Herder and Herder, 1971).

[3] Bernard Lonergan, *Verbum: Word and Idea in Aquinas*, ed. David Burrell (Notre Dame, Ind.: University of Notre Dame Press, 1967).

[4] Bernard Lonergan, *De Verbo Incarnato* (Rome: Gregorian University Press, 1964).

[5] Bernard Lonergan, *De Deo Trino I: Pars Dogmatica* and *De Deo Trino II: Pars Systematica* (Rome: Gregorian University Press, 1964).

[6] Bernard Lonergan, *Insight: A Study of Human Understanding* (London: Longmans, Green & Co., 1957).

[7] *Method in Theology.*

[8] Bernard Lonergan, *Collection* (New York: Herder and Herder, 1967); *A Second Collection*, ed. William F. J. Ryan and Bernard Tyrrell (Philadelphia: The Westminster Press, 1974) and *A Third Collection*, ed. Frederick E. Crowe (New York: Paulist Press, 1985).

[9] "Dimensions of Meaning," *Collection*, pp. 266–67.

Bernard Joseph Francis Lonergan
Selected Events and Major Writings

1904   Born December 17 in Buckingham, Quebec, Canada

1922   Entered the Society of Jesus

1922–26 Novitiate and Classics at Guelph, Canada

1926–29 Philosophical Studies at Heythrop College, England

1930   Received B.A., University of London

1930–33 Taught at Loyola College, Montreal

1933–37 Theological Studies, Gregorian University, Rome

1936   Ordained priest

1937–38 Tertianship (Spiritual Formation), Amiens, France

1938–40 Doctoral Studies, Gregorian University, Rome

1940   Received S.T.D., Gregorian University; Dissertation: *St. Thomas' Thought on "Gratia Operans [Operative Grace]"* (Published in 1941–42 in *Theological Studies* 2, 3)

1940–46 Professor of Theology, Loyola College, Montreal

1944   *An Essay on Circulation Analysis* (Publication in Process)

1946–49 "The Concept of 'Verbum [Word]' in the Writings of St. Thomas Aquinas," *Theological Studies* 7, 8, 10

1947–53 Professor of Theology, Regis College, Toronto

1949   Cardinal Spellman Award, The Catholic Theological Society of America

1953–65 Professor of Theology, Gregorian University

1957   *Insight: A Study of Human Understanding*

1957   *Divinarum Personarum Conceptio Analogica [The Analogical Understanding of the Divine Persons]*

1959   *Lectures on Education* (Publication in Process)

1960   *De Verbo Incarnato [On the Word Incarnate]*

1961   *De Deo Trino [On the Triune God]*

1965   Surgery for cancer, lung removed

1965–75   Research Professor, Regis College

1967   *Collection*

1969–71   Member of International Theological Commission

1970   Companion of the Order Of Canada

1970   International Symposium on Lonergan's Thought, St. Leo College, Florida

1971   Lonergan Research Center established at Regis College

1971–72   Stillman Professor, Harvard University

1972   *Method in Theology*

1973   John Courtney Murray Award, C.T.S.A.

1974   *A Second Collection*

1975   Fellow of the British Academy

1975–83   Visiting Distinguished Professor, Boston College

1983–84   Retirement, Jesuit Infirmary, Pickering, Ontario

1984   International Symposium on Lonergan's Thought, Santa Clara University, California

1984   Died November 26 at Jesuit Infirmary, Pickering

1985   *A Third Collection*

Seventeen honorary doctorates
were conferred on Father Lonergan

Robert M. Doran

Introduction—
Lonergan: An Appreciation

A thorough introduction to the thought of Bernard Lonergan would occupy several volumes. Moreover, such a work cannot be written for a number of years, since many of Lonergan's writings are as yet unpublished, important notes and fragments are still to be made available and in some instances still to be deciphered, and some of his lectures are still to be edited from tape in a publishable form. But already it is clear that the work of few if any other twentieth-century thinkers has a comparable range of implications for various fields or a comparable importance for the future of thought and indeed of human living. It can reasonably be argued that Lonergan penetrates more directly and swiftly to the heart of the matter than do most, if any, other contemporary figures.

That "heart of the matter" is, for the early Lonergan, the act of human understanding, and, for the later Lonergan, the events that constitute intellectual, moral, and religious conversion. Lonergan says on the opening page of his first great book, *Insight,* that to grasp the act of understanding "in its conditions, its working, and its results, is to confer a basic yet startling unity on the whole field of human inquiry and human opinion."[1] And at the turning point of a later great book, *Method in Theology,* he writes that "the basic idea of the method we are trying to develop takes its stand on discovering what human authenticity is and showing how to appeal to it."[2]

Lonergan's work is formidable. Most of his readers find *Insight* an enormously difficult work. The mastery of this one book alone would be, for most of us, the task of a lifetime. The book cannot adequately be taught in one semester, not even in an entire year, even to the most talented and advanced doctoral students. Only a series of seminars over several years, such as have been devoted occasionally to Hegel's *Phenomenology,* could begin to do it justice. Many readers are easily discouraged especially by the opening five chapters, with their exploration of the nature of understanding in mathematics and contemporary physics. And if they breathe a sigh of relief when

1

the more familiar terrain of common sense begins to be discussed in the sixth chapter, it it is not long before another kind of challenge is posed, an existential invitation to the major personal transformation that is Lonergan's primary intention in all of his work. The transformation is to an authentic personhood or subjectivity, whose intellectual, moral, and religious constituents are explored with rigorous consistency and ever more comprehensive inclusiveness as he moves from an account of understanding to a position on judgment, then to an analysis of the constituents of responsible choice, and finally to a description of religious love.

Preceding *Insight* Lonergan wrote two ground-breaking, perhaps definitive, interpretations of Aquinas;[3] and following *Insight* he worked out a theology of the Incarnate Word and the Trinity,[4] moved ever so slowly and carefully to a theological method that, if implemented, will entail the complete reconstruction of Catholic theology,[5] and returned to earlier work elaborating a macroeconomic theory whose implications, many believe, are as important for economics as his earlier work is for philosophy and theology.[6] His unpublished papers and as yet unedited lectures delivered over a period of some twenty-five years only add to the list of materials to be studied by anyone who would reach up to the mind of a genius and bring that mind to bear on the problems of our day.[7]

Fortunately, I have been asked to write an introduction, not to Lonergan, but to a book of essays on Lonergan. It is the burden of these essays, and not of my introduction, to explore in some detail the contribution that Lonergan makes to the solution of various pressing questions, especially in theology. The present volume is intended to meet the need for an interim introduction to Lonergan's work that would begin to point to its implications for theology, and that would show the central importance of the invitation to transformation and self-appropriation that is the unifying theme throughout his work. That leaves me free to devote my attention to a matter that is perhaps more elusive, but that will probably attract increasing attention over the next years and decades as others begin to reap the rich harvest of Lonergan's work. What sort of commitment lies behind this monumental achievement? What values motivated Lonergan? What atmosphere would he promote in the academy, the Church, and the wider society?[8] Why did he undertake to do what he did? What were his fundamental convictions?

What I will say in response to these questions I discovered first by reading Lonergan's works, and only later confirmed during the years when I was privileged to know him personally. But the items that I single out in response to these questions are what drew me to Lonergan in the first place. And they are perhaps even more important today than they were at the time I first encountered his work. I will mention three interrelated items: tradition and modernity in thinking, the promotion of a "perhaps not too numerous center" in the church,[9] and the detachment of a long-range point of view in society, a "withdrawal from practicality to save practicality."[10] The three are related in that they are analogous embodiments in Lonergan's own life and thought of the creative tension that constitutes for him the immanent intelligibility of human genuineness or authenticity.[11]

1. TRADITION AND MODERNITY

A former student of mine, who has continued to read Lonergan for many years after he was first introduced to *Insight*, recently commented to me, after having read a collection of some of Lonergan's later writings,[12] what a remarkably sane and balanced attitude these papers show toward modernity. Lonergan's attitude contrasted with my former student's own pre-conciliar Catholic upbringing, with its fear of modern developments and its long-standing rejection of modern methods of inquiry. But I remarked in response that Lonergan's critical and discerning respect for modern advances—a respect at least partly rooted in his love of mathematics and science—is balanced by an equally pervasive, if also equally critical, reverence for the best in the classical intellectual tradition of the West: for Plato and Aristotle, Augustine and Aquinas, the Greek breakthrough to theory and the medieval synthesis of faith and reason. Here is a mind, one of the few I have encountered, that is *equally* at home in both the old and the new,[13] and equally critical of both.

To illustrate this, I need only turn to the book of essays that my friend had been reading. It manifests both ever deepening interpretations of Aristotle and Aquinas and a penetrating and appreciative reflection on the emerging religious consciousness of our time; both an affirmation of the Nicene and Chalcedonian doctrines regarding Christ and a reinterpretation of those doctrines in terms of modern notions of the subject and subjectivity; both a retrieval of the Aristotelian notion of *praxis* and a socially transformative commitment to the overcoming of contemporary alienation and determinism. The list could go on and on. In fact almost all of Lonergan's published writings can be filtered through the hermeneutic grid of his respectful attention to, learning from, and critical reorientation of, both tradition and modernity.

Behind this balanced and comprehensive attitude there lies a profound reverence for the life of the mind, the spirit of inquiry, the desire to understand, wherever and under whatever circumstances human questioning is exercised. Yet this reverence is neither uncritical nor atemporal. It combines with perhaps the most lucid understanding yet achieved of the actual workings of the inquiring mind, to enable an appreciation of classical and modern thinkers that sorts out what is to be brought forward from what is to be reoriented or left behind. And it acknowledges with pinpoint accuracy how *a priori* structures develop with historical advances in understanding. The calculus, for example, originated at a precise and easily identifiable time in the history of modern mathematical inquiry; but differential equations are now a dimension of the physicist's heuristic anticipations "from above" of the immanent intelligibility of the data investigated "from below."[14]

Working hand in hand with this respect for the life of inquiry at any time and place we find a commitment to honor the charge of Pope Leo XIII's encyclical on the revival of Thomist studies, *Aeterni Patris:* a commitment, in the Pope's own words, *vetera novis augere et perficere,* to augment and complete the old with the new. To my knowledge, Lonergan first cites the Pope's mandate in a letter to his Jesuit provincial in 1935, and he adds, "I take him at his word."[15] He mentions the encyclical again in the last of his *Verbum* articles, where he explains what he was about as follows:

> My purpose has been the Leonine purpose, *vetera novis augere et perficere,* though with this modality that I believed the basic task still to be the determination of what the *vetera* really were.[16]

A third mention of the same papal challenge appears at the very end of *Insight,* where the determination of what the *vetera* really were has given way to a methodological anticipation of what the *nova* could be. Neither the scholarly research that establishes texts nor the intellectual penetration that reaches to the development of another thinker's mind and to its motives and causes is sufficient.

> After spending years reaching up to the mind of Aquinas, I came to a twofold conclusion. On the one hand, that reaching had changed me profoundly. On the other hand, that change was the essential benefit. For not only did it make me capable of grasping what, in the light of my conclusions, the *vetera* really were, but also it opened challenging vistas on what the *nova* could be.[17]

2. THE NOT TOO NUMEROUS CENTER

Mention of a papal encyclical and of the commitment that it inspired in the mind and heart of a modern thinker is an obvious springboard to my next topic, Lonergan's attitude toward the Church and its *aggiornamento.*

Lonergan was a *peritus* at the Second Vatican Council. He was named by Pope Paul VI as an original member of the International Theological

Commission. He served other special Vatican commissions, including the Secretariat for Non-Believers. But I think it accurate to say that his main ecclesial concern after the Second Vatican Council was with the depth, both religious and intellectual, to which the Church must penetrate if it is really to achieve "Pope John's intention."[18] That depth is manifest in the centrality of the notion of authenticity in all of his writings bearing on *aggiornamento*.[19] But it is clear, too, in his reflections on the forces within the Church that would militate against a real renewal.

> There is bound to be formed a solid right that is determined to live in a world that no longer exists. There is bound to be formed a scattered left, captivated by now this, now that new development, exploring now this and now that new possibility. But what will count is a perhaps not numerous center, big enough to be at home in both the old and the new, painstaking enough to work out one by one the transitions to be made, strong enough to refuse half-measures and insist on complete solutions even though it has to wait.[20]

If the scattered left dominated some aspects of the Church's life during the first twenty years following the council, it is no secret that the solid right is flexing its muscles today. Lonergan understood the difficulty as a crisis of culture, and referred to the problematic mentality of the right as "classicism." If he was distressed by the "scattered left," he also was fearful of the "solid right." For if he could describe himself as "a Roman Catholic with quite conservative views on religious and church doctrines,"[21] he also could write the following about "the shabby shell of Catholicism":

> There are two ways in which the unity of the faith may be conceived. On classicist assumptions there is just one culture. That one culture is not attained by the simple faithful, the people, the natives, the barbarians. None the less, career is always open to talent. One enters upon such a career by diligent study of the ancient Latin and Greek authors. One pursues such a career by learning Scholastic philosophy and theology. One aims at high office by becoming proficient in canon law. One succeeds by winning the approbation and favor of the right personages. Within this set-up the unity of faith is a matter of everyone subscribing to the correct formulae.[22]

The other way of conceiving the unity of faith is to find the "real root and ground of unity" in "being in love with God—the fact that God's love has flooded our inmost hearts through the Holy Spirit he has given us (Rom. 5,5)."[23] Then one will find the function of Church doctrines to lie within the function of Christian witness. And

> . . . the witness is to the mysteries revealed by God and, for Catholics, infallibly declared by the church. The meaning of such declarations lies beyond the vicissitudes of human historical process. But the context, within which such meaning is grasped, and so the manner, in which such meaning is expressed, vary both with cultural differences and with the measure in which human consciousness is differentiated.[24]

The essential, again, is the human authenticity that begins with the acceptance of the gift of God's love that "constitutes religious conversion and leads to moral and even intellectual conversion."[25] And this authenticity, ever precarious, is twofold:

> There is the minor authenticity or unauthenticity of the subject with respect to the tradition that nourishes him. There is the major authenticity that justifies or condemns the tradition itself. In the first case there is passed a human judgment on subjects. In the second case history and, ultimately, divine providence pass judgment on traditions. . . . [T]he unauthenticity of individuals becomes the unauthenticity of a tradition. Then, in the measure a subject takes the tradition, as it exists, for his standard, in that measure he can do no more than authentically realize unauthenticity.[26]

It is not simply with the tradition, then, but with the authenticity of the tradition that Lonergan was concerned, and more precisely with the communication of an authentic religious tradition in the pluralistic context of modern culture. Essential to this communication is the distinction between classicist and modern notions of culture, and the clean break that the Church must make with classicism, so as to become "all to all."[27] On the difficulties attendant on this challenge, Lonergan wrote, in words that comprise aspects of his campaign against both the solid right and the scattered left:

> On the one hand, it demands a many-sided development in those that govern or teach. On the other hand, every achievement is apt to be challenged by those that fail to achieve. People with little notion of modern scholarship can urge that attending to the literary genre of biblical writings is just a fraudulent device for rejecting the plain meaning of scripture. Those with no taste for

systematic meaning will keep repeating that it is better to feel compunction than to define it, even if those that attempt definition insist that one can hardly define what one does not experience. Those, finally, whose consciousness is unmitigated by any tincture of systematic meaning, will be unable to grasp the meaning of such dogmas as Nicea and they may gaily leap to the conclusion that what has no meaning for them is just meaningless.[28]

It was against "the real menace to unity of faith" that Lonergan struggled, against "the absence of intellectual or moral or religious conversion."[29] And it was in the interest of promoting those conversions of mind and heart that he made his extraordinary contribution to the differentiation of consciousness through the process of self-appropriation. For with sufficient differentiation of consciousness, one can exercise a pluralism of communications without falling prey to the threefold peril of a distinct kind of pluralism resulting from lack of conversion:

> First, when the absence of conversion occurs in those that govern the church or teach in its name. Secondly, when, as at present, there is going forward in the church a movement out of classicist and into modern culture. Thirdly, when persons with partially differentiated consciousness not only do not understand one another but also so extol system or method or scholarship or interiority or slightly advanced prayer as to set aside achievement and block development in the other four.[30]

3. THE LONG-RANGE POINT OF VIEW

The extraordinary balance that Lonergan's mind reached between fidelity to tradition and respect for modernity, between fidelity to doctrine and the promotion of responsible pluralism, is a function, I think, of what perhaps more than anything else characterizes both his own mode of thinking and the cognitive authenticity that he would encourage in others: his approach to practicality or praxis.

The seventh chapter of *Insight* is our main source of data on this facet of Lonergan's thinking and mentality. This complex text, I have come to believe, is a fairly sustained and quite subtle reorientation of Marx. It was this chapter that first persuaded me I had encountered not only a brilliant mind, but a thinker with a message of profound importance for our time. But the practical upshot of Lonergan's work was already indicated in the Preface to

Insight. One quotation will suffice to show what Lonergan thought to be the ulterior finality of what he was about.

> . . . insight into insight brings to light the cumulative process of progress. For concrete situations give rise to insights which issue into policies and courses of action. Action transforms the existing situation to give rise to further insights, better policies, more effective courses of action. It follows that if insight occurs, it keeps recurring; and at each recurrence knowledge develops, action increases its scope, and situations improve.
>
> Similarly, insight into oversight reveals the cumulative process of decline. For the flight from understanding blocks the insights that concrete situations demand. There follow unintelligent policies and inept courses of action. The situation deteriorates to demand still further insights and, as they are blocked, policies become more unintelligent and action more inept. What is worse, the deteriorating situation seems to provide the uncritical, biased mind with factual evidence in which the bias is claimed to be verified. So in ever increasing measure intelligence comes to be regarded as irrelevant to practical living. Human activity settles down to a decadent routine, and initiative becomes the privilege of violence.[31]

Lonergan told me in several conversations during the year before he died that the chapters on common sense (Six and Seven) and on judgment (Nine and Ten) were the first chapters of *Insight* that he wrote, that they contained what he most wanted to say, and that it was in order to substantiate his point in these chapters that he wrote the first five, which treat of insight in mathematics and modern science.[32] What he most wanted to say, then, included preeminently a position on the role of human intelligence in history and society, and on the relation of intelligence to social and cultural progress and decline, especially in view of the distinct dangers confronting human society today.

Lonergan's concern with these questions can be traced back at least to the same 1935 letter to his Jesuit provincial in which he mentions Pope Leo XIII's *Aeterni Patris.* Indeed, the charge *vetera novis augere et perficere* is there appealed to, precisely in order to explain his "excursion into the metaphysic of history." He admitted the "enormity" of the influence of Hegel and Marx on his position on history, but maintained that his own position, already drafted, would go quite beyond them. "It takes the 'objective and inevitable laws' of economics, of psychology (environment, tradition) and of progress (material, intellectual; automatic up to a point, then either deliberate and planned or the end of a civilisation) to find the higher synthesis of these laws in the mystical Body."[33] Between the lines one can read the basic sketch of what later would become a quite thorough position on the structure of history.

The reorientation of Marx that Lonergan's position entails locates the basic social dialectic, not between forces and relations of production, but between practical common sense as it erects technological, economic, and political structures, on the one hand, and vital intersubjectivity, on the other hand. The political dimension of society is located, not in the superstructure, as in Marx, but in the infrastructure. The superstructure is constituted by the reflective, objectifying dimension of culture that steps back from everyday practicality and exercises critical, dialectical, and normative judgment on the workings of practical common sense. The forces that militate against a harmonious or integral dialectic of practicality with intersubjectivity—individual, group, and general bias—are examined, and the stress is laid on the distorting influence of the general bias against long-term consequences, ultimate issues, and theoretical questions.

Of this analysis, Lonergan wrote many years later that it was worked out on the model of a threefold approximation. He used the analogy of Newton's planetary theory to explain what he meant.

Newton's planetary theory had a first approximation in the first law of motion: bodies move in a straight line with constant velocity unless some force intervenes. There was a second approximation when the addition of the law of gravity between the sun and the planet yielded an elliptical orbit for the planet. A third approximation was reached when the influence of the gravity of the planets on one another is taken into account to reveal the perturbed ellipses in which the planets actually move. The point to this model is, of course, that in the intellectual construction of reality it is not any of the earlier stages of the construction but only the final product that actually exists. Planets do not move in straight lines nor in properly elliptical orbits; but these conceptions are needed to arrive at the perturbed ellipses in which they actually do move.

In my rather theological analysis of human history, my first approximation was the assumption that men always do what is intelligent and reasonable, and its implication was an ever increasing progress. The second approximation was the radical inverse insight that men can be biased, and so unintelligent and unreasonable in their choices and decisions. The third approximation was the redemptive process resulting from God's gift of his grace to individuals and from the manifestation of his love in Christ Jesus.[34]

A later expansion and refinement of the theory appears in Lonergan's paper, "Natural Right and Historical Mindedness."[35] There the "dialectic of history" is set forth under six headings. First, human meaning develops in human collaboration. Second, there is a succession of plateaus on which expansions of meanings occur: the development of common sense or practical intelligence; the specialization of intelligence in theory; and the move to interiority and method. Third, there are quite specific ideals proper to the third plateau, which was the one on which Lonergan himself was working. These ideals are:

> . . . such self-awareness, such self-understanding, such self-knowledge, as to grasp the similarities and the differences of common sense, science, and history, to grasp the foundations of these three in interiority . . . and, beyond all knowledge of knowledge, to give also knowledge of affectivity in its threefold manifestation of love in the family, loyalty in the community, and faith in God . . .

and

> . . . such self-transcendence as includes an intellectual, a moral, and an affective conversion. As intellectual, this conversion draws a sharp distinction between the world of immediacy and the world mediated by meaning, between the criteria appropriate to operations in the former and, on the other hand, the criteria appropriate to operations in the latter. Next, as moral, it acknowledges a distinction between satisfactions and values, and it is committed to values even where they conflict with satisfactions. Finally, as affective, it is commitment to love in the home, loyalty in the community, faith in the destiny of man.[36]

Fourth, there is needed a critique, in the light of the first three headings, of what our past has made us. Fifth, ambiguity arises "when first-plateau minds live in a second-plateau context of meaning, or when first- and second-plateau minds find themselves in a third-plateau context."[37] And sixth, beyond all dialectic, there is the dialogue in which this ambiguity can be resolved.

> Dialectic describes concrete process in which intelligence and obtuseness, reasonableness and silliness, responsibility and sin, love and hatred commingle and conflict. But the very people that investigate the dialectic of history also are part of that dialectic and

even in their investigating represent its contradictories. To their work too the dialectic is to be applied.

But it can be more helpful, especially when oppositions are less radical, for the investigators to move beyond dialectic to dialogue, to transpose issues from a conflict of statements to an encounter of persons. For every person is an embodiment of natural right. Every person can reveal to any other his natural propensity to seek understanding, to judge reasonably, to evaluate fairly, to be open to friendship. While the dialectic of history coldly relates our conflicts, dialogue adds the principle that prompts us to cure them, the natural right that is the inmost core of our being.[38]

If Lonergan here mentions "natural right," it is, I believe, in order to relate his position to that of Leo Strauss and his followers.[39] The latter position, for all its acumen in retrieving the tradition of classical political philosophy, both remains on the second plateau, and is unable to adopt a balanced attitude toward modernity. But Lonergan's third plateau, which would recover and integrate the advances toward which modernity has been moving, at the same time does not reflect modernity's rejection of the classical tradition. The move to interiority enables the recovery and reorientation of the *vetera* and their integration with a critically reoriented set of *nova*. For modernity, no less than the classical tradition, moves on the second plateau. The "second stage of meaning" comes to its term, perhaps, in Hegel. The advance to a third plateau grounded in the self-appropriation of interiority is required if humanity is not to fall victim to the series of ever less comprehensive syntheses that today threaten civilization with destruction.

There is to be distinguished in the structure of human history, then, a shorter cycle and a longer cycle. The distinction marks another contrast with Marxist analysis. The shorter cycle turns on the ascendancies to power of various groups or nations and their subsequent replacement by other groups who champion the rights of the previously downtrodden. The longer cycle cuts through all such reversals of power, to reveal a sustained decline that results from the neglect by all groups of long-term consequences, ultimate issues, and theoretical questions. It is to responsibility for the longer cycle that Lonergan would call his readers. And it is the awareness of this responsibility that again enables him to strike such a delicate balance in his thinking. The balance is not only between the old and the new, the classical and the modern, but also between the political "right" and "left," "conservative" and "liberal," liberal and Marxist. In historical thinking Lonergan reaches and invites to a higher synthesis of the liberal thesis and the Marxist antithesis[40] in a philosophy of history that accounts for both and moves beyond them by criticizing their defects.

Lonergan's historical and political thinking has yet to be appreciated to the same extent as have other dimensions of his work. But in many ways it represents what may be the most important aspect of his remarkable achievement. A case can be made that his entire life's work may be understood from and organized around the six points that I summarized above on the dialectic of history. If that summary seems more obscure than the rest of what I have written here, perhaps it is because his thought in the area of a philosophy and theology of history is so comprehensive and far-reaching. But with this excuse I must end this section, for any further explication would make my introduction far lengthier than it should be.

4. CONCLUSION

I close by reflecting on a strange phenomenon that perhaps has not escaped the attention of some readers. Lonergan's thought meets with an intensity of emotional response that, it seems, is more vehement than that given to the work of most other thinkers. This is true both of those who accept his work and of those who reject it. While the reasons for opposition to Lonergan's work are no doubt multiform and complex, I suggest that they may be partly due to the extraordinary balance that I have tried to focus on here.

In other words, if one finds oneself firmly planted on one side or the other of the various dichotomies that Lonergan manages to transcend by a higher synthesis, if one belongs to one or other of the various groups that achieve ascendancy and then are supplanted in the shorter cycle, whether in the academy, the Church, or the wider society, will one not resent and reject a thought that would relativize one's own position by sublating it into a higher viewpoint, a viewpoint that brings forward what is to be brought forward and leaves behind what is to be left behind? Lonergan's thought meets with resistance from the advocates of both the old and the new, the right and the left, the reactionary, the liberal, and the Marxist. And the resistance is not due to the fact that, transcending these oppositions, he stands for nothing at all, but is rather the manifestation of an all too human tendency to oppose moving beyond the limitations of one's own position, especially when the achievement and maintenance of that position have already cost one dearly in terms of the politics of everyday living.

Perhaps this represents as well as anything the point that I have been trying to make. Lonergan is an important, and indeed vitally significant thinker precisely because he does invite us all beyond the narrow confines of less inclusive viewpoints to the achievement of a horizon capable of meeting responsibly the immense problems of academy, Church, and society with which we are confronted in our day. This is not to say that he has given us the last word, so that all we need do is make our own some Lonerganian "system." He comments any number of times in *Insight* that his own account of the processes constitutive of human knowledge will and must be improved upon in the light of further advances of human understanding. It is more accurate to say that he has given us a first word, a foundational word on which even the improvements and nuances that are required can be built. So I close by expressing my own persuasion that, if one wants to find one's way amidst the welter of conflicting opinions with which we are confronted today, one can do no better than to spend years reaching up to the mind of Bernard Lonergan before one sets out on one's own. As Lonergan's own reaching up to the mind of Aquinas changed him profoundly, and as that change was the most important thing, so reaching up to the mind of Lonergan will transform our own approach to every serious issue with which we attempt to come to terms; and precisely that transformation will be the most important ingredient that we can bring to the resolution of the issues with which we must be concerned today.

NOTES

[1]Bernard Lonergan, *Insight: A Study of Human Understanding* (paperback ed., San Francisco: Harper and Row, 1978), p. x. The page numbers of the Preface differ by one from those of the hardcover edition (London: Darton, Longman and Todd, 1973), where this quotation appears on p. ix.

[2]Bernard Lonergan, *Method in Theology* (New York: Seabury, 1979), p. 254.

[3]Bernard Lonergan, *Grace and Freedom: Operative Grace in the Thought of St. Thomas Aquinas,* ed. J. Patout Burns (New York: Herder and Herder; London: Darton, Longman and Todd, 1971); *Verbum: Word and Idea in Aquinas,* ed. David B. Burrell, C.S.C. (Notre Dame, IN: University of Notre Dame Press, 1967). *Grace and Freedom* is an edited version of articles on operative grace in Aquinas which first appeared in *Theological Studies* 2 (1941), pp. 289–324; 3 (1942), pp. 69–88, 375–402, 533–578. *Verbum* is an edited version of articles on the concept of *verbum* in Aquinas which first appeared in *Theological Studies* 7 (1946), pp. 349–92; 8 (1947), pp. 35–79, 404–44; 10 (1949), pp. 3–40, 359–93.

[4]Bernard Lonergan, *De Constitutione Christi Ontologica et Psychologica* (Rome: Gregorian University Press, 1964); *De Verbo Incarnato* (Rome: Gregorian University, *ad usum auditorum,* 1964); *De Deo Trino* (Rome: Gregorian University Press, 1964).

[5]Lonergan, *Method in Theology.*

[6]Bernard Lonergan, *An Essay in Circulation Analysis*, currently being edited from several versions, 1944–1983.

[7]Cf. Lonergan: " . . . it is only through a personal appropriation of one's own rational self-consciousness that one can hope to reach the mind of Aquinas and, once that mind is reached, then it is difficult not to import his compelling genius to the problems of this later day." *Insight*, p. 748.

[8]On the academy, the Church, and the wider society as theological "publics," see David Tracy, *The Analogical Imagination: Christian Theology and the Culture of Pluralism* (New York: Crossroad, 1981).

[9]Bernard Lonergan, "Dimensions of Meaning," in *Collection: Papers by Bernard Lonergan* (New York: Herder and Herder, 1967), p. 267.

[10]*Insight*, p. 241.

[11]See *Insight*, pp. 474–79.

[12]*A Third Collection: Papers by Bernard J. F. Lonergan, S.J.*, ed. Frederick E. Crowe, S.J. (New York: Paulist, 1985).

[13]See "Dimensions of Meaning," p. 267.

[14]See *Insight*, pp. 38–39.

[15]Letter to Very Rev. Henry Keane, S.J., 22 January 1935, available in archives, Lonergan Research Institute, Toronto.

[16]*Verbum*, p. 215.

[17]*Insight*, p. 748.

[18]Bernard Lonergan, "Pope John's Intention," in *A Third Collection*, pp. 224–38.

[19]See, for example, Bernard Lonergan, "*Existenz* and *Aggiornamento*," in *Collection*, 240–51; "The Response of the Jesuit as Priest and Apostle in the Modern World," in *A Second Collection*, eds. William F. J. Ryan, S.J. and Bernard J. Tyrrell, S.J., pp. 165–87.

[20]"Dimensions of Meaning," pp. 266–67.

[21]*Method in Theology*, p. 332.

[22]*Ibid.*, pp. 326–27.

[23]*Ibid.*, p. 327.

[24]*Ibid.*

[25]*Ibid.*

[26]*Ibid.*, p. 80.

[27]*Ibid.*, p. 329.

[28]*Ibid.*, pp. 329–30.

[29]*Ibid.*, p. 330.

[30]*Ibid.*

[31]*Insight*, p. xv (paperback), xiv (hardcover).

[32]On one occasion, Lonergan said "Chapters Six through Nine," and on another occasion, "Chapters Seven through Ten." Thus it may be that he

included in this enumeration the important and difficult Chapter Eight on "Things."

[33]Letter to Henry Keane.

[34]Bernard Lonergan, "*Insight* Revisited," in *A Second Collection,* pp. 263–278; quotation from pp. 271–72.

[35]Bernard Lonergan, "Natural Right and Historical Mindedness," in *A Third Collection,* pp. 169–83, esp. pp. 176–83.

[36]*Ibid.,* p. 179.

[37]*Ibid.,* p. 181.

[38]*Ibid.,* p. 182.

[39]Leo Strauss, *Natural Right and History* (Chicago: University of Chicago Press, 1953).

[40]*Insight,* p. 241.

======

I. "The Desire To Know: Intellectual Conversion"

THE NAMING OF DESIRE

"In the ideal detective story the reader is given all the clues yet fails to spot the criminal."[1] With this low-key introduction Bernard Lonergan begins his own detective work in *Insight: A Study of Human Understanding*. What he is searching for, and what he invites us his readers to search for with him, is not a criminal but rather our own dynamic power of inquiry itself, a power which can indeed search for a criminal but which can also search for much more besides. It is that "dynamic power of inquiry" and the "much more besides" which is the focus of Lonergan's work throughout his life and will be the focus of this introduction to his thought.

"Though I cannot recall to each reader his personal experiences, he can do so for himself and thereby pluck my general phrases from the dim world of thought to set them in the pulsing flow of life."[2] The pulsing flow of life to which Lonergan refers is the life of our desires: their frustrations and their fulfillments, their tragedies and their ecstasies. Lonergan's work is in many ways a grammar of those desires. He helps us to understand and to take reflective possession of their pattern and their dynamic structure, the sweep of their interests and the complexity of their interrelationships. We will look at his work as it illuminates the range of desire in its many phases: in the sensible texture of our everyday lives, in the excitement and persistence of our search for knowledge, and in the immediacy and the richness of our search for God. Desire, Lonergan suggests, comes to consciousness in four distinctive ways: in the scope of our experiencing, in the insight of our understanding, in the truth of our judging, and in the goodness and beauty chosen or created in our deciding. Yet although divided in their specific functions, "the many levels of our consciousness are just successive stages in the unfolding of a single thrust, the eros of the human spirit."[3] Not only are our bodies erotic, our spirits are erotic too. Or rather we are body-spirits and the energies of desire permeate our being. The desires and longings which we have for what is beautiful, for what makes sense, for what is true, for what has value, and for what has ultimate value are at the heart of what it means to be human. Lonergan invites us then to become familiar with this range of our desires and comfortable with it.

Desire, its struggles and its triumphs, is the clue to Lonergan, and not any desire, but your own desire, and my own, and his. For Lonergan's work is not only a theory about human desire, though it certainly is that, but it is also and especially an invitation to name our own desires and not only to name them but to enhance their freedom to choose what is good.

THE LEVELS OF CONSCIOUSNESS

Deciding

Judging

Understanding

Experiencing

METHOD AND OURSELVES

Lonergan is perhaps best known for his work on method, method both in the human and natural sciences, and especially in theology. But what has method to do with desire? Everything, if method is not basically something we learn or are taught but is, rather, ourselves, ourselves as we search for what is true and good, ourselves as we engage in every facet of life. And that is precisely Lonergan's point. He suggests, and invites us to verify for ourselves, that there is a dynamic structure, a method, operating in our engagement with life, in our urge to discover what is true and valuable and to create what is worthwhile. That method, spontaneous yet free, invites and leads us, when we are face to face with the experiences of life, not only to attend to those real experiences fully but also to seek to grasp their meaning. And not to be satisfied with the meaning that might first occur to us but to pursue our questions until we have confidence that the meaning we have discovered is the true meaning of the experience. And not to stop there either, but to seek to evaluate the quality of the experiences. Does this experience fit into my life? Do I want it to? Is it worthwhile?

Lonergan suggests then that there is an unfolding of our consciousness from experiencing to understanding to judging to deciding, and that this unfolding operates in every area of our lives, from our day to day decisions to our most crucial choices. He suggests too that it operates in every aspect of scholarly pursuit. In reading a book, for example, one gets the point of a passage, though perhaps on second thought one becomes unsure, then one confirms the original or a new understanding, and then one evaluates the worth of what one has discovered. The same pattern applies to scientific work. One gathers the data, formulates an hypothesis, attempts to verify it, and decides how to use what one has discovered. The social sciences use the same pattern as well, or rather social scientists use the same method, for it is the method of persons and, because of that, the method of the various disciplines. The reader's own special areas of interest can provide further examples in which the existence of this pattern can be tested. Lonergan wrote *Insight* to lay out a series of strategic exercises whereby one can verify this pattern for oneself by seeing it operative in the manifold areas of human pursuits.

If Lonergan is indeed correct in his assertion that there is a method, a general pattern of inquiry, which transcends all the particular areas of life but is operative in each, then there is an actual, if frequently unrecognized, dynamic structural unity in all our diverse human efforts. The diversity of our enterprises is certainly real: the physician is not the tailor, the scholar is not the astronaut, the politician is not the chemist; but there is an underlying core in all our pursuits, and we do well to recognize it. The uncovering of that common core might encourage dialogue among the various sciences and between the humanities and the sciences. That dialogue becomes both the more necessary and more difficult as the various fields which human ingenuity has created become increasingly complex and diversified. Without our seeking after unity, even our best scholarly and technological advances can serve to fragment us. Seeking after and discovering unity in our various pursuits, however, can make the diversity of our interests and skills not a source of confusion and conflict but a source of enrichment.

LEVELS OF CONSCIOUSNESS

The pattern of inquiry, the method, which we have identified is frequently referred to by Lonergan as the four "levels of consciousness." This formulation highlights two significant features of human knowing and deciding. The first is that the levels are stages; each level builds on the preceding one: without experience there is no understanding, without understanding no judgment, without judgment no decision. The second feature is that these levels are conscious: we are *aware* in our experiencing, *aware* in our under-

standing, *aware* in our judging, *aware* of deciding. These two features need
to be examined in some detail, since, although once pointed out, they are
relatively easy to recognize, their implications need elaboration.

Not only does each level depend on the previous level, understanding
on experience, judgment on understanding, decision on judgment; but once
a particular level has achieved its goal, one spontaneously goes on to the next
level. For example, once a scientist thinks he has formulated an accurate
hypothesis, he tries to verify the one he has formed. If the results of the experiment he then performs don't bear out his theory, only then does he return to the level of understanding, to seek another explanation for the data.
The same is true for each of the levels. Further, not only do we go on to the
next level when the goal of the level we have been engaged with has been
reached, but we don't go on, or at least can't satisfactorily go on, to the next
level until that goal of the level we have been on has been reached. Until I
have experienced something, I haven't experienced it, and I know I haven't
experienced it, and no amount of argument by myself or others is going to
persuade me otherwise. Until I have understood something, I haven't understood it, and I know I haven't understood it, and no amount of self-deception
is going to really satisfy me. Until I've established on the basis of evidence
that my hunch or my theory is really correct, I know it is still only a hunch
or a theory, and no amount of rationalization will really convince me otherwise, even if I try and even perhaps succeed in convincing others. Until I
have discovered the right course of action, I know I haven't yet found it, and
no amount of persuasion, no amount of repetition of the wrong actions, is
going to convince me otherwise. "The drive to truth compels rationality to
assent when evidence is sufficient but refuses assent and demands doubt
whenever evidence is insufficient."[4] Each level then has its own criterion of
adequacy. The truth of this is the base of our confidence in our own judgment, in our own conscience. There is an internal compass in each of us
which is targeted to the true and the good, and we know when we have found
it and when we haven't. Our desires to know and to act have a home and we
know when we have reached it.

These levels of our desires are also conscious, and conscious in two distinct but interrelated ways. We are conscious of *what* we are attending to
and we are conscious that *we* are attending to it. In other words, whenever
we experience, understand, judge, or decide, we are not only aware of what
the object is we are attending to, e.g., the marks on this page, but we are
aware that *we* are attending to it. We are present then both to ourselves and
to the objects of our inquiries. But lest that seem as though we are suggesting
that our consciousness has two objects at the same time, it is important to
point out that "the presence of the object is quite different from the presence
of the subject. The object is present as what is gazed upon, attended to, in-

tended. But the presence of the subject can be conscious, as attending, and yet give his whole attention to the object as attending to."[5] By way of example of the two linked types of presence, there is never only an isolated experiencing of the marks on this page; rather there is always also a person, a subject, aware of doing the experiencing. Human consciousness always involves both elements. Our personal consciousness is always an engaged consciousness.

Further, the quality of the consciousness changes and develops as we move from level to level. More of us is at stake, because more of us is involved, as we go from experiencing to understanding to judging to deciding. This can be seen perhaps most vividly in the increasing responsibility we feel when we must acknowledge failure at the various levels. To acknowledge that we haven't noticed something that others have noticed is generally an easy admission to make; to acknowledge we haven't understood something that others have understood hits closer to home; to acknowledge that our judgment has been wrong is an even more personal admission of some failure in ourselves; and to acknowledge that one has chosen, embraced, or done what was evil addresses the core of who one is. But it is not the possibility or reality of failure which is our real concern at this point but rather the fact that as we move from level to level "it is a fuller self of which we are aware and the awareness itself is different."[6] As we consciously move from level to level, not only are our operations different, we ourselves are different. In fact, there is a dual creation in anything we engage in. We not only create relationships or objects, we create ourselves in so doing. Whenever we act, our own character is formed as well.

We are and choose to be the receptive consciousness which takes in the impressions of our world and of our inner states. We are and choose to be the inquiring consciousness which is not satisfied with mere impressions but which tries to grasp their meaning. We are and choose to be the verifying consciousness which is not content with bright ideas but looks for the evidence that our understandings are true and correct. Finally we are and choose to be deciding consciousness which is not content to have discovered the truth, or even the value of the truth we have uncovered, but chooses to act upon it or to work to achieve it. In a word, consciousness is not a mere fact, it is a many-leveled achievement. The desires of our humanity, when they are consciously assented to, seek their goals and thereby establish our character. Lonergan refers to these various dynamic operations of our consciousness, respectively, as the empirical (experiencing) level, the intellectual (understanding) level, the rational (judging) level, and the responsible (deciding) level, to highlight the various rich dimensions of who we are, which operate on the successive interlocking stages.

The names for these four levels are actually a short-hand for a series of operations at each of the levels. The experiential* level consists of all of the operations of receptivity or attending, generally the operations of our sense faculties, but including as well the "interior senses" which attend to our states of consciousness. The intellectual level consists of all operations which are necessary for understanding. That includes asking questions, the imaging which aids understanding, understanding itself, and conceptualizing and formulating our understanding. The rational or judging level consists of all operations which are involved in verifying our understanding. That includes reflection on how to prove the truth or falsity of our understanding, the gathering and weighing of the evidence on the issue, and the actual act of judging what the truth is. The responsible or decisional level consists of all operations which are involved in acting on truth and value. That includes deliberating what courses of action are possible, evaluating which would be best, the actual deciding on the course to be pursued, and the pursuing it to completion. And even this list of operations really only exemplifies what is involved in the four basic ways in which our human consciousness engages life.

CONFIRMING THE FOUR LEVELS

It would be helpful at this point if the reader would explicitly try to confirm whether his or her own desire to know and to act consists of the pattern which Lonergan suggests. If one can actually confirm it in whole or in part, then one has a basis to build on as one follows the development of Lonergan's reflections. If one can disconfirm it in whole or in part, then one has a basis to criticize the development of Lonergan's reflections.

Lonergan suggests that in seeking to evaluate his understanding of knowing and choosing, one first attend to the experience of one's own experiencing, understanding, judging, and deciding. You might choose some decision you have made e.g., a job decision, an educational decision, a personal decision, and recall in some detail if those four levels were operative in it. After reflecting on the stages leading to your decision, you might then try to understand the pattern and relationship of the operations to one another. Do the operations, did they, lead in a spontaneous and natural sequence from one to another? You might then examine the evidence you have brought forward and make the actual judgment that this is how your knowing

---

*The word "experience" for Lonergan bears the twofold meaning, as it does in common usage, of referring either to the receptive state, namely, Lonergan's first level, or to the whole range of all conscious activity, including receptivity, namely, any or all of Lonergan's four levels. One must attend to the context to know which meaning is being used when. In other words, there is double usage of the word "experience." It refers both to a stance of passivity to data, most frequently sense data, and also to the rich texture of all human activity.

and choosing work, or at least worked in that case. But since one example can be deceptive, it would be well to consider a second or third example or even more. Finally, if this is indeed the way your consciousness operates in the examples you have considered, then it is likely the way your consciousness operates in general. You are faced then with the question of whether you will act in accord with the full range of these dynamic operations of your mind and heart. Concretely, acting in full accord with the pattern of the operations means that one has to ask oneself, first, if one will gather all the data pertinent to an issue one wants to understand and hopes to act on; second, if one will not be content with the first bright idea one has, but will seek as full and as adequate understanding as possible and as the issue calls for; third, if one will take the time and effort to verify one's understanding before moving to action; and finally, if one will only act on what one considers to be true and valuable, and that when one sees what is in fact true and valuable, one will indeed act. In a word, one has to ask oneself if one will be a truth-seeking and an ethical person.

But why does this follow? Why does affirming the existence and structure of the four levels of consciousness lead to a moral question, even to a moral imperative? Because if the pattern we are considering is indeed the method of our consciousness, then it is our way to be human, and to deliberate about whether to follow its injunctions is to deliberate about whether to grow in our humanity and to work with others to help grow with them.

I have mentioned injunctions since there is in fact an imperative quality to the dynamics of our consciousness. We have already suggested that earlier by indicating that our consciousness is always a directed consciousness. Recall that you as conscious are always intending something, whether the gathering of evidence, the point of a question, the truth of a statement, or the value of a course of action. Recall too that each level of your consciousness has its own criterion of when it is satisfied. But the natural dynamism of the levels of your consciousness does not mean that you can't decide to give only passing attention to one or another of the operations of the various levels. You can refuse to gather all the data and therefore face understanding with the probability of an incomplete or erroneous insight; or you can rush understanding so that it must settle for the first bright idea or one can divert intelligence from some of the data to avoid an unpleasant realization; or you can refuse to consider some of the evidence when drawing a conclusion and therefore arrive at a false judgment; or finally you can decide not to act, or choose to act wrongly, or at least half-heartedly. In other words, you can impede or derail the deepest desires of your human mind and heart.

Why any of us might do that, we will consider in some detail later. Suffice it to say at the moment, and each of us can readily verify this for himself or herself, that we do in fact at least on occasion work against the dynamic of our own deepest desires. That is why these four levels of our consciousness are precisely imperatives and not necessities. We are indeed called to: Be attentive. Be understanding. Be reasonable. Be responsible; but we need not respond to the call. In that possibility of choice lies our freedom. Lonergan's invitation to us to attend to the spontaneous yet free method of our understanding and our deciding is an invitation and a challenge to the highest form of self-knowledge, the knowledge which encourages and facilitates our responsibly and lovingly fulfilling our desires.

METHOD AS RECURRENT

Our focus so far has been on the four levels as stages in a pattern and on those stages as operating in the whole range of human activity. But this pattern does not operate only once in each of those areas. The word "method" which Lonergan employs for the levels implies that there is a process involved which is done not only once but can be done over and over again. And he further suggests that the results are not repetitive but cumulative. Every piece of knowledge gained becomes the base for further knowledge, as, for example, in learning a language or in doing an experiment. Knowledge builds on knowledge, discovery on discovery. Every decision one makes sets the context for a new decision. In other words, the method which is the four levels of our consciousness is recurrent, and not only recurrent but expansive. Certainly there are methods in which routine is the goal—a Big Mac should taste like a Big Mac wherever or whenever it is bought—but even here the mind that devised the method or process for making that hamburger will also change the process if customers' preferences change. But in contrast to the setting up of a routine and recurrent process, there are the progressive results of the mind's own method. This can be seen in such diverse ways as one historical discovery leading to another, the understanding of one text of Scripture leading to the meaning of others, the finding of one genetic key leading to the uncovering of other genetic secrets. As Lonergan defines it, method then is "a normative pattern of recurrent and related operations yielding cumulative and progressive results."[7] The levels of our consciousness are such a method.

Of course one can think one has made a discovery and find out, in trying to prove it or to apply it, that one is wrong. But the mind's method is a self-correcting process, if we let it be, and an error can be used to call one's attention to new experience, or to old experience in a new way. It can challenge us to come up with new understandings. Sometimes in fact discovering an error or a mistaken assumption can itself lead to an important breakthrough whether in Scripture studies, or in physics, or in a personal relationship. The levels of our consciousness, then, not only operate in diverse fields but operate recurrently and progressively in each of the diverse fields. Not even error need be looked on as a dead end, but can point the way to the need for a new beginning.

REVISION OF THE LEVELS

Lonergan suggests that there is a sense in which the levels he has named are revisable and a sense in which they are not. They are certainly revisable in terms of the names he has given them. Might they be better called receptivity, inquiry, affirmation, action, thereby highlighting different aspects of the four levels? Perhaps. Perhaps not. But the naming of the pattern is one thing and the reality which is named is another. It is the reality which is named, the processes themselves, which is unrevisable. Even here Lonergan is not saying that knowing and choosing *must* be the way he describes and explains them, but only that they are *factually* that way, and he asks you to verify that for yourself. If knowing would factually change, then obviously the description would need to change as well.

But might Lonergan be wrong about the facts of our knowing and our choosing? How would one prove him so? Perhaps one could point to data he hasn't attended to or point out new elements in the data he has attended to. But that is to affirm the crucial importance of the data gathering or experiencing level. Perhaps instead one discovers meanings he has not grasped. But that is to affirm the crucial importance of the understanding level. Perhaps one discovers evidence which disproves his understanding. But that is to affirm the crucial importance of the judging level. Perhaps, finally, one makes a different decision than he makes about what to do about what one has discovered. But that is to affirm the crucial importance of the deciding level. In other words, one would have to use the very method that he describes in any attempt to prove him wrong. But that would be only to affirm in practice what one was trying to deny in theory. One would be involved in self-contradiction. So basic, then, to all our inquiry is the dynamic structure which Lonergan is describing that one actually affirms it in practice in trying to refute it in theory.

TRANSCENDENTAL METHOD

These levels then are so foundational to all that we are and all that we do that even our attempts to revise our understanding of them must use them. Because they are so foundational, Lonergan refers to the levels as transcendental method. They are transcendental because they transcend all other methods and are operative in all other methods. For example, to decide on the technique (method) to build a bridge or the procedure (method) one will use in filling out one's income tax, one first gathers the data, seeks to understand the data, etc. That is, one first uses the method which one is, the transcendental method, to establish any other technique or procedure, any other method, one will use. But it is again important to note that this transcendental method which one is is no mere technique or procedure; rather it is ourselves, the dynamic structure of our creativity. It is the method behind all of our methods, it is ourselves creating all other procedures, processes, techniques, and methods. It is ourselves open to the whole range of reality.

Each of the levels of the transcendental method is open to reality under a different aspect. The first level is open to reality as it can be experienced. The second level is open to reality as it is intelligible. The third level is open to reality as it is true. The fourth level is open to reality as it is good. Each level then can be considered to be a question searching for reality under a specific aspect. Traditionally the aspects which have been afforded most attention are the last three: the intelligible, the true, and the good. They are called the transcendentals because they transcend any specific content. The periodic table of chemistry, the departments of a university, the list of NFL teams, etc., are all intelligible categories. They all fall under divisions of reality which our capacity to understand can either comprehend or create. But our capacity to understand transcends any specific field of data to which we apply it. That is why it is called a transcendental orientation of our consciousness, or, as Lonergan calls it, a transcendental notion. The transcendental notion of the intelligible, our second level of consciousness, is open to everything that is intelligible; the transcendental notion of the true, our third level of consciousness, is open to everything that is true; the transcendental notion of the good, our fourth level of consciousness, is open to everything that is good. This transcendental openness of our consciousness is why we are ultimately open to the question of God. The transcendental notions are our capacity to search for any and everything that might be intelligible or true or good and our capacity to recognize when we have found it. This first chapter is focusing particularly on the notions of the intelligible and the true, and is an invitation to the reader to recognize the intelligible structure of his or her own dynamic pattern of consciousness and to affirm the truth about it. The second chapter will focus particularly on the notion of the good. The third chapter will focus on the ultimately good.

INTELLECTUAL CONVERSION

The recognition and affirmation that the dynamic structure of one's own knowing and choosing consists of the compound set of operations—experiencing, understanding, judging, and deciding—Lonergan refers to as intellectual conversion. He uses that strong term, conversion, because he considers the recognition to constitute a decisive break with a pervasive misperception about knowing, namely that it is like "looking." If knowing is like looking, then all one has to do is open one's eyes and one will not only see but also know. Nothing could be further from the truth. When I look at an x-ray of my chest, I see a series of light, of shaded, and of dark areas, i.e., a recognizable skeletal structure. When a radiologist looks at the same x-ray, he or she is not only more alert at noticing aspects of the visual presentation, but also is able to interpret (understand) what is seen. That barely discernible line means, to the physician, a fractured rib, and that type of fracture takes about three weeks to heal. Knowing is not merely looking, it is also understanding and judging. It is not only using the capacity of your first level of consciousness, experiencing, it is using the capacity of your second level, understanding, and of your third level, judging, as well. It might seem strange, given the commonly accepted division between subjectivity and objectivity, that the more one employs the full range of one's subjectivity, the more objective are one's conclusions, but it is in fact true. The radiologist's tutored subjectivity arrived at an objectivity that I, merely by looking at the x-ray, could not arrive at. Knowing is not merely taking a good look, it is attending *and* understanding *and* judging.

But why is recognizing that knowing is not merely looking so important? Because if knowing is just looking, then what is seen becomes the most important reality. What can be seen becomes "objective" and everything else becomes "subjective." And it happens that trust and love and care and understanding and truthfulness and fidelity can't be seen in a physical sense. Surely they will manifest themselves, but one always needs understanding and judgment to recognize their presence. At a certain stage in the development of the physical sciences, the view was common that only what could be sensed was real. This view was called empiricism. But when it was realized that scientific theories themselves couldn't be sensed but had to be understood—$E = MC^2$ is just marks on a page if one doesn't understand it—this view lost credibility. Empiricism is taking one of the components of knowing, experiencing, as if it were the whole reality of knowing. Knowing is not just looking, a capacity which we all have if our visual organs are intact and our eyes are open, but also involves our capacity and indeed our willingness to understand and to affirm our understanding in judgment. Not only is our first level of consciousness involved, our second and third levels are involved as well.

It is not only personal and interpersonal values such as love, fidelity, and trust which become "subjective" if knowing is just looking. The whole social order vanishes as well. One does not really *see* a nation, or a city, or a university. One does not *see* a wife, or a president, or a criminal. Surely one sees land and buildings, but one only understands and judges that a particular expanse of land is under the jurisdiction of a particular group of people. Does a disputed plot of land really *show* you which nation it belongs to? The same group of buildings which you call a college or university can become a low security prison with a change of ownership (a change of understanding and meaning) and look exactly the same. Surely ones sees a woman but recognition of whether she is wife or president or criminal is a matter of understanding and judgment and not merely of vision. No, knowing is not merely looking, it is experiencing *and* understanding *and* judging. The real world we live in consists of facts such as the weather and the earth beneath our feet, and of facts such as nations and marital status, but these latter facts, which are no less real, are facts principally in the world of understanding and of meaning. To confine knowing to looking is to arbitrarily declare our personal, our interpersonal, and our social worlds unreal, or "subjective" in a pejorative sense. No people in fact live their lives that way; they couldn't. But thinking that way leads to further errors whose consequences are quite serious.

If one thinks knowing is like looking, then any field which has a strong and obvious visual or sensory component, such as the natural sciences, is taken, in a naive sense, to be the model of knowing. If knowing is experiencing and understanding and judging, then the natural sciences are one example of knowing; the social sciences are another example; the humanities, including ethics and religion, are still another example. And the conclusions of each of the fields are either objective or subjective depending on whether or not each of us, when we engage in them, employ our full capacity to experience, to understand, and to judge. Whenever we use the full capacity of our subjectivity, all of our levels of consciousness, all of our desire to experience, our desire to understand, and our desire to find the truth, then our conclusions have a claim to objectivity. If we don't use all that we are, then our conclusions are merely arbitrary and "subjective" in the pejorative sense. Lonergan makes the point of the relationship between objectivity and subjectivity quite strikingly in his statement: "Objectivity is the fruit of authentic subjectivity."[8] The full use of all of our capacities leads to objectivity, and nothing less than that leads to objectivity. Intellectual conversion is the recognition that that is true.

In sum, intellectual conversion is the awakening to the realization that we will only discover what is true when we use our most personal human capacities, when we devote ourselves to experiencing, understanding, judging with all the resources available to us. Intellectual conversion implies as well the further realization that the world we live in—the personal, interpersonal, and social dimensions of our existence referred to earlier—is principally constituted not by sense data but by human understandings, judgements, and decisions. The world we live in is constituted by human meanings.

PROGRESS AND DECLINE

Up until this point, the focus on the method of our consciousness has emphasized the fruitfulness of using our resources to their full extent. If we and others did that, then advance would follow advance; or if an honest mistake were made, then one's best efforts would be used to correct it. But that description does not fit either the world that Christianity or any other of the major religions presents to us or the world of our personal and communal experience. Advance frequently does not follow advance, and errors and other worse evils are often not honest mistakes but rather are careless or willful choices. Our real world is an often confusing and even disheartening mixture of progress and decline. Lonergan is not blind to that. Rather it is precisely because he is acutely aware of the moral complexity of our world that he wants to aid us to distinguish progress from decline and to challenge us to contribute to the one and to help to reverse the other. His presentation of progress and decline (and later also of healing) is an ideal type, namely, a set of ideas, which, though never found fully realized in actual experience, can be extraordinarily helpful in understanding our actual experience because of the clarity they can give to the underlying issues. Such ideal types, which were originally employed in sociology, are often used in the social sciences to aid in the understanding of complex situations.

The nature and structure of progress is relatively easy to grasp. It is the cumulative effect of our personal and communal response to the imperatives of our consciousness: Be attentive; Be intelligent; Be reasonable; Be responsible. It is the cumulative effect of our being true to ourselves. Its flourishing means that new understandings of experiences are discovered, new truths are verified, and new decisions which genuinely improve the situation are made. It is individuals and societies, healthy and growing, meeting problems and challenges and surmounting them.

What then is decline? It again is a cumulative result, but, this time, of inattentiveness, of failures to understand, of wrong judgments, and of evil choices. It is the consequence of refusing to follow the imperatives of our experiential, intellectual, reasonable, and responsible consciousness. It brings about a personal and social situation where confusion and disvalue abound, and where it is hard to know where to begin to set things moving again in a positive direction. In fact, that is one of the worst aspects of decline. It tends to discredit and ridicule the type of intelligence, judgment, and responsibility that could reverse the situation. It creates an inertia which is difficult to reverse. A person in a spiraling drug habit would be a good example of decline and of decline's massive resistance to change. A physically or emotionally abusive family would be another example. On a broader scale, nations on the verge of revolutions are often examples of countries in decline. Unfortunately, often after revolutions, even greater decline can set in. Decline tends to be intractable to remedy.

Why do we choose decline? Or perhaps better, why do we make the types of choices which bring about decline? Decline itself is surely rarely, if ever, chosen. But what motivates the choices which bring it in their wake? Why we would choose in accord with the orientation of our consciousness toward what is true and good is self-explanatory. But why would we act against that orientation? What is the triggering mechanism or mechanisms of our evil choices? Why do we and others choose to be inattentive, uncomprehending, unreasonable, and irresponsible?

Lonergan suggests that there are four biases to which we are subject as the unique type of beings we humans are. He calls them: neurotic bias, egoistic bias, group bias, and the bias of common sense. We will first consider what they have in common. As human we are, each of us, a concrete, individual, sensing, and sensitive person, by our physical constitution always and spontaneously alert to a certain type of good, namely, what gives us pleasure and not pain. In addition, we are also gifted with the special capacity of being able to understand, if we want to, what is, in a more complete sense, good and valuable for ourselves and for others as well. There can be, and often is, a tension between the immediately satisfying and what is more ultimately good. That tension can be profound. And with too striking frequency, we choose immediate gratification for ourselves over what is genuinely valuable, in the long run, both for ourselves and for others. The strength of this natural and spontaneous physiological tendency to be focused on short run satisfaction frequently enough leads to our inattention to the needs and concerns of others, to our refusing to understand or to tell the truth about a situation which would be to our detriment, and to our refusal to choose what is really right if the price is too high for us personally. In other words, we with some regularity resolve the tension, which is ingredient in who we are, by choosing to violate the more inclusive imperatives of our consciousness; we choose to be inattentive, uncomprehending, unreasonable, and irresponsible in the service of the immediately physically and psychologically gratifying. The recognition of this tendency in ourselves is, for example, why the law insists that judges must step aside, not only in the obvious case of judging themselves, but even in the case of judging those to whom they have any significant personal contact. And why legislators are not to vote on matters in which they have significant personal interest. It is generally and correctly acknowledged that, given a choice between our own immediate self-interest and the general good, we will only too frequently at least seriously entertain choosing our own self-interest.

It is important to realize precisely what Lonergan's point is here. It is not that we should not pursue both what is valuable and what is satisfying. It is that the immediately satisfying is not always what is valuable, and what is valuable is not always immediately satisfying. And that in those instances, the correct choice is to choose what is valuable. It is delightful to have a delicious meal, but not during the time one has promised to drive someone to the airport. It is valuable for oneself, and eventually for others, to study consistently in a course, but it is frequently not immediately gratifying. There is, therefore, a tension in our persons. The tension is that, in addition to our being oriented toward what is valuable, we are also, as physical and psychological beings, oriented toward what is satisfying and pleasing in a physiological sense and oriented against what is unsatisfying and unpleasant. Both tendencies, toward the valuable and toward the satisfying, are good in themselves; and the second is, in fact, indispensable for living. In the extreme, the lack of the pain reaction is always a medical nightmare, since it means that the spontaneous trigger to avoiding injury is gone. Often, in fact, the two orientations work hand in hand. It is physiologically necessary and desirable to get exercise, rest, and relaxation. It is physiologically and psychologically necessary, and when not necessary, certainly desirable, to have food that is appetizing, and relationships that are gratifying. But our physiological and psychological responses are not geared toward grasping the whole picture. That is not their role. But in those instances when we are faced with a conflict between ourselves as physiological/psychological beings and ourselves as beings who grasp the whole picture of what is really good for ourselves and others, there can be a strong tendency to choose the immediacy of the tangibly satisfying over what is the truly valuable. It is that tendency which is at the root of the biases. Each of the biases in its own way involves a choice of satisfaction over value. Those choices often indeed bring immediate satisfaction, but they likewise bring both a bad conscience and some measure of individual and/or social decline. Lonergan expresses the heart of the tension that leads to the biases in a striking manner:

> Intersubjective spontaneity and intelligently devised social order
> have their ground in a duality immanent in man himself. As intel-

ligent, man is the originator and sponsor of the social systems within which, as an individual, he desires and labors, enjoys and suffers. As intelligent, man is a legislator but, as an individual, he is subject to his own laws. By his insights he grasps standard solutions to recurrent problems, but by his experience he provides the instances that are to be subsumed under the standard solutions. From the viewpoint of intelligence, the satisfactions allotted to individuals are to be measured by the ingenuity and diligence of each in contributing to the satisfaction of all; from the same high viewpoint the desires of each are to be regarded quite coolly as the motive power that keeps the social system functioning. But besides the detached and disinterested stand of intelligence, there is the more spontaneous viewpoint of the individual subjected to needs and wants, pleasures and pains, labour and leisure, enjoyment and privation. To each man his own desires, precisely because they are his own, possess an insistence that the desires of others can never have for him. To each man his own labors, because they are his own, have a dimension of reality that is lacking in his apprehension of the labours of others. To each man his own joys and sorrows have an expansive or contracting immediacy that others can know only through their own experience of joy and sorrow.[9]

In sum, there is a tension in us which provides a point of vulnerability for bias in its many forms.

The particular dynamic in each of the biases merits exploration. Neurotic bias works primarily on an unconscious basis. Lonergan in fact calls it on one occasion the bias of unconscious motivation. It is caused by a major trauma to our physiological/psychological constitution. Anything touching the trauma is so emotionally loaded that one avoids dealing with it. The consequence is that certain experiences do not get attended to, and therefore do not get understood, and the truth is not discovered nor is the way to heal the trauma discovered, and effective action is not taken. Blind spots and sore spots in ourselves and others usually have to do, at least to some extent, with neurotic bias. Our "first work of art is [our own] living"[10] and the bias of unconscious motivation distorts the dramatic, active, pattern of our living. Depending on the seriousness of the bias, either a part of one's life or almost the whole of one's life can be lived askew. Neurotic bias is caused by our unconscious desire to avoid pain. Its consequence is a tragic distorting of value. In addition to the early neuroses which psychoanalysis has so thoroughly examined, there are later traumatic events which cause aberrations in perception, understanding, judgment, and decision-making. Experiences connected with the Vietnam War led to a high degree of psychological confusion and disturbance in such a number of veterans that a post-Vietnam syndrome was identified, and assistance was made available to the service men and women. The disturbances of neurotic bias generally lead primarily to individual decline, but one can wonder whether certain intense forms of racial prejudice do not have a base in a neurotic bias of an entire culture or social class, and therefore whether neurotic bias can lead and has led directly to social decline.

Egoistic or individual bias is almost self-explanatory. It is the choice to attend to matters that pertain to my own self-interest rather than to the general good. When we act from this bias, we use our intelligence to ferret out solutions to problems which will serve us and our concerns; and we turn away from the further questions of how or if those solutions will help or harm others. Even in neurotic bias, there is some measure of unease over one's actions, although the originating conflict remains largely unconscious; in egoistic bias, there is greater reason for disquiet, since the motivation of acting for self over others has become conscious.

Egoistic bias is an incomplete development both of intelligence and of willing. It is refusing both to understand and hence to choose the world of value, because of a prior choice for self-interest and personal satisfaction. Its consequence is often some measure of that satisfaction, but ultimately it results in an isolation of oneself from others and a conscience that knows the quality of one's character.

Whereas egoistic bias finds us working indifferent to the concerns of our neighbors and our community, and therefore in opposition to normal intersubjective feeling, group bias is supported by others—others of our own group, that is. Groups in themselves are essential for the development and smooth working of society, farmers, engineers, physicians, professors, students, etc. Community forms spontaneously among those who share interests and skills. Groups, therefore, are one of the goods of society. The difficulty arises when a group begins to attend to its own self-interest, in a narrow sense, rather than to the overall good of society and to its creative role in society. Again, spontaneous feeling, this time not solely for oneself but for those who are near and dear, can find itself in tension with our capacity to understand and to choose the greater good. Group bias is precisely the choice of the group's interest when it is in conflict with the good of society. "The group is prone to have a blind spot for the insights that reveal its well-being to be excessive or its usefulness at an end."[11] Groups, like individuals, tend to rule data and ideas out of court when they would challenge in any substantial way the group's hold on some aspect of society. If societal progress is groups working together, attentively, intelligently, reasonably, and responsibly, then decline is the cumulative result of groups working against one another, and trying to keep both from themselves and from the public forum whatever might call into question their own particular status. The implications of group bias will be treated further in Chapter XIV on social ethics. Here it is sufficient to note that while individual bias generally can be dealt with by the group of which one is a part, and therefore can be handled on a small scale, the effect of group bias is, by definition, social and can result in massive public consequences. The Middle East, Central America, Northern Ireland, and South Africa are but some of the more notable examples of the effects of the bias of groups.

The fourth bias that Lonergan treats, he calls the bias of common sense or general bias. It is the tendency in all of us to seek short term and immediate solutions even to complex problems. If there is a difficulty, solve it now with the means at hand. That is precisely the common sense solution. But common sense doesn't ask the further questions. Will solving it this way cause more problems down the road? What is the cause of the problem? Will certain structural changes in the manufacturing process, or in the institution, or in society keep this type of problem from occurring in the first place? Famines are occurring with significant frequency in various parts of the world. Certainly wherever and whenever they occur, immediate aid is needed. But what are the long term solutions which would make famines less likely, or would structure assistance to areas of likely famine before the problem became major or even catastrophic? These are the questions that common sense doesn't ask. It stays with the short term, at hand, solutions rather than raising the long term, often complex, theoretical and scientific questions which could provide truly adequate and ultimately satisfying solutions. This general bias of common sense has at its root the same type of tension which is involved in all of the other biases: our tendency to follow our propensity as physiological beings for the im3diate and the gratifying rather than to follow our capacity as intelligent and valuing beings to choose what is ultimately worthwhile. Hopefully what is ultimately worthwhile will include what is gratifying—for the gratifying is also a good, although not the ultimate good—but whether the gratifying is included or not in any particular worthwhile goal, it is still what our moral sensibility urges and even requires us to choose.

The bias of common sense, along with group bias, will be further considered in the chapter on social ethics. Both of them pose problems of national and global social order. It is sufficient to note here that they both, along with the other biases, involve violations of the deepest orientation of our consciousness to be attentive, intelligent, reasonable, and responsible. They are more or less conscious decisions not to attend to; and, therefore, not to try to understand; and ultimately not to act on what is ultimately worthwhile because of a prior decision to choose what is more immediate and gratifying to my psyche, or myself, or my group, or my ease of action.

They are decisions which bring in their wake personal and societal decline, or some combination thereof. How this decline can be overcome will be a principal concern of Chapter III: the healing role of religious, spiritual, and moral transformation.

CONCLUSION AND SUMMARY

This chapter has invited you to reflect on some of your own deepest and most pervasive desires: your desire to experience, your desire to understand your experiences, your desire to be satisfied only with a true understanding of your experiences, and your desire to choose and to act on what is really valuable. The chapter has tried to show that these desires are a structure, a method, operating in all our pursuits, from the most personal to the most theoretical and scientific. It has invited you to confirm that structure for yourself and to indicate some of the consequences of confirming that structure. That structure, those desires, is our way of coming to understanding, to truth, and to value, and, therefore, that structure underlies our recognition and pursuit of moral values and so constitutes our most basic set of moral imperatives: Be attentive, Be intelligent, Be reasonable, Be responsible. In addition, to be aware of the range and structure of those desires is to be freed from a pervasive myth, that knowing is like looking, and therefore that only what can be seen in the most obvious ways is real, to the detriment not only of the most personal values but of the whole structure of meanings which constitute families, communities, and societies. To recognize the implications of the method, which is our desires, is to undergo a change of perspective radical enough to be called a conversion, an intellectual conversion. We have also seen, however, that while following the dynamic orientation of our consciousness leads to progress, not following it or refusing to follow it leads to decline. We examined the basic tension between the immediate and the really valuable, which is the occasion for wrong and even evil choices, and we presented the four specific forms, the biases, which the tensions which lead to decline can take. We can all discover in ourselves the conflicting orientations and forces of neurotic, of egoistic, of group, and of common sense bias. And we can easily recognize how they can and do lead to decline.

In sum, the basic understanding of the dynamic structure of our desires and of the principal aberrations of those same desires, which we have invited the reader to attend to in this chapter, will provide the foundation for the further implications which will be explored in the succeeding chapters.

NOTES

[1]Bernard Lonergan, *Insight: A Study of Human Understanding* (New York: Harper and Row, Publishers, 1978), p. x. The date of original publication was 1958.

[2]Lonergan, *Insight,* p. xix.

[3]Bernard Lonergan, *Method in Theology* (New York: Seabury Press, 1979), p. xix. The date of original publication was 1972.

[4]Lonergan, *Method,* p. 35.

[5]Lonergan, *Method,* p. 8.

[6]Lonergan, *Method,* p. 9.

[7]Lonergan, *Method,* p. 5.

[8]Lonergan, *Method,* p. 292.

[9]Lonergan, *Insight,* pp. 214–15.

[10]Lonergan, *Insight,* p. 187.

[11]Lonergan, *Insight,* p. 223.

II. The Desire for Authenticity: Conscience and Moral Conversion

THE STRUCTURE OF MORAL CONSCIOUSNESS: PRACTICAL KNOWING AND DECIDING

Our desire to know and our achievement of knowledge is not an end point. There is more. Our knowing is oriented toward action: we desire to know because we desire to act, and act intelligently. Our experiencing, understanding, and judging are directed not just to what is, but to what is to be done, not just to knowing reality, but to creating reality, and creating ourselves in the process. The contemporary theological emphasis on *praxis*, on intelligent action, is a direct reflection of this basic human desire not only to know but to act, and to act knowingly.

In this chapter we focus on the fact that the radical dynamism of the human spirit that drives us to cognitive self-transcendence, to going beyond ourselves in affirming what is true, also thrusts us to going beyond ourselves in action. The spirit of attentive, intelligent, and critical inquiry becomes on the fourth level of personal consciousness the spirit of responsible decision and action. The radical dynamism of our spirit which manifested itself cognitively as a search for meaning and a demand for evidence now reveals itself on the level of moral consciousness as a quest for value and an insistence coming from within us on self-consistency in knowing and doing. In other words, because the "I" who must decide what to do is the same "I" who has judged that I should do "X," I feel a demand to do "X." But the demand is subject to my consent and decision. It is not necessary; I can do otherwise. Such is the familiar human experience commonly known as conscience, and the concrete possibility for a crisis of conscience. This, for example, is what John F. Kennedy had in mind when he conceived *Profiles in Courage*: striking instances of elected representatives voting for what they judged to be right, regardless of the serious personal costs they could anticipate for so doing.[1] To document political conscience in the three decades since Kennedy's slim volume would require an encyclopedia, with individual volumes for topics like civil rights, Vietnam, and abortion. Politicians, of course, are professionals; at our most innocent moments we expect them to make tough judgments and stick by them—that is what they get paid for. Fortunately, professionals have no corner on conscience and on the crises of conscience which inevitably arise. Just out of the spotlight the amateurs have struggled with the same issues simply because they would be authentic; their stories would fill not encyclopedias but whole libraries.

DYNAMIC QUESTIONING:
THE TRANSCENDENTAL NOTION OF VALUE

Perhaps we should review this practical pattern of knowing and deciding in a slightly more detailed fashion, this time in terms of the dynamic questions which embody our drive for self-transcendence. The previous chapter focused on the questioning which strives to make sense of our experience and on the questioning which aims to sort out the insights that really hit the bull's-eye from all the other bright ideas that fade under tough scrutiny. We saw the dynamism for self-transcendence first show itself as the question searching for understanding, then, after hitting upon an idea, transform itself and appear as the question that demands verification, casting its critical eye on the latest brainstorm and asking, "Is it really so?" "Will it work?" "What evidence is there?"

Because of the ethical focus of this chapter, however, we have moved beyond our experienced desire to know the universe to our experienced need to act in it. So, beyond the questions for intelligence by which we reach out for meaning, and beyond those for critical reflection by which we attempt to establish true meaning, we must also take into account now what Lonergan calls questions for deliberation, by which we seek to determine what is to be done. When we are oriented in a practical direction, in other words, understanding regards not just what is, but also what might be. But a possible course of action grasped by practical insight is not automatically translated into action. Practical reflection scrutinizes it from every angle, including the important angle of probable consequences. Still, even consequences are factual, and we may ask how desirable they would be in terms of the human good. A new job possibility, for example, may have a higher salary, greater sense of achievement, more personal stress, and increased strain on family relationships as its foreseeable factual consequences; one must still evaluate these consequences in terms of the fuller human good. Practical reflection, then, moves from the realm of fact into that of *value* when we deliberate about the goodness of a possible course of action. As factual questions of practical reflection are answered by judgments of fact, evaluative questions of deliberation are answered by judgments of value. For Lonergan, value judgments are objective in the same way factual judgments are, insofar, that is to say, as they proceed from a self-transcending subject, from a person who is actually achieving what is true and what is good.

But practical deliberation is directed not just to the knowledge of value but also, and especially, to the realization of value in action. In deliberation we ask, "Is *this* course of action, beyond all personal pleasure or pragmatic advantage, truly valuable and one *I* should follow?" Ultimately, if the answers to these questions are affirmative, we must also face what can be the toughest question of all: "What am I going to *do* about it?" This question demands neither a judgment of fact nor a judgment of value, but a *decision*. And because this question is pressed by the same drive for self-transcendence which urged the questions for understanding and judgment, it is realized concretely as an exigence or drive for self-consistency in knowing and deciding, as an imperious demand arising from within us that we conform our decision to our best judgment of what we *should* do. Even if we judge that the new job is not desirable when all its foreseeable consequences are assessed in light of our wider human values, we still must *decide* to pass it up, overcoming the powerful attraction of a higher salary. Clearly, then, we are drawing a sharp distinction not only between the fourth level of moral consciousness and its cognitive predecessors on the basis of value, but also between two different phases of self-transcendence within the fourth level itself on the basis of the differences between judgments of value and decisions. At the same time we recognize that these two phases are intimately linked by the dynamic thrust for self-transcendence which urges us to decide to act in line with our judgments of value.[2]

In tracing the dynamic questions which embody the radical drive for self-transcendence—What is it? Is it so? What do I do about it?—we have been explicating the basic orientations of our consciousness, our orientations to the intelligible, the true, and the good. Lonergan calls them the transcendental notions since they transcend any particular area of questioning and apply to all areas. We seek for what is true in biology and psychology, in world affairs and in our daily lives. In contrast to categories, such as the different species of animals or the periodic table in chemistry, which involve asking specific questions and giving determinate answers through experiencing, understanding, judging, and deciding, transcendentals are the dynamic ground of questioning; they are the radical intending in our questions for intelligence, reflection, and deliberation that constitutes our capacity for development and self-transcendence. Our desire to understand is the intention or transcendental notion of intelligibility. And just as our desire to understand becomes a desire to understand correctly, the intention of intelligibility becomes the intention or transcendental notion of being. Finally, as our desire to know reality becomes a desire of the good, so the intention of being becomes the intention or transcendental notion of value. In Lonergan's account, then, the transcendental notions are the successive, unfolding stages of a single, dynamic principle that not only promote us to full consciousness, but in so doing thrust us toward ever fuller knowledge of reality and ever fuller realization of the good. These transcendental notions, then, direct us to appropriate goals; in questions for deliberation, for example, we are intending value even though we are not yet knowing or realizing value. And they also provide criteria for the attainment of these goals; the drive to value, Lonergan says, "rewards success in self-transcendence with a happy conscience and saddens failures with an unhappy conscience."[3] Recalling times when deciding to act in accord with their best judgment resulted in a happy conscience should help readers begin to identify these transcendental notions in their own experience. Reflection on instances of unhappy conscience is also a valuable exercise toward greater authenticity.

CONSCIENCE: THE MORALLY CONSCIOUS SELF

This is the structure, then, of our drive for self-transcendence, the practical pattern of our desires oriented toward action: the questions for intelligence, critical reflection, and deliberation which concretely embody the drive; and the responding operations of understanding, judging, and deciding which effect it. This is really, of course, the structure of the conscious self oriented actively in a world of meaning and value. Notice how, especially at the point of deliberation for decision, we keep coming back to the *self.* While the self is present at the center of every phase of the drive for self-transcendence, that presence takes on greater significance at each higher level of conscious activity. I may easily complain about my deplorable memory and failing eyesight, but I am more touchy about my powers of discrimination, and I get downright defensive if you question my rationality. And, finally, at the level of moral consciousness, of deliberation and decision, criticism of my sense of responsibility becomes fighting words. Because now you are not just criticizing my moral responsibility, you are attacking *me,* or so it seems to me! In a very important way I *am* my moral consciousness, my conscience.[4] And now, because of this identity, it is not just some more or less important aspect of me that is at issue, but my integrity, my authenticity, indeed my very self is at stake. "Honor" may be an old-fashioned word, but when it is used in its deepest sense, rather than the superficial one of social face-saving, it points to the core reality of responsibility at the center of moral consciousness. And, as Robert Bolt showed so vividly in *A Man for All Seasons,* that reality is no respecter of linguistic fashions.[5] Bolt portrays Thomas

More as a man with an adamantine sense of self, a man of conscience, which is to say the same thing. For to More, conscience *is* self, and to betray one is to betray the other. Discussing with Norfolk the Apostolic Succession of the Pope, which he understands to forbid the required Oath, More admits it is a theory, and says, "But what matters to me is not whether it's true or not but that I believe it to be true, or rather, not that I *believe* it, but that *I* believe it. . . . " When a man takes an oath, More says, "he's holding his own self in his own hands." Again, "In matters of conscience, the loyal subject is more bounden to be loyal to his conscience than to any other thing." And when his daughter asks More if he has not already done as much as God can reasonably want, he answers: "Well . . . finally . . . it isn't a matter of reason; finally it's a matter of love." To this point we must return before long, for love, as we shall see, is the very heart of the moral matter.

VALUE AND FEELINGS

Having claimed that conscience is the morally conscious self in its drive to go beyond itself, we must now stress that this radical drive for self-transcendence is a dynamism of the whole person. Any intellectualist suggestion of the foregoing cognitive-structural sketch notwithstanding, the personal drive for self-transcendence is affective at its very core. Lonergan insists that our feelings—joys and sorrows, fears and desires—give our intentional consciousness its mass and momentum, its drive and power. These and countless other feelings dynamically orient us in a human world mediated by meaning.

We cannot imagine the experience of discovery apart from the enthusiastic anticipation that precedes it, the ecstatic excitement that accompanies it, or the joyful satisfaction that follows it. If this is true on the cognitive levels, it is even more so at the fourth level of evaluation and deliberation, where we grasp values within feelings themselves. Indeed, such apprehension of value—especially the ontic value of persons—is the very ground of moral consciousness.[6] We should therefore examine Lonergan's consideration of the point in some detail. His basic statement sets the structural context of our inquiry quite directly: "Intermediate between judgments of fact and judgments in value lie apprehensions of value. Such apprehensions are given of feelings."[7]

Lonergan first distinguishes in the realm of feelings between "non-intentional states and trends" and "intentional responses." Non-intentional states are fatigue, anxiety, bad humor. Trends or urges include hunger, thirst, sexual discomfort. Such states and trends have causes or goals, but they require no perceiving, imagining, or representing of the cause or goal. We simply *feel* tired or hungry. Later we might diagnose the problem as lack of rest or food. Values are apprehended not in these states and trends, but in the intentional responses which answer to the intended, the apprehended, the represented, and which relate us not simply to a cause or end, but to an object. Loving someone is not like having a stomach ache. A stomach ache is a state; love is a response to value.

But values are not apprehended in every intentional response, for even these responses regard two kinds of objects: the satisfying or dissatisfying, pleasure or pain, on the one hand, and on the other, the valuable, the truly good. Feelings, then, even those that respond to objects intentionally, are ambiguous. Sometimes the valuable and the satisfying coincide, and self-transcendence comes easily. But often enough, as we all know too well, the valuable is dissatisfying, disagreeable, and then self-transcendence means overcoming the disagreeable for the sake of doing the good. Not having that second or third drink so that one can drive home safely is choosing value over satisfaction. Thus, while feelings are the source of values, they are not an unambiguous source, and require critical discernment. Yet, when feelings do respond to value, we can be moved effectively toward self-transcendence, for then we respond not just as knowers but as whole persons with, as Lonergan puts it, the stirring of our very being at the possibility of moral self-transcendence. Indeed, feelings can be so strong and deep that they shape our horizon, give direction to our life. We can be consumed by hatred, but also driven by love.

Feelings not only respond to value, but, in Lonergan's analysis, they respond according to an ascending scale of preference. *Vital* values such as health are usually preferred to avoiding the effort and cost of maintaining them (ask any jogger). *Social* values such as caring for the environment condition the vital values of a whole community (unpolluted air is good for everyone, joggers and the sedentary alike). *Cultural* values, such as education and art, though dependent on vital and social values, go beyond them, just as the meaning and value we search for in our living go beyond that living (not on jogging alone do even joggers live). *Personal* value is the self-transcending person: loving, creating value, inspiring others to the same loving life of value (even joggers need and can become role models). *Religious* values, finally, lie at the heart of the meaning and value of our living and our world; because our desire is unrestricted, we are finally satisfied with nothing less than ultimate meaning and value (even winning a marathon does not bring ultimate fulfillment).

Lonergan notes the moral significance of recognizing that feelings develop. Though fundamentally spontaneous in their origin, not lying at the beck and call of decision, once arisen, feelings may be reinforced by approval and curtailed by disapproval. Because of the centrality of feelings in moral consciousness, this discriminating process of enriching, refining, and pruning of feelings is the heart of moral education. Besides development, there are also aberrations of feelings, and because self-knowledge is of the whole person, authenticity requires that we take cognizance of all our feelings, however deplorable they may be. Values, after all, are not purely rational, abstract realities; they are rooted in our feelings at the depths of our psyche, and share the limits as well as the strengths of those feelings.[8]

In order to summarize our discussion of value to this point, we may note with Lonergan that in judgments of value three components unite: knowledge of reality (human possibilities, probable consequences, etc.), intentional responses to value, and the judgment of value itself.

THE STRUCTURE OF THE HUMAN GOOD

We have discussed the transcendental notion of value which dynamically urges us beyond ourselves toward moral self-transcendence. And we have just considered in some detail the components which come together in judgments of value. But all of this, as we said, is aimed at the realization of value through decision and action. Now we must explain how, in the final unfurling of the transcendental notion of value, the value affirmed in judgment becomes a *terminal* value, an achieved goal, through decisive choice and action in what we specified as the second phase of the fourth level of consciousness. To do this we will situate terminal value within the overall structure of what Lonergan calls the human good, as outlined in the following chart.[9]

Individual		Social	Ends
Potentiality	*Actuation*		
capacity, need	operation	cooperation	particular good
plasticity, perfectibility	development, skill	institution, role, task	good of order
liberty	orientation, conversion	personal relations	terminal value

As individuals we actuate our capacities for operation and thus fulfill needs through realizations of *particular goods*. Because we live in groups much of our operating is cooperating: performing role-tasks within an institutional framework (teaching or learning in an educational system). Because the capacities of individuals are plastic and perfectible, there is the possibility of developing skills, especially those demanded by institutional roles and tasks (so there are not only those dreaded workshops for teachers, but even required courses for college students).

Besides the institutional basis of cooperation, however, there is the actual, concrete way cooperation functions—what Lonergan calls the *good of order* (education, like marriage, is a wonderful institution, but some classrooms remind us of dentists' offices; for that matter, some spouses, I am told, remind their mates of dentists).[10] This good of order is distinct but not separate from instances of the particular good. If particular goods satisfy my needs here and now, the good of order in the realm of meaning regards all particular goods as related and recurrent (reading about Lonergan's theology might be a particular good for you, but education for everyone who wants it is part of the good of order). This sustained succession of recurring particular goods requires an ordering set of "if-then" relationships linking effective desires to properly coordinated operations of cooperating individuals. Beyond the particular good health that jogging gives me, there is the issue of good communal health. This requires the fulfillment of many conditions. Well informed and seriously motivated individuals must together effectively demand an efficient and just system of health care. Such a system of health professionals must be complemented by good personal habits of diet, exercise, rest, etc. and an unfouled environment. If we want the good result, we must fulfill all the conditions. The good of order is based in institutions, then, but most concretely it is also the result of skillful people working together to meet one another's needs against all obstacles within constantly changing circumstances.

We fulfill roles and perform tasks to meet needs, then, but, Lonergan insists, we do so freely. Any course of action is only a limited good; there are always alternatives. Thus evaluation and deliberation are not in themselves decisive. We must bring deliberation to an end through a decisive exercise of liberty—actively choosing one course of action and executing it. Beyond particular goods of desire, then, and beyond the common good of order, there are *terminal* values: true instances of the particular good *actually chosen* in a true good of order.

We exercise our liberty within a matrix of personal relations—common needs, feelings, experiences, understandings, judgments, commitments, orientations, and expectations. But each of these has its opposite; so while personal relations can bind communities together, they can also tear them apart. But in freely choosing terminal values we not only act to meet common needs, we create ourselves as authentic originating values. Since we can know and choose such self-transcending authenticity, originating values can be terminal values. And when each of us both opts for authenticity in ourselves and promotes it in others, then originating and terminal values intertwine in a conspiracy for the human good. But opting for authenticity is moral conversion, a radical change in orientation; and this is the topic of the following sections. So here we should briefly summarize our discussion of conscience and value.

INITIAL SUMMARY

We began with the structure of moral consciousness and have moved in the space of a few pages to its objective correlative in the structure of the human good. We now review that route. We first noted that in a practically oriented pattern of knowing we desire to know in order to act intelligently. We further noted that the same radical dynamism that drives us to move beyond ourselves in realistic knowing also grounds the moral demand we experience to make our decisions for acting conform to our best judgment of what we should do in any given instance. This is what we mean by conscience—specifically, the exigence to make our doing consistent with our knowing; more generally, the morally conscious self evaluating, deliberating, deciding in response to the drive of its spirit for self-transcendence in the realization of value. With Lonergan we named that drive the transcendental notion of value, the full flowering of that questioning eros which in children can drive parents to the brink of lunacy. We stressed that this drive for value is a dynamism of the whole person, and that value is apprehended in feelings. Finally, in our outline of Lonergan's structure of the human good, we specified three dimensions: particular goods of desire, the common good of order, and terminal values. Conscience is our metaphor for these fundamental human phenomena: in the transcendental notion we intend value; in intentional responses of feeling we grasp value; in judgments we affirm value; in decisions we choose value; in actions we realize value.

We perform all these activities in a social context of personal relations, but while they are thus thoroughly interpersonal, social realities, they are in freedom and responsibility radically personal. While we reach for value and choose freely, however, we may not do so arbitrarily, for all our deciding is done under the imperious demand of authenticity. If we are to realize our self-transcending humanity we must choose in line with our judgments of what we should do, which judgments themselves must be made—within a critical community—in fidelity to the demands of our drive for understanding, truth, reality. For on that symbolic day of final judgment, when the ultimate criterion of love takes the shape of personal authenticity, we will be asked how genuine we have been in forming our conscience as well as how faithful we have been in following it.

Finally, we should emphasize: because the radical drive for self-transcendence is dynamic, our personal being is becoming; our very existence is a fundamental process of development. If physical growth is more obvious, moral development reaches more deeply into our being. From the first glimmer of understanding and glimpse of goodness in the young child, through the older child's education into the human world, to the adolescent's blossoming in self-awareness, the development of knowledge and the development of moral feeling, writes Lonergan, "head to the existential discovery, the discovery of oneself as a moral being, the realization that one not only chooses between courses of action but also thereby makes oneself an authentic human being or an unauthentic one. With that discovery," he states, "there emerges in consciousness the significance of personal value and the meaning of personal responsibility."[11] So, finally, we have come to the question of moral conversion. Stay tuned.

HUCK FINN'S MORAL CONVERSION: "YOU CAN'T PRAY A LIE"

One straightforward way of saying what Lonergan means by moral conversion is that in it one discovers one's conscience and begins to take it seriously. Few writers have captured the early budding of this experience as sharply as Mark Twain did in describing the precocious Huck Finn's moral struggle over his friendship with Jim, the runaway slave.

Every reader of his *Adventures* will remember how one day during their raft trip down the Mississippi, Huck, having helped Jim escape, begins to feel the pangs of what he calls his conscience for "stealing a poor old woman's nigger."[12] Huck tries to pin the blame on his wicked upbringing, but cannot avoid the realization that he could have gone to Sunday school where he would have learned that such deeds are punished by everlasting fire. All this makes him shiver, and he resolves to pray, to see if he "couldn't try to quit being the kind of a boy [he] was and be better." He kneels down, but the words will not come. And Huck knows why: his heart is not right, he is "playing double"—only "letting *on* to give up sin." He is trying to say he will do the right thing—write to Jim's owner of his whereabouts, but "deep down" he knows it is a lie: "You can't pray a lie."

After much anguished reflection Huck decides he will write the letter, and *then* see if he can pray. With this decision his troubles disappear and he feels "as light as a feather right straight off." Excited, he quickly writes the letter, and immediately feels "all washed clean of sin for the first time" in his life. Now he knows he can pray. But before he does, Huck starts thinking about how well all this has worked out, and about how close he had come to being lost and going to hell. And as he goes on thinking, he reviews the trip down the river. He recalls in detail how good and kind and loving Jim has always been to him. And as he recalls how Jim had once told him that he was the best friend he has ever had, and now the only one, Huck's eyes fall on the letter. We should turn to Huck's own words at this point. "I took it up, and held it in my hand. I was a-trembling, because I'd got to decide, forever, betwixt two things, and I knowed it. I studied a minute, sort of holding my breath, and then says to myself: 'All right, then, I'll *go* to hell'—and tore it up. It was awful thoughts and awful words, but they was said. And I let them stay said; and never thought no more about reforming."

FROM SUPEREGO TO CONSCIENCE

Turning from Twain back to Lonergan now, how can Huck's experience help us to understand moral conversion? First, in light of our earlier remarks about moral development, we should note that Huck's struggle involves a transition from a moral consciousness defined by socially imposed rules and dominated by the fear of punishment attached to disobeying them, to a moral orientation defined by concern for value and liberated by a loving care that reaches out to others. Though the name "conscience" is often given to both orientations, we might distinguish them by identifying the rule-oriented moral consciousness with the Freudian superego and the value-oriented consciousness with the radical drive for value and self-consistency in knowing and acting we have called the transcendental notion of value. Developmentally, we may speak of this distinction as a transition from an immature to a mature moral consciousness, naming, for the sake of simplicity, the immature phase "superego" and the mature phase "conscience." In saying that moral development is from superego to conscience, from rule-oriented to value-oriented consciousness, however, we should not think of the transition as one that is ever fully completed. It is more a question of emphasis than of one or the other exclusively.

What we see in Huck's experience initially, then, is tension between the moral rules of Huck's superego and his behavior in violation of those rules: one should not take another's property, including slaves. Huck fails in his attempt to escape his feelings of guilt. Fearing the punishment of hell, he wants to straighten out his life. He tries to pray to this end but fails in this, too, because his heart is not in this renunciation of sin. The problem, of course, is that Huck does not really believe he has done wrong in helping Jim escape. He has not yet made this discovery, however, so he writes the letter in proof of his amendment. This is a nice psychological move, and it seems to work, though not for long. Huck is finally too sensitive to be able to deceive himself that easily.

FROM SATISFACTION TO VALUE AND RESPONSIBLE FREEDOM

If we were to stop Huck's story at this point, we would seem to have an example of Lonergan's basic definition of moral conversion: a shift in the criterion for decision from satisfaction to value. Against his careless disregard of justice involved in helping Jim's escape and against the pleasure of their companionship on the river, Huck will opt for the social value of private property. But would he really be opting for value? Is he not tempted rather, out of fear of punishment, to superego conformity to social rules? Writing the letter does make him *feel* better—light as a feather, washed clean of sin. He does seem to have dealt pretty well with his superego guilt. His superego is satisfied.

But Huck does not stop here; his deeper sensitivity to value will not let him. As soon as he allows his attention to shift from his own guilt feelings to his feelings for Jim, Huck's true moral dilemma presents itself to him in starkly clear, existential terms: "I was a-trembling, because I'd got to decide, forever, betwixt two things, and I knowed it." And the "two things" he must decide between are not, he realizes, just two possible courses of action in this situation, one right and one wrong, but two radically different modes of moral existence. Huck is, in other words, confronted with the possibility of a fundamental moral conversion definitive of his very self, of his character, of the kind of person he will be. The full meaning of Lonergan's understanding of moral conversion is at stake: the choice of value as criterion for decision *and* the choice of oneself as a free and responsible moral self. And Huck is "a-trembling" because he knows it. In Lonergan's meaning, moral conversion is not something that just incidentally happens to a person; one deliberately chooses. And, as with Huck, one chooses oneself as a free and responsible creator of value not abstractly, but in the concrete situation of a very specific action decision.

So Huck holds his breath, studies for a minute, and makes his decision. Tearing up the letter, he affirms that if standing by your friend in his search for freedom means going to hell, then he will *go* to hell. In this breath-holding minute of reflection focused on the loving friendship he and Jim share, Huck brings together all the elements of deliberation we examined earlier, and chooses the value of Jim's personal freedom and dignity. In so doing he also chooses himself as free and responsible. Although Huck cannot explain it this way, he has, as we put it above, discovered his conscience and taken it seriously. Because Huck identifies his conscience with the rules of his socially imposed superego, he thinks he has done the "awful" thing of violating his conscience, and he is ready to take whatever punishment that deserves, even the fires of hell. Happily, though it surely was scary for him at the time, Huck casts aside for good all thought about reforming. Huck will need a good course in moral theology to straighten out the language of conscience and moral conversion, but the reality is there. And that, as Huck might put it, is for sure. Of course no one ever said that having a sensitive conscience is easy; and confusion about its function makes it all the more difficult. For example, a bit later in his *Adventures,* Huck, after failing to warn them in time, sees the rapscallion Duke and King cruelly tarred and feathered. He feels terrible, somehow to blame, though he knows *he* had done nothing wrong. He complains that "it don't make no difference whether you do right or wrong, a person's conscience ain't got no sense, and just goes for him *anyway.*" Then Huck expresses his utter contempt for this worthless conscience as only he can. "If I had a yaller dog that didn't know no more than a person's conscience does I would pison him. It takes up more room than all the rest of the person's insides, and yet ain't no good, nohow. Tom Sawyer he says the same."[13]

DEVELOPMENT AS SELF-CREATION

For Lonergan, personal development is to an important degree a process of self-creation. When authentic, this self-creation is a personal realization of the radical dynamism of the human spirit for self-transcendence. Basic to this process of self-creation, as Lonergan explains it, is the fact that "by deliberation, evaluation, decision, action, we can know and do, not just what pleases us, but what is truly good, worthwhile."[14] In other words, as morally conscious the personal subject is "at once practical and existential: practical inasmuch as he is concerned with concrete courses of action; existential inasmuch as control includes self-control, and the possibility of self-control involves responsibility for what he makes of himself."[15]

Self-control can be rooted in quite different personal realities, however. If the ground be mere selfishness, then evaluation and deliberation are limited to determining what is most pleasurable, most advantageous. But self-control can also be rooted in concern for value; and to the extent that our living is a response to value, we effect a real self-transcendence. In every decision, every action that responds to value, we move beyond ourselves, transcend ourselves in a real way. We all have experienced instances of such moral self-transcendence. But it is one thing to transcend ourselves in response to value occasionally. It is another to do it consistently. Only after many years of development does there emerge the *sustained* self-transcendence of the virtuous person. Normative personal conscience is never given as an accomplished fact from the beginning; we have to develop it the "old-fashioned way."

From the earliest years of childhood even our most primitive moral sense must be developed. Our sense of responsibility, indeed, only begins to emerge at around the age of three as we gradually move into the world mediated by meaning and regulated by values. If we supposedly reach the "age of reason" by seven, the reason we reach is still far from maturity. So as children we must be persuaded, ordered, even compelled to do what is right. But as our being is becoming, a degree of autonomy gradually appears, and we want to do, decide, and discover things for ourselves, without adult interference. Tragically, our desire (and before long, need) to do things for ourselves quickly outruns our ability to reasonably judge and responsibly decide for ourselves. Still, despite the time and pain involved, we do gradually grow in knowledge and develop our response to value; we become more and more ourselves, straining toward authenticity.

Precisely in this developing drive toward authenticity lies the possibility of moral conversion. For, in Lonergan's view, it is within this long and gradual process of personal becoming and increasing autonomy that we may reach that crucial point, that existential moment when we discover for ourselves that our deciding and acting affect ourselves no less than the objects of our decisions and actions, and that it is up to each of us to decide for ourselves what we are to make of ourselves. In such a discovery we recognize ourselves as originators of value who create ourselves in every deed, decision, and discovery of our lives, for the subjective effects of these personal acts accumulate as habits, tendencies, and dispositions determining the concrete shape of our very selves. Such a discovery demands that we take hold of and, in radical freedom, responsibly choose ourselves precisely as the originating values we have recognized ourselves to be.

This choice of ourselves as free and responsible creators of value is not forced; it is a radically free, and indeed most difficult, choice. But if we do make it, we establish for ourselves an entirely new personal horizon specified by value as the criterion for our decisions and choices, indeed, for our lives. Of course, even before this discovery and choice of ourselves as responsibly free, we are always creating ourselves. The essential point of moral conversion is that after it occurs, our creation of ourselves is open-eyed and deliberate. In Lonergan's words, "autonomy decides what autonomy is to be."[16] The fact that, before conversion, we make ourselves what we are, without any significant awareness of what we are doing, offers us no escape from responsibility after conversion. For now we can re-create ourselves in the light of better knowledge and fuller responsibility. If we refuse this opportunity for re-creating ourselves, we assume the responsibility, whether we want it or not, for whatever we had made of ourselves before discovering our responsible freedom.

In contrast to open-eyed, deliberate, autonomous persons, there are what Lonergan calls "drifters." Drifters have not yet found themselves. They have not yet discovered their own deeds or their own wills or their own minds, so they are content to do and choose and think what everybody else is doing and choosing and thinking. The point is not that drifters go about deliberately doing evil; the problem, rather, is that they do nothing very deliberately. Either they have never discovered the meaning of human authenticity in themselves, or, if they have, they have never summoned the courage to opt for it—to choose themselves as free and responsible.

FREEDOM, MORAL IMPOTENCE, AND LIBERATION

The unhappy fact is that in describing the drifter Lonergan is really telling the common human story. For most of us are caught somewhere in the tension between drifting and autonomous living. Few of us actualize our essential freedom in anything like its fullness. We may not be compelled to do what we judge best, but, as St. Paul reminds us so forcefully, neither are we completely free to do what we judge best. Our effective freedom is limited in many ways.[17]

Physical and external constraints on our freedom are obvious (most of us are about as free to run a marathon as we are to fly to the moon), but psychoneural limitations are perhaps more telling. There is a fundamental human truth to the old joke that asks, "How do I get to Carnegie Hall?" Even we who are psychically normal and perfectly adjusted must do more than wish to develop a good second serve, let alone master the Goldberg Variations. Of course, not everyone is perfectly adjusted; unwanted insights can be unconsciously rejected, leading to conflict between intellectual and psychoneural development and to the resulting neurotic restriction of our capacity for effective deliberation and choice. Further, the development of understanding is itself limited; we must struggle through the process of learning. The range of possible courses of action we can even consider is subject to the present limitations of our practical intelligence. Finally, like our understanding, so too is our willingness to act limited. Willingness can be expanded by persuasion, but persuasion, like learning, takes time. Meanwhile, we are closed to otherwise possible courses of action.

Beyond the superficial restriction of freedom resulting from external circumstance and psychic abnormality, then, Lonergan specifies the profound limitation of freedom rooted in the incomplete development of our capacities to understand and decide. During the long and difficult process of personal development we must live and make decisions in the light of underdeveloped intelligence and under the guidance of incomplete willingness. And in this radical limitation Lonergan locates moral impotence: the gap between our potential effective freedom and our actual effective freedom. Because continuous growth is rare, our desire for greater effective freedom is vitiated in countless ways: from neurotic aberrations and refusals to give up settled routines to the devious attempts to quiet an uneasy conscience by undermining values. Then our feelings become soured, our value preferences distorted. Our outlooks are corrupted by bias, our morals by rationalization, our thought by ideology.

Our evaluations are biased not just by unconscious motivations, but also by egoistic disregard of others, group loyalty hostile to outsiders, and humanity's common bane of overlooking long-term costs by concentrating on short-term benefits.[18]

And rationalization is not the only way we try to dodge the exigence for self-consistency in knowing and doing. Besides that attempt to revise our knowing into conformity with our doing, there is the common escape of avoiding self-consciousness. We remember how Huck tried unsuccessfully to slip moral scrutiny by blaming his wicked upbringing. Finally, there is the attempt to escape through moral renunciation: a virtuous life is a beautiful ideal, but one does have to live in the real world. And so, in all these ways, rather than responding to the motives that lead to ever fuller authenticity, we ignore them, and drift into an ever less authentic selfhood. Of all the forms of ideology, the deepest is the justification of this radical alienation from our drive for self-transcending authenticity.

Where, in all of this, is the possibility of liberation? Effective freedom must be won, but how? We must reach a willingness to persuade ourselves and to submit to others' persuasion. But this is no easy task. How can we be persuaded to openness to rational persuasion if we are not yet open to persuasion? In *Insight,* Lonergan states that the solution lies in a higher integration of human living. We shall see, in the following chapter, that this higher integration is effected by the power of transcendent love experienced in religious conversion. Here, as a first approximation of that ultimate transformation, we shall follow some hints Lonergan drops in *Method in Theology* and consider the personal reality of affective conversion.

AFFECTIVE CONVERSION AND AUTHENTICITY

Moral conversion, it should by now be clear, is no easy matter. Indeed, it is extremely difficult to overcome the resistance with which the psyche responds to the possibility of conversion, of moving into a radically new horizon. For our horizons define not abstractions but the concrete shape of our living. And to contemplate a radical change in the style of our concrete living is to invite an experience of dread. The spontaneous and powerful resistance generated by this dread defends the challenged horizon with a logic rooted in its own meanings and values, and therefore unimpeachable on its own grounds. Thus conversion to a new horizon must be a non-logical leap, effected not principally by logic but by symbols which tunnel under the logical defenses to reach our horizon's imaginative and affective center, our hearts. While moral conversion is a matter of discovery and decision, then, it is also a matter of *desire:* of feeling in the demand to respond to the call to responsible freedom a joy over the prospect of growth toward more authentic life.

As difficult as the leap of moral conversion may be, however, it is more a beginning than an end, more a challenge than an achievement. To be morally converted is not to be morally perfect. Conversion must be ongoing. For insofar as moral conversion reveals how drastically limited our effective freedom really is, we must commit ourselves to the endless task of continuing conversion. The problem of moral impotence and liberation, then, is not just a question of experiencing moral conversion, but also the issue of meeting the challenge posed by moral conversion—the challenge of becoming an ever more authentic source of love dedicated to the ever greater realization of true value. If, given the radical limitations on our freedom, this challenge appears impossible, we may well ask if indeed there is a real possibility of *living* a morally converted life. For Lonergan, that possibility lies in the reality of love, just as it did for Thomas More.

A person is affectively self-transcendent, Lonergan points out, when the isolation of the individual is broken and he or she spontaneously acts not just for self but for others as well. Further, when a person falls in love, his or her love is embodied not just in this or that act or even in any series of acts, but in a dynamic state of being-in-love. Such being-in-love is the concrete first principle from which a person's affective life flows: "one's desires and fears, one's joys and sorrows, one's discernment of values, one's decisions and deeds."[19] Falling-in-love, in other words, is a more or less radical transformation of a person's life: affective conversion.[20] Such conversion turns one's self, shifts one's orientation, from an absorption in one's own interests to concern for the good of others. If moral conversion is the recognition of the possibility and thus the felt challenge, of becoming a living principle of benevolence and beneficence, affective conversion is the transformation of personal being which actualizes that possibility, which makes effective response to that challenge a reality. Affective conversion, therefore, is the concrete possibility of overcoming moral impotence, of not only being able to make a decision to commit oneself to a course of action or direction of life judged worthwhile and personally appropriate, but of being able to execute that decision over the long haul against serious obstacles.

The reality of falling-in-love, of course, has as many versions as there are love stories. There is the beaming love of young parents for their newborn child; there is the love of sons and daughters for mothers and fathers which grows through years of responding to the wonders of parental self-transcendence. Such familial self-transcendence grounds the possibility, too, of the intimate love between a woman and a man—from the boundless dreams and reckless self-giving of young lovers to the gentle touch and knowing smiles of a peaceful couple remembering a half-century through which they have grown together in each other's love.

Life, of course, is made of more than love stories. Right alongside are ugly tales of hatred and brutality, misunderstanding and resentment, indifference and bitter disappointment—tales which too often end without a hint of forgiveness, reconciliation, hope. At the end of a century that has witnessed human atrocities of the most staggering proportions, a story that ignores the full potential of the human heart for evil is less credible than a fairy tale. Still, if life is not an innocent story in which prince charmings and fairy godmothers always emerge triumphant, there are indeed instances of self-transcending love. As the lives of individuals as different as Martin Luther King and Mother Teresa of Calcutta remind us, when the mutual love of families and friends is authentic it does not remain absorbed in an *égoisme à deux* or three or more, but reaches out beyond itself to the neighbor, not to "humanity," but to the concrete person in need, whoever or wherever that person is.

Affective conversion should be understood as a matter of *both passion and commitment*. Affective conversion *is* the transformation of our deepest life of feeling. Without the radical reorientation of our passionate desires from obsession with self-needs to concern for the needs of others, there is no affective conversion. But because fundamental conversion is always a fully personal reality, affective conversion is not exclusively a matter of passion, feeling, emotion. The centrifugal reorientation of the passionate desires of our affective life, having been nudged and coaxed by symbols, briefed and guided by reflection, finally needs to be thoroughly personalized in the decision of commitment to love. Such commitment is powerful when it crystalizes the other-centered reorientation of feeling. Still, loving commitment is directed toward service; the criterion, then, for passionate commitment to others, for authentic affective conversion, lies in action.

Such, according to Lonergan, is the story of our moral life writ by conscience. Our desire for the authenticity of a self-transcending life demands responsible choice consistent with critical, realistic judgments of fact and value. But, despite our drive for truth and value, both our knowing and our choosing are riddled with the limitations of incomplete development. Any serious attempt at the sustained self-transcendence of authentic living, then, faces the stubborn fact of moral impotence: desire straining under the burden of leaden weights. But if feeling, the locus of value, gives our conscious life its mass and momentum, as Lonergan says, the radical transformation of feeling in affective conversion gives the power of sustained self-transcendence, of authentic living. In this transformation we realize that personal development is only partially self-creation; it is also, and centrally, a radical gift. The fullness of this transformation, and therefore of its power, lies in religious conversion.

NOTES

[1]John F. Kennedy, *Profiles in Courage* (New York: Harper & Row, 1956).

[2]In this section I have integrated into a single explanation Lonergan's somewhat different discussions of the material in *Insight* (ch. 18) and *Method in Theology* (ch. 2).

[3]Lonergan, *Method in Theology*, p. 35.

[4]We must remember, of course, that on the basis of the principle of sublation, each higher level of consciousness (self) incorporates the preceding levels; see Lonergan, *Method in Theology*, p. 340.

[5]Robert Bolt, *A Man for All Seasons* (New York: Random House Vintage, 1962); for quotations below, see pp. 53, 81, 89.

[6]For a particularly helpful discussion of the affective dimension of moral consciousness, see Daniel C. Maguire, *The Moral Choice* (Garden City: Doubleday, 1978), esp. ch. 9, "The Feel of Truth."

[7]Lonergan, *Method in Theology*, p. 37. Lonergan's analysis of feelings is explicitly dependent on the work of Max Scheler and Dietrich von Hildebrand.

[8]See Lonergan's discussion of dramatic bias in *Insight*, pp. 191–206.

[9]Lonergan, *Method in Theology*, p. 48.

[10]Some of my best friends are dentists.

[11]Lonergan, *Method in Theology*, p. 38.

[12]Mark Twain, *The Adventures of Huckleberry Finn* (New York: Grosset & Dunlap, 1948 [1884]); quotes in this section are from ch. 31.

[13]*Ibid.*, ch. 33.

[14]Lonergan, *Method in Theology,* p. 35.

[15]Bernard Lonergan, "Faith and Beliefs" (mimeographed paper presented at the Annual Meeting of the American Academy of Religion, Newton, Mass., October 1969), p. 6.

[16]Bernard Lonergan, *Collection,* ed. F. E. Crowe (New York: Herder and Herder, 1967), p. 242. Moral conversion may be *critical* or *uncritical.* In other words, in moral conversion we can critically recognize and accept the responsibility of discovering and establishing our own values (in dialogue with our community), or we may merely turn uncritically toward and accept some *given* set of values of whatever conventional source. Critical moral conversion involves our tacit but nonetheless real recognition and choice of self as criterion of the real and the truly good in our own self-transcending judgments and choices (an at least implicit intellectual conversion). Though uncritical moral conversion is a real enough conversion (from satisfaction to value), it presupposes no conversion of knowing, only sufficient cognitive development to make possible a clear distinction in the good been "value" and the "good for me." For a detailed analysis of the critical and uncritical forms of moral conversion, see Walter E. Conn, *Conscience: Development and Self-Transcendence* (Birmingham: Religious Education Press, 1981), pp. 190–94.

[17]See Lonergan, *Insight,* pp. 622–23.

[18]On individual, group, and general bias, see *ibid.,* pp. 218–42.

[19]Lonergan, *Method in Theology,* p. 105.

[20]On affective conversion, see Bernard Lonergan, "Natural Right and Historical Mindedness," *Proceedings of the American Catholic Philosophical Association* 51 (1977): 132–43, at 140–41; and Walter E. Conn, "Bernard Lonergan's Analysis of Conversion," *Angelicum* 53/3 (1976): 362–404, at 385–91.

FURTHER READING

Carmody, John. *Reexamining Conscience.* New York: Seabury, 1982.

Conn, Walter. *Christian Conversion: A Developmental Interpretation of Autonomy and Surrender.* New York: Paulist, 1986.

Conn, Walter E. (editor). *Conversion: Perspectives on Personal and Social Transformation.* New York: Alba House, 1978.

Gilligan, Carol. *In a Different Voice: Psychological Theory and Women's Development.* Cambridge: Harvard University Press, 1982.

Haughton, Rosemary. *The Transformation of Man: Conversion and Community.* New York: Paulist, 1967.

Kegan, Robert. *The Evolving Self: Problem and Process in Human Development.* Cambridge: Harvard University Press, 1982.

Kohlberg, Lawrence. *The Philosophy of Moral Development.* San Francisco: Harper & Row, 1981.

Nelson, C. Ellis (editor). *Conscience: Theological and Psychological Perspectives.* New York: Paulist/Newman, 1973.

III. The Desire for Transcendence: Religious Conversion

Bernard Lonergan's fullest discussion of precisely religious issues occurs in Chapter 4 of *Method in Theology*. To focus that discussion on religious conversion and extend its implications into the world religions and explicit Christianity, I shall deal with the following topics: God, Religious Experience, The Word, Faith, World Religions, and Christian Religion.

GOD

True to his intellectualist cast, Lonergan approaches God by way of human questioning. God lies within the horizon of our interests and competence because God arises quite naturally as a question. Even if we were not to hear about God in church or from television and radio, we probably would ask questions (about the overall meaning of life, the choice between good and evil, the ultimacy of death, and the like) that imply God (usually in the form of The Beginning or The Beyond).[1] Since Lonergan is a quite precise thinker, who rivets onto the dynamics of human consciousness that offer us a universal tool (transcendental method: the normative pattern that emerges when we take our lead from the core cognitional structure of experiencing-understanding-judging-deciding), he locates the question of God precisely at the term of a reflection on the drives of the human spirit to transcend itself and understand its world. Specifically, Lonergan shows how God emerges when we inquire about the possibility of fruitful inquiry, reflect on the nature of reflection, and deliberate on the worth of deliberation.[2]

If we study the fact of human inquiry, the actual phenomenon as it occurs in both ourselves and any other animals capable of writing ragtime, we find that our inquiries assume that the world is intelligible. When we set off to the bank to find out why our checkbook balance is $57.62 less than that of Mid-Kansas Federal Savings and Loan or Manufacturers Hanover Trust, we assume that an answer is possible; the nature of banking is rational. So too when we go to the dermatologist to get rid of an irksome rash, go to a professor to map out a seminar paper, open Escoffier to find out the composition of Bernaise sauce. Our world is intelligible. It makes sense to probe and search. But could our experiences of probing and searching report this back if the universe had no intelligent ground? Could what makes sense but is partial be as it is without God, that which is full and makes complete sense?

Lonergan says, then, that God is ingredient in any thorough questioning of what human inquiring implies. We cannot study the phenomenon of people searching the world, scientists and den mothers trying to gain order, without coming to the bottom line question of where the intelligibility of the world, our confidence that inquiry is worthwhile, comes from. This bottom line question is the question of God.

Equally, God becomes a question when we reflect on the fact that human beings reflect. Human beings reflect in order to determine what probably is or is not so. In Lonergan's terms, reflection is the process of judgment, which heads toward a virtually unconditioned—a reality or state of affairs that possesses the requisites for existing. But to speak of a virtually unconditioned is to raise the question of a purely unconditioned—that which has no outside or extrinsic requisites for existing but exists on its own, necessarily. Such a being is God. So when we examine the process of reflection or judgment we enter upon a line of thought that, if we take it to its logical end, raises the question of God. To think as human beings do, ponder as bankers and lawyers, generals and artists, parents and offspring all can, is to perform an activity which, under analysis, reveals the human being's orientation to or possible dependence upon "God," a reality that would fix the process of reflection, take the judgmental chain out of thin air and pound it into solid ground.

Finally, God becomes a question when we deliberate about whether deliberation is worthwhile. Deliberation is the familiar process of asking ourselves about the value of something. Is all the toil and pressure of a college education worthwhile? Does raising a family justify the hard work and worry? What makes the Church worthy (or unworthy) of membership? What gives the arms race its justification (or lack thereof)? So deliberation is quintessentially human, an activity characteristic of *homo sapiens*. But what are the implications of this characteristically human activity? If we study it through, chew on its assumptions and consequences, where do we come out? Lonergan thinks that we come out at the question of God.

Initially, God may be implied in the query whether the word "worthwhile" has any ultimate meaning. Does the world actually justify our praise of progress and reasonableness, our denunciation of decline and sin? Is the universe on the side of this moral evaluation that we so regularly make? This question is but the obverse or front-facing side of the question of God as the final and guaranteeing Good. Is there a final cause, an unambiguous value, to ground the universe as deserving our moral strivings, matching up with our efforts to pursue what is good and contest what is evil? Such a final cause is what we mean by God, so the question of God is at the marrow of our deliberations about deliberation, our search for the foundations of an ethical or moral life.

On Lonergan's reading, the question of God clearly follows from the way that people actually live. It is a question natural and proper, not heterogeneous or contrived. Thus any merely verbal analysis of "God" that prescinds from the actual occurrence of human inquiry, reflection, and deliberation about worthwhileness misses the point. God is not a name or term so much as the grounding mystery to which all names and terms point when they reach the Beginning and Beyond of human light and love.

The question of God will have different colorings and textures in different cultures and historical epochs. Sometimes it will be badly framed, distorted by secondary issues, not seen for what it is: the central interrogation that our constitutive drives naturally raise when we let them unfold systematically or passionately. Only by restricting human inquiry, reflection, or deliberation so that they do not become self-conscious and self-critical can we ward off the question of God. Unless we truncate the human spirit, it spontaneously asks about the whole, the ground, the origin, the term of itself and the world. Thus few (if any) human cultures have not produced sizable testimonies to a prolonged struggle with the question of God. Even atheists and agnostics testify to the weight and pull of this question. Whenever the human spirit stretches out to its full span, unfurls its natural unrestriction, at least implicitly it raises the question of God.[3]

So for Lonergan God is part and parcel of human authenticity, because human authenticity requires constant self-transcendence or unfurling. Unless we are moving beyond our narrower capacities, refusing to let lower levels of consciousness determine our meaning, we are not living authentically human lives. But such self-transcendence soon raises the question of God, because it soon runs into the issue of what grounds its experiencing, understanding, judging, and deciding. And if specific loves, such as friendship or the love of marriage, actualize important parts of our capacity for self-transcendence, the love of God actualizes its ultimate basis, the unlimited potential of our knowledge and love. The love of God that Christian Scripture describes (Mk 12:30; Rom 5:5) is God's own doing. There the divinity that was a question reaches into our midst to become an answer. There the question that might be terrifying becomes wonderful. No longer may we try to justify our inquiry, reflection, or deliberation in a narrowly scientific or detached way, as though we could manipulate God. The love of God makes us humble and encourages us to think of the unconditioned holistically, a question posed as much to our hearts as our minds.

For Lonergan the God of the philosophers is not different from the God of Abraham, Isaac, and Jacob, the fathers of biblical faith. What the philosophers seek by the path of inquiry, reflection, and deliberation, the biblical fathers experienced as a living mystery capable of changing their lives. The questions that change lives are those most mysterious ones that challenge our deepest assumptions. If, for instance, we assume that God is limited to the significances accorded divinity in our particular religious tradition or national culture, we can be in for a pleasant surprise. In place of the legalistic or remote entity that our tradition may have described we can find a thickness of significance so rich that it elevates our whole sense of self and destiny. Frequently that is how God becomes real for people who previously barely entertained the question of divinity.

Sitting beside the sea on a lovely day, or beside a sick child through a desperate night, we may sense that "it all" hinges on the ultimate character of the universe, what sort of source and term the world has. Is the void, the ultimate, the formless Beginning and Beyond solid and benevolent? Can it be a surplus of meaning, not poorer than what we imagine but far richer? Or does our drive for ultimate meaning, for a purely unconditioned, make our existence in space and time absurd? Are we useless passions, as Jean-Paul Sartre once put it, beings that burn after meaning and love to no avail? Does the mystery that hangs over every truly crucial question, both obscuring and intensifying what we ought to treasure and do, lure us toward holiness or depravity, authenticity or self-destruction?

Lonergan's testimony clearly is that God's love is the crux of human authenticity, the fullest flowering of human self-transcendence. It is the warmth and light poured forth in our hearts by the Holy Spirit, the Christian God as given to us and received by us, that most brings our spirits aglow. By the logic of human life, the whole pattern of our thrusting, striving consciousnesses, we reach out to a God, a whole, that would purify us of our limitations and disorders, give real rest to our restless hearts. By the richer logic of revelation, God reaches into our lives, becomes himself our spiritual meat and drink, bringing a telltale peace and joy. Like the amazingly good father who rushes out to meet the prodigal son (Lk 15), Lonergan's God takes the initiative, has in Christ drawn closer, become more interior, than our questioning alone would ever have expected. Loving this God can offset pain and privation, keep us going through humiliation, failure, and disease. Such love is not a sop but an encouragement, not a rest that undercuts responsibility but a rest that increases our resistance to evil and injustice.

Without the question of God, human culture stands starved and twisted, denatured into spastic forms. Without the love of God, individual human beings become trivial and frustrated, their capacities shriveled for lack of deepest challenge and fulfillment. Then fun, ruthlessness, despair and the like wreak havoc right and left. Then what should be a cathedral with soaring walls and rose windows becomes a bomb shelter or a prison. The question of God and the mystery that answers by pouring forth love are the very crux of human existence. What we mean and are worth lie squarely in their balance. People who neglect the question of God neglect the one query necessary for their peace. People who miss the love of God cannot be authentic, are bound to end up butchers or fools.

RELIGIOUS EXPERIENCE

Self-transcendence and God's love structure Lonergan's discussion of religious experience. The two meet because we experience God's love in a context of unrestriction. What the Spirit poured forth in our hearts prompts by way of response is a love that is unwilling to set limits. Our love for God is the one warmth and light that has no concern to study the fine print in the contract, rejects limiting our generosity because that would betray the generosity that God has first shown us. This sort of unrestricted self-giving fulfills the capacity for self-transcendence manifested in our limitless questioning. The mystery that we come upon when we keep pushing at our inquiry, reflection, and deliberation is what comes into our hearts and prompts their utter response. When we are in love with God our constant going-beyond has engaged with a worthy beloved. We can keep going-beyond with God endlessly. There is always more light, life, and love to serve, admire, and desire.

The love of God, of course, does not occur apart from the rest of our intellectual and emotional concerns. It can and does play through our work, family life, citizenship, church membership, and the rest. But its own peculiar touchstone is unrestriction, response worthy of an infinite Creator who gratuitously has chosen to be an infinite love. Still, being in love with God does change all the rest of our lives. No work, family life, citizenship, church membership, and the like cannot be seared or burnished by its flame. In Lonergan's terms, the unrestricted love that is the heartbeat of genuine religion sets up a new horizon. It resets our values and alters our knowing. The pieces of our lives do not so much alter their individual identities as find themselves set into new relationships. Like the pieces of glass in a kaleidoscope, which shift as one alters their border, religious conversion makes the pieces of our lives give off new light and color.

For example, study is no longer either an end in itself or something unmysterious. A math problem is still a math problem but it can be *sublated* into the larger contexts of human culture and divine reality. So on occasion we may praise God for the human mind that can work the marvels of mathematical rigor and complexity. We may see that the drive of the mathematical mind to understand what may be is an inquiry consonant with the philosophical quest for an explanation of the universe. Indeed, it is even consonant with the religious love of a mysterious universe, a world so vast and deep that its explanation could only be the understanding of God. Thus mathematics need not be mere games or mental gymnastics. Without losing its proper autonomy, the good that comes when one concentrates only on its own rules and demands, mathematics can become a remarkable instance of the human light that seeks a fullness of explanation, the human capacity that can only be fulfilled by a limitless object or partner of love.

Religious conversion is the turning-around that resets our consciousnesses in terms of unrestricted love. When we are religiously converted, our hearts, the centers of ourselves, open to embrace whatever is good, noble, true, humanizing. If so, religious conversion is a yes to the mystery of God, an acceptance of the Creator's ground-rules or conditions. We have been made to be beyond all partial goods and truths, to reject all idolatries. If we are to be authentic, we must refuse to worship anything less than the unlimited, infinite goodness that whispers in our limitless questioning. Lonergan-ian religion therefore is a capital part (indeed the foundation) of human authenticity. It is an orientation of consciousness to the love that gives a good conscience, a joy and peace that stabilize all our other knowings and loves.

When Lonergan describes religious experience he makes his own such cognate descriptions as Rudolf Otto's view of the holy, Paul Tillich's view of being grasped by ultimate concern, Karl Rahner's description of Ignatius Loyola's consolation without previous cause. These are variants on Lonergan's own portrait of unrestriction. Like his love without limits, they stress the personality's openness, acceptance of mystery, willingness to plunge into the dark depths of the creature-Creator relationship where a God too vast and good for our comprehension takes us into the divine interiority. There we are in love with Dante's love that moves the stars. There we are wedded to our Maker. With whole mind, heart, soul, and strength we try to honor the primordial fact that we are not our own, have been fashioned by an Other of a quite different order, will only be "home" when we rest in an unlimited embrace. This religious experience is not something that we can know or understand as we can know or understand finite experiences, work out their meanings and realities. But it is the fulfillment of our fourth level of human consciousness, of the choosing and loving that complete what our prior experiencing, understanding, and judging have sought.

Religious conversion therefore explicates a love affair. It turns us into people whose joy and fulfillment are contemplating and serving the holy love that is divinity. Thus religious conversion leads to prayer and practical love of neighbor. It leads to our opposing what is ungodly, even our willingness to suffer for divine standards. To be sure, all but the most dazzling saints among us are very imperfect religious lovers. The rest of us neither pray nor pursue justice with the generosity that our divine lover deserves. So for most of us religious progress, growth in authenticity, is dialectical: three steps forward and two steps back. For those who have at least somewhat appropriated the *world of interiority,* however, progress is nothing external, not at all assimilable to an accountant's balance sheet. They realize that the love of God produces a dynamic state of *being* in love, that the grace of God that communicates divine life becomes the inmost definer of what the religious person is.

At this point, religious conversion has become effective, quite actually has taken hold. It is nothing to brag about. We remain unprofitable servants who must give all the glory to God. But we are in a relationship, a love affair, that has uttered its nuptial vows, made a lifelong and exhaustive commitment. For better or worse, richer or poorer, in sickness or health we know that the love of God ought to be our main treasure and reliance. In the dialectical way mentioned above we try to let the love of God assist the full ripening of our authenticity. If we keep to our prayer and efforts at social service, we discover dozens of ways in which we continue to sin and fall short of God's glory. All of these call us to transcend our present imperfections, hold back less because of selfishness and fear.

Perfect love casts out fear and selfishness. Even imperfect but honest love disavows the places where it remains closed to the divine invitation to self-transcendence, admits that there can be no valid stopping short of whole mind, heart, soul, and strength. Still, Lonergan stresses the many aberrations that religious expressions of being in love unrestrictedly can generate. We must let God strike a balance between immanence and transcendence, being with us and being ever beyond. We must make good use of such materials as food and drink, sex and work, ritual and politics, not letting them block or become substitutes for our self-transcending pursuit of the divine mystery itself. The dialectic of religious advance is therefore a demanding maturation. The balance we seek is rarely achieved, testifies impressively to how different the world would be were God's grace regularly to meet with human generosity.

Among the many different expressions of religious experience and conversion Lonergan numbers the major world religious traditions. In all their diversity and lengthy development they amount to a museum in which we can study the many stages of religious meaning. The oldest traditions, for example, tend to start with a symbolism in which the spatial predominates over the temporal, the specific predominates over the generic, the external predominates over the internal, and the human predominates over the divine. The result is a rich treasury of outward occasions when the holy manifests itself—a great wealth of *hierophanies*.

Shinto, the native religious tradition of Japan, is a good example. Its 800,000 gods represent an incalculable number of times and places where the holy broke into human consciousness, people were seized by God's otherworldly love. Perhaps the power of a storm or the beauty of a mountain scene occasioned a sense of the divine presence. Or maybe the divine was sensed to be involved with the fate of the clan, especially the burial of an old generation and the birth of a new. In terms of expression, its concepts and symbols, Shinto seems less *differentiated* or sophisticated than what the overall unrestriction of the divine love requires. Nonetheless, through its forms and testimonies people often have led good lives, found sanctifying contact with the creative divine love.

Drawing on the work of the comparative scholar of religion Friedrich Heiler, Lonergan ventures a general description of what the world religions hold in common. If we were to move across the board of the different traditions' senses of the divine, Heiler suggests, we would compose a portrait something like this: There is a transcendent (otherworldly) reality that helps to put the natural cosmos and our human affairs in healthy perspective. This transcendent reality is also immanent in human hearts, has a presence in the deepest yearnings and best loves that stir in any culture. Such a God or ultimate reality coincides with the supreme beauty that we extrapolate from our sensual and intellectual lives. We know beyond doubt that "God" must be splendid, for God is the source of snowy mountains and beautiful women, striking sunsets and dear, dear kids. This God is also the best instance of truth, righteousness, and goodness that we can imagine, conceive, or hope. Just as the beauty that we meet tells us of God, so do the instances of truth, righteousness, and goodness that we experience. God is also love, mercy, and compassion. Each of these has something pure in it, something calling for self-transcendence.

To advance toward this transcendent reality, the traditions agree, we must repent of our refusals to keep developing in knowledge and love, abhor the ways we mire ourselves in what is less than God. We must deny our sensuality, increase our prayer. The path that is straight, as Islam calls it, is a path that takes us to a love of our neighbors, even a forgiveness and love of our enemies. Indeed, the transcendent is so good and pure that only its unlimited sort of love can be our model.

Finally, the religions agree that human fulfillment is nothing less than union with the transcendent, loving God and being loved by God in return. Muslim Sufis, Jewish Hasidim, Buddhist monks, Hindu yogis, Taoist sages and many more have contributed to this sketch that Lonergan takes from

Heiler. In their different symbolisms, stages of meaning, degrees of differentiation, Lonergan thinks, they suggest the widespread presence of a core religious experience of unrestricted love. Thus we might expect that future dialogues among the world religious traditions would profit greatly from focusing on the experience and mystery of unrestricted love.

THE WORD

Thus far we have discussed Lonergan's approach to the question and love of God, and we have reflected on his views of religious experience and conversion. In this section we follow his thoughts about the expression of religious meaning, especially the expression that is verbal or linguistic.

The words of the religions are the means by which religious experience comes into the world that is mediated by meaning and regulated by value—into the world as precisely human or cultural. From Lonergan's description of religion as the fulfillment of human interiority on its fourth and highest level, it follows that the words of religion are the main means by which the precisely human world deals with its deepest meanings and highest values. Were there no objectifying descriptions of religious experience, of being in love in an unrestricted fashion, we could not discuss this phenomenon with one another, could not even reflect on it or analyze it by ourselves. It is the "word," the expression of religious experience, that makes religious experience effective in the world.

However, we must not equate the outward words of the religions with the inner experience of God's self-communication in love. That inner experience is prior and unmediated. The outer expressions are later and mediating. The outer expressions also are historically conditioned, forms of communication that vary from time to time and place to place. Thus to consider the word of religious expression is to discover another call to balance. On the one hand, religious experience can only become socially effective and fully personal through the expressions that allow us to get some handle on it. On the other hand the unmediated experience of God is always something prior to our mediating expressions. Indeed, the core of religion, God's love poured forth in our hearts, occurs in a world of immediacy where image, symbol, language, doctrine and the rest lose their relevance. When we are directly experiencing God no mediators can do justice to the mysteriousness that overshadows us. We must abide in a cloud of unknowing, as one of the Christian contemplative classics calls it, letting divinity itself, in all its darkness or thickness or surfeit of being, be our whole concern.

On the other hand, once again, we need words and other expressions if our love even of God is to unfold fully. Lonergan uses the analogy of love between a man and a woman. Were they never to express their love, always keep it immediate, it would not bind them together, could not become the new, wonderful source of a shared, enriched meaning and life. Similarly, religious experience, love of God both unrestricted and immediate, needs expression. If only to sustain the person who struggles in the cloud of unknowing, stumbles along in the dark of God's pull toward holiness, words of the religious traditions, expressions of what other pilgrims have been through, are a great need and much appreciated blessing. Thus in Christian religion the word of the Gospel, the liturgical words that create fellowship at Christ's table, and the like become the more precious as one fights not to misunderstand or abuse or be twisted by a love that runs so silent and deep that we are more swept along than in control.

Thus the words of religion, as such religious figures as the priest and the prophet enunciate them, serve both the individual and the body social. As well, such words are historical. They take their place amidst the other words of their cultures, must communicate with expressions of other realms of meaning and sorts of experience. At this point Lonergan's careful distinctions among such different realms of meaning as common sense and interiority, theory and transcendence, pay rich dividends. For these distinctions enable us to understand why and how expressions of religious meaning vary not just from such other expressions of meaning as the economic or the scientific but from one another as well.

A terse summary of Lonergan's correlation of these realms of meaning with religious expression runs as follows: "When the realms of common sense, of theory, of interiority, and of transcendence are distinguished and related, one easily understands the diversity of religious utterance. For its source and core is in the experience of the mystery of love and awe, and that pertains to the realm of transcendence. Its foundations, its basic terms and relationships, its method are derived from the world of interiority. Its technical unfolding is in the realm of theory. Its preaching and teaching are in the realm of common sense."

Using this little summary, Lonergan offers a brief typology of the various world religions, a shorthand sketch of what their words tend to stress. Eastern religions, for instance, stress religious experience. Semitic religions (e.g., Islam) stress prophetic monotheism (the proclamation of what the sole God is doing and wants). Western religion has stressed transcendence in its piety and religious life, theory in its scholarly theology and jurisprudence. Today its great task is to develop the foundation of both theory and common sense in interiority and use this foundation to communicate its experience of transcendence to the common culture, the world mediated by meaning. The world of interiority therefore becomes the crux of future Western religious development. If we are to conjoin piety and theory, common sense with science and technology, we must better appropriate the subject of these different worlds, ourselves as makers of meaning.

FAITH

Much of what a religious tradition wants to communicate to the culture at large comes under the aegis of faith: the knowledge born of religious love. With this beautiful characterization of faith, Lonergan has laid a bridge between his tradition and his own fresh stress on interiority. Catholic tradition has tended to deal with faith as authoritative knowledge: doctrines, propositions, elaborations of divine revelation. Lonergan has moved below the common-sensical and theoretical realms in which such a faith usually has been located, focusing on the gift of divine love that is not only prior to propositions about God and the religious life but also their generative source. As Vernon Gregson recently has shown very well, Lonergan has shifted theology onto a more experiential foundation, moved it from propositions to spirituality.[4]

But what sort of knowledge is born of religious love? In first approximation, it is the knowledge that Pascal called "reasons of the heart." When we are in love, feelings carry our responses to the values, the goods, that have seized our hearts. These feelings give tone and life to our personalities, integrate us (on the fourth level of consciousness) that we may more effectively embrace what is beautiful and true, combat what is ugly and false. Faith is the reoriented view of things, the new evaluations–judgments–appreciations that come when we feel the love of God, are moved by the divine beauty and truth. For example, a faith-filled view of the poor people in our society goes beyond mere economics and sociology, helping us to "know" that life below the poverty level is evil and destructive. As well, it helps us to "see" the victories that the human spirit may win even below the poverty line: the pot of geraniums on the slum window, the continuing toil that one's kids may have a better life.

Thus faith is centrally not the mastery of a catechism but the acquisition and exercise of a new horizon, a renovated outlook, in terms of which both catechetical matters and humanistic matters gain deeper resonance. Ultimately, faith reaches out to the unrestricted goodness of God, from whom its new light and zest derive. The reconstituted values that come with religious conversion are due to the shifts in the kaleidoscope that otherworldliness, genuine transcendence, brings about. Alternatively, they are due to a sharpening of the question of God, a personal pointing. Experiencing God's love, being invited to a new angle or light on the world, I must make a decision. Shall I accept this invitation, agree to the undertow of God's romancing and demanding, or shall I hold back, cling to old treasures and old lights? When religion gets down to business it is nothing merely interesting, a far cry from what is dealt with in most academic courses. The mystery that defines all of our lives, hovers in all of our depths, holds the key to our joy and peace has become insistent, imperative, demanding. Not to choose for it is to choose against it. To drift along in confusion or fear is to miss the great opportunity of one's time.

From the transcendent, unrestricted love of God come the further dimensions that religion gives to the world mediated by meaning. When faith expresses itself to the common culture, trying to evoke the workings of grace in all people's lives, it speaks of such more-than-secular matters as the worth of the whole universe, a consistent ethic in defense of life, the justice that is only approached by sacrifice, the holiness that goes beyond self-interest, the worship that has no utilitarian cause, the prospect of life beyond the grave. Further, it draws from its tradition dicta to the effect that God's glory is human beings fully alive, creation has come about not for God's sake but for ours, humanity is cast in the image of God, only an inner eye of love can spy out enough goodness to make the world fit to embrace, grace is necessary to sustain human development, making these dicta persuasive expressions of things felt and glimpsed at prayer. Explicitly, Lonergan makes faith the power to undo human decline, outwit and outpersuade propaganda and ideology. For faith, hope, and love, the virtues (strengths) that come with God's grace, are what enable us to take the measure of human sinfulness, look our depravities in the face. If we are ever to escape our dead-ends of violence and recrimination we need a power and vision beyond what reigns in secular life. Our problems are too vast and deep. We will not solve them within restricted horizons, by anything less than a love willing and able to go as far as human authenticity requires.

Finally, faith encourages a prudent acceptance of the beliefs that a worthy religious tradition has developed. In the light generated by God's love it seems good to accept what other intelligent and moral people have found, to join a community centered on religious values. The narratives, ascetical teachings, political programs, communal disciplines, and the like that arise in such a community can greatly help our efforts to answer the call to love of God and neighbor. We are historical and social beings, as much condemned as invited to form traditions and cooperative ventures, dependent upon one another's testimonies. Most of us in the West have been addressed by a God creative of such traditions as the Jewish and the Christian—a God believed to have entered time and space. If religious people understand the relation between faith and beliefs, core knowledge born of love and historically conditioned expressions, they have a good basis for inter-religious dialogue. As well, they have the capital distinction needed for keeping their traditions authentic, rooting themselves in what is central and continually purifying what is derivative or changing.

WORLD RELIGIONS[5]

Apart from his use of Friedrich Heiler's list of the convictions about God or ultimate reality common to the world religions, Lonergan does not deal much with Hinduism and Buddhism, Judaism and Islam. His sketch of religion completely applies to traditions other than Christianity, however, so it seems well to reflect now on a Lonerganian approach to religious conversion in non-Christian contexts.

The central thrust of this reflection, I find, is the commonality of both unrestricted questioning and being in love without limitation. These are both simply human phenomena, nothing limited to any particular time, tradition, or culture. Some times, traditions, and cultures may explicitate unrestricted questioning or love more clearly or fully than others. In terms of their words or beliefs some peoples may make a great deal of the divine mystery and others much less. But if we analyze the actual performances of people the world over, how they in fact live, pray, and suffer, we find that all human beings evidence the drives to know and love that constitute humanity's call to self-transcendence. Similarly, we find that all religions that deal with ultimate matters, discourse about the Tao or Buddhanature or Brahman or Allah, report experiences of transport, wonder, being silenced, being loved.

The Eastern traditions, whose main sense of the ultimate is impersonal, speak less of love than of light. Nonetheless, enlightenment, *bhakti* (devotional love), harmony and the rest of their words for peak states all admit of interpretation as modes of unrestricted love: opening one's soul to the ultimate, giving over one's lesserness to that which is great.

The Western traditions, whose main sense of the ultimate is personal, vary in the stress they place on love, but they too speak of mystical or foundational experiences that fold nicely into Lonerganian unrestricted love. For instance, Islam, whose basic diction for the creature-Creator relation is submission, still speaks of a God compassionate and merciful. The Sufis, Islam's most mystical branch, go further, detailing the many stages by which one may progress to union with Allah. Judaism, too, knows a great deal about the heart to heart relation between God and God's people. Thus Jeremiah spoke of God's reconstituting the human heart, plucking out its stone and giving it a flesh that would feel and love. The end of rabbinic disciplines, Torah in the sense of ethical prescription, is sanctifying God's name, being as worthy as limited human beings can of the covenant that the Lord of the Universe has struck.

One could give similar instances from the religions of non-literate small-scale societies or the religions of the pre-Christian West (Greece, Rome). Without making these traditions run together uncritically, a thick night in which all cows are black, we could easily show that a similar human consciousness works in each, a similar ultimate mystery defines all. Just as all human beings are mortal, and thereby have a strong basis for compassion, so all human beings have minds and hearts, consciences, that are lured by the divine light, solicited by the divine love. Any human mind that can have an insight has the potential to ask about transcendence, the reality that is more than the limited things of space and time. Any human heart that can love has the potential to follow love's purifications to their term, open up to the mystery of human longing for total goodness and let the divine Spirit have its way.

The consequence of this common human condition most germane to our purposes here is the equivalence we find among the world religions' various calls to conversion. Islam and Judaism, for instance, both want the creature to leave the idolatries of untranscendent living, face clearly and embrace generously the sovereignty of the sole God. In its famous *shema* or call in Deuteronomy 6, Judaism has linked the sovereign Lordship of the one God to a command of radical love: "Hear, O Israel: The Lord our God is one Lord, and you shall love the Lord your God with all your heart, and with all your soul, and with all your might" (Dt 6:4–5). Prophetic monotheism, as the Western traditions deriving from biblical Israel are generally called, says that there can be no human prosperity, no good common life, without obedience to and love of the sole ultimate holiness, the single treasure worth a total love. They say, in Lonerganian interpretation, that until we let go of our refusals to love unrestrictedly we shall not be whole, healed (saved), or authentic. Conversion in the prophetic traditions is answering the word of God that calls us to turn around, reform, get our minds straightened and our hearts purified so that God again becomes God, the sole lovely and lightsome mystery deserving our adoration.

The Eastern traditions also call for a turn-around, an enlightenment, a new path. Indian religions tend to stress the ignorance and bad karma that distort current human culture. Only when one calms the mind and purifies the passions, lets go of one's cravings and desires, can ultimate reality come into view, moksha or nirvana (states of complete fulfillment) become realistic. In East Asia harmony and beauty receive greater play. There the world moves to a rhythm, along a path, that crushes those who are foolish but blesses the wise with longevity and peace. Thus the beginnings of Confucian, Taoist, and East Asian Buddhist religious progress involve a rejection of this-worldly ambitions, a moving out to the way of the cosmos and the ancients that better mediates the ultimate mystery. All of this, too, I find amenable to description in terms of unrestricted love. In each of these religious traditions, too, success involves letting go of purely worldly wisdom, taking direction from the whole or ultimate that one meets at the end or in the depths of human knowledge and love.

CHRISTIAN RELIGION

Lonergan is a Christian theologian, so it is not surprising that his layout of religion in *Method in Theology* frequently uses examples from Christian spirituality or renders further explanations by reference to Christian views of grace, the theological virtues, and the like. Still, *Method in Theology,* as its name implies, is methodological rather than theological. It concentrates on the patterns of inquiry that will best connect theology to contemporary culture, and best allow the different theological functional specialties to collaborate, rather than on formally theological questions such as Christian conversion. To take up the question of explicitly Christian conversion is therefore to assume a task that Lonergan himself tends to deal with only partially or suggestively.

In my view, the key to a Lonerganian notion of Christian conversion is specifying religious love, being in love in an unrestricted fashion, through the person and program of Jesus Christ. In other words, the same religious conversion to the mysterious God who is worthy of all love that occurs under different names and with different nuances in Judaism and Islam, Hinduism and Buddhism, occurs in Christianity. But where Judaism correlates its conversion with Torah and the history of salvation, and Islam correlates its conversion with Muhammad and the gift of the Qur'an, Christianity correlates its conversion with Jesus. If the warrant for Jewish conversion is the biblical story and living religious experience of Israel as the people of God, and the warrant for Buddhist conversion is the experience and teaching of the Buddha that one may verify in personal meditation, the warrant for Christian conversion is the love of God manifested in Christ, the wisdom of God immortalized in Jesus' death and resurrection. Christians are the people who try to love God with whole mind, heart, soul and strength, and try to love their neighbor as themselves, because of Jesus and in communion with him.

Hans Küng is right, then, when he says that the distinctiveness of Christianity completely derives from and rivets upon Jesus.[6] Without Jesus of Nazareth, the prophet who his contemporaries thought spoke like no predecessor, the victim who shed his blood and was ratified by being taken definitively into the divine sphere, there would be no Christian religion. Jesus' God is not different from the God of the biblical fathers or from the ultimate holiness that draws the Hindu mystic. Jesus' humanity has no special goal apart from the ultimate that draws the Hopi or the Hottentot. But the incarnation of the divine goodness in Jesus, and the sweet power of Jesus' Spirit, convince Christians that he is the one to whom they must go for the words of immortal life. So, Christians are converted to Jesus. Their path to God takes them into the union with Jesus of which Paul spoke when he likened the Church to Christ's body. Christians abide with Jesus, abide in Jesus, as branches abide in the vine.

When Christians take these biblical and spiritual expressions to heart, linking them with the traditional development of Trinitarian theology, they come to words that characterize their core religion, their being in love in an unrestricted fashion, as a sharing in the divine nature. This sharing is such that the unbegotten Father connects with the mysterious fathomlessness of ultimate reality, the only-begotten Son (Jesus as the eternal Word) connects with the intrinsic expressiveness and communication of the ultimate mysterious reality, and the processive Spirit connects with the circular giving and receiving of divine unrestricted love, sealing Father and Son like a holy kiss. This is the further sense, the rich amplification, that the holy mystery receives when one ponders on the Christian life in terms of the deepest traditional appreciations. Conversion to Jesus then becomes surrendering to the communal embrace of the Trinitarian God from whom Jesus cannot be separated. It becomes entering into what Greek Christianity has called divinization (*theosis*): our being taken up into God's life, made partakers of the divine nature (2 Pet 1:4).

From another point of view, Christian conversion to God, Christian yea-saying to the divine undertow of unrestricted affection, admiration and self-giving, is an entry into a familial or marital communion with God that, if we characterize its dynamics theologically, is a process of sanctification and redemption. Life with Jesus and Jesus' God remakes our human natures, purifying them of some of their sin and raising them into interpersonal relations with the holy Beginning and Beyond. True, Christian yea-saying can be as constipated, reluctant, or niggardly as any other religious turn-around. On the other hand, its warrants are at least as splendid and powerful as any other.

If we think of conversion as turning toward what we have been made or called to be, Christian conversion sings that we have been made and called to be children of God, intimates of the Ultimate, the Wholly Good, the Absolute, the Holy. If we think of conversion as rejecting dysfunctional ways, throwing off of what frustrates human development and community, Christian conversion presents itself soberly as a disavowal of sin, a rejection of absurd self-centeredness, a move away from the strong man Satan toward the much stronger Bringer of Salvation Jesus, God's anointed. Jesus is the first born of the dead, the prototype of humanity remade, Adam redone and gotten right. Christian conversion is the gateway to Christogenesis, as Teilhard de Chardin called it: the becoming of the whole Christ, all the members of God's incarnate body. Finally, in Lonergan's own terms, Christian conversion is making Christ the way and life of authenticity. Jesus is self-transcendence personified, incarnated, divinized. The unrestriction of Christ's love is the life that all people hunger to enjoy. The cross of Christ is the law of redemption, the way that conversion passes on to putting one's body and spirit on the line for authenticity and self-transcendence, a good God and a good world.

NOTES

[1] See Eric Voegelin, *Order and History, Vol. 4: The Ecumenic Age.* Baton Rouge: Louisiana State University Press, 1974, pp. 7–11.

[2] See, in addition to *Method in Theology* pp. 101–103, *Insight*, chapter 19, and *Philosophy of God and Theology.*

[3] See Karl Rahner, *Foundations of Christian Faith.* New York: Seabury, 1978, pp. 44–89.

[4] See Vernon Gregson, *Lonergan, Spirituality, and the Meeting of Religions.* College Theology Society: Studies in Religion. Lanham, Md.: University Press of America, 1985, pp. 59–78.

[5] See Denise Lardner Carmody and John Tully Carmody, *Ways to the Center,* third edition. Belmont, Cal.: Wadsworth, 1989.

[6] See Hans Küng, *On Being a Christian.* Garden City: Doubleday, 1976, pp. 119–44.

IV. Theological Method and Theological Collaboration I

It is clear from the preceding chapters that Lonergan assigns great importance to the four levels of consciousness. They are our way to arrive at truth and value. It should also be clear that they are not simply personal imperatives. They certainly are that, but they are also, in addition, imperatives to a community. Communities must be authentic, too. The imperatives apply, therefore, to all human endeavors.

It is very difficult, if not close to impossible, to personally Be attentive, Be intelligent, Be reasonable, Be responsible, when the community one is a part of consistently violates any or all of them. For example, if certain types of data are suppressed by a community, how can an individual come to investigate that data; or if certain types of questions are ruled out of court by one's community, how can the individual find the support to pursue an understanding of the suppressed questions? The achievement of truth and value, then, is not only a personal but a communal achievement. We cannot rule out the lone hero who stands out above others or stands as a critic of a society in decline. But such persons are rare, and the lone hero will not, in fact, accomplish much in the long run, if others do not eventually join him or her in a communal effort to accomplish significant change.

What is true about seeking truth and value in general is also true about seeking truth and value in the area of religion, and, specifically to our point here, in the area of theology and in the work of theologians. Theologians are men and women who study in order to understand the origins and sources of a religion and who try to communicate the meaning and significance of that religion to the culture in which they live, or to which they direct their concern. As Lonergan puts it, theologians mediate "between a cultural matrix and the significance and role of a religion in that matrix."[1]

Theologians, as persons, are members of multi-faceted communities and their role or task as theologians is to bring the resources of religion and of religious tradition to bear on the culture and communities they are an integral part of, and also to bring the resources of their secular communities to bear on the religious tradition. Theologians are, therefore, mediators between the riches of the past and the riches of the present. But that mediating must also be a discerning and an evaluating, for not everything in the past of a tradition is something to be treasured, sometimes far from it, nor is everything in the present culture something to be treasured, again sometimes far from it.

But how does the theologian go about this mediating and this evaluating? Lonergan suggests that in doing theology there are eight different tasks that the theologians engage in, eight specialties which are functionally related to one another. Each theologian does not necessarily engage in all of the tasks, at least to any full extent, because the field of religion has become too extensive for any one person to do all the tasks well. Theology has become a collaborative endeavor. Just as one individual historian would rarely engage in detached documentary research, and also write grand overviews of history, and also spell out the implications of history for present politics, and one scientist would not do basic laboratory research, formulate new theories, and also develop and implement the practical applications of his or her theories, so one individual theologian would also rarely engage in basic archeological research, and also formulate new theories, and also work out the implications in practical policy for the community. The eight tasks that Lonergan delineates for the theologian, then, are principles for collaboration among theologians.

These eight tasks of theology which Lonergan articulates are best seen in relation to the levels of consciousness, of which they are a *specific implementation*. Like the levels of consciousness, the tasks of theology build one upon another.

FUNCTIONAL SPECIALITIES

4. DIALECTIC	*DECIDING*	5. FOUNDATIONS
3. HISTORY	*JUDGING*	6. DOCTRINES
2. INTERPRETATION	*UNDERSTANDING*	7. SYSTEMATICS
1. RESEARCH	*EXPERIENCING*	8. COMMUNICATIONS

The first four tasks principally concern the retrieval of the past: gathering ancient artifacts and texts (Research); discovering the meaning of what one has gathered (Interpretation); constructing a history of the time (History); and evaluating the significance of what one has arrived at in the first three levels (Dialectic). The relationship of these four operations to the levels of consciousness should be relatively clear. The goal of Research is data gathering or Experiencing. The goal of Interpretation is Understanding. The goal of History is arriving at what really happened in the past, which is an exercise in Judging. And the goal of Dialectic is considering the significance of what the past has to offer and determining when there are conflicting views of the significance of the past, which is the most accurate and valuable; this is an exercise in Deciding. Although the goal of each of the specialties is one of the levels of consciousness, in fact, all of the levels are used in each specialty. For instance, the researcher must use his or her understanding, judgment, and decision to arrive at the goal of Research, establishing accurate data.

An example may be helpful to clarify at least in a preliminary way these first four specialties of theology. A scholar might be interested in the original meaning of the passage in Matthew's Gospel in which the following words are attributed to Jesus: "I say to you that whoever divorces his wife, except for immorality, and marries another, commits adultery" (Mt 5:32). Research would involve establishing the accurate Greek text of the passage, and comparing it with other parallel passages in the New Testament. One would discover that Mark's Gospel does not make any exception for remarriage, even for immorality. Interpretation would involve understanding the meaning of the words during the first century A.D. and their use in Matthew's Gospel. Precisely what type of immorality justifies divorce? Is there a different standard for men and women implied in the passage—whoever divorces *his wife*? Can the wife initiate divorce? History would involve placing the statement attributed to Jesus in the context of the Jewish, Greek, and Roman views of the time which would further clarify its meaning. Is Jesus' statement going against the current of the time or is it in accord with other Jewish or Greek or Roman views? Does it continue a tradition or does it begin one? Dialectics would involve discerning the specific value or values the passage is seeking to affirm. How does the passage relate to the other teachings of the Gospel? Is the value of fidelity the point of the passage? Is Jesus seeking to raise the status of woman by limiting the reasons a man can divorce her? When the further question is asked, "Is this a teaching that has relevance only to Jesus' time or to the time of the writing of the Gospel, or to our own time as well?" one has moved on to the second four specialties.

A thorough study of the passage would take skill and training and intelligence and time and effort. It would be undertaken only by someone who values understanding the past, and, in this instance, particularly someone who values the message of Jesus and the early Church, and, in addition, its possible significance for us today. Any text of whatever religion could be examined in the same way. Lonergan's contribution here is not principally in terms of the operations of each of the four specialties—the first three are well recognized disciplines—but in showing the functional relationship of the specialties to one another and to the later specialties—and, as well, in showing the relationship of work in the four specialties to work in the natural sciences. But more on this later.

The second four specialties principally concern the present and the future. They involve reaping the fruits from the study of the past to create the present and the future. "Foundations" is articulating the change that has taken place in oneself or in one's community as a result of seriously confronting the values of the past. "Doctrines" is affirming the values one has discovered. "Systematics" is relating and integrating (making systematic) the values one is now affirming with one another and with the other values and meanings in one's life. "Communications" is passing on what one has arrived at, and what one values, to others. These four specialties also bear relationship to the four levels of consciousness. "Foundations" is Deciding on one's values after, and often through, evaluation of the past. "Doctrines" is affirming the truth of those values, which is an act of Judging. "Systematics" is placing the values one has affirmed in intelligible relationship to other values, which is an exercise in Understanding. "Communications" is passing on to others what one values, fleshing out one's values in Experience.

Short-circuit or attempt to bypass any of these specialties, and all the following ones will rest on an inadequate base. One will be building on sand. To build one's Foundations on what one would like the past to have been, or on what the past at first sight might seem to have been, is to build on a shaky foundation indeed. One of the reasons for the development of Scripture studies in the last hundred years is the recognition that a first reading of a text written almost two thousand years ago in a very different culture and in another language and with a community facing far-different problems is not going to reveal its meaning without careful and thorough study. The last four functional specialties depend on the first, therefore, for their integrity and richness. But the first four specialties are barren for the present and the future unless the further questions of the last four specialties are also attended to. To know the past but not to bring its values into the future is a great waste of one's time and effort.

To continue with our example of the prohibition in Matthew on divorce and remarriage, except for immorality: Foundations would involve articulating the ground for the change in one's own attitude toward marriage and divorce, if it differed from what one discovered the Gospel to mean. And if it has not differed, Foundations would ground one's previous evaluation more deeply. Doctrines would involve affirming the truth of one's new position. Systematics would be bringing this new truth into relationship with one's other positions and values. And Communications would be passing on, in as concrete and persuasive a manner as possible, one's new-found or renewed value.

For simplicity's sake, the above example was developed in terms of an individual theologian. In the real order, one's Foundations are usually not articulated in isolation but in community. The same is true with regard to one's formulation of Doctrines, Systematics, and Communications. Theologians work on the values discovered in the past in collaboration with one another, with their faith community, with those in other fields, and with the community at large. And if theologians find that their views diverge in a substantial way from those of the community of which they have been a part, they seek to change the consensus of their present community. If that fails, and the matter is truly substantial, they may be led to seek community among those who share their new values. Recall John Henry Newman's decision to become Roman Catholic and Luther's decision not to submit to the Roman Catholicism of his time, but to work for a renewed church community. This process then can have very serious consequences, for in going through this process of the eight functional specialties, one is constituting who one is, who will be one's companions, and what one will labor to bring into being in the future.

The brief analysis with regard to divorce and remarriage is only an example of the type of significant question from the past which can perhaps shed substantial light on today's questions. You should try to supply some of your own. Some that I would suggest would be the following:

What was Jesus' attitude toward those who sincerely, religiously differed from him—what is the meaning of "He who is not against us is for us" (Mk 9:40)? What relevance might Jesus' attitude have today?

What is Jesus' attitude toward abortion? Is it significant for today, or is it not, that the subject is not mentioned in the Gospels?

What is Jesus' attitude toward violence? Is it clear and unambiguous? What are the implications for us today, if Jesus' attitude is clear, or if it is not?

Did Jesus concern himself with the structure that the community of disciples would have after he left them? If so, what did he envisage? What normative value should that have for us today?

These questions are offered as examples of significant matters about which light from the past would be valuable. They are questions which, if they are to be answered adequately and accurately, require full investment of the energies of the inquirer and significant collaboration with others. Lonergan's articulation of theological method can provide clear guidelines to the theologian, to the scholar, and to the ordinary believer who is seeking answers to these questions, and who does not shy away from the complex series of tasks necessary to arrive at answers. Knowing is not looking; it is carefully experiencing, understanding, and judging.

Lonergan's understanding of theological method exposes two common errors. One is the tendency of scholars and academics to seek knowledge of the past and then to stop there and not to ask the further difficult but relevant questions concerning the significance of those discoveries for the present. It is the error of stopping at History and not doing an evaluation of the significance of what one has discovered (Dialectics) and performing the other tasks necessary to bring the meanings and values of the past into the present and the future. It is the failure to let oneself be personally challenged by the past and the failure to seek to integrate the values of the past in oneself and in one's community. In terms of Lonergan's four transcendental imperatives, it is: Being attentive, Being intelligent, Being reasonable, but not Being responsible for what one has discovered. It is truncating one's subjectivity by failing to raise the question of value.

The other error has tended to characterize not so much the scholars as the religious leaders. It is to disregard the first five functional specialties and to begin with Doctrines and to pass on the Doctrines of the Church(es) from generation to generation without the challenge that comes from renewing again, in each generation of laity and clergy, direct contact with the original sources which gave rise to the Doctrines. These sources might challenge the handed-on traditions or might renew their relevance for today. The uncritical handing on of tradition to new generations might have been understandable and inevitable before the methods of critical investigation of the past were widely known and developed. But in the present state of historical awareness, the attempt to pass on the tradition without the critical study of the originating texts of the traditions cannot help but give rise to the suspicion of defensiveness, or of laziness, or even of bad faith.

In sum, Lonergan's enumeration of eight functional specialties in theology serves as a challenge, then, to both Historical and Doctrinal theologians, a challenge to broaden their horizons to the whole related set of questions that alone can lead one from the riches of the past (Research) to that kind of action which responsibly creates the future (Communications).

Although we have focused particularly on theology, it is important to realize the full breadth of the functional specialties which Lonergan articulates. Just as the four levels of consciousness, studied in the first chapter, apply to everything we might attend to, understand, verify, and decide about, so the eight functional specialties apply to every creation and construction of human meaning, in all historical and pre-historical places and times. Lonergan develops particularly their relevance to theology and religion, because he is a theologian, but their application to religion is simply a specific example of their general relevance to all fields in which human meaning is the subject matter. Just as the natural sciences are one example of the operation of the levels of consciousness, so theology is but one example of the relevance of the functional specialties.

The social sciences,[2] such as sociology, and political science, have their own Research, Interpretation and Verification (the tasks of traditional sociological and political science research), but these spontaneously lead to questions of social philosophy and social ethics (Dialectics and Foundations) and these are followed by questions of social policy (Doctrines and Systematics) and social action (Communications). The operations from Research to Communications, then, follow a sequence of questions which lead, in any discipline which studies human meaning, from one functional specialty to another. The eight functional specialties are really answers to eight basic questions: (1) What are the relevant data? (2) What is the meaning of the data? (3) What does it tell us (verify) about its time? (4) What value(s) does it reveal? (5) Where do I stand with regard to its value(s)? (6) What will I affirm about its value(s)? (7) How does this relate to my own or my community's other values? (8) What and how will I communicate this to others? The functional specialties, then, partake of the transcendental and open-ended character of the levels of consciousness, of which they are simply the specification with regard to human meaning and human history. Religion is one important aspect of human meaning and human history and, as such, is a suitable subject for the functional specialties, but it is not the only subject.

We will examine now in more detail Lonergan's understanding of each of the functional specialties. Again, as with regard to the levels of consciousness, it is important to realize that Lonergan is not creating an arbitrary, even if very helpful, method; rather he is trying to elucidate elements in the natural sequence of questions which lead one from Research through to Communications. He is not trying to create a new method but to indicate the intricate but purposeful relationship of tasks which those who do theology necessarily engage in. By making these tasks explicit, he suggests a meaningful division of labor and encourages mutual respect and cooperation among those who do each of the various tasks of theology.

RESEARCH

The aim of research is to gather the data which is relevant to the inquiry one wants to pursue. Research can be a relatively simple or an exceedingly complex task, depending on whether others have investigated the same area before you, and have carefully preserved and catalogued what they discovered. To date events referred to in the Hebrew Scriptures or to explore the ruins of ancient cities might take decades of arduous on-site archaeological digging and sifting. To study a text of Jewish or Christian Scripture, on the other hand, is relatively, but only relatively, simple. First, one need only find a critical edition of the text in the original language(s) with the variant readings of different manuscripts carefully noted. These editions are available, however, only because extensive work (Research) has already been done on establishing the biblical texts. But even here one must learn what is the best critical edition, one which includes references to manuscripts which even now continue to be discovered. And one must also, of course, have taken years to have thoroughly studied the pertinent ancient languages. Then one is prepared to research the specific text one is interested in.

Research is a specific and concrete skill which is one that is best learned under the guidance of a master in the field. One apprentices oneself to a skilled scholar, follows him or her in the research the scholar is personally engaged in, and then engages in one's own research under the teacher's guidance. It is a long and arduous but for many a very rewarding process, for one has advanced the field of knowledge for everyone; what one has learned can be made available to others.

Again, it is important to recognize that although the aim of Research is the assembling of relevant data (the experiential level), the researcher uses all four levels of consciousness in order to do it.

To discover, for example, what is the most accurate biblical text, researchers must *choose* to investigate those manuscripts which will most likely give the earliest versions of the texts so that they can *understand* and then *affirm* what the original text most likely was. "So the textual critic will select the method (level of decision) that he feels will lead to the discovery (level of understanding) of what one may reasonably affirm (level of judgment) was written in the original text (level of experience). The textual critic, then, operates on all four levels, but his goal is the end proper to the first level, namely, to ascertain the data."[3] The same is analogously true for each of the eight functional specialties. The scholar in each speciality uses all four levels of consciousness to achieve the goal of the particular level or specialty he or she is working on.

But where does one begin Research? With what data should one start an inquiry? With the data one considers at the time to be relevant to the question one is asking. One can only start from where one is. No neutral, omniscient position is open to humankind. Later attempts to understand the data might reveal that the present data are irrelevant and one must search elsewhere. We have all had the experience of having to begin a research project over again. But that is the self-correcting process of learning, the self-correcting process of being attentive, intelligent, reasonable, and responsible. Dead ends and wrong directions will gradually or even suddenly and sharply reveal themselves to an inquirer who is using all of his or her intentional capacities. For instance, one might begin to understand Roman Catholicism by gathering data on papal infallibility and only in the course of one's investigation realize that this is a late and derivative notion. One would then turn to more basic questions and to the data relevant to them.

To conclude this section on research a word needs to be said about the difference between the research data pertinent to the natural sciences and the research data pertinent to human studies, including religious studies. The natural sciences search for universally valid laws, laws that pertain to each and every instance of the element or process under consideration. In principle, then, one element or process can be replaced by any other of the same type. This allows for experiments to be replicated and verified by others. Human studies in general, on the contrary, deal with the unique, with the single instance, with what happened at a specific time and place. It is concerned not with the universal but with the particular historical event or historical text. As such, Research in human studies is concerned to preserve intact, as best it can, the evidence of the unique instance, so others can understand it and interpret it, so others can also discover its meaning and its value.

Research is no easy task. But if it is not done adequately, all that follows will be incomplete and partial, or simply wrong.

INTERPRETATION

The aim of Interpretation is understanding the meaning of the data, often a text, which has been discovered in Research. Some texts which are mathematical or scientific in nature, such as Euclid's geometry, require little or no interpretation. Such texts are written in a formal and systematic manner and it is clear when one has understood them correctly and when one has not. Most texts, however, are not of this type. Rather, they are narrative, descriptive, or symbolic such as the Gospels.

While a text might be readily understood by a person of the time when it was written, it might be very obscure to people of another time, culture, or language. In this sense, texts from the past might be considered to be very much like jokes, which are obvious and funny in one context, but obscure and pointless in another context. To follow that analogy, the aim of interpretation is to understand the context in which the joke originally made sense and to get the humorous point. Not so easy a task when twenty or more centuries have elapsed since the text was written or one doesn't know the original context in which the joke was told. It indeed is a difficult task to understand cultural and religious texts from the past. If we sometimes have difficulty understanding our peers and those of the immediately previous generation, how much more difficult to understand the meaning of even some of the most apparently simple texts of centuries ago.

Lonergan suggests that the full understanding of a text has four component aspects. One must understand the object or objects the text is referring to. One must understand the words used in the text. One must understand the author who wrote the words. And finally one must understand oneself. Each of these tasks will require considerable dedication and labor.

First, with regard to understanding what an author is referring to. Lonergan rejects what he calls the Principle of the Empty Head, namely, the view that the less one knows about what an author writes about, the better position one is in to understand the author accurately and not impose one's own ideas on a text. Few would actually formulate such a principle explicitly, but it is often implied when one is warned about reading one's own view into what an author has written. That imposition of one's own view certainly is a danger that must be avoided. But knowledge is a cumulative enterprise. In fact, the more one knows, the better one is in the position to know even more.

All a text is, is spatially separated marks on a page. Just looking at a text in a language one doesn't know can quickly bring that fact home. One's ability to make sense, to give meaning, to those spatially separated marks comes, significantly, from one's previous learning, one's previous experience, understanding, and judgment. Knowing is not just looking, as the material in the first chapter made clear; it is a compound set of operations, using all of the levels of consciousness, with one increment of knowledge building on and fitting in with other knowledge. That is why long years of study in languages, history, and culture are necessary to understand accurately a text of another time and place. Lonergan's view on this matter follows from his theory of cognitional processes. Knowing is not just taking a good look, it is experiencing and understanding and judging, and doing this one's whole life long.

Second, with regard to understanding an author's words: We have all had the experience in conversation of thinking someone was speaking about one thing and halfway through the conversation realizing the individual was speaking of something else. If that can happen in conversation in the present, it can even more readily happen in trying to understand the meaning of a text written centuries ago. What the author is saying might seem false or foolish, when the real problem is in the interpreter and not in the author. In such instances, we can be controversialists who relish finding an apparently absurd statement and avidly criticize the author. An interpreter, on the other hand, considers that he or she might be in error and carefully retraces the path of understanding until his or her own error is found, or until it becomes clear that the author has indeed, to the best of one's understanding, ventured off into absurdity.

There are certain rules that have been developed to aid in understanding a text. Consider the author's purpose, the occasion on which the author wrote, the style and literary form, etc. But no sequence of rules can guarantee understanding. Understanding is a creative act of intelligence, deriving from the desire to know and one's native gifts, which finally allows one to make sense of a word, a sentence, a paragraph, a section, and finally the whole work. Understanding a text is, at its root, an exercise of the second level of consciousness, our capacity to arrive at the liberating and expanding joy of insight.

Third, in addition to understanding the object an author is referring to and the author's words, the interpreter wants to understand the author himself. For to fully understand a text one needs to understand how people at that time thought and acted. Gradually, as one becomes familiar with an author through his or her works, one begins to get a feel for how he or she perceived things and responded to them. In a sense, authors can become like familiar friends who, although they lived in very different times, can be understood and appreciated. Their common sense way of thinking and acting with regard to the concrete circumstances of their time does not become our way of thinking and acting, but we learn to understand why and how it made sense for them. And in understanding this we have the rich experience of passing over into another place and time and of gaining perspective on our own circumstances.

Fourth, understanding the objects referred to by an author, the words of an author, and the author himself or herself finally leads, or at least can lead, to a new understanding of oneself. Great works of the past and of the present, classics, whether in religion, philosophy, or literature, require a change, and sometimes even a significant change in ourselves, even to understand them. The Scriptures, Plato, Aristotle, Shakespeare, the great novelists, etc., challenge us to alter our own view of ourselves and of our values, if we are to appreciate what they have to offer. They challenge us to a conversion, sometimes intellectual, sometimes moral, sometimes religious. We have all had the experience of picking up a book and not appreciating it or seeing its point and then, months or years later, picking it up again and having it speak to our experience. The spatially separated marks on the page haven't changed, we have. Great works in a field have the power to challenge us to that change. We know when we are reading certain texts both that we do not understand them and that they have much to offer. At such times, a person "will come to know [the meaning] only in so far as he pushes the self-correcting process of learning to a revolution in his own outlook. He can succeed in acquiring that habitual understanding of an author that spontaneously finds his wavelength and locks on to it, only after he has effected a radical change in himself."[4]

In brief then, interpretation is no easy task. Not only does it require painstakingly entering into another time and culture, it can face us with a personal challenge to our own religious, moral, and intellectual values. Enter at your own risk. But avoid entering, and this also is at your own risk as well.

There is a special challenge that also accompanies trying to understand a classic. It is that a classic usually establishes a tradition of interpreting it. Secondary texts are written by others to help explain it. If those texts are written by those who really understand the original, are authentic to it, they can be enormously helpful. If they miss the point of the original, however, they can lead many astray. The Jewish and Christian Scriptures have established such a tradition of interpretation but periodically someone arises who challenges the accepted meanings and uncovers what he or she considers to be more authentic interpretations. For example, what does "The just man lives by faith" mean? What does the tradition of interpretation, before Luther, say it means? The tradition after Luther?

"Blessed are you, poor, for yours is the kingdom of God" (Lk 6:20). "You are Peter and upon this rock I will build my church" (Mt 16:18). "This is my body, which is about to be given for your sake. Do this as my memorial" (Lk 22:19). Each of these passages has a history of interpretation which has developed over centuries. Sometimes different Christian traditions have different histories of interpretation of these passages. Which of these interpretations, if any, is meant by the original text? The task of discovering the answer to that question is the task of the functional specialty, Interpretation. And a difficult task it often is. It involves using all of one's personal resources, all of one's desire to know the truth. It calls for personal authenticity.

Personal authenticity and communal authenticity are both the means and the goal of the functional specialties. And achieving authenticity, affirming what is really true and what is really valuable, involves a double burden. "There is the minor authenticity or unauthenticity of the subject with respect to the tradition that nourishes him. There is the major authenticity that justifies or condemns the tradition itself."[5] In other words, the task for each of us is not primarily to achieve the goals of the tradition that we are a part of, but rather to judge the very authenticity of the tradition itself. Traditions can become unauthentic over time by inadvertence or by willfulness. "So the unauthenticity of individuals becomes the unauthenticity of a tradition. Then in the measure a subject takes the tradition, as it exists, for his standard, in that measure he can do no more than authentically realize unauthenticity."[6] The task of the functional specialty, Interpretation, is then, no less than the task of authenticity. For that is what is necessary in order to come to an accurate understanding of the texts which ground a tradition.

How does a scholar, or anyone else, know that his or her own interpretation of a text is correct? There is no magic to resolve the issue. There is no disembodied "objective" viewpoint that can solve the problem. "Nor may one expect the discovery of some 'objective' criterion or test or control. For that meaning of the 'objective' is mere delusion. Genuine objectivity is the fruit of authentic subjectivity. It is to be attained only by attaining authentic subjectivity."[7] One brings questions to a text. When all the relevant questions have been answered, one has achieved the meaning of a text. That is more arduous than it might sound. For the question one first brings to a text might or might not be what the text is trying to answer. For example, one might be interested in the relevance of the passage, "You are Peter and upon this rock I will build my church" to present day discussions of the role of the Pope in Catholicism or in Christianity in general. Perhaps the passage is very relevant to those discussions, perhaps not. But one must first ask what Jesus and/or the early Church meant to convey by that passage in their own situation. It is in answering the interlocking set of questions posed by a passage itself, and by its context, that one arrives at the meaning of a text, not by insisting that a text first answer one's own, perhaps extraneous, questions.

In addition, knowing how to ask the right question is something that needs to be learned. A physician can sometimes ask only three or four questions and arrive at a proper diagnosis. A layman might ask fifty questions and not know what is wrong. Similarly, a trained scholar in a field can sometimes ask only three or four questions of a text and understand its meaning, and a layman in the field can ask fifty questions and make little headway.

In sum, one arrives at a correct interpretation of a text by answering all of the relevant questions that the text poses. And one gets to that point by using all of one's intellectual capacity, all of one's desire to know, and all that one has learned from others who have used their capacities before you.

HISTORY

While Interpretation aims at understanding particular texts, History uses all the understandings of the texts of a period to establish with some probability the events and currents of the time. Historians, when they do their tasks well, in some way know more about what happened in the past than the people who actually lived at the time, for historians are in a position to understand aspects of the whole picture. For example, in having access to both sides of the correspondence and other documents in a dispute, or of the battle plans of generals on each side of a conflict, historians can construct a more complete and objective account of what was taking place than the participants could.

The achievement that good critical history can accomplish in expanding our knowledge of what actually took place in the past and correcting our misperceptions can perhaps best be shown by contrasting pre-critical with critical history. Pre-critical history is the type of story of origins and heroes that every group writes to bolster the pride and sense of identity of the group. Nations do this, peoples do this, religions do this. In itself there is nothing wrong with it, but its aim is not to achieve knowledge of the truth of what happened in the past, but to achieve coherence and enthusiasm in the group.

More specifically, Lonergan suggests that the aim of pre-critical history has five characteristics. It is *artistic, ethical, explanatory, apologetic,* and *prophetic.* It is artistic, since it is written in such a way as to catch the reader's interest, to persuade and to convince. It is ethical, since it establishes villains and heroes, clearly indicates what was good behavior and what was not. It is explanatory, since it accounts for the way things are in a group by telling of their origin and development. It is apologetic, since it shows why the way the particular group does something is right, despite what those in other groups say. And finally it is prophetic, since it suggests how things should progress in the future.

However understandable the purpose of pre-critical history is, its aim is not the achievement of real knowledge of the past. To write pre-critical history one does not engage in the type of thorough research for data and careful interpretation of texts that Lonergan envisages in the first two functional specialties. In fact, one positively avoids such activity, for who knows what one might turn up? Certainly one doesn't want the facts to obscure the persuasive picture one wants to paint.

The reader might recall the situations when he or she has been told or may have read pre-critical history. Stories told to children in grammar school about the Revolutionary War are often of this type. Much of the historical narratives of the Jewish and Christian Scriptures are pre-critical history. But one must avoid passing the same judgment on texts written before the norms of critical history were developed, or on stories told to children, and texts written for adults after the development of critical history.

In contrast to pre-critical history, however, objective history aims at presenting what actually happened in the past. Lonergan suggests such history has seven characteristics. It is *heuristic, ecstatic, selective, critical, constructive, reflective,* and *judicial.* It is heuristic, since it searches for relevant data. It is ecstatic, since it brings the historian out of his or her original perspective into the perspective of the time being investigated. It is selective, since it chooses only the data relevant to the inquiry. It is critical, since it discerns the context in which it is appropriate to understand the data. It is constructive, since it establishes on the basis of the data an interconnecting set of questions and answers which bring to light what happened in the past. It is reflective, since it is open to data arising from new discoveries which would revise its conclusions. Finally, it is judicial, since it will risk making affirmations about the past, when it considers all the relevant questions have been answered, even though the judgments might be open to later modification based on fresh investigations.

The contrast between pre-critical and critical history makes clear the very specific goal of critical history. This is to know, as best we can, what happened in the past, what was going on. Its aim is the aim of the third level of consciousness, judgments of truth and falsity: what was so or not so. Obviously the critical historian uses all four levels of consciousness to arrive at those judgments, but the goal is knowledge, accurate knowledge of our past.

The use such knowledge of the past will be put to is certainly also important, and is, in fact, the ultimate social goal of investigating the past. But if historians focus primarily on that in the process of doing their historical investigation, it will both distract them from what they are doing and perhaps also lead them, consciously or unconsciously, to arrive at historical conclusions which will only bolster their own previous positions, sometimes only their own biases or the biases of their group. Again, the use that the knowledge of the past will be put to is of extraordinary importance, but the historian must not explicitly emphasize that during his or her investigations or else the historian will not arrive at conclusions worth using.

A matter that Lonergan sees as important in evaluating the objectivity of history is the challenge of relativism. Determining the character and quality of the knowledge gained in historical research is of utmost importance in our deciding what weight to give the results of historical investigations. Is it actually possible to gain accurate knowledge of the past? How can we really have verifiable knowledge with regard to an event of any complexity in the distant past? Are we not in the final analysis caught in our own merely subjective perceptions of the past?

If relativism is true, then we are ultimately unable to get out of ourselves and our own time to enter in understanding into another time and place. "[R]elativism has lost hope about the attainment of truth."[8] Lonergan's whole cognitional analysis is in contrast to relativism. For Lonergan—and he asks you to verify this in your own operations of consciousness—careful attentiveness, conscientious understanding, and verifiable judgments precisely lead one out of oneself into knowledge of what really is so. Authentic subjectivity leads not to relativism but to objectivity.

There is no question that objectivity with regard to history is difficult to attain. But to affirm a full relativist position, namely, in this instance, that one view of the past is as good as another, flies in the face of significant experience to the contrary. If relativism were correct, the most off-handed view of the past should deserve the same respect as the most careful and thoroughgoing study. And no one should bother to correct his or her own previous view on the basis of new evidence, since the second understanding has no more claim to being correct than the first. No one can live a complete relativist position, for no growth of knowledge would be possible. Even a relativist considers his position on relativism more correct than the position he opposes, or the position he held before.

But if full relativism is self-contradictory, relativism does call attention to the difficulty of attaining real knowledge, and, in this instance, real knowledge of the past. And that difficulty must be borne in mind lest the historian claim more than greater or lesser probability for his or her conclusions. While the attainment of real knowledge in any field requires careful effort, there are some particular difficulties for historical knowledge. Investigations in the natural sciences can be checked out in various ways, e.g., other experiments can be run. Also, the accumulated insights of science became part of a well-defined system, allowing for indirect verification. In addition, scientists attempt to define their terms systematically, formulate precise hypotheses, and carry out elaborate experiments.[9]

Historians, on the other hand, cannot systematically formulate all that they bring to an historical investigation. Human self-understanding does not permit complete formulation. We never know ourselves fully. In addition, the data that historians investigate is one of a kind and does not allow for replicated experiments, only different attempts to explain the same data.

Also, after the data available are assembled, historians express their conclusions in descriptions and narratives, not in the systematically formulated style of the natural scientist. All of these features call for modesty on the part of the historian in stating his or her conclusions. But express them the historian must, for knowledge of our past, however incomplete, is invaluable. Every increment of knowledge reveals something about human achievement or human failure. Every increment allows us to understand better the human institutions and forms which we have inherited, and which it is our responsibility to carry forward, to renew, to abandon, or to recreate.

But if there are views which overly stress the subjectivity of history, there are also views which would imply a facile objectivity in historical research. In these views, the work of historians would be to assemble the data of their historical research and let the results speak for themselves. These views too would appear to have some plausibility. For the data that historians assemble can, in principle, be examined and seen by all. But to take such a view is again to fall into the error of considering that knowing is like looking. If you can see it, you can understand it and know what it means. It is a scissors and paste view of history.

In actuality, however, observing the data (experiencing), while an essential component of knowing, is only one component. The capacity to interpret texts (understanding) requires both native intellectual ability and training, as does the capacity to verify an historical construction of our past (judging). Data just sits there, quite dumb, if there is no interpreter to give voice to it. No, history is not as "subjective" as relativists would have us believe, nor as "objective" as naive realists would also have us believe. Lonergan suggests that the truth in this instance is in a third position. He calls that position, which we have described, "perspectivism."[10]

Perspectivism points out that not all elements of historical knowledge are equally subject to revision. The motivations for Brutus' killing Caesar will likely never be all known, but it is quite improbable that later history will discover that it was not Brutus that killed Caesar but rather that Caesar killed Brutus! In other words, historical knowledge approaches certainty with regard to many events and situations, even if it only establishes probable correlations in other instances. "If I have been led to adopt the view that the techniques of critical history are unequal to the task of eliminating historical relativism totally, I affirm all the more strongly that they can and do effect a partial elimination."[11]

Ironically, the very fact that an historian in his or her work is, in fact, unable totally to escape his or her own pre-suppositions and those of the times in which the history is written allows later historians to use the indirect self-revelation of earlier ones as evidence of the very times in which the earlier historians wrote. An historian does indeed then write from a perspective, but careful attention to understanding the data allows him or her, to a greater or lesser extent, to transcend the limits of the original perspective.

In sum, the discipline of History uses the data assembled in research and the understanding of the data achieved in Interpretation to establish as accurately as possible what was taking place in the period being investigated. The three disciplines of Research, Interpretation, and History, then, although they each have distinct particular goals, functionally relate to one another to help us achieve greater knowledge of the human enterprise that our ancestors were engaged in, and which it is our burden and opportunity to carry forward.

The three functional specialties studied in some detail in this chapter form a unit of traditional academic disciplines. Lonergan's account of them serves to indicate the issues involved in each, to correlate these disciplines with Lonergan's own position on how we come to knowledge, and to indicate in a general way these disciplines' relevance to religion and theology. The remaining five functional specialties, which we will treat in the next chapter, will begin with two less traditional specialties or disciplines, where Lonergan's account brings a number of new issues to light.

NOTES

[1]Lonergan, *Method in Theology*, p. xi.
[2]*Method*, pp. 248–49.
[3]*Method*, p. 134.
[4]*Method*, p. 161.
[5]*Method*, p. 80.
[6]*Method*, p. 80.
[7]*Method*, p. 292.
[8]*Method*, p. 217.
[9]*Method*, p. 219.
[10]*Method*, p. 220.
[11]*Method*, p. 195.

V. Theological Method and Theological Collaboration II

After experiencing, understanding, and judging comes deciding. Accordingly, after researching the data of the past, after trying to interpret the data accurately, and after determining as best one can what historically happened, one is faced with the question: "What effect will I let this have on my life?" or "What will I do about what I know?"

An example may clarify. You have studied the life and teachings of the Buddha and have come to the conclusion that he has profound insights into the human condition, that what he said is true and good. Will you let it stop there? Will you let your knowledge remain a piece of cultural or religious history, or will you let the Buddha challenge your life personally. Will you let his lived insights become your own lived insights? What will you decide?

Another example. You have studied the life of Jesus and seen the depth and power of his teachings. You have seen the intimate terms with which he spoke to God as a loving Father. Will you let that knowledge remain "notional," or will you let it become "real"? Will you turn to God in prayer, and say as Jesus said, "Our Father . . . "? What will you decide?

In each of these examples, after one has become convinced that something is true and good, one is faced with the challenge of personal decision. Lonergan suggests that there are two moments to that personal decision: evaluation and choice. He calls them: Dialectic and Foundations.

Dialectic	*Foundations*
History	Doctrines
Interpretation	Systematics
Research	Communications

Dialectic involves evaluation. But evaluation of what? An evaluation of differing accounts of the past or the present, an evaluation of the relative worth of different viewpoints. In short, an evaluation of the different movements and currents of human history. For example, is Confucius' view of our relationship to God more accurate or truer than Mohammed's or Jesus' or Buddha's? Or is that the right question? Are their views complementary or contradictory? Are their differences largely cultural, one teaching at one place and time, and another at a different place and time? Or are the differences more significant than this? These are questions for evaluation. But who will evaluate? You and I. And on what grounds? On the grounds of what we already know and what we already value and on that "more" which our study of the lives of the great teachers (or saviors) challenges us to recognize and to value.

But surely there must be more solid ground than this. Should we not rely on the judgment of those who are more knowledgeable and who are better than you or I? Yes. But we are the ones who decide who knows more than we do and who is better than we are. The matter still comes down to us and our evaluation. And what if those who know more than we do or who are better than we are disagree. Who will decide then? We will or there will be no decision. In the final analysis, do we not bear responsibility for our lives? We must ourselves decide among conflicting alternatives, for even if we adopt someone else's view, we are the ones who have chosen that person as the expert.

The whole point of Lonergan's analysis is to help us to grasp that our own knowing processes orient us toward truth and our own valuing processes orient us toward what is good. The criteria of our own consciousness, if we will but follow them attentively, intelligently, reasonably, and responsibly, will lead us to true judgments both of fact and of value. Our evaluations then, our Dialectics, partake in objectivity insofar as we give ourselves authentically to seeking truth and value.

DIALECTIC

Lonergan suggests that there are three basic perspectives or horizons which characterize a person who really desires truth and value. Each of these perspectives involves a change in the person, either from an erroneous perspective to a correct one, or at least from a less adequate perspective to a more adequate one. Lonergan uses the term "conversion" (and by that meaning a major alteration in viewpoint) to describe each of these changes.

INTELLECTUAL CONVERSION. The first conversion he considers is an intellectual one. We explored this personal change in the first chapter of this book. It involves the realization that our knowing process is not like the process of looking. "Do you 'see' what I mean?" can be a very misleading question. Opening our eyes to observe the data or "opening" our ears to hear the words is necessary, but it is only the first stage in knowing. We must also try to understand the data or the sounds, and judge the correctness of our understanding. The importance and implications of this we have considered earlier, in Chapter I and in Chapter IV. The reason for referring to it again here is to indicate that this viewpoint on knowing provides a criterion, indeed a crucial criterion, for deciding truth in the type of issue which one faces in Dialectic.

For example, anyone who says that a text from the past (other than a mathematical text) has only one meaning and that that meaning is clear without studying history, but just by looking at it, is by that very fact wrong. A person who makes that type of statement might be a very morally good person, but what he or she is affirming about our knowing is simply wrong. And that in itself raises questions about any substantive point of meaning that one is affirming about the text. The people, however intelligent, who equate knowing with merely looking or listening lack intellectual conversion. This viewpoint is characteristic of many who call themselves, or are called, "fundamentalists," but it is not limited to those who are designated by that name. The view that these individuals and groups have about truth is in error. Human beings just do not know meaning and truth by looking and seeing. That is only the beginning.

All fundamentalisms, all literalisms, which hold the viewpoint that there is "clear" truth, that the meaning of the texts of the past are obvious, if one would but open one's eyes, are mistaken on the very basic way we human beings gather knowledge and affirm the truth. This is so whether the fundamentalisms are religious or are political. The assurances that such people give that they have the real meanings from the past can surely be appealing and comforting. In reality, however, those who proclaim these fundamentalisms are building on sand, rather than on the sure-footed rock they think they are building on. Even when the substance of what they say is true, it is not true for the reason they say it is. And that causes significant problems. Their statements are meant to end inquiry. In reality, their statements should stimulate the beginning of inquiry. How do fundamentalists know that what they say is true and why should you or I believe them?

There are fundamentalisms of the left and of the right. There are liberal and conservative fundamentalisms. The issue is not one of political or religious direction, but an issue of what counts as evidence for one's position. If careful examination of the data, diligent efforts to understand, and thoughtful attention in judging are integral aspects of any position, then one does not have a literalism or a fundamentalism. One indeed might well have serious disagreements among people, but one will have the evidence, the understandings, and the judgments to go back to in an effort to resolve the disagreements. Fundamentalists who are in disagreement can only fall back on proclaiming ever more stridently that they are right and others are wrong. If they are Christians, they may keep repeating "The Bible *clearly* says. . . ." They lack the ability to call on the full range of evidence (historical and contemporary), the full range of understandings, and the full range of judgments which could either mediate the disputes or provide accessible grounds to substantiate their own viewpoint.

A question may have arisen in your mind about the consistency of what I have said so far. In the beginning of this chapter I spoke of the great teachers, such as Buddha and Jesus and Confucius and Mohammed. Did they not establish the type of fundamentalisms that I raise questions about? I don't think so, though some of their followers speak and act as if they did. First, these great teachers were originators of meanings and values. As individuals, they surely arose out of traditions, but they reshaped those traditions and contributed new vitality and vision to them. The past became "new" to their visions. They did not give new answers to old questions. They raised new questions.

Second, most of what they taught was in the form of stories or parables, which are particularly effective and striking ways to reveal values, their principal concern. Their interest, then, was not primarily discursive truth. In other words, the "truths" which they taught were truths about living. And they indicated how one might find evidence for and verify these truths, by trying to live them oneself. This was their challenge to their followers.

Third, their own lives were the best narratives, the best stories, to reveal the depth of their own characters and to give evidence of the goodness, the beauty, and the rightness of what they stood for.

The above critique of fundamentalism is an example of the way that the elements of intellectual conversion can serve as criteria in evaluating various competing positions. Habitual awareness of the elements of intellectual conversion alerts one to be cautious about any position that prescinds or tries to prescind from the criteria of evidence and of careful understanding. Needless to say, Lonergan's own position that these are the basic criteria to be applied to positions must itself be subjected by you to those same criteria. The evidence for his position will not be re-presented here, however, since it can be found in Chapters I and IV of this book and in his own work, *Insight*.

Lonergan's criterion of intellectual conversion is not meant to be some "new" criterion. Rather it is meant to be a reflective grasp of the natural and active criteria of our own minds. These criteria manifest themselves spontaneously as questions: "What is the evidence for what you say?" "Why do you understand it that way and no other?" "On what do you base your assurance that your understanding is true?" That really is what intellectual conversion is about: knowing how basic those questions are, and using them. Using those questions not only calls fundamentalisms into doubt, but helps one to resolve many another dispute. "What is the quality of your evidence?" "Are you sure you have all the relevant data, or are you leaving something out?" "If so, what?" "Why must the evidence be understood in the way you are proposing, and not in some other way?" "Are you sure the evidence supports your hypothesis?" It is just such awareness and sensitivity to these issues of how we know that constitute intellectual conversion.

MORAL CONVERSION. In addition to the criterion of intellectual conversion, Lonergan suggests that the criterion of moral conversion can serve to resolve disputes that one is faced with in Dialectic. The principal element of this criterion was treated in Chapter II. Moral conversion is the change in us from using the criterion of sensitive satisfaction for what is really good, to using the criterion of value, of which sensitive satisfaction is a real part, but only a part. It is the change from the seeking of pleasure and the avoidance of pain criterion of children to the mature criterion of what is really worthwhile, even if it is sometimes painful, which characterizes adults.

Economic materialism, scientific determinism, early Freudian *id* psychology, and many forms of behaviorism use as a basic criterion in their theories that human beings are at base sophisticated stimulus/response mechanisms. Such views attempt to reduce human beings to creatures responsive merely to pleasure and pain. These views can be appealing both because of their simplicity and because they can indeed explain much of our behavior, and surely much more than we are usually willing to admit. But they cannot explain all.

The advocates of those views can appear courageous, and can in fact be so, for proposing views which people do not like to hear about themselves. But the views are flawed and partial. In fact, the very courage and creativity of their proponents reveals the partial nature of their discoveries. Who is courageous but one who is willing to risk the pain of loss of reputation or the scorn of others to stand by what he or she considers to be true? But to be willing to do this is to show by one's actions that not all human beings use the pleasure/pain principle to control their behavior. The proponents of these theories contradict the exclusive or universal quality of their discoveries by their very act of brilliantly formulating them and, against all opposition, proposing and defending them. Their very activity is most convincing evidence that their theories contain only partial truth. These individuals are generally not immoral persons. Rather they are often moral and conscientious persons who have partially, but only partially, reflected on their own moral experience.

It is well to recall, however, that many of those who formulated "materialistic" views of human motivation did so by observing the actions of those persons and institutions which proclaimed a higher view, but were not all that successful at living it. In other words, those who proclaim a higher view often are not willing to admit how much human motivation in general and their own in particular can be understood in terms of the seeking of pleasure and the avoidance of pain.

Moral conversion then can be a criterion for deciding among differing viewpoints in two ways. As formulated, it is a criterion for calling into question any theoretical view of human motivation which is exclusive, whether that view is solely materialist or solely value-related. In addition, and equally or even more importantly, moral conversion as lived by us can provide the criterion for evaluating those persons and movements which are in fact morally responsive to the range of values. Moral conversion, as lived, challenges us to use our own value consciousness to help decide between competing economic, political, medical, ethical, and social theories and policies and, further, challenges us to ourselves propose new theoretical and practical solutions. Moral conversion of its very essence is oriented toward action.

RELIGIOUS CONVERSION. In addition to intellectual and moral conversion, Lonergan suggests that religious conversion provides an important criterion in the evaluative task of Dialectic. By religious conversion he does not mean moving from one religious group to another. That may or may not be of religious significance. Rather he means the actual broadening of our own personal perspective from focusing only on the realities of our finite world to attending as well to matters of ultimate meaning and value. Religious conversion then, for Lonergan, means that interior change whereby our ordinary cares are placed in the larger context of transcendent meaning and value, whether that meaning and value is experienced in personal or transpersonal terms.

As a criterion in Dialectic, religious conversion, both as lived and as reflected on, serves to distinguish between views that promote meaning and present value and those which take a deeper and longer-ranging perspective on the worth of our world and of our actions in it. Religious conversion orients us to a vision of the whole and to a valuing of each person and event in themselves and in the ultimate significance they have. Religious conversion grounds a "more" of trust, a "more" of hope, a "more" of love both in our attitude and in our action. It is by no means, however, blind to the complexities, the ambiguities, and the evils of our human experience. Rather, precisely because it is alert to a larger and more beneficent meaning, it is able, at least in its saints and in its other holy men and women, to face evil vigorously and courageously because it does not fear that evil will be the final word. For religious understanding, our world is not just fact, it is also gift.

Many scholars in economics, in ethics, in the natural and human sciences, etc. make no secret of either denying or prescinding from the type of religious perspective indicated here. With regard to those persons who explicitly deny a religious perspective, it is helpful to distinguish between those whose professional insights are in themselves incompatible with religious views and those whose are not incompatible. For instance, although Freud himself understood many of his psychoanalytic insights to be incompatible with taking the religious perspective seriously, yet even at his own time, and certainly now, a number of analysts see many of his psychoanalytic insights as quite compatible with, although often purifying of, religious consciousness. Dialectic often means not taking things at their "face" value.

With regard to those views which do not deny, but only purport to prescind from religion, one must also evaluate with care. Sometimes these views are actually incompatible with religion, such as certain exclusively economic views of human relationships. At other times there is simply a genuine scientific prescinding from religion, such as in mathematics and in much of medicine. Views which do in fact actually prescind from the religious perspective can often be quite compatible with it, when looked at from a more comprehensive perspective. Mathematics and medicine, as referred to above, are two such endeavors.

What are perhaps most challenging and difficult to evaluate are views which call themselves religious, but perhaps are really not. All cases are not as obvious, at least in retrospect, as Jim Jones and the mass suicide he ordered or Charles Manson and his cult of killing. Until fairly recently, Christians in general considered all other religious traditions, at best, as inferior to their own and, at worst, as demonic; and sometimes, when they could, they acted accordingly. It is clear now that that perspective had more to do with cultural chauvinism and Western imperialism than with "religious" insight. We are just now getting to a place where genuine historical and comparative dialogue can begin.

There is one criterion of religious authenticity which Lonergan suggests could be applied to all viewpoints that call themselves religious. At first glance this criterion may appear to be a minimalist one. I would suggest that it is not. It is the criterion of whether the religious perspective encourages among its followers and manifests in its followers: attentiveness, understanding, judgment, and responsibility. Lonergan's work, and our study of it in this book, reveals just how integral these qualities are to human growth and to overcoming decline. If a religious tradition seeks to narrow attentiveness, intelligence, reasonableness, and responsibility, it is to that extent inauthentic. It to that extent manifests the fear of the "more" and the "good" which should characterize a perspective which aims to encompass the whole in love and in compassion.

Finally, religious conversion should be able to discern the perspective of religious value in those who manifest the "more" in their thought and in their lives, even though these same persons, for whatever reason, do not use the name of religion. True religion does not need to possess, but only recognize and rejoice in the "good" and the "more" wherever they are to be found.

THE SIGNIFICANCE OF THE CONVERSIONS. It should be clear from the reflections above on intellectual, moral, and religious conversions that the degree of their presence or absence both in ourselves as we evaluate and in the views which we evaluate is of immense significance. To the extent that we lack the attitude of openness which characterizes each of the conversions, we cannot recognize their lack in the views and positions we are evaluating. If we are "colorblind" either to how we know, or to how we choose what is really valuable, or to what is of ultimate value, then we will hardly be able to be guides either for ourselves or others on these matters. We will more than likely mistake the false for the true, and the true for the false, the really valuable for the apparently valuable, and the apparently valuable for the really valuable.

But we are not locked into where we are. When we come face to face with real excellence in the intellectual, in the moral, and in the religious spheres, we can know that we are in the presence of some reality that is perhaps at present beyond us, by the confusion and the heightening of feeling which they provoke in us. We can, of course, dismiss such feelings, and the persons or objects which provoke them, much as some adolescents dismiss or ridicule what they or their group are not comfortable with. But we can also recognize our present ignorance and be willing to make those interior and exterior changes necessary in order to learn and to grow. The presence of real intellectual, moral, and religious excellence can challenge us to real intellectual, moral, and religious excellence ourselves. We are capable of the kind of expansive exercise of freedom, which allows us to reach new and richer horizons.

OTHER CRITERIA. In addition to the criteria of intellectual, moral, and religious conversion which separate out issues dialectically, there are other considerations which can in fact lessen apparent differences. Not all perspectives differ dialectically; some perspectives are complementary and others differ genetically.

For example, physicians, professors, engineers, business executives, and lawyers, despite some appearance to the contrary, basically inhabit, in their professional work, not opposed but complementary worlds. They need one another, and we all need them. Dialectic would not heighten the differences between these professions, but would seek to understand how they can better work together. Lonergan's own work in understanding the transcultural and trans-professional character of the levels of consciousness would be an example of understanding these fields in a complementary manner. The real dialectical opposition would not be between physicians and lawyers as such, but between physicians who are morally converted and those who are not, and between lawyers who are morally converted and those who are not.

Similarly, some differences are genetic, i.e., they are stages in a process. One need not put the stages of fetus, infant, child, adolescent, young adult, adult, and older person against one another. They are successive stages in a developmental process. Likewise, in the history of ideas one need not dismiss or put down ideas of an earlier time which may have been a necessary precursor for the ideas of today. Some earlier ideas do need to be criticized, but not because they were earlier. Studying those earlier stages of ideas might in fact give necessary or at least helpful perspective on later ones.

Dialectic then is our evaluative activity with regard to the options that the past and the present have established. It is an ecumenical version of the type of apologetics which the churches used to engage in. It is in addition an activity which can call for growth and development in ourselves to meet the challenges of the genuine achievements of the past. Foundations, the next functional speciality, consolidates and builds on the personal growth and change which has begun in and been stimulated by Dialectic.

FOUNDATIONS

Foundations reflects on the new horizons—intellectual, moral, and religious—which we have arrived at and chosen through our encounter with the truths and values discovered in Research, Interpretation, History and Dialectic. Or, more precisely, Foundations reflects on who we have become by the choices we have made through our careful understanding and evaluation of the past. For when we are faced with evaluative decisions and make them, we not only determine the matters at hand we also establish our own character.

> . . . foundations occurs on the fourth level of human consciousness, on the level of deliberation, evaluation, decision. It is a decision about whom and what you are for and, again, whom and what you are against. It is a decision illuminated by the manifold possibilities exhibited in dialectics. It is a fully conscious decision about one's horizon, one's outlook, one's world-view.[1]

Who we have become by our decisions has not been an arbitrary choice or series of choices, or at least ought not to have been. If we have followed the transcendental imperatives—Be attentive; Be intelligent; Be reasonable;

Be responsible—then what we have discovered through the first four functional specialties is not arbitrary and subjective but is, rather, objectively true and valuable, or is as close to truth and value as we are able to come. To have been arbitrary and subjective would have been not to have attended to all the relevant data, not to have understood carefully, not to have verified fully, and not to have chosen responsibly. It is *our* choice whether, in our searching for truth and value, we act in such a way as to achieve greater personal authenticity or less.

Further, however intensely personal our decision-making has been, if it has not been arbitrary, then it has not been purely or merely private. Others can make similar decisions. In addition, our decisions are social because they have been made with regard to cultural heritages, which are the achievement of many persons over long centuries. Our choices then will not only be personal, with personal consequences, but will also be social and have social and interpersonal consequences. Through our decisions we will share new horizons, perhaps with new people, and sometimes, as a result, we will also cease to share horizons with others with whom we have long been one with. This can lead to inevitable, but nonetheless painful choices.

Not all such achievements of new horizons need lead to such radical personal and interpersonal change, however. Often one's new horizon is the achievement of a personal authenticating of a tradition or traditions of which one has been a part. But if one takes the road to personal authenticity, then one must be willing to undergo the pain of growth and change which often includes moments of confusion and doubt, and which can call for difficult realignment of one's values and one's life.

Consider the difficult choices and their consequences faced by the Gentiles when confronted by Paul's preaching of the good news about Jesus Christ; the choices faced by Christians in Europe at the time of the Reformation; the choices faced by Germans at the time of Hitler; the choices faced by young Americans at the time of the Vietnam War; the choices faced by South African Christians at the present time. These are but dramatic instances of the real and significant choices which all of us face, generally on a smaller scale, if we follow the road of authenticity in our searching for truth and value.

It is with regard to difficult choices that the close connection between Dialectic and Foundations becomes especially clear. It is actually in the process of evaluating (Dialectic) the range of choices before us, and placing the value of one above the other, that we show, and indeed create, our character (Foundations). Dialectic and Foundations then are really names for two poles of the same process. Dialectic is the name of the pole which is the content of our evaluations, and Foundations is the name of the pole which is who we have become through the process of making those evaluations.

For instance, those who were faced with the choice (Dialectic) between almost certainly being killed or letting themselves be conscripted into Hitler's army, and who chose, for moral and religious reasons, to die rather than fight with Hitler, were establishing their foundational stance by the very process of their evaluation of the options before them. One's Dialectic, therefore, establishes one's Foundations. The only further point that needs to be made is that the functional speciality, Foundations, also includes explicit reflection on the new foundational reality we have become by our Dialectic.

In the section on Dialectic, we gave an analysis of the three conversions. They are indeed operative in Dialectic, which is why Lonergan discusses them there. But it is only in Foundations, when one is reflecting on the criteria that are now operative in one's life, that these conversions would actually get fully articulated.

Theologically, Lonergan's emphasis on the meaning of Foundations as the personal achievement of a new horizon by each of us contrasts sharply with the common Roman Catholic theological view before the Second Vatican Council. Before the Council Foundational or Fundamental Theology was generally considered to be a series of basic propositions from which one could deduce conclusions.

The example Lonergan gives of this previous view is a striking one. At its extreme it would have made faith the conclusion of a syllogism, rather than a personal act of a response to and a choice of ultimate value. The syllogism which Lonergan suggests would characterize the previous view is the following:

> One must believe and accept whatever the bible or the true church or both believe and accept. But X is the bible or the true church or both. Therefore, one must believe and accept whatever X believes and accepts. Moreover, X believes and accepts a, b, c, d. . . . Therefore, one must believe and accept a, b, c, d. . . . [2]

Nothing could be further from Lonergan's view that one finds theological Foundations not in propositions but in persons. Faith is not the conclusion of a series of apparently logical statements, but the personal act of valuing and deciding, which is experienced as gift from the Divine. Valuing the Bible or Church is not a conclusion of irrefutable reasoning, but rather a shift of horizons which is a transformative response to the goodness and truth one finds in the Bible and Church. "The threefold conversion [religious, moral, intellectual] is not a set of propositions that a theologian [or religious believer] utters, but a fundamental and momentous change in the human reality that a theologian is."[3]

PLURALITY OF RELIGIOUS EXPRESSION. If Foundations is not a set of propositions, but rather the new personal reality that we are as a result of our decisions, then our expressions of that personal reality are going to be manifold. We will manifest that new personal reality in deeds and in words. And our deeds will be creative and our words will be rich and varied.

Lonergan indicates some of the many forms that expression will take. All of us will express ourselves in everyday language, which Lonergan refers to as the language of common sense. In addition, if we are artists, we will also express ourselves in poetry or in music, in painting or in architecture. If we have been trained in Aristotelian and Scholastic philosophy and theology, we will also express ourselves in the technical language of theory. If we have been trained in a contemporary philosophy and theology of reflection on interiority, such as Lonergan's own, then we will express ourselves in words that speak of personal transformation. If we are gifted with a profound prayer life, such as the mystics have, then we will express ourselves with the subtle observations about spiritual growth. In other words, our forms of religious expression will only be limited by the extent of our conversions and the extent of our literary, artistic, and scholarly gifts.

But religious expression must not be isolated from the other aspects of our lives. Rather, it needs to be integrated with them, if we are to be whole and if religion is to have its full effect in our lives. Historically that means that religious living and religious expression must be integrated with the other cultural achievements of the period.

For example, when Christianity encountered the intellectual world of the Greeks and the Romans, questions arose about who Jesus was ontologically and what was his relationship to God, questions which were not asked or answered in the Jewish and Hellenic worlds of early bibical Christianity. How many persons were there in God? Was Jesus as the Son of God one person or two? Did Jesus as the Son of God have one nature or two? These were all questions from the theoretical orientation of consciousness. It was a cultural context which Christianity had to enter, or it would remain on the fringes of Greek and Roman life and thought.

Now, however, the Greek and the Scholastic worlds with their model of science as what is necessary and with their concern for substance and accidents are no longer significant cultural realities, although they were important human achievements both in themselves and as stepping stones for later cultural achievements. They are not at present, though, the partner that religious living and religious thinking need principally to be in dialogue with.

Culture has moved from concern with static and necessary systems, to interest in historical development and in what constructs systems, namely, method. Fascination with classic cultural achievement has given way to concern about the ongoing process of cultural creation. Science is not now about the necessary, but about the possible and the probable, and how we can ever keep increasing our knowledge. This new cultural context is the one Lonergan wishes particularly to address. And it is in terms intelligible and relevant to this culture that Lonergan calls on the religious believer and theologian to express himself or herself.

Specifically, this means our expressing the foundational religious reality, which we are, in terms of interiority and in terms of method. This has the advantage of presenting religious development in terms which correlate religion with other cultural issues, for it is interiority and method which locate our scientific and historical knowing on the same trajectory as our ethical and religious knowing and deciding. That will call for treating religious experience from the perspective of interiority, namely, in terms of who we are as religious in relation to who we are in the other dimensions of our lives.

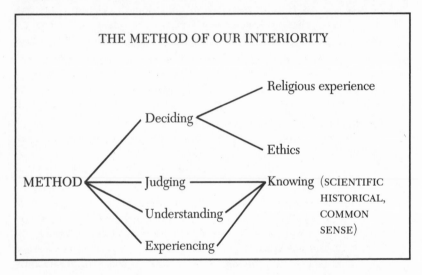

THE METHOD OF OUR INTERIORITY

Lonergan treats religious experience as decisional openness. Religious experience, therefore, is awareness, i.e., experience or consciousness, of our decisional openness to the Transcendent. By thus locating religious experience at the decisional, fourth level of our consciousness, Lonergan also clearly indicates how religious experience operates in relation to the other operations of our consciousness. Religious experience is at the controlling level of our consciousness.

The fourth level of consciousness is our level of valuing; as religious consciousness it is our response to transcendent value. Although feeling is found, and in fact is constitutive of, each level of consciousness—one has genuine feeling when an insight into a difficult matter finally comes—it is particularly characteristic of the fourth level. Feeling is the specific and appropriate response to the perception of value. This is true whether the value responded to is the world of finite value—ethics—or the world of infinite value—religion. "[A]pprehensions [of value] are given in feelings."[4]

In fact, it is in our feelings that we first have the apprehension that something is valuable. Contrary to some contemporary philosophical disparagement of feelings, Lonergan affirms their essential importance in our discovering and responding to value. But it must be clear that by feelings, Lonergan does not mean the volatile emotional responses of the pleasure-pain continuum, but the deeply experienced intentional orientation of our being to the worth of what we are evaluating.

Foundational theology for Lonergan, then, is reflection upon ourselves as experiencing religiously, i.e., as experiencing our decisional responsiveness to the divine. Our fourth level controls by its choices what we will attend to, understand, and verify. And this is so, not only with regard to what we will attend to in the area of religion, but what we will attend to in the other aspects of our lives. Certainly, not all persons who experience religiously actually make that orientation determinative of their actions in the rest of their lives. In fact, those who do so are called "saints." But the orientation to ultimate value, which is religious experience, has the power to be so determinative, if we let our responsiveness to the divine be whole and pervasive.

This is not to say that if one is wholly responsive to ultimate value, or as wholly responsive as humans can be, one will go about the *process* of understanding and knowing the world in some different fashion than those who are not responsive to the divine. Far from it. Knowledge comes from attention, intelligence, and reasonableness both for those who are religious and for those who aren't. The difference for those who are religious would not then be in the process of knowing, but, first, in what these who are religious choose to attend to, and, second, in the dedication that they ought to devote to what they have chosen to understand. The actual process of understanding is the same for all. In fact, religious persons do religion a disservice to claim to have hidden sources of knowledge about the world.

The difference for the genuinely religious person is not in the process of knowing, but in the motivation for knowing and in the freedom for knowing. For if we really experience ourselves as being gifted, graced, by the divine, we can begin to let go of our neurotic, egoistic, group, and common sense biases. These biases are ultimately based on our fear that we will be hurt, or further hurt, and so we narrow our focus to what is for "me," or for "us," or for "now." Knowledge, which does not have "us" at the center, simply is not relevant. For a genuinely religious person, however, all knowledge about the real world is significant, whether it impacts me directly or not.

There are surely those, however, who are open to the divine, even if they are not reflectively aware of it. Just as one could be acting out of anger that one was not explicitly attending to, but which could be controlling one's actions [others might notice it], so one could be experiencing religiously without explicitly attending to that reality [again others might notice it]. And in fact, as with anger, it could be the controlling motivation of one's actions; but, if asked, one could actually even deny that it was operating. Jesus was quite aware of this distinction. "It is not those who *say* 'Lord, Lord,' who enter the kingdom of heaven, but those who do the will of my Father."

It might be well to conclude this discussion of Foundations with an ecumenical and even universalist consideration. Lonergan by recognizing that the true foundational reality is who persons have become by their response to transcendent value has opened up ecumenical dialogue and the dialogue of world religions to reflection upon spirituality. Christianity in particular has tended to focus on differences in Doctrines between religious communities rather than on the religious experience which grounds Doctrines. Lonergan's work indicates why attention should first be focused on Foundations, on the spirituality which grounds affirmations or Doctrines, rather than beginning reflection immediately on the differences of the Doctrines themselves.

Beginning dialogue in this way allows for exploring the question whether and to what extent varying Doctrines perhaps express the same or similar religious experiences in different terms, rather than necessarily expressing different religious realities. Perhaps sometimes indeed even the same Doctrines express not the same but different religious experiences, and different Doctrines in fact express the same experience, but in different cultural circumstances. In other instances, although the experiences are different and the Doctrines are different, both the experiences and the Doctrines stand in a complementary and not in a dialectical relationship to one another. Lonergan's focus on the priority of the foundational reality of the person's own spiritual transformation suggests a way to explore and to help resolve the issue of the diversity of Doctrines both within Christianity and among the world religions.

With that brief reflection on the significance of our understanding of Foundations for an understanding of Doctrines, we turn to that topic.

DOCTRINES

Doctrines are the judgments of fact and of value which we make from the stance we have taken in Foundations. We can make those judgments either as an individual or as a community. Foundations has established a new horizon. Doctrines are the affirmations we make from that new horizon. Because of the range of meaning that Lonergan gives to Doctrines, it is important not to exclusively identify this functional speciality with the doctrines or dogmas of a particular religious community. Doctrines as a functional speciality is much broader. It refers to the affirmations of a person, of a group of persons, *or* of a formally constituted community in which that person, those persons, or that community expresses its basic values and truths.

The recognition of the broader scope of Doctrines is also important to emphasize that Doctrines flow out of the struggle for authenticity which we have been exploring in each of the functional specialities. The function of Doctrines is to bring one's Foundations into greater concreteness. Doctrines clarifies both for oneself and for others where one stands.

The content of a Doctrine arises from the issues one has reflected on and evaluated in Dialectic. For instance, if the issue a theologian was considering was the contemporary issue in Roman Catholicism about the ordination of women, he or she would have posed the pertinent questions in Research, Interpretation, and History on that subject. What do we discover from Scripture on this question? Is the question explicitly addressed or even implicitly addressed? What roles have women had in the Church in the various periods of history? Has the question of ordination ever been explicitly addressed? If so, how authoritative in the tradition was the answer? Has the growing equality of women in every aspect of society changed the context of the question or shed new light on it?

All of these questions and more the theologian would address about this question and only then make his or her evaluation in Dialectics. Foundations would address and reflect on any new horizon the theologian had come to from his or her investigation of the question. Doctrines would be the affirmations that the theologian would now make on this subject, after he or she has personally examined all of the facts and values involved.

I have deliberately chosen an example which focuses on an issue upon which there is significant division. A person investigating this question may well come up with his or her personal Doctrine on this issue before the Church as a whole makes a final authoritative pronouncement. Perhaps the Church never will make a definitive pronouncement on this issue.

Doctrines, then, as Lonergan understands them, are not just definitive Church affirmations, they also include one's own affirmations about significant issues.

A necessary preliminary to understanding any particular doctrine of any person or any tradition is to understand the specific cultural context in which it was affirmed, since cultural contexts obviously change and develop throughout history. In addition, different cultural and intellectual contexts can and often do exist at the same time. If we do not understand this we may well consider that two different formulations about the same matter are necessarily affirming two different realities, when in fact the matter may simply be being affirmed in two different ways.

For instance, a great deal of the ecumenical advance between Roman Catholicism and the Reformation Churches has come about from the discovery through historical research that key affirmations of the Council of Trent and of Protestant Confessions were aiming at the same truth about God's saving activity, but that they were formulated from different theological and intellectual perspectives. The animosities of the time tended to blind the participants on both sides to what they shared in common.

Clearly, then, in discussing different doctrinal formulations about the same subject matter, one must understand the particular historical context of each of the affirmations. There are some general historical shifts which are particularly important, however, and which Lonergan considers need special emphasis. With regard to Western Christianity, Lonergan understands those cultural stages to be as follows.

STAGES OF WESTERN CULTURE. First is the stage of common sense, the stage when things are spoken of in direct relation to ourselves. This stage, that of biblical and pre-biblical times, is largely symbolic in its language. For instance, it is quite anthropomorphic in the way it speaks about God. God walks in the garden; God shows anger at sin, and can repent of his actions.

The second stage is post-biblical. It is largely influenced by Greek thought. It is the world of theory, in which things are spoken of in relation to one another. The question with regard to the Trinity in this stage is not who are God the Father, Jesus Christ, and the Spirit as we experience them, but who are they in themselves? It is in such a world of thought that the questions and answers with regard to person and nature in the Trinity and in Christ were formulated by Church councils. These questions had not been asked in the Bible, but once the Christian Church took root in the Hellenic world, they were inevitable questions. And if Christianity was to become integral to and grow within that culture, those questions needed to be answered.

The third stage is our present cultural context. This context is an outgrowth of that Greek advance in thought, but with some notable differences. The Greek interest in necessary correlations has given way to the realization that the correlations we discover are only probable. Because of this, further research, hypotheses, and verification are always called for, and the methods for doing this must always also be further developed and refined. Scientists, therefore, still explain data in terms of theory, in terms of the relationship of data to one another, e.g., the structural relationships of the elements of the atom, but instead of searching for necessary correlations, scientists search for ever better understandings. Necessity has given way to probability and interest in method has, therefore, increased.

In the human sciences, as well, there has been change. In place of the exaltation of any one particular period as a norm for all times, a form of classicism, there is a respect for the richness of each cultural and historical period. Correspondingly, there has also been a concern for method, since historical method is the only way we can come to increasingly accurate understandings of the different cultures which are studied.

Theology too is faced with the same questions which call for attention to method. Historical study has entered deeply into the field of religion. This need for attention to theological method, therefore, arises not only or even principally from a need to speak to contemporary culture, but precisely because historical studies of religion and of theology themselves raise the question of the method operative in the creation of theologies. History clearly indicates that different theologies have developed over the centuries. How and why do theologies grow, develop, and change? What is the method of theology?

But there is another, perhaps even more important reason for theology to attend to method. With the development of method in the human and natural sciences, and with the proliferation both of disciplines and of knowledge, the question of whether there is any possibility of the unity of knowledge or of the unity of disciplines arises. Are we simply to be overwhelmed by the knowledge from the diverse disciplines which we have created? Lonergan's whole body of work is directed toward answering those questions. Unity in knowledge is to be discovered by attending to the one who is doing the knowing and the choosing, namely, ourselves. We are the method in all disciplines, humanistic, scientific, and religious, through the activity of the four levels of our consciousness.

The special role that religious reflection on method can bring to the issue of the possible unity of methods is its capacity to consider the full range of human subjectivity. Religious reflection on the full dimensions of the human subject reveals the method behind all methods, ourselves operating as experiencing, understanding, judging, and deciding persons with regard to any field of data, whether of sense or of consciousness, that we attend to.

In addition, religious reflection also reveals that it is at the decisional level that we give in to the biases, the self-protecting narrownesses, which can distort all our knowing operations with regard to any field. But religious reflection further reveals that it is with the healing that comes from experiencing ourselves accepted and loved by the Absolute that we can be slowly freed from the narrowness of bias to operate without the blinders of what is in "my best interests" with regard to whatever we attend to.

Reflection on the full range of subjectivity then reveals both the method behind all other methods and the dynamics both of the biases that impede the exercise of those other methods and the healing process which can release their creativity. The challenge of theology in our cultural context then is to work out with fullness the correlations between religious interiority [method] and the interiority [method] of all other fields. In Lonergan's words, "[Theology] has to construct the common basis of theory and of common sense that is to be found in interiority and it has to use that basis to link the experience of the transcendent with the world mediated by meaning."[5]

PLURALITY OF DOCTRINAL EXPRESSION. As there are different cultural contexts, so there will be different forms of doctrinal expression appropriate to each. Classicism focused on the second stage described above, the world of theory, as normative for Christian theology. That claim is no longer credible. The Western cultural context has changed. The questions and problems are different now. The three stages of culture presented above are but illustrative of the historical as well as the contemporary diversity of cultures throughout the world. For Christianity, as well as for any religious tradition with a universal intent, the religious message of the tradition needs to be communicated in terms appropriate to the different cultural contexts it addresses. What Lonergan says so forcefully below about Christianity applies to any universal religious tradition.

> . . . if the Gospel is to be preached to all nations . . . still it is not to be preached in the same manner to all. If one is to communicate with persons of another culture, one must use the resources of their culture. To use simply the resources of one's own culture is not to communicate with the other but to remain locked up in one's own. At the same time, it is not enough simply to employ the resources of the other culture. One must do so creatively. . . . Doctrines that really are assimilated bear the stamp of those that assimilate them, and the absence of such an imprint would point to a merely perfunctory assimilation.[6]

The consequence of this understanding of the diversity of cultures and the diversity of development within each culture is clear. Doctrinal expression will of necessity be diverse. A further, quite important consequence is implicit in this recognition of diversity. Only those who share the perspective of the communicating culture and of the culture which is being communicated with are in a position to judge the adequacy of a doctrinal formulation in that new culture. Those who do not understand the context of the "communicated with" culture are not in the position to judge the new doctrinal expression. As Lonergan wrote in his chapter on Doctrines, which was originally written for the papal Theological Commission of which he was a member, " . . . no one should pass judgement on matters he does not understand, and no one with a less or differently differentiated consciousness is capable of understanding accurately what is said by a person with a more fully differentiated consciousness."[7]

But in addition to Doctrines in which a person or a community expresses its basic affirmations, there is a further theological task, which is both to explore the connections between the individual doctrines one affirms and also to explore the relationship between one's doctrines and the other aspects of one's life. That is the task of Systematics.

SYSTEMATICS

The task of the theologian in Systematics is understanding. More precisely, the task of the theologian is to understand what one or one's community has affirmed in Doctrines, and to understand it in terms that can communicate with the culture one is living in. The distinctions among cultural periods, then, which was discussed in Doctrines, are also, and perhaps particularly, relevant in Systematics.

Understanding is not disembodied. Each period has certain cultural forms and certain cultural challenges. There are cultures which are characterized almost solely by common sense, cultures which have both common sense and theory, and cultures, such as our own, which include common sense, theory, and, increasingly, method and interiority. If one's own, or a community's, basic affirmations, Doctrines, could be found, even by believers, to have no meaning to a particular culture and to its problems, that would not bode well for the future of that community or for the value of its affirmations. Systematics then is the exploration of the cultural meaning of Doctrines.

One of the principal tasks of a theologian, therefore, is precisely to provide the mediation between the basic affirmations of his or her community and the culture in which the theologian lives. Much of Lonergan's own most creative theological work was in the area of Systematics. Most of the second half of this book will be a retrieval of his systematic insights into the basic Christian affirmations. That work will not be repeated here, but an example may be helpful to show both the power and the relevance of Systematics.

That Jesus brings salvation to humankind through his death and resurrection is a basic Christian doctrine. But that teaching has given rise over the centuries to many understandings (different Systematics) about how that takes place. A number of those understandings are both fantastic and grotesque. Jesus by his death pays the price the devil demands to release us from the devil's power into which we have fallen by our sins. In this scenario, God bargains with the devil and sacrifices his Son to the devil! Another attempt at understanding, which is still unfortunately being preached, is that God's justice was offended by our sins and that, to pay the penalty incurred by that offense, God in his mercy sent Jesus to die in our place. Here we have two of God's attributes in conflict with one another: we have mercy capitulating to justice's demands, and we have God sacrificing his own Son to himself. One might perhaps worship such a God out of fear, but it is hard to conceive how one would worship this God out of love.

Lonergan proposes a quite different Christian understanding of the dynamics of salvation. (1) Jesus dies because human beings reject him and his message and put him to death. This statement summarizes the facts of the bibical account. (2) Jesus by the manner of his death, his submission and his love, and by his forgiveness of his killers transforms the apparent victory of evil over good into the moral triumph of good over evil. (3) God confirms this victory of Jesus by Jesus' resurrection appearances to the apostles and disciples. (4) The disciples and we ourselves see starkly the thrust and the ugliness of evil (sin) in its power to kill Jesus, God's anointed. (5) We are moved by the power of Jesus' example and by its confirmation by God to identify with Jesus in overcoming evil with good in our own lives. In fact, the death of Jesus can empower us to begin to act in like manner, to transform evil into good, stopping and reversing the cycle of evil by forgiveness. By the quality of our response to evil, we continue in our own lives Jesus' work of redeeming our world.

This brief summary cannot indicate the richness of the treatment of what Lonergan refers to as "the law of the cross." What our example can show is the function of Systematics. Systematics seeks the meaning of Doctrines. Lonergan's own succinct statement of the meaning of the Christian Doctrine of salvation is: "God wisely decided and lovingly chose to take away the evils of the human race not by an act of power but by transforming those evils into a supreme good through the working of a just and mysterious law of the cross."[8]

Notice some of the elements of Lonergan's understanding:

(1) Lonergan's law of the cross sticks close to the phenomenology of the experience the Christian has in contemplating the crucified Jesus. We see his love and forgiveness and are moved by it, identify with him, and are empowered to imitate him. The terminology of penalty to be paid and legal justice disappears. God does not sacrifice his Son either to the devil or to himself. (There is a power to sacrificial and legal language which does speak to certain aspects of the definitive character of the liberation which the Christian experiences, but interpreted literally, it is incoherent and offensive.) For Lonergan, God sends his Son to us; we take him into our hands

and we see him transform our evil into good, and, in the process, transform our understanding of our human task and our challenge in living it.

(2) The mystery of salvation is no abstract and merely cognitive teaching to be affirmed. It calls us to a transformation in our own way of acting, and not only to assent to a truth about Jesus. The dynamics of salvation, as Lonergan suggests we understand it, is a complex and rich drama of values which we are challenged to acknowledge, to respond to, and to participate in. Christians experience in the death and resurrection of Jesus God's answer, his personal response, to the problem of human evil and his invitation to us to actively share in the overcoming of evil.

(3) Lonergan's understanding of the transforming power of Jesus' death is open to a universalist interpretation. It does not make exclusive claims about the power of Jesus' death to lead us to the transformation of evil into good. It only affirms what Christians experience in the death of Jesus. It makes no comment about what others experience. Christians' knowledge about Jesus does not in itself give knowledge about the experience of God that others might have. It does implicitly, however, call for Christians to collaborate with all others who transform evil into good.

(4) Lonergan affirms the meaning of salvation in terms of our interiority. Salvation is grace, i.e., it is experienced as gift. It is the gifted transformation of our decisional consciousness by which, in response to the loving death of Jesus, we are empowered to respond to the evil which confronts us with forgiveness and love. Christians experience such a personal transformation as beyond the power of their own willing. As a consequence of this gifted transformation of our willingness, we can begin to let go of our various self-protective biases, which we cling to because we do not experience ourselves as sufficiently loved, and, therefore, try to protect ourselves. In the death of Jesus we experience ourselves loved in a way in which God precisely does not demand a penalty for our sins, but rather freely grants forgiveness. Jesus dying, and yet loving and forgiving, manifests the unconditional forgiveness of God. Jesus' death does not cause God to forgive us; rather it unmistakenly manifests that God has forgiven us. It is we who needed to experience Jesus' death, not God. God did not need it nor want it in itself, but only for our sake. But only with such a forgiving death of God's own Son, in response to human evil, could we really believe we are unconditionally loved and forgiven by God.

(5) Lonergan by his law of the cross, then, shows the powerful relevance of the death of Jesus to the power of evil in the world. Evil in human affairs seems to generate more evil. Resentment breeds more resentment; killing, more killing. Jesus represents an ending of that cycle by his active reception of the evil meted out to him and his transformation of it into forgiveness. The

cycle of decline which we live out and extend through our biases receives a powerful initial transformation by Jesus' refusal to give in to it or to continue it. By accepting the love manifested in Jesus' death, we can become active collaborators with him and the Father in the transformation of evil into good.

This Systematics of salvation which Lonergan develops shows the creative power of Systematics to be faithful to the insights of tradition, and yet to render Doctrines understandable in our present context. Doctrines enshrine in language the experience of transcendent mystery. Language is never adequate to this task. Systematics can point in the direction of the mystery, however, and provide us, and those we communicate with, some understanding of the mystery.

COMMUNICATIONS

The final challenge the theologian has is to communicate what he or she has discovered. Theology cannot be effective in the Church or in the world unless it is communicated. Therefore, although Communications is the last functional speciality, it is clearly as essential and integral to the theological task as the others are. In fact, the case could no doubt be reasonably made that Communications is the most significant of the functional specialities, since all the previous ones prepare for it.

Theology reflects on the facts of good and evil in our world, on interpretations of these facts, and on the transcendent resolution of the issues which are raised by these incontrovertible elements of our human condition. And it reflects on these facts, interpretations, and resolutions not only theoretically, but as challenges to action in the world. The last functional speciality is the forum for the communication of both the theoretical and practical insights of the previous specialities. Lonergan points out in a striking way the challenge and subtlety of Communications:

> [T]eaching is the communication of insight. It throws out the clues, the pointed hints, that lead to insight. It cajoles attention to drive away the distracting images that stand in insight's way. It puts the further questions that reveal the need of further insight to modify and complement the acquired store. It has grasped the strategy of developing intelligence, and so begins from the simple to advance to the more complex. Deliberately and explicitly, all this is done by professional teachers that know their job.[9]

> . . . [Communication] is a work of art; and it has at its disposal not merely all the resources of language but also the support of mod-

ulated tone and changing volume, the eloquence of facial expression, the emphasis of gestures, the effectiveness of pauses, the
suggestiveness of questions, the significance of omissions. . . . [I]t
can also take on all the delicacy and subtlety, all the rapidity and
effectiveness, with which one incarnate intelligence can communicate its grasp to another by grasping what the other has yet to
grasp and what act or sound or sign would make him grasp it. . . . [10]

[F]ar more impressive than talking is doing. Deeds excite our admiration and stir us to emulation. We watch to see how things are
done. We experiment to see if we can do them ourselves. We watch
again to discover the oversights that led to our failures. In this fashion, the discoveries and inventions of individuals pass into the possession of the many, to be checked against their experience, to
undergo the scrutiny of further questions, to be modified by their
improvements.[11]

Communications, then, is the way to pass on to the next generation the
achievements of the present and previous generations. What is Communications for the present generation, however, becomes the data for Research for
the next generation. Method in theology, just as method in general, is a recurrent process. And what appear as present achievements must eventually be
evaluated by future theologians, as they will attempt to pass on the valuable ac-
complishments of the past to *their* present generation.

The concrete context for theological Communications is one's religious
community in the world. For Christians, that is the Church; and Lonergan, in
fact, reserves his treatment of the Church for this functional speciality, Communications.

In his treatment of the Church, Lonergan departs from the traditional
Roman Catholic view that both the Church and the state are "perfect" societies, i.e., that each possesses, in its own sphere, ultimate authority to achieve
its own goals. Such a view is disembodied and results in a conceptual duality
between Church and state. The Church, rather than being a "perfect" society,
separate from the state, is a community of persons within the context of other
communities of persons in an increasingly intersecting world. The Church is a
community with a specific function in society. Although as a human community it is subject to all the biases that any human community has, yet as a community brought together by the experience of God's forgiving love, it has a
goal proportionate to that origin:

The church is an out-going process. It exists not just for itself but for
mankind. Its aim is the realization of the kingdom of God not only

within its own organization but in the whole of human society and not only in the after life but also in this life.

The church is a redemptive process. The Christian message, incarnate in Christ scourged and crucified, dead and risen, tells not only of God's love but man's sin. Sin is alienation from man's authentic being, which is self-transcendence, and sin justifies itself by ideology. As alienation and ideology are destructive of community, so the self-sacrificing love that is Christian charity reconciles alienated man to his true being, and undoes the mischief initiated by alienation and consolidated by ideology.[12]

The Church then is a community, committed by its origins, to serve the whole human community in overcoming our manifold human biases and the alienation they engender, by preaching and by living the forgiving and redemptive message of Jesus. As such, it is called to work together with all other communities which are grounded in the experience of transcendent love and compassion and which work for the healing of the human condition.

Since this goal of healing is world-wide, the Christian message is to be preached and witnessed to in all cultures and to every development of consciousness. To do this is the task of Communications. There will necessarily result from this a rich plurality of religious expression, which will give evidence that the message has indeed taken root in the various soils where it is preached.

Since the human community consists of persons skilled in every branch of human and natural science and since our world needs the skills of the human and natural sciences to deal adequately with our increasingly complex world, theological Communications must include dialogue with these people and with these disciplines. " . . . [T]heology is not the full science of man . . . the church can become a fully conscious process of self-constitution only when theology unites itself with all other branches of human studies."[13]

Communications, then, makes theology concrete by challenging theologians to be in dialogue with every aspect of the human condition. We, as the human community, need for the healing of our brokenness all of the resources of creativity available in religion and in every other field. We need the cooperation of all men and women who are meeting the challenge to intellectual, moral, and religious conversion.

CONCLUDING REFLECTIONS

Lonergan's achievement in delineating the stages of theological method is one of his most significant contributions. His treatment of theological method establishes a correlation between theological method and the method operative in each of the human and natural sciences. The dialogue between disciplines, which Lonergan recognizes as so important, is established on the base of common method. The task of each of the theological functional specialities is shared analogously by the functional specialities of each of the human and natural sciences. The sharing of similar tasks establishes a firm base for dialogue and for mutually helpful advances.

In addition, Lonergan's emphasis on method rather than on specific solutions is appropriate in the light of the ongoing and recurrent challenges facing religion and every area of human life. In a continuing process, today's achievements or failures will provide the basis for future Research which Lonergan's attention to method envisages.

Specifically in terms of religion, Lonergan's analysis of method challenges the perspective both of those who would stress the importance of the first three historical disciplines and of those who would stress the importance of the last three doctrinal disciplines. To those who would stress the historical disciplines, Lonergan points out that unless one's study has an effect on one's life and on what one will affirm for the future, one's study is sterile. To those who stress the doctrinal disciplines, Lonergan points out that unless one's doctrines are informed by ongoing study of the past and the present, one runs the risk either of affirming doctrines which have no firm base in tradition or of teaching to a culture which no longer exists. The historical and doctrinal disciplines need one another, then, if the human project is to advance. These two types of disciplines meet in the persons who, by engaging in Dialectic and Foundations, evaluate and take a stand with regard to the past, and decide what they will bring forth or modify from that past to create the future.

The particular significance of Lonergan's analysis of method is that his analysis is grounded on the set of spontaneous and interlocking questions which move us from Research through Communications. As such, the method which Lonergan explicates is not an optional one. Rather it is grounded in who we are as human beings, with our capacity to ask and answer questions in meaningful sequence from experience to understanding to judgment to decision and to return from decision to judgment to understanding to experience:

Research	What data are significant for answering the question I have?
Interpretation	What is my understanding of these data or these texts?
History	From my understanding of the texts, what can I affirm was going forward at that time?
Dialectics	What evaluation do I make of the differing historical accounts of the same period?

Foundations	Where do I stand with regard to the values I have discovered through Dialectics?
Doctrines	What do I want to affirm as true and valuable from the stance I have arrived at?
Systematics	How does what I now affirm in Doctrines relate to my other basic affirmations?
Communications	What and how do I share with others about what I now affirm and understand?

Finally, the asking and the answering of these questions are a collaborative enterprise. The sheer mass of material involved with regard to any religious tradition makes it impossible for any one scholar to engage in all of the disciplines. One cannot establish the authenticity of ancient texts and engage in archaeological digs in Palestine—to mention only two of the tasks of Research—and be the same person who labors over the meaning of texts in numerous languages, and then engages in all the other specialities. Theologians need to collaborate, then, with one another in ways and for the reasons that natural scientists collaborate with one another. Without one another the field cannot advance. What one person has done well, another need not repeat.

Theologians, then, need to respect the diligent work of one another and to respect the unique contribution which each functional speciality gives to the whole theological project. Researchers need to respect communicators; historians need to respect systematicians; and vice versa. There will of course be substantive differences among theologians, however, and inadequate work, but that will be revealed and can be remedied by the self-correcting process of learning. If something doesn't fit or make sense, ask "why?" and pursue it till one gets a satisfactory answer, or one recognizes that one's own question was wrongly put. The problem of error will certainly not be remedied, however, by each person repeating every other person's work. Theology, then, is a collaborative exercise in which men and women work together to explore the religious meaning of the past and present, and to pass on to others the fruits of their labors.

NOTES

[1] *Method in Theology,* p. 268.
[2] *Method,* p. 270.
[3] *Method,* p. 270.
[4] *Method,* p. 37.

[5]*Method,* p. 114.
[6]*Method,* pp. 300–301.
[7]*Method,* p. 330.
[8]Lonergan, *De Verbo Incarnato,* p. 524.
[9]*Insight,* p. 174.
[10]*Insight,* p. 177.
[11]*Insight,* pp. 174–75.
[12]*Method,* pp. 364–65.
[13]*Method,* p. 354.

VI. Philosophy, Theology, and God

Theologians have no monopoly on discourse about God. Philosophers too, from Plato to Whitehead, have had something to say about deity, and this common interest has been the topic of a long conversation. Not always a harmonious conversation, certainly; now and then it has become a quarrel, and there have been times when theologians and philosophers were scarcely on speaking terms at all.

Today seems to be one of those times. Gone are the days when Christian thinkers, convinced that faith illuminates reason, welcomed the philosophy of God as a powerful (if subordinate) ally of theology, queen of the sciences. The last two hundred years or so have seen that alliance fall apart as both sides broke off diplomatic relations. On one hand, theologians have insisted that what philosophy calls God has nothing to do with the Holy One of Israel whom Jesus addressed as Father, or with the mysterious, personal Other who touches human hearts in religious experience; on the other hand, philosophers have argued that there can be no such thing as a science of God, that theology is at best a kind of poetry, and that the clear light of reason needs no further illumination from religious faith.

Lonergan's stand on the topic of this chapter is clear: philosophical questions about God are best regarded today as belonging to theology; more specifically, to the functional specialty he refers to as Systematics, which aims at understanding the doctrines that religious men and women believe and live by. This means, among other things, that proving on strictly philosophical grounds that God exists no longer takes priority over everything else. Logically speaking, no doubt, proof comes first. Religion, after all, is supposed to have something to do with God, and so before investigating any religion it would seem reasonable to make sure that God is real—which is exactly what the traditional theistic arguments of "rational theology" did. But this logically impeccable view leaves one thing out: the name "God" takes its meaning, in the first instance, not from discursive reasoning, but from religious experience. Once theology is conceived empirically, as a disciplined reflection on religion, it becomes apparent that acknowledging that God *is* involves far more than asserting the truth of a conclusion; it involves worship, a worldview, a whole way of life. Only in the abstract, then, does establishing God's existence stand as the first item on the agenda; concretely, it is religious conversion that gives theology its specifically theological foundations.

Such is the position Lonergan develops in *Method in Theology* and *Philosophy of God, and Theology*. What then becomes of *Insight*'s philosophy of God, especially the much-discussed theistic proof in chapter nineteen? In later writings, Lonergan admits that this chapter does not depart from the traditional line. Its purely objective treatment of God's existence and attributes omits both the religiously converted subject and the horizon of meaning that conversion opens up. But subjectivity and meaning can safely be omitted only on the classicist assumption that human nature is pretty much the same always and everywhere—an assumption that Lonergan explicitly disavows in the first few lines of *Method*. Does it follow that he thereby disavows, at least by implication, his own earlier argument for theism?

Not at all. The problem with *Insight* is not chapter nineteen as it stands. It is that chapter nineteen stands *where* it stands, namely as a bridge between the earlier chapters, in which Lonergan consistently appeals to experience, and the theological method he sketches in chapter twenty and the epilogue, where religious experience is deliberately bracketed.[1] In the fifteen years between this sketch and *Method in Theology*, Lonergan did change his mind. But it was not so drastic a change as it is sometimes made out to have been. Everything in chapter nineteen, read in light of Lonergan's later work, still holds good; only what it is good *for* is different. It no longer heads the theological agenda, but neither can it simply be dropped, for reasons that I will try to suggest in the final section below. In any case, it simply will not do to suppose that *Method* abandons the God of the philosophers for the God of Abraham, Isaac, and Jacob. They are still, as in fact they were in *Insight*, one and the same God, a God who is to be loved with all one's mind as well as all one's heart.

That being so, anyone seriously interested in Lonergan's philosophy of God will eventually want to tackle chapter nineteen of *Insight*, which I propose to introduce here. Along the way, however, I shall have to bring in quite a few other topics, for Lonergan's philosophy of God is at the same time a philosophy of the world of human experience. How we know that world, what we know about it, what we can know about its Creator and Redeemer—these are not three mutually isolated questions. Each is linked to the others. Since all of them are vast and intricate, what I want to say about their connectedness will have to be said in a condensed and commonsense way, yet I hope that by the end of this chapter I will at least have managed to indicate the breadth and beauty of Lonergan's answers. If I have, the price paid by oversimplifying them will perhaps be justified.

PROVING GOD AND EXPLAINING THE UNIVERSE

Like so much else in *Insight*, chapter nineteen is at once old and new—old, in that it stands within a tradition that goes back by way of Thomas Aquinas to Aristotle; new, in that Lonergan also brings this tradition into the richer context resulting from modern developments in philosophy and natural science. From the standpoint of continuity with the past, his proof of God's existence can be regarded as an up-to-date version of what tradition calls the cosmological argument, or more accurately the argument *a contingentia mundi,* "from the contingence of the universe."

The reasoning used in arguments of this type is not especially abstruse. Saying that the universe is contingent amounts to saying that it does not explain itself. Whole and parts, the universe might have been otherwise; it might not have been at all. But since it does exist, the fact that it exists is a fact that needs to be accounted for. Yet nothing *in* the universe can account for it. This presents two alternatives: either the existence of the universe is just a sheer, inscrutable, brute fact, or else it can be understood; either there is an explanation of its contingence, or else there is not. But because the universe is not intelligible on its own, such an explanation exists if and only if the whole universe is related to something else. And this "something else" has got to be something that can account for its own existence as well as for the existence of the universe, because otherwise it too would need to be explained. A fact that explains the contingence of every other fact cannot itself be contingent; it must simply *be.* It needs no explanation, because it cannot be other than it is. But such a necessary fact could only be the existence of God. *Q. E. D.*[2]

So goes the argument from contingence. Examples abound, the most famous being the five arguments that Thomas Aquinas mounts at the beginning of his *Summa Theologiae.* All of them are quite brief, and while Thomas' reasoning is by no means simplistic he does give the impression that it is not all that difficult to mount a convincing case for the existence of God. Lonergan would agree. Each of Thomas' "five ways," he notes, is a particular instance of the general statement that the universe cannot be completely understood on its own terms, yet nothing short of complete understandability will do. From this it follows that there are as many proofs of God's existence as there are cases of incomplete intelligibility. Any fact whatsoever, simply by being a fact, can prompt us to ask *why* it is a fact, and in the long run this question is answered only by affirming that God, the *because* of every *why*, exists.

The long run, however, is longer today than it was for Thomas, thanks to philosophers who have thought up countless ways to disprove, discredit, or dismiss the existence of God. One of these objections can usefully be mentioned here. Immanuel Kant is still regarded by many as the philosophical gladiator who laid the cosmological argument to rest for good and all. Yet the important thing about his *Critique of Pure Reason* is not, in Lonergan's judgment, the explicit refutation of theistic proofs at the end. It is the cognitional theory at the beginning. "Intuition," Kant asserts, is our only immediate relation to the objects we know, and we have this direct contact with them only through our senses. Grant that, and the philosophy of God is already doomed. For if our knowing is confined within the bounds of sense, as Kant claims it is, then obviously we can know nothing whatever about a reality "without body, parts, or passions," such as God is generally supposed to be. A transcendent being is precisely not a possible object of sense-experience.

Kant's claim, then, is not that we can be certain there is no God, only that we cannot be certain there *is* one. For practical purposes, however, we can and indeed must act *as if* there were a God. Thus he can insist, somewhat paradoxically, that his restrictions on the scope of reason leave room for faith: the existence of God, although it cannot be known as a fact, is nevertheless a good idea. The catch is that by "faith" Kant evidently means a kind of untested and untestable assumption, which need never conflict with intelligence for the very good reason that it has nothing to do with the intelligible universe. In spite of this, however, quite a few theologians since Kant's time have swallowed his *as if* whole and done their best to digest it. Others have tried instead to make his argument more palatable by stretching "intuition" so as to include not only sense-experience but also some kind of direct contact with God. Still others have played the ostrich, ignoring Kantian philosophy altogether. And then there is Lonergan.

His response to Kant's argument is to meet it on its own turf—cognitional theory. Lonergan agrees that assertions about the objects we know have got to be rooted in what we are doing when we are knowing. But knowing, he adds, is not a matter of simple "intuition." It is a process of raising and answering questions, and to understand that process is, ultimately, to know that God exists. Anyone who genuinely denounces obscurantism is adoring God without naming him; anyone who declines to dismiss a possibly relevant question is, to that extent, an anonymous theist; anyone who has grasped why a cartwheel is round has glimpsed the eternal rapture that explains the universe.

But none of this goes without saying. How Lonergan can say it will occupy the next several sections here.

THE NATURE OF GOD AND THE
NATURE OF UNDERSTANDING

From the roundness of cartwheels to the contingence of the universe to the existence of God: such is the path Lonergan lays out in *Insight*. It is long and difficult, but perfectly straight. From cover to cover *Insight* is a book about "the nature of . . . "—the nature of fire, photosynthesis, freedom, or what you will. To speak about "the nature of" this, that, or the other takes no great philosophical acumen. We do it all the time, and we know what we mean. But, like the Athenians who knew quite well what they meant by courage, without being able to *say* what they meant when Socrates asked them, most of us would probably be hard put to state very cogently just what we do mean by "the nature of . . . " Lonergan's Socratic aim is to guide his readers toward a clear understanding of what they already grasp more or less vaguely. But most people also understand the name "God"—again, without being able to spell out precisely what they understand God to be—and there is a connection between knowing exactly what "the nature of . . . " means, and knowing exactly what "God" means. Making this connection explicit is the whole purpose of *Insight*'s nineteenth chapter.

"The nature of" such-and-such is what we know when we have gone beyond describing all the data pertinent to such-and-such, to explaining these data correctly. In order to help explanatory understanding become a cumulative and progressive process, *Insight* assembles a method, an all-purpose box of conceptual tools for inquiring about every aspect of everything we understand, or have yet to understand, on the basis of our experience. To use Lonergan's own metaphor, this generalized empirical method provides one blade of a pair of scissors. The other is provided by sensible data or conscious data or both. Questioning provides the energy that brings the two blades together. In principle, there is no question about the universe of our experience on which this scissors will not work—except one. Why does it work at all? Why do things, events, and processes *have* natures? Why *can* they be understood? What explains the explainability of the universe of our experience?

In *Insight*, that is *the* question about God, and as I have already noted it is also the theme on which every version of the argument from contingence rings a variation. The exceptional thing about chapter nineteen, then, is not that Lonergan rests his case for God's existence on the fact that the universe does not explain itself. It is that he rests his case for the contingence of the universe on the nature of human cognition. More specifically, the argument in chapter nineteen is based on what I shall refer to here as three "relevant features of knowing." They are:

first, that our knowing is propelled by a desire, distinct from other desires and independent of them, which manifests itself in questioning;

second, that this desire to know comes to rest only when all the relevant questions have indeed been answered; and

third, that all our questions, insofar as they concern factual knowledge, are either questions for understanding (What? Why? How many?) or else questions for reflection and judgment (Is it so?).[3]

All three of these statements are treated elsewhere in this book. Here the point to be stressed is that all of them can be verified. Unlike Kant, Lonergan does not simply assume at the outset that he knows what knowing is. Instead, he invites me, the reader, to find out what it is, by asking, "What *am* I doing when I am knowing?" The answer—that I am experiencing, understanding my experience, and judging the correctness of my understanding, in that order—is not a take-it-or-leave-it speculation. It is an hypothesis. As such it has to be confirmed, and the only person who can confirm it is myself. In order to decide whether it is correct, I must ask a further question: "Is that so?"

Thus, after leading me through a series of "five-finger exercises," which get me to attend to my own experience of myself in the process of knowing and to understand that experience, *Insight* invites me to affirm, "Yes, that *is* so: I *am* a knower, a complex unity of conscious activities occurring on three successive levels." "Up to that decisive achievement," Lonergan writes, "all leads. From it, all follows"—including the affirmation of God.[4]

The reason why everything follows from the judgment "I am a knower" is that it is the primary instance of knowledge by identity. The affirming and the affirmed are one and the same: my knowing of myself as a knower consists in a related set of conscious acts, and what I know is the related set of contents of the very same acts. Such a judgment, once made, cannot be overturned. I cannot get around the identity it affirms by claiming to know that I am *not* a knower. That would be like sawing off the branch I was sitting on. My only escape hatch is silence, "the complete silence of the animal that offers neither excuse nor explanation for its complacent absorption in merely sensitive routines."[5] On the other hand, having made the privileged judgment that I am a knower, I know at least one fact that I cannot coherently deny. And since a single fact is all it takes to build a theistic proof, it ought to be possible to argue from my own existence as a knower to the existence of God as the explanation of *why* that is so.

In a sense, that is just what *Insight* does. The self-affirmation of the knower in chapter eleven is still Lonergan's base of operations in chapter nineteen. In between, however, he expands that base to include the whole intelligible universe. "The nature of" the knower who is myself is enough to lead to an affirmation of God, but Lonergan—with good reason—prefers to make a thorough job of it.

THE UNIVERSE AS UNDERSTANDABLE

The reason is this. I have pointed out that the strategy of cosmological proofs is to argue from some defect in the intelligibility of the universe. What this strategy assumes, usually without stating it, is that the universe *is* intelligible, though not completely so. The opposite assumption—that the universe is utterly *un*intelligible, a chaos rather than a cosmos—defeats any cosmological argument before it begins. Now until fairly recently, the idea that nothing makes any sense at all would have been scorned as unworthy of a reasonable being. But reasonable beings we are not, according to some of the most influential thinkers of modern times. Nor does the world into which we have been tossed hold any awe or mystery. Instead of eliciting our wonder, moving our minds toward what we do not yet know, the universe evokes only cynicism and despair. No crumb of understanding we happen to pick up can alter its mindless, meaningless absurdity.

Lonergan's answer to this dark view of things is implicit in the way his account of human understanding always goes hand in hand with an account of what there is to be understood. The gist of the seven chapters in *Insight* that follow the self-affirmation of the knower is that what I know about myself tells me something about the rest of the universe, because it tells me something about what I will know whenever I understand correctly. For, if I am a knower, if the dynamic structure that Lonergan lays out so patiently is in fact the pattern of my own conscious operations; if, further, I cannot help understanding similars in a similar fashion; and if, finally, my understanding of myself is similar to my understanding of what is given in the presentations of my senses and the representations of my imagination—if all that is true, then two things follow.

First, what there is for me to know by intelligent insight and reasonable judgment is not only the reality of myself *qua* knower, but also the reality of anything and everything else there is to be understood. Second, the immanent, inherent structure of anything and everything there is to be understood will turn out to be similar to the structure of my cognitional activity. To use Lonergan's term, there is an *isomorphism*, a sameness of pattern, between what I know and what I am doing when I am knowing.

That is the sense in which the broad lines of all there is to be understood follow from a thorough understanding of what it is to understand. A *thorough* understanding, please note. There is no royal road to self-affirmation. It is only because of what leads up to "I am a knower" that from it, all follows. Lonergan's cognitional theory does not appeal to the data of consciousness alone. Also, and equally, it appeals to actual developments in human understanding. The natural sciences are especially relevant here, and that for two reasons.

In the first place, twentieth-century physicists have had to "envisage the possibility that the objects of their science were to be reached only by severing the umbilical cord that tied them to the maternal imagination of man."[6] What these scientists understand is not imaginable, still less sensible. But since what they are doing as scientists *is* understanding, a distinction has got to be drawn between understanding on one hand, and sensing and imagining on the other. What there is to be understood, Kant notwithstanding, is not the same as what there is to be "intuited."

In the second place, the modern sciences accept no hypothesis, however brilliant, without verification; in cognitional terms, no understanding without judgment. Insights are a dime a dozen, and they may or may not be correct. But since judging the correctness of insights is a different kind of activity from both understanding and experiencing, a further distinction has got to be drawn within the process of coming to know. Moreover, since that process is not complete until the question of verification (Is it so?) has been answered, this further component is no mere ideal. Judgment is an actual constituent of knowledge, not an unhittable target to aim at.

In sum, modern science lends its support to the second and third of the "relevant features of knowing" listed a few pages back. By so doing, however, it allows and even calls for a view of the world as intelligible *and* mysterious, elegantly ordered yet for that very reason astonishing, tremendous, and fascinating. Since this is not at all what science is supposed to do—not, anyhow, according to certain firmly ensconced views of what science is all about—some further comment will be appropriate.

THE UNIVERSE AS CONTINGENT

In order to draw even a rough sketch of the argument in *Insight*'s nineteenth chapter, I have already had to outline the self-affirmation of the knower, the cognitional theory it confirms, and what it implies about the general structure of everything there is to be known. Yet all of this does bear on affirming the existence of God, because it all bears on the contingence—the mysteriousness—of the universe.

Here the key is judgment. It so happens that I am a knower. It need not have happened so, but in fact it does. If I have raised and answered all the relevant questions about my own knowing, I know as a matter of fact that I know. I am a knower, in other words, because certain conditions have been fulfilled. The same goes for any other judgment based on intelligent insight into experiential data: if the relevant questions are answered, if the conditions for making a reasonable judgment are fulfilled, then and only then do I affirm that while it might have been otherwise, it is not; that while these conditions did not *have* to be fulfilled, still they are; in short, that it *is* so. Not necessarily so. Just so. This is a typewriter. Never mind who made it or what it is made of or what I use it for. Those questions may be quite relevant in some other connection. Here they are beside the point, which is simply that this, as it happens, is a typewriter and nothing else.

The difference between correctness and necessity is worth a bit of elaboration. Ever since Aristotle asserted that knowledge, properly so called, is knowledge of what cannot be other than it is, the idea that "true" means "necessarily true" has haunted Western thought. The makers of the "scientific revolution" still clung to it, even while scorning every other aspect of what they took to be Aristotelian science. Hence it was supposed (and still is) that scientific laws of the kind Lonergan names "classical" are, in themselves, true statements about the way the world runs and predictions about how it is necessarily going to run. Not so. In themselves, classical laws are abstract. For instance, "What goes up must come down," one of Newton's laws in its popular version, says nothing at all about what it is that goes up, about the conditions under which it goes up, or even about whether it goes up at all. Accordingly, the misleading word "must" means simply that *if* something goes up, it comes down—unless something interferes with it. The only necessity involved is what logicians call a contingent necessity, one that depends on the fulfillment of certain conditions. *If* Socrates is sitting, as the stock example puts it, he is necessarily sitting, in the sense that while the conditions for his assuming this posture are being fulfilled he cannot, say, be turning somersaults. What he *is* doing, whether he is sitting in point of fact, is a different question. So is the question whether anything does go up.

Classical laws, then, are hypothetical—not in the sense of being mere speculations, but in the sense of being ideal formulations that hold true, concretely, only "on condition." It so happens that our solar system behaves pretty nearly in accord with Newton's laws. But there is nothing necessary about the fact that it does. That depends. Among other things, it depends on whether there are any planets. As it happens, there are. But that fact too depends on the fulfillment of certain conditions; they, in turn, have still prior conditions that may or may not be fulfilled—and so on, as far as you please. There are always *ifs*, and the *ifs* keep fanning out like branches on a tree. Consequently there neither is nor could be a combination of classical laws that grasps all of them in a single explanatory system.[7]

The point at present is that classical laws such as Newton's always carry a proviso. They hold *caeteris paribus,* "provided other things are equal." This leads to a further question of a different sort. How often is the proviso met? When are the "other things" going to be equal? It is a perfectly valid question, but the answer to it will not be a classical law. It will be an ideal frequency, an every-so-often, a *statistical* law. Actual events will diverge from it, but they will not diverge in a way that can be understood systematically.

What this last sentence means would take a book to explain.[8] Suffice it to say that Mark Twain went too far when he grumbled about "lies, damn lies, and statistics." The dubious purposes to which statistics are sometimes put does not alter the fact that frequencies do express what is grasped in insights of a certain kind, and what they grasp can be verified. Understanding statistical laws correctly, therefore, has exactly the same claim to the status of knowing that knowing classical laws has. Moreover, statistical and classical laws complement each other. On one hand, every classical law holds good "other things being equal," while explaining how often they *are* equal is the concern of statistical laws. On the other hand, statistical laws pertain to events that classical laws define and classify.

This complementarity is quite important for the topic at hand. As I have already noted, there is an isomorphism or structural analogy between our knowing and what we know. Add to this the fact that both the classical method of inquiry and the statistical method unfold from one and the same cognitional structure, and the result is nothing less than a worldview. Because statistical as well as classical laws are needed to explain the universe of our experience, it has an inherent, intelligible pattern that Lonergan names *emergent probability.*

THE UNIVERSE AS EMERGENTLY PROBABLE

Consider an aquarium. It contains a certain number of plants, all taking in carbon dioxide and turning out oxygen, and a certain number of fish, all using up oxygen and getting rid of carbon dioxide. Ideally, there is no need to pump in any air; the plants supply just enough oxygen to support the fish, which in turn supply the carbon dioxide needed by the plants. What is going on is a "scheme of recurrence," a sequence of events that depend on other events in such a way that the dependence is circular. In this case, photosynthesis keeps on occurring in the plants as long as respiration is occurring in the fish, and vice versa.

Ecology provides the most familiar (though by no means the only) examples of what Lonergan is referring to. An "eco-system" is a combination of interdependent schemes of recurrence, and the phrase "balance of nature" points to the fact that such systems keep going on unless they are interfered with. Each cyclical scheme, that is, survives *caeteris paribus,* other things being equal. Its survival depends on the fulfillment of certain conditions, among which is the recurrence of other schemes. By way of illustration, consider the situation portrayed on a poster I once saw. It showed a little fish, about to be devoured by a bigger fish, about to be devoured by a still bigger one, about to be devoured by a very big fish indeed. *There's no such thing as a free lunch,* as the caption put it; but in that case, what did the smallest fish lunch on? To generalize, what if all animals were carnivorous? Pretty soon, obviously, there would be no lunch at all. Meat-eating is one of the events in a nutritional scheme that can recur only so long as there is meat to be eaten. No fish, no fish-eaters. So, somewhere along the line, the survival of carnivorous schemes of nutrition depends on animals with a strictly vegetarian diet.

This dependence, however, is one-sided. Plant-eating could get along quite well if meat-eating never occurred, but not vice versa. Presumably, therefore, meat-eating is a latecomer on the ecological scene, compared with plant-eating. Only when herbivorous schemes of nutrition were already going strong did any carnivorous scheme have a chance of starting up. More generally, the recurrence of earlier schemes is one of the conditions of the emergence of later ones. No photosynthesis, no corn; no corn, no turkeys; no turkeys, no Thanksgiving dinner. But schemes of recurrence are circular, and so once all the conditions of a given scheme are fulfilled and it has in fact occurred, it is far more likely to happen a second time round. The probability that any scheme will survive, in other words, is higher than the probability it had of emerging in the first place.

For present purposes, the chief thing is the way Lonergan is able to show that schemes of recurrence can be understood only by employing a statistical method. There is no guarantee that any particular scheme will occur or that, having occurred, it will recur. There is, however, a specific probability of its emerging, and a higher probability of its surviving once it has emerged. Thus, as my rough outline may already have suggested, there is a certain resemblance between emergent probability and Darwin's theory of evolution. But while Darwin did recognize that probabilities have a part to play in explaining the universe, the significance of his insight has tended to be eclipsed by the stubborn idea that there is nothing about the world which classical laws will not eventually account for.

Lonergan, by showing that probabilities are intelligible and that statistical laws complement classical, brings the process of biological evolution within a wider explanatory context. In his more precise formulation, "chance variation is an instance of probability of emergence," while "natural selection is an instance of probability of survival."[9] But biology is not the only area of empirical investigation on which emergent probability can shed important light. Economics is another, and here too the notion that there are "iron laws" stems from what Lonergan would call an oversight of insight. As his own essay in macroeconomic analysis shows, Adam Smith's "invisible hand," which somehow orchestrates the activities of independent entrepreneurs, is in reality "a conditioned series of more or less probably emerging and surviving schemes of recurrence."[10]

These and other concrete applications of emergent probability are waiting to be worked out in detail. Here there are five general implications that are worth taking note of, for reasons that will appear shortly.

First, the world-process characterized by emergent probability is open. Schemes of recurrence are not the mechanical turnings and grindings of a cosmic clockwork; nor are they capricious or arbitrary or "random" as the word is usually construed. Their emergence and survival are more or less probable, and even extremely improbable things are likely to happen, given enough time and space. What has a thousand-to-one chance of occurring can be expected to occur a thousand times, given a million opportunities. Dinosaurs and dandelions are both pretty unlikely, if you think about it; but then, they took a long time to show up.

Second, in such a world-process there are successive levels of intelligibility. Events that defy any systematic explanation in themselves become intelligible at a "higher" level, that is, within a more comprehensive scheme. There is no reason why the methods proper to chemistry could not eventually get around to explaining, one by one, each and every molecular event that goes on in an amoeba. But the only result would be a very long list of explanations, none of them related to any other in a systematically intelligible way. Move up to the organic level, though, and there *is* a systematic pattern to be grasped, and grasping its intelligibility compensates for the lack of system at the molecular level. Not that amoebas emerged by somehow bewitching an otherwise coincidental stew of molecules into "breaking the laws" of chemistry. As molecules, they still go on with business as usual; otherwise there would be no amoebas. At the same time, each amoeba goes about *its* business, its schemes of nutrition and reproduction and so on, as a biological organism with an irreducible intelligibility in its own right.

Third, the hierarchical nature of such a world-process implies a hierarchy of empirical investigations—a point to which I shall return in a later section. As many as are the levels of intelligibility—physical, chemical, botanical, sensitive, intellectual, moral, religious—so many are the independent sciences that explain the nature of the world.

Fourth, the properties of the emergently probable universe that Lonergan outlines are quite general. No amount of empirical investigation is going to upset them. This is because the very events that constitute every empirical method, insights and judgments, are themselves subject to statistical explanation. Insights need not occur. They are more or less probable. An orchard of apples might have fallen on Newton's head without his discovering any laws of motion. On the other hand, the probability of insights can be enhanced, especially if they become elements in a recurring scheme such as the one that emerged in *Method in Theology*'s cycle of eight functional specialties. It remains that you can read *Method* (or *Insight*) till you know it by heart without ever getting the point of getting the point.

The fifth and most important thing worth noting about emergent probability leads back to the main thread of my discussion. What there is to *be* known, by such knowers as we are, is the intelligibility formulated in classical and statistical laws, the intelligibility of emergently probable schemes, developments, and cycles of progress and decline.[11] All of these *are* known, however, if and when their conditions are fulfilled, because they are known by intelligent grasp *and* reasonable affirmation. That is, they are known as matters of fact. None of them is necessary. The world-process, whole and parts, might be otherwise. It is contingent through and through. To understand all the methods by which the universe of our experience can be understood is to grasp that it is intelligible, yet incompletely intelligible. Emergent probability itself is a genetic explanation of this universe, and this universe includes among its processes the human process of understanding emergent probabilities. Thus the one thing that emergent probability does not explain is why it can explain everything else. Lonergan's worldview, in other words, is not self-explanatory. Emergent probability does not explain itself.

With that we come to the threshold of affirming God's existence. In order to cross it, only one thing needs to be recalled, namely the first of the "relevant features of knowing" listed earlier—the desire to know.

FROM INCOMPLETE INTELLIGIBILITY
TO UNRESTRICTED INSIGHT

This desire, the *eros* of our minds, is intentional, a desire *for* something. It is cognitional, a desire that unfolds consciously, intelligently, reasonably. And it is a desire without limits, a desire to know everything about everything—not just to think about it, but to understand it correctly. What we are yearning for as we raise question after question, Lonergan names *being.*

Only being, in this sense, can satisfy the wonder that prompts us to ask "Is it so?" because to have answered every "Is it so?" question would be to know all that is so, and all that is so *is* being. It follows that being is intelligible; otherwise it would not be what this particular desire, the desire to understand correctly, heads for. It also follows that being is not just intelligible but completely intelligible; otherwise it would not be the objective of a desire with no restrictions, including the restrictions imposed by imagination and the restrictions imposed by other sorts of desires.

Being, then, can only be defined at one remove. It is what would be known by the totality of true judgments. Notice, however, that this indirect definition leaves quite a few questions open. It does not say whether our desire to know is ever fulfilled. Nor does it say whether to *be* is to appear, or to be present, or to be experienced, or what have you. All of these questions depend on another: *Are* there any true judgments? Is there any correct, albeit partial, understanding of all that is so? Is there any knowledge of being?

Indeed there is. There is the privileged, inescapable judgment "I am a knower." At one and the same time, my self-affirmation establishes that I do know, and also that what I know I do *not* know because it appears, because it presents itself, or because it is experienced. I know what I know because I have intelligently grasped it and reasonably affirmed it; because there are no more nagging questions that clamor for my attention; because the conditions for a true judgment have been fulfilled. In a word, I know what I know because it is a fact, just as I know as a fact that I know.

But there is more. What I know by answering the question "Is it so?" is objectively real. I would still be a knower even if I did not understand what I am doing when I am knowing. And if intelligent grasp and reasonable affirmation are the conditions for knowing what really is, then what really is—the real, everything that is so, reality—is the same as what there is to be known by true judgments. But the totality of true judgments would be knowledge of being. Therefore, to know the real and to know being are one and the same. Therefore the real, and only the real, is identical with being. But being is completely intelligible. And if the real is completely intelligible, God exists.

I ought perhaps to apologize for the preceding paragraph, especially as there is another one like it coming up. But the alternative to writing a full-length commentary (which Bernard Tyrrell has already done, and done admirably) is throwing nuance to the winds as I have thrown it just now. Needless to say, Lonergan himself is not to blame. Still, it may be worth pausing on the last eight words of the paragraph in order to fend off the worst of many possible misunderstandings.

If the real is completely intelligible, God exists. What does that mean? Logically speaking, the meaning of the *if*-clause depends on Lonergan's definition of being and on identifying being with the real. Thus the premise of his argument is the basic tenet of every realist philosophy—to be, to exist, is to be real; and reality exists irrespective of whether anyone knows it does. Put it that way, and "the real is being" seems quite obvious. After all, most people are realists.

So they are. But there is realism and realism. For the good Dr. Johnson, knowing what is real was on a par with kicking a stone—which only shows that his was the "incoherent realism, half animal and half human" that most people settle for. Not that stones are illusory. They are real enough. But so are photons, although you could not kick a photon even if you had very, very tiny feet. Strangely enough, however—startlingly strange, as Lonergan puts it—there is another kind of realism, an intelligent and reasonable realism. For those who achieve it, knowing is not a matter of kicking or of any other sort of contact; reality means something quite different from the palpability of bodies such as stones; and objectivity does not consist in being located somewhere out there, ready to be confronted.

That, to say it once more, is why chapter eleven of *Insight* is so crucial. To affirm as a fact that I am a knower is at the same time to affirm that when I am knowing I am judging as well as understanding. To move from this fact to an affirmation of God's existence, I need only note that my being a knower *is* a fact, and only a fact. The same is true of every other fact in the whole factual universe. Each of them is intelligible, for until I understand "the nature of" something, its *so*-ness, I am in no position to ask "*Is* it so?" Yet none of them is completely intelligible, for even when I affirm that in point of fact this or that is so, I am left with the problem of explaining why facts are facts.

What makes it a problem is this. If facts are mere facts, brute facts that admit of no further explanation, then they are apart from being, because being is completely intelligible. But being is also identical with the real. Consequently, an unexplained and inexplicable fact is just—well, just nothing at all.

In this way Lonergan arrives at the alternative I mentioned at the outset as the mainspring of the cosmological argument. *Either* the whole universe of our experience, a universe shot through with contingence and facticity, amounts to—well, just nothing at all, *or* it has an explanation. And if there is an explanation, it can be no part of the universe. It must be an explanation that goes beyond anything and everything we can imagine, anything and everything we can know by correctly understanding any and all of the data of sense and of consciousness. Besides "proportionate being," the conditioned world of things and events and processes that are isomorphic with human knowing, there would have to be a reality whose existence does not depend on the fulfillment of any conditions whatever, a being which is therefore self-explanatory and which also grounds the explainability of every other being.

Quite a job description, this. What would the being that could fill it be? Such a being, Lonergan proposes, would be an unrestricted act of understanding. Why? I can only offer another rapid-fire summary.

To affirm the intelligibility of the real is to affirm the intelligibility of all there is to be affirmed. But to affirm anything is to know its existence, and so affirming that the real is completely intelligible is knowing that complete intelligibility exists. But complete intelligibility would be the content of an unrestricted insight, one that grasps everything about everything, and so knowing that complete intelligibility exists is knowing that the content of such an insight exists. But the primary content of any act of understanding is that act itself, and so knowing that the content of an unrestricted insight exists is knowing that there exists an unrestricted act of understanding, "the eternal rapture glimpsed in every Archimedean cry of Eureka."[12] But an unrestricted act of understanding, as Lonergan proceeds to show at length, has all the attributes associated with the name "God." And there you have it. *The real is completely intelligible. Therefore God exists.*

Summarizing Lonergan's argument is not all that difficult, and having already apologized for doing it so hastily I would only observe that no summary on its own—for that matter, not even chapter nineteen itself—can be more than ink on paper, unless the reader makes it something more. That is what matters, and like most things that matter it is hard work. In Lonergan's words, it is quite true that

> *if* I am operating in the intellectual pattern of experience, *if* I am genuine in my acceptance of the domination of the detached, disinterested desire to inquire intelligently and reflect reasonably, then I have no just grounds for surprise if I find myself unable to deny that there is a reality or that the real is being or that being is completely intelligible or that complete intelligibility is unrestricted understanding or that unrestricted understanding is God.[13]

But those are two very big *ifs*. No one is born in the intellectual pattern of experience. No one reaches it without a fight. No one, having reached it, goes on operating in it on automatic pilot. There are other patterns, and when one of them takes over, the self that is self-affirmed and the universe of being both tend to melt away, to say nothing of the God who is an unrestricted act of understanding.

Yet such a God is the most real being of all, the *ens realissimum,* even though—no, *because* there is nowhere in Lonergan's argument to plug in the umbilical cord of imagination. The God whose existence grounds the intelligibility of being is precisely not tangible, visible, or measurable. He is the first agent and final cause, the Creator of heaven and earth, of all that is, seen and unseen; yet in none of these attributes as Lonergan applies them is there any trace of anthropomorphic picture-thinking.

This God really is *God.*

Is such a God even conceivable? Yes; though, as Austin Farrer rightly observed, the conceiving "strains to the uttermost the powers of the human mind. How could it be otherwise, if God is God?"[14] Why anyone should consider the strain worthwhile is a question to which I shall return. First it will be appropriate to mention some conclusions that follow from conceiving God as Lonergan does.

GOD AND THE INTELLIGIBLE UNIVERSE

The content of an unrestricted act of understanding, as I said in the previous section, includes as its primary component the act itself. Otherwise stated, God understands God. Moreover, God understands every possible world order, every single intelligible pattern of things and events, in every aspect and every detail. Yet he need not affirm and decide for any particular universe of being. If he does not, he is no less God.

This point ought to be emphasized. It is true that any decision is an act of self-transcendence. It is also true that, in us, deciding is also the act by which we change ourselves. But the act that is God is an unrestricted act; otherwise it would not account for the contingence of other acts. Because such an act lacks nothing, it does not change. By deciding for some universe, then, God does transcend but does not alter himself.[15] There is admittedly something mysterious about the idea of a gift that does not change the giver. But that is just the point. The universe *is* mysterious, because it is purely gratuitous, and a changeable deity, far from illuminating the mystery, merely turns it into a myth. The notion of God as just another item within the cosmos has a certain imaginative appeal, especially in an age of imaginative starvation such as our own. But the ancient Israelites got beyond it, and in the Christian tradition a clear distinction between creatures and their Creator had emerged by the time of the Arian controversy. There are pressing reasons for improving on these achievements of the human spirit: there is no pressing reason to reverse them.

To resume, however. Any universe of being that God does decide for is, for that reason, real. It need not exist, but it does, precisely because God wills it to exist. This means that it is exactly the same thing to affirm the existence of any being other than God, and to know that God is its Creator, its preserver, and its efficient, exemplary, and final cause.[16] If, for instance, God decides for a world order whose intelligibility has the general form of emergent probability, then such a world order exists, and for it not to exist would be an impossibility. Vice versa, if such a world order exists, then God wills it, although he might very well have decided for a completely different universe, or for no universe at all.

What this amounts to is simply the assertion that *if* such a world order exists, then it exists and cannot but exist. It exists necessarily, in the same conditional sense that if Socrates is sitting he is necessarily sitting, and what I have already said about Socrates applies here too. Whether he is sitting is another question altogether, and the same goes for whether ours is an emergently probable universe, whether I am a knower, and whether my decisions are free. If any of these is a fact, it cannot be anything else. *Is* it a fact? Is it so? The answer to that depends on intelligent inquiry and reasonable reflection. Filling up the gaps of science and scholarship is *not* the point of affirming the existence of God.

Furthermore, God knows all this. Since he understands every possible world order, God knows what every intelligent, reasonable, responsible being in an emergently probable world order would think, affirm, and decide for *if* that world order were real—that is, if God were to will it. But God also knows that he is intrinsically the same, irrespective of which world order (if any) he chooses to bring into being; God knows that any world order which does exist exists because he chooses it; and God knows that were he to decide for an emergently probable universe, there could emerge in that universe a species of beings characterized by intelligence, reasonableness, responsibility, and freedom in the fullest sense of the word. Their being free to choose would in no way be compromised by—on the contrary, it would wholly depend on—God's choosing of just that particular kind of world order.

This difficult and important assertion can be stated somewhat differently. In the universe that actually exists, every event that actually occurs is related to God in exactly the same way. That is what it means to affirm that God is the First Agent. The Big Bang, biological evolution, my writing this chapter and your understanding it—if any of these is occurring or has occurred, it is intelligible, and God is the reason *why* it is intelligible. But the same thing is true, in the same way, of miracles, revelation, religious conversion, and the Incarnation. The sense in which these are acts of God is no different from the sense in which falling sparrows and lilies of the field are acts of God. Even "salvation history," in other words, belongs to the intelligible, emergently probable universe.

This calls for some elaboration. As Philip McShane has shown in detail, the complementarity of classical and statistical laws that lies behind the notion of emergent probability resolves an issue that philosophers of science have long and heatedly debated. How can there be emergence without duality—real novelty that does not "overrule" the intelligibility of classical laws? The theological counterpart of this debate is that hardy perennial, the problem of grace and freedom. How can God initiate salvation in a way that does not "overrule" human decision? The most basic answer is that God does not "overrule" anything, because God is not a conceptualist. He does not first think up the parts of the universe, and then assemble them like building-blocks; he thinks up the universe, salvation included. The notion of God as a supernal bricklayer, however refined, is just another piece of picture-thinking. As for the specific question of grace and freedom, it was solved in the thirteenth century when theologians posited two "entitatively disproportionate" orders. Faith, charity, and God's favor belong to the higher, "supernatural" order; reason, good will, and reputation to the lower, "natural" one. But this solution, the "theorem of the supernatural," involves a philosophy that was scorned by the Reformation, implicitly challenged by the scientific revolution, and explicitly undercut by the rise of critical philosophies. Today, as a result, "supernatural" tends to be a word with no very clear meaning.

Lonergan gives it one. Having recovered the theorem of the supernatural in his doctoral dissertation, he went on to introduce it into a contemporary context, beginning with *Insight*. For there is a sense in which emergent probability generalizes the notion of disproportionate orders: each successive level of proportionate being is functionally disproportionate to the one below. Molecular activities enter into organisms, to use my earlier example, yet an organism is not just a very big molecule, because processes such as ingestion, excretion, development, and reproduction, which belong to "the nature of" organisms, are not continuous with "the nature of" the molecular processes that organisms integrate. Quite properly, then, the emergence of organic life can be called *super*natural in relation to molecular events. In the same sense, activities at the level of intentional consciousness, the raising and answering of questions, are supernatural with respect to the nature of the psychic events that consciousness integrates. Likewise, decisions are supernatural compared with factual judgments about possible courses of action; that is the sense in which decisions are free. And finally, beyond the whole series of discontinuities that reaches from sub-atomic particles to human freedom, there is one that is supernatural in the fullest and most definitive sense: grace, which is out of proportion to even that highest integration of human being, conscience. So it is that the existence of a number of intelligent, reasonable, responsible, religious beings can be the material for a still higher integration of human living, which Christian theology knows as the Mystical Body. Having emerged "in the fullness of time" with the Incarnation, the pure instance of grace, this integration is now recurring in God's adoption of men and women as his own children.

REDEMPTION AND THE INTELLIGIBLE UNIVERSE

In the last few paragraphs, without announcing it, I have moved from philosophy to the theological specialty that Lonergan calls Systematics, by suggesting how he himself understands some of Christianity's central doctrines in relation to the emergently probable universe whose intelligibility depends on an unrestricted act of understanding. But there is more to it than that. Grace, the supernatural properly so called, is a reality in the world as it actually exists, and from this it follows that any worldview which omits grace will be incomplete and distorted. But in order to indicate why this is so, I need to back up a bit.

One of the implications of emergent probability is that every biological species is a solution to a problem of living in a given environment.[17] For an animal species, an entirely new way of living would *be* an entirely new species of animal. For the human species, however, the emergence of inquiry and insight "are not so much a higher system as a perennial source of higher systems, so that human living has its basic task in reflecting on systems and judging them, deliberating on their implementation and choosing between possibilities."[18] Ours is the problem of making both ourselves and the environment, the world of meaning and value, in which we live. How we solve this problem depends on whether our choosing is intelligent, reasonable, and responsible. If it is, the result is progress; if not, decline. But the fact of the matter is that although we are free to live in accordance with the normative unfolding of consciousness, from insight to judgment to decision to action, we do not. Evil is a fact, and moreover it is not an exception but the rule, the "reign of sin" that Lonergan speaks of in chapter twenty of *Insight*.

But if evil is a fact, it is a peculiar one, a "false fact." All that intelligence can grasp about it is that, at bottom, there is nothing to *be* grasped. "What is basic sin? It is the irrational. Why does it occur? If there were a reason, it would not be sin."[19] There is no understanding it in relation to any aspect of proportionate being—a serpent in a garden, or the ills inherent in an emergently probable universe—and neither can it be understood in relation to transcendent being, God. True, God is the first agent of every event. But sin is not an event. It is the failure of an event, a lack of intelligent love, that warps and unmakes the events brought about by human decision. "Why does God cause sin?" is a meaningless question. Sin has no cause, no intrinsic intelligibility. What can be asked, however, and must be, is what God is doing about the problem sin has spawned. Is there a higher integration, which compensates for the unintelligible surd of sin?

Thus *Insight* ends as a search for faith. A "sincere acceptance of scientific presuppositions and precepts," Lonergan writes, "mounts to a conception and an affirmation to God, only to be confronted with a problem of evil that demands the transformation of self-reliant intelligence into an *intellectus quaerens fidem*."[20] To put this in a metaphor that appears in Lonergan's later writings, *Insight* moves "from below upwards." By taking the complementary route, "from above downwards," *Method in Theology* acknowledges not only that God's solution to the human predicament has been and is being given, but also that awareness of the gift more often than not precedes searching for it. The question of God *can* arise as a question about the contingence of the universe, but if so it is likely to arise in response to that fulfillment of the desires of the human heart which Lonergan identifies with sanctifying grace. Whereas *Insight* tends to go along with a dictum at least as old as Augustine, "Nothing is loved unless it is known," Lonergan later reverses it to read, "Nothing is truly known unless it is already loved."

This applies above all to the God whose heart-flooding love is the solution to the problem of evil. That it is *God's* love, those who experience it may not and often do not know. They may be moved to find out, however, and if so their inquiry will lead toward either theology or philosophy, or perhaps both. If it is philosophy, they will be inquiring about the world of experience as, "more than all else, a mystery that signifies God as we know him and symbolizes the further depths that lie beyond our comprehension."[21] If it is theology, they will be inquiring about the "outer word" by which religious experience enters the human world of meaning and value, and which, in the case of the biblical religions, includes as well "specific meaning, the word of God himself."[22] And if the theology is Christian, they will be inquiring about the intelligibility of the Gospel, which Lonergan has set out as the "Law of the Cross."

Either way, their inquiry will be faith's search for understanding. Without faith, as Lonergan uses the word in *Method*, "the world is too evil for God to be good, for a good God to exist."[23] And, I venture to add, without faith Lonergan's own philosophy of God is too difficult for the effort of mastering it to be worthwhile. That does not mean there is no real need to argue philosophically for God's existence; it means there is no need to do it in a way that "produces the rabbit of theistic proof from the hat of impartial cosmology."[24] For in a very real sense there *is* no impartial cosmology. You either love the universe or you do not.

Still, loving the universe is not enough. Faith, the knowledge born of love, is the horizon within which any discourse about God is credible, but modern culture is dominated by other horizons. That is why the crisis Christianity faces is not a crisis of faith but of belief. People are not unwilling to believe; they know what Christianity teaches; but they want to know what these doctrines could possibly mean, and there is no shortage of psychologists, sociologists, and historians who are quite ready to explain what Christians believe—that is, to explain it away. Why? Because it does not fit into the horizon of nearly all modern intellectual endeavor, a horizon that stops short of anything like transcendence, contains only what is inherently conditioned by space and time, and acknowledges scientific statements alone as meaningful. But science quite properly limits itself to explaining data, and there are no data on God. Therefore "God" must be the name of a comforting but childish illusion, or an ideological tool, or the imaginary *as if* that focuses human aspiration, or the "depth dimension" of everyday living—take your pick. They are none of them really real; but then, for God to be real is too much to ask, if science has got the reality market cornered.

If ever a philosophy of God was needed, one that could meet these issues squarely and thoroughly, now is the time. A religion that promotes self-transcendence to the point of self-sacrificing love will have, Lonergan writes, "a redemptive role in human society inasmuch as love can undo the mischief of decline and restore the cumulative process of progress."[25] The question is, can any theology, committed to mediating such a religion to such a culture as ours, do its job without showing how and why the human sciences on their own have yet to find a solution to the human predicament? And can any theology do *that* unless it can show in no uncertain terms that no solution is going to be really practical so long as it leaves the reality of God out of account? Without a thorough and convincing way to articulate divine transcendence, it would seem that theologians can only go on "arriving on the scene a little breathlessly and a little late."[26]

NOTES

[1]Chapter eighteen, "The Possibility of Ethics," has some of the same problems as chapter nineteen, but I will not try to show how they bear on the topic at hand. Suffice it to say that, as *Method in Theology* adds religious experience to Lonergan's earlier philosophy of God, so also it adds feelings to his earlier view of ethics.

[2]For a very readable discussion and reworking of the argument from contingence, see Mortimer J. Adler, *How To Think About God* (New York: Macmillan Publishing Co., Inc., 1980). A useful exercise in the functional specialty that Lonergan calls Dialectic would be to figure out where, how, and why Adler's restatement of the argument differs from Lonergan's.

[3]The further question about value (Is it worthwhile?) is not treated as distinctly in *Insight* as it is in *Method,* and I shall have to return to it later.

[4]*Insight,* p. xviii.

[5]*Insight,* p. 329.

[6]*Insight,* p. xxi.

[7]Laplace is famous for claiming that such a systematic explanation would be possible, for a sufficiently vast intelligence, given knowledge of the positions of every particle in the universe and all the forces acting on it. He was wrong. For the reasons why, see Patrick H. Byrne, "Relativity and Indeterminism," *Foundations of Physics* 11 (1981), pp. 913–932.

[8]For the book that explains it, see Philip McShane, *Randomness, Statistics and Emergence* (Dublin: Gill and Macmillan, 1970).

[9]*Insight*, p. 132.

[10]Bernard Lonergan, "Questionnaire on Philosophy" [1976], *Method: Journal of Lonergan Studies* 2 (1984), no. 2, p. 17.

[11]For a more accurate statement, see *Insight*, p. 652.

[12]*Insight*, p. 684.

[13]*Insight*, p. 675 (emphasis added).

[14]Austin Farrer, *Finite and Infinite: A Philosophical Essay*, 2nd edition (London: Dacre Press, 1958; reprint, New York: The Seabury Press, 1979), p. 60.

[15]On God's self-transcendence, see *Method in Theology*, pp. 116–117. The point, so to say, is that God created the universe for the sheer joy of it— not because he needed something to love. Notice that Lonergan's remark here is set, quite deliberately, in a Trinitarian context.

[16]Not its formal cause, however, and not its "quasi-formal" cause. Each thing and event has its own formal cause—its own intrinsic intelligibility— which is another way of saying that it is *not* God.

[17]See *Insight*, pp. 263, 265.

[18]*Insight*, p. 266.

[19]*Insight*, p. 667.

[20]*Insight*, pp. 744, 731.

[21]*Insight*, p. 692.

[22]*Method in Theology*, p. 119.

[23]*Method in Theology*, p. 117.

[24]Farrer, *Finite and Infinite*, p. 6.

[25]*Method in Theology*, p. 55.

[26]*Insight*, p. 733.

FOR FURTHER READING

1. Articles by Bernard Lonergan

"The Absence of God in Modern Culture." In *A Second Collection*, pp. 101– 16.

"Finality, Love, Marriage." In *Collection*, pp. 16–53; see especially pp. 18– 22.

"Mission and the Spirit." In *A Third Collection*, pp. 23–34.

"The Natural Desire To See God." In *Collected Works of Bernard Lonergan*, vol. 4, pp. 81–91.

"Natural Knowledge of God." In *A Second Collection*, pp. 117–133.

"On God and Secondary Causes." In *Collected Works*, vol. 4, pp. 53–65.

2. *Secondary sources*

Byrne, Patrick H. "God and the Statistical Universe." *Zygon* 16 (1981), pp. 345–363.

———"Relativity and Determinism." *Foundations of Physics* 11 (1981), pp. 913–932.

Hefling, Charles C. "Science and Religion." In *The New Dictionary of Theology.* Edited by Joseph A. Komonchak, Mary Collins, and Dermot A. Lane. Wilmington, DE: Michael Glazier, Inc., 1987, pp. 938–945.

Lawrence, Frederick "Method and Theology as Hermeneutical." In *Creativity and Method: Essays in Honor of Bernard Lonergan, S. J.* Edited by Matthew L. Lamb. Milwaukee: Marquette University Press, 1981, pp. 79–104; see especially pp. 94–96.

McShane, Philip *Randomness, Statistics and Emergence.* Notre Dame: University of Notre Dame Press, 1970.

Melchin, Kenneth R. *History, Ethics and Emergent Probability.* Lanham, MD: University Press of America, 1987, esp. pp. 59–121.

Meynell, Hugo *The Intelligible Universe: A Cosmological Argument.* London: Macmillan, 1982.

Tyrrell, Bernard *Bernard Lonergan's Philosophy of God.* Notre Dame: University of Notre Dame Press, 1974.

VII. A Note on Scholasticism

Lonergan's Latin works have left a puzzle to posterity. The puzzle is not just that they were written in Latin, a language now not nearly so widely known and practically nowhere now used for speaking, teaching or writing. That fact strikes the imagination, but it is not the real obstacle to those works being widely known and used today. After all, Bultmann and Barth wrote all their theology in German, but they have had an enormous impact on American and English religious thought.

Nor is the problem merely one of a specialized terminology or even jargon. Heidegger's works are filled with both, but they have been successfully translated and are widely read in a multiply-hyphenated English version.

The real problem is perhaps that Lonergan's Latin works are written in two foreign languages simultaneously: in Latin and in the language of Scholasticism. Scholasticism is not just another set of specialized terms and jargon. Terms can be defined, point for point, and added to existing languages. But Scholasticism, like a foreign language, represents a completely different thought-world. Those who merely render its ancient terms out of Latin into English find themselves more and more met by stares of amazement, incomprehension, boredom. Putting Scholastic Latin into scholastic English is to make only one of the two translations needed; and a complete two-track translation of Lonergan has not yet been attempted and will certainly prove harder than one would expect.

Scholasticism was the style of theology and philosophy in Catholic Jesuit seminaries during the period before Vatican II when Lonergan did the bulk of his theological writing. Looked back on today, it indeed seems a different world. To satisfy those who wonder why Lonergan's Latin works have not been simply translated and published, and to make clear why here I do not include in my chapters on Trinity and Grace more sizable excerpts from the original, it may be well to describe a little of that world.

The Scholasticism of nineteenth and early twentieth century Catholicism was not the same as the Scholasticism of the Middle Ages, though it

144

presupposed the existence of that earlier Scholasticism, as well as assuming its name. The earlier Scholasticism, reaching its high point of development with Thomas Aquinas in the thirteenth century, had been basically a technique of investigation or of research. Pre-Vatican II Scholasticism in Catholic seminaries had been reduced to little more than a technique of presentation, of exposition. That exposition aimed at an overwhelming impression of solidity and clarity, because it was part of the training of the clergy of the teaching Church.

For clarity, all of theology was divided into treatises according to fields of subject matter. Each treatise normally was the work of one semester or two in a four-year theology curriculum: "The One God," "The Triune God," "God Creating," "Grace," "The Word Incarnate," "The Blessed Virgin," etc.

Again for clarity the substance of each treatise was divided up into a limited number of short, usually one-sentence propositions. Twenty to thirty of these was a common number for a single course. These propositions, called "theses," were the heart of the course. The daily lectures (in Latin) progressed through them one at a time and in sequence. Periodic reviews took the form of calling on one or the other student to defend theses already learned. The exams at the end of the term made the theses the one subject of examination.

During the exam each student had before him a printed sheet listing all the theses of the course. The examination (oral and in Latin) would normally begin by his being asked to read one thesis, arbitrarily selected by his examiners (a board of three or four professors); and the outcome of the exam depended on how well the student showed himself able to explain and defend that thesis, as well as any others to which the discussion with the examiners might lead.

At the end of four years, the student faced a longer exam in which he was expected to show the same mastery of all the theses he had learned in all the dogma courses of his four years. These courses were the heart of all theological training. In comparison to them, courses in Scripture and moral theology were distinctly secondary. Pastoral courses, prayer, mysticism, Church history, etc. were tertiary concerns. One could do poorly in all of those and still graduate with honors. But nothing else could ever substitute for mastery of the theses of dogma.

The system aimed at clarity and solidity. It was presumed that at least each graduating cleric would come out knowing what the Church holds on all essential matters, how to explain it and how to defend it. The difference from a typical theology course today hardly needs to be touched on here.

Such a system was mandated by Rome for all seminaries, and though not all complied completely in practice, all had to at least report to Rome year by year the names of the approved textbooks they used in all their dogma courses. How carefully each textbook was read by Roman censors there is no way of knowing; but it is clear that by simply skimming the list of theses proposed a censor could see almost at a glance whether or not safe traditional doctrine was being inculcated in safe traditional formulae.

The bulk of the typical textbook was devoted to the explanation and defense of the individual theses. These explanations too followed a rigid format which promoted the sense of solidity and clarity, and which at the same time made the text easy to spot-check for orthodoxy.

The explanation typically began with a statement of the general point of the thesis and its link with the preceding and following theses. Then would follow a page of formal definitions of every word used in the thesis. Then came the author's judgment as to the degree of theological certainty which should be ascribed to the thesis: Had the Church defined it, so that all Catholics should know it was true and could be denied only by heretics? Was it, if not defined, nevertheless the clear teaching of Scripture or/and tradition? Was it at least a conclusion which all would grant followed from Scripture or tradition? Or was it at least the general teaching of theologians? Of the greater number of theologians? Of the "better" theologians? In this section were collected, as "the teaching of the Church," all possible statements from councils and from recent Popes which seemed to echo or favor the words of the thesis. During the exam the student could have at his side a standard printed collection of such official Church statements of possible relevance to the theses of theology. The statements were indexed and numbered, and the student was expected to be able to refer to them with ease in defending his thesis.

Next came a catalogue of those who had opposed the thesis: the "adversaries." These could be drawn from any century. Adversaries included anyone who had taught a different solution or given a different expression to the subject matter of the thesis, whether or not they had ever heard of the thesis under discussion. The point of the section was not historical. There was no attempt to explain or understand the doctrine of these others in its own context, but only to single out that aspect in which they "erred," i.e., said something different, used different words, from those of the thesis.

The final step was the "proof" of the thesis. If the preceding preparatory sections had been well done, the proof seemed obvious and easy.

The proof too aimed at absolute clarity and solidity. It was divided into three parts, according to the traditional three sources of theological argument: proof from Scripture, proof from tradition (especially of those noted writers of the second through eighth centuries called the Fathers), and proof from reason.

The proof from Scripture was a collection of texts, with as much exegesis as was deemed necessary to show that some texts at least, if carefully interpreted, could be found to say substantially the same thing as the thesis said. The student was expected to be able to cite enough of these texts to produce the same impression, and had a Bible at hand during examinations to appeal to as necessary.

In the proof from the Fathers or tradition, selected texts again were cited which sounded basically like what the thesis itself was saying. The student was expected to be familiar enough with these to use them convincingly and to that end could have at hand during exams a book of selections from the Fathers commonly used in support of standard theses. The texts, usually short paragraphs, were numbered and indexed. The student learned these numbers just as he learned the most frequently appealed to chapter and verse references for Scripture.

The final proof was from reason. Here the argument was expected to be laid out in syllogisms: major premise, minor premise, conclusion, with further demonstrations added where necessary to clarify either or both premises. The reasoning and the metaphysical principles to which appeal was made were borrowed from Scholastic philosophy, which the student was expected to have mastered substantially before beginning the course.

The exposition closed with a set of objections in the form of syllogisms whose conclusions contradicted the thesis. The answers to these showed either that there was a logical flaw in the syllogism or that the objector's syllogism did not use words in exactly the same sense as they were being used in the thesis.

Clearly this Scholastic thought world was one that put an extraordinary premium on logic, clarity, the mechanics of exposition, on precise divisions and subdivisions of material. It presupposed the possibility of perfect and exact definitions of everything. It excluded emotion and rhetoric as rigorously as any treatise in the physical sciences. It insisted that the bones of the argument always show through. The chain of reasoning can always be followed, if one has the patience and stamina to pursue it. This was its strength but also its weakness. For so much emphasis on form could easily allow form to replace substance. Ideas and names are always sharper and clearer than reality, and a world of definitions, divisions and logic could soon become a world of words alone.

It is obvious that the system was not devised to promote innovation. Of course, what a teacher did inside an individual classroom could not be so completely controlled as could the written textbook. Nevertheless, classrooms were hardly private places. The students were always examined by boards of examiners, so it soon became public knowledge if an individual teacher had not been actually teaching the theses which the textbook prescribed. The students, too, for their own safety and future advantage, out of fear of the exams or sometimes just out of normal student preference for what is orderly and clear, often insisted just as much as the most rigorous censor on careful adherence to the assigned theses.

Moreover, everything took place in a general context where everyone involved was thoroughly conscious that they were preparing spokespersons for an official doctrine, priests who would teach, preach and counsel in the name of the Church. Innovation was not only undesirable, it was a derogatory term. Theology consisted in learning, appreciating and passing on what the Church had always taught. One could expand its content by applying it to new situations or by drawing logical conclusions from it. But no one would have dreamed of advertising a new theology book in the way which has become familiar since Vatican II: "Full of new insights . . . "; "exciting . . . "; "revolutionary . . . "; "casts doubts on the whole procedure of the past . . . "

That sort of thing was simply not theology. A second century Bishop of Rome had summed up the Catholic ideal in a phrase which became almost a motto of the seminaries: "Nihil innovetur nisi quod traditum est . . . " "Let nothing be started except what has been handed down . . . " It was a world in which the councils of the Church and the Popes and the Vatican Congregations spoke the truth, and to be able to quote them in support of your position was the best confirmation you could find. If such an "authority" had clearly said something you did not like, you tried to show that it could still be interpreted in your sense. You never challenged a traditional authority head-on.

The use of the collections of texts—scriptural, patristic and ecclesiastical florilegia—promoted the sense of secure continuity. In dogma courses you did not do independent historical research, reading through the originals in the context of their own times. You read and pondered selections in the manuals. These selections were the texts which the Church wanted to remember. For these there was a living tradition of interpretation, into which you had to fit your own thoughts and arguments.

What if not everything a textbook author had to say could be fitted into twenty or thirty theses? For this situation the device of the scholion existed. The scholion was a long specialized note, an appendix to a thesis. Other appendices could be added to the text as well. So could "special questions" and long introductions to the book or to individual theses be made the repositories of one's own thought. Into such odd corners, too, all genuinely historical reflections had to be tucked, because the structure of the thesis itself was devised to foster only an impression of eternal, unchangeable truth.

Lonergan made abundant use of these standard devices to insert his own personal emphases. But he also learned to bend the intricacies of the system itself to his own purposes. Often a thesis will sound much like the standard thesis in any course, but his statement of the point, his definitions of terms, his groupings of the adversaries, his intricate divisions and subdivisions of the arguments actually convey something startlingly different to whoever is willing to work through the entire exposition patiently line by line and word by word. His most drastic modifications, however, are only the inevitable result of the fact that "the meaning of *every other term* changes with changes in the meaning of the terms 'knowledge,' 'reality,' 'objectivity' " (*Insight* 426, emphasis added). All of Lonergan's arguments in his Scholastic works presuppose the philosophy of St. Thomas interpreted according to the critical realism of *Insight*. In this he stands alone.

In *Insight* Lonergan touches more than once on the irremediable problem of communication for someone with a major new insight. The words with which to express the new insight may simply not exist. They will be created only slowly and with the help of disciples as a new thought-world grows up around the insight and works out its implications. But at first the idea can be communicated only imperfectly, indirectly, obscurely.

Now much of Lonergan's creative genius lies doubly buried in his Latin Scholastic works. It is hard for the average reader to believe that anyone with something new and important to say would go about writing it in Church Latin in a seminary textbook in the structured language of a medieval disputation. After all, we don't expect new automobiles to resemble a surrey with a fringe on top. If there are many who have never been able to put forth the effort to work through *Insight* because they take it for granted that a Catholic and a Jesuit is not ever really going to say anything really different from what Catholics and Jesuits always ultimately say, how much more will they overlook writings which even on the surface show they have nothing to say to the modern world?

In *Insight* Lonergan makes the point that real metaphysics must always begin wherever the person attempting it actually is. And similarly in *Method* he explains that real theology can have no other starting place. Clearly this implies that we must be ready to dialogue with non-Christians and with Christians of different persuasions from ourselves, letting them begin from their own starting places. But it also implies an openness even to the narrow conservative Catholic mind of pre-Vatican II Scholasticism. That was the mind Lonergan wanted to reform, and so he had to begin with it just where it was with its own presuppositions. Because it was there.

VIII. Three Persons—One God

A short summary like this cannot consider in detail each of Lonergan's works on the Trinity or attempt to reproduce in a few pages a theology which took him five volumes to express. All we will do here is pick out a few (five) central features of his trinitarian theology, tell where they appear, describe them briefly, and finally relate them to the stages of theological reflection which Lonergan eventually called "the functional specialties."

THE FIRST FEATURE

1. *Separating the Questions.* The first reform Lonergan made in the theology of the Trinity was to refuse to treat all kinds of questions at the same time and on the same level. Scholasticism might be satisfied with an orderly presentation of all that the future priest should know. But for Lonergan, coming to know was answering questions, and questions must be answered one at a time. He flatly announced that his course on the Trinity would have only one aim: understanding. That is, taking for granted that he and his students stood within a living tradition, he wanted only to answer the question: What does this Church tradition mean? What sense can it possibly make? The reform sounds methodological, but its implications for content were enormous.

First of all, it meant simplifying and abbreviating the course seriously, eliminating material devoted to other aims than just understanding. Secondly, it meant further pruning according to the demands of an exigent intellect, removing all dead ends, obscurantism, useless and trivial questions.

For, when one aims exclusively at understanding, one answers questions of meaning and intelligibility: What? Why? But one leaves questions of fact, truth, reality: Is it so? to be answered elsewhere, in another step, in a different set of operations.

Now the standard course in Scholastic theology of the Trinity started with the given truth and reality of one God and three Divine Persons as part of the Catholic faith which the students brought with them from the creeds and the catechism. But the bulk of the course was devoted to a long series of other items never mentioned in Scripture, creed, catechism or ordinary sermons. These were such things as: processions, relations of origin, subsistent relations, notional acts, personal properties, attributions and missions—to use the shortest possible list. The course seemed to present those and dozens of other *theologoumena* as additional facts about God, known only to theologians, part of an esoteric tradition, unfamiliar to the ordinary layperson. Each of these items, moreover, was the occasion for numerous subtle disputes and further distinctions among various schools of theologians, though their principal usefulness to the student seemed to be only as a key to passing exams.

In Lonergan's course, aimed solely at understanding, it became clear that none of those mysterious beings represented any additional factual information about God. They were all merely elaborations of a single basic theorem: the hypothesis that God is conscious in a dynamic way (cf. Step IV under point 5, below). The theologian sets up that hypothesis, according to Lonergan, because by means of it all the statements about the divine Persons in Scripture, the Creeds and theological tradition can be clarified and so related to one another that they can be held before the mind in a single integrated grasp.

The series of technical terms listed above are only logical steps in a process of clarification. They are parts of a scaffolding, helpful in designing a coherent pattern. They are not dubious facts taken partly on faith, partly out of respect for tradition and ultimately accepted only as a set of hurdles along a semester-long exercise in memory. They flow logically out of a single basic supposition and out of one another. But they flow only as an enlargement of understanding. They are implications, consistent with the givens of faith. But they are neither givens of faith nor conclusions from faith. They are not themselves in the realm of facts. They are true or false only as an understanding is true or false, not as a judgment is. They have only the truth or falsity of definitions, not of propositions.[1]

If the aim of the course is achieved, the student will be able to grasp as a unified whole the entire tradition on the Trinity, know why these items have become part of the treatise through its normal historical development, and know how to use them as helps in answering ordinary questions about the Christian triune God. Moreover, the student will gain an integrated grasp of the role of the Trinity in Christian life, prayer and spirituality.

Is all this worthwhile? Well, it is not the whole of human life. But it is something which a normally curious intelligence would not want to turn away from either. Whether or not it is a good aim for a course depends on whether or not the course delivered what it promised. One has to ask the testimony of students who have taken the course and achieved the understanding. Obviously not all did achieve it. Many students came away from Lonergan's treatise with no more than the Roman censor got from it—the feeling that they were being exposed to just one more sample of the same old thing. At the same time, many who were to become outstanding teachers and theologians in their own right came away from Lonergan's classes thoroughly excited over the prospects being opened before them.

THE SECOND FEATURE

2. *The Point of the Mystery.* Separating out the question of understanding made it clear that other questions too needed individual attention, especially the question: What exactly are we going to try to understand?

In *Insight* Lonergan had demonstrated that a reasonable person would accept a part in a world-wide collaboration for transmitting and applying God's solution to the problem of evil. Being a part of such a collaboration would involve accepting the truths passed on in the collaboration, even when these were about "objects beyond the natural reach of any finite understanding . . . that man never could discover for himself, nor, even when he assented to them, could he understand them in any adequate fashion" (*Insight,* 725). The Trinity is certainly one such truth, and Lonergan and his theology students assented to it as part of their participation in their world-wide collaboration, the Roman Catholic Church.

But the question remains: What exactly is "the mystery of the Trinity" proposed by the Church? How formulate precisely that to which one must give intellectual assent in order to be a part of this collaboration? Different biblical authors, different Church councils, different Fathers of the Church, different theologians have said many different things about the Trinity. No reasonable person takes all of them as equally "of faith." But how distinguish among them and specify exactly where the revealed mystery lies?

Moreover, good theology for Lonergan is always personal, subject-conscious and subject-centered. Even a theology written down in a textbook to be used by thousands is still only this one author's theology. It is therefore always incumbent upon the author to explain exactly why he or she takes this and not something else to be faith doctrine in the midst of the enormous differences which history reveals among religious traditions and within religious traditions.

Therefore Lonergan devotes another book[2] to spelling out exactly what it is he feels obliged to take on faith as a Catholic Christian and why. The book is not in the form of a personal confession. It has the superficial appearance of a history of doctrine. After all, what he intends to describe is not "my faith," but "the Catholic faith." Nevertheless, Lonergan always remains aware that the statement "This is the Catholic faith" always means "insofar as I have understood it" and "if I am presenting it correctly."

His account is certainly not based on feelings. It follows on lengthy historical studies, reflections, comparisons, which then ground his judgments and choices. He describes the sweep of possibilities which people have seen for stating the Catholic faith on the Trinity. Out of that wide sweep he picks out the doctrine which he summarizes in five propositions. These come down to the formulae defined by various Church councils as still preserved in the creed recited at Sunday Mass: that Christ is one in being (consubstantial) with the Father and that the Holy Spirit is to be adored equally with Father and Son; that the Son is from the Father and that the Spirit is from Father and Son united; that this is a mystery beyond human understanding.

Even this needs further specification as to the exact sense of the word "consubstantial" as an object of faith. Using a phrase from Athanasius and a profound metaphysical dialectical analysis as his justification (cf. point 3, immediately following), he maintains that the word means exactly and only this: "Whatever is predicated of the Father is predicated of the Son and of the Spirit, except that he is Father."

THE THIRD FEATURE

3. *Accounting for Diversity of Viewpoints.* This third feature is closely related to the second, and is found treated within the same book.[3] Lonergan is concerned to give a full, plausible account of why so many others have failed to specify the mystery or the object of faith in exactly the same way as he has himself.

Here his point is not to list all that others have held, nor to determine by historical research what exactly they said and meant. That would be an historical study, and would have required a very different kind of research from that which he did for this section.

Here Lonergan began simply from the standard texts from the Fathers and theologians available in the manual-collections. He applied to these the criterion established in *Insight:* whether or not their language implied notions on the real, on knowing and on objectivity which were consistent with how the human mind actually knows, identifies the real and judges objectivity (*Insight* 387–390). Here, as always, natural tendencies of a many-sided human consciousness led thinkers to err on one side or the other of a long back-and-forth process of statement, reaction and counter-reaction. But over the years, within a community whose lives centered on the truth, objectivity and reality of him in whom they believed, these errors tended to work themselves out, the expressions gradually were corrected, purified.

Concretely, a variety of incompatible concrete images gradually gave way to a privileged example drawn from human spiritual experience (knowing and loving). The truth that God is not a body—not in any sense (cf. *Insight* xx–xxi)—finally became more than words; and instead of somehow trying to imagine a three-in-one, thinkers settled on a rule of predication which was purely intelligible and which gave as little to the imagination as do Maxwell's equations for the electro-magnetic field in the realm of physical science. [The comparison is explicitly drawn: *De Deo Trino* I, p. 86; note the same favorite example in *Insight* 25, 45, 68, 80, 443.]

THE FOURTH FEATURE

4. *Emphasizing the Sendings.* One would expect a systematic treatise in the Scholastic manner, especially one which placed so much emphasis on the understanding of mystery, to be painfully abstract. But this would violate Lonergan's principles of abstaining from speculation about merely possible universes and confining oneself on the one hand to what is explicitly revealed and on the other to what can be verified in human consciousness (*Insight* 733–734). Therefore it should not be surprising that Lonergan's theology of the Trinity gives special emphasis to those realities in Christian experience which the Scriptures describe as the sendings of Christ and of the Spirit.

Besides the large part necessarily given to the sendings in his *Pars Analytica,* he also devotes 45 of the 195 pages of his *Pars Systematica* to them; that is, about twenty-two percent of a text aimed exclusively at understanding the revealed mystery is devoted to the actions of the divine Persons in the world. Of the thirty-two "questions" in his *Systematic,* eleven are questions on the sendings, and four of his eighteen theses are on them. This is not usual in the tradition of Scholastic textbooks. A single thesis, sometimes only one or two scholia, would be more normal. But Lonergan wanted to show the "fruitfulness" of right understanding, and he felt that appeared especially in consideration of the sendings.

For the educated Christian may avoid discussions of the inner life of God. But it is hard to be a Christian and have nothing definite or clear to say about Christ, salvation, forgiveness of sin. But to discuss those as a Christian is to speak of the workings of individual divine Persons in the world. That demands some intelligible grasp of what "divine Persons" might mean, especially in a religion which claims to be monotheistic.

The world's great religious traditions start from different sets of experiences which were perceived to be God's actions in the human world. In

Christianity those special experiences were first Christ's life, death and resurrection, and then the Spirit-filled life of the early communities. "Incarnation and redemption" and "grace" are the objects of other treatises in
theology. But because they are in Christian experience the work of distinct
divine Persons, they also provoke further questions which the treatise on the
Trinity must answer.

What does it mean to believe that God really did certain actions in time,
"became man," "dwells in our hearts"? How do such notions differ from tales
about the gods of Olympus? What is the difference between saying "the
Spirit" and simply saying "God"? Can God have a Son? All the rest of theology would hang in the air unless the course in the Trinity answered such
questions.

Lonergan's basic account of God's action in the world and in time is that
of *Insight* 661–662, but here he expands it to include the faith-reality of the
three Persons.[4] The sendings are explained in a non-mythological fashion
(avoiding the defects listed on *Insight* 681), but remain supremely real. The
Son's being sent is his very being as Son; the Spirit's being sent is his being
as Spirit—each conceived according to the basic analogy of the treatise (cf.
point 5, below).

Since the reality of their being sent is their own eternal being (reality),
it is obvious that any new reality implied in the sending is a new reality not
in God, but in us. We are changed when Father and Son send the Spirit. We
begin to love God and others in a new way. This change in us occurs because
of God's eternally loving and choosing the highest and best and choosing that
in our time we might share it. Again, the Father's sending his Son means that
a human figure in history became our key to knowing God as only God can
know himself. This happens because God eternally, perfectly does know
himself and expresses himself to himself and chooses that in time that expression might be shared with us.

The sending of the Son and the Spirit was also the revealing of the Trinity. It made possible personal relationships between us and God. For, first
of all, apart from Father, Son and Spirit, there is no "person" of God.[5] The
divine Persons are three; there is no fourth—"God"—to whom one can have
a personal relationship. Reason indeed may argue convincingly that the one
God must be intelligently conscious and therefore personal. But this consciousness is utterly transcendent. Philosophically affirming God as the transcendent, unrestricted act of understanding (*Insight* 19) is a far cry from the
fullness of the Christian experience and hope.

The sendings of the Son and the Spirit open to us the relationships
which the Persons have with one another and invite us to share those relationships. God loves us in the Spirit and loves us as he loves his own Son.
And we reciprocate. Our being redeemed and being graced are our sharing

in God's knowing and loving; created shares of the being of the Son and Spirit are ours. This reality of being loved in the Spirit as the Son and in return loving God as children is the way the divine Persons dwell in us—that is, as objects of our transformed knowing and loving.[6]

Thus all is discussed without conjuring up entities beyond those which experience provides, faith presents or logical conclusion makes inescapable. The sending, the indwelling and other activities *ad extra* of the divine Persons are located in terms of conscious human activities of knowing and loving, in conformity with the criterion of meaningful metaphysical and theological predication of *Insight* 524–525 and *Method in Theology* (343–344).

Finally, in these pages, the last part of the treatise, Lonergan writes passages which interweave scriptural sentences and references into a demonstration through poetic example of how all the New Testament can be read movingly and devoutly as a meditation on the sending of the Son and the Spirit. This is not exegesis, as Lonergan knows well. This is not asking what the Johannine school held or what Mark's redactor alluded to. This presents only what most people hope for from Scriptures preserved and read in the Church as God's inspired word: an illustration in moving, sensitive style of the realities in which the Church believes.

THE FIFTH FEATURE

5. *A Revolutionary Analogy.* It is time to be precise about this understanding of which we have been speaking. How can a treatise be aimed exclusively at understanding the mystery of the Trinity, when standard Catholic doctrine maintains that a revealed mystery cannot be understood? The same council of the Church which defined that mysteries cannot be understood in themselves (Vatican I, 1869–70), also defined that there are certain ways in which "some understanding, and that most fruitful" can be attained by reason helped by faith. One of those ways is by "analogy with things naturally known." Lonergan's treatise on the Trinity leads the student along that way of understanding through analogy.

Now the way of analogy can be purely literary, as when a religious poet finds a reminder of a Trinity wherever a group of three appears. Analogy may mean merely a devout or a dogmatic reading of Scripture, as when patristic commentators see the Trinity in Abraham's three guests (Gen 18) or in the fact that Isaiah's seraphim cry "Holy, holy, holy" (Is 6:3). But those uses of analogy have little to contribute to fruitful understanding.

The use of analogy for understanding is the use familiar to any teacher. When something new and difficult has to be explained, the teacher analyzes it to find exactly what is likely to cause difficulties for the student. Then the teacher looks for places within the student's present knowledge and experience where something like that material occurs but seems familiar to the student as something already known.

Thus St. Patrick is said to have illustrated the Trinity by holding up a shamrock: three leaves, one plant. His point was not just that here we have another instance of the number three, but to offer an instance in human experience where something is already known as simultaneously three and one. That analogy limps badly, because each leaf of a shamrock is only a part of the whole, and the leaves of the shamrock do not come from one another, while in God each Person is truly and wholly God, and the Son and the Spirit do come from Another. But it was an attempt to illustrate something of what the doctrine meant, and it was an attempt to make the doctrine seem not quite so absolutely remote from the normal world of human thought and experience.

Other early writers proposed examples like ice, steam and water, or a fountain and the streams that flow from it, or a burning lamp, its brightness and its warmth. Augustine proposed the human analogy of memory, intellect and will in one human mind.

As a good teacher, Lonergan begins the process by first pinpointing the difficulties, that is, the apparent contradictions in the Church's doctrine of the Trinity which make necessary an appeal to some analogy. The apparent contradictions are, in brief:

1. That the Son is from Another (from the Father, whose Son he is). But the Son is truly God, and God cannot be from another.

2. That the Spirit is from the Father and the Son. But the Spirit is God, and God cannot be from another.

3. That there must be a difference between the way the Spirit is "from another" and the way the Son is "from another" (for the Son is the "only begotten"). But there cannot be differences in God.

Even an ideal analogy would not explain the Trinity or prove from reason that the Trinity exists. It would at best indicate something which seems to be like the Trinity and would at best suggest that what we affirm in faith might not be an utterly inconceivable flat contradiction. In technical terms, it would make possible not direct but indirect understanding.[7]

Lonergan holds that there is only one analogy in all human experience which has these necessary qualities. It is the psychological analogy, based on the workings of the human mind. But even that analogy will do what it should only if it starts from an accurate analysis of those workings. That right analysis is the analysis of *Insight*.

Getting the analogy exactly right is terribly important to Lonergan. He devotes 49 of the 195 pages of his Systematic to explaining it, and adds another thirty pages in the form of two appendices on the subject. Moreover, his entire massive research project of the *Verbum* articles was devoted to establishing that this one cognitional analysis (later developed in *Insight*) was the only key to Aquinas' writings on the Trinity. Lonergan maintained that, although Aquinas had not explicitly described the conscious psychological process of "What do I do when I know?" his writings on the "intelligible emanation" of the divine Persons clearly presupposed an awareness of it.[8]

The heart of the analogy is an event in human consciousness. Understanding what Lonergan's *Pars Systematica* is about depends entirely on being able to identify that event in one's own consciousness. Lonergan insists that it is in itself a simple thing to do. But the prejudices of language, as well as the influence of incomplete or erroneous philosophic accounts of knowing, are so all-pervasive that very few people ever do it successfully. There is nothing more fundamental for understanding Lonergan, and nothing more indispensable for grasping his major contribution to the theology of the Trinity.

We will study the analogy in four steps. The first two describe the psychological fact; the last two show its use as a Trinitarian analogy.[9]

THE FIRST STEP: IDENTIFYING THE ACT

I. The first step is to identify in our own experience the act of understanding. It is the act which *Insight* explains "occurs reasonably often in the normally bright, rarely only in the stupid." It is commonly overlooked as obvious.

We are each aware that there are things we understand and other things we do not understand. Those we understand seem fairly obvious and clear; things we do not understand seem puzzling, foreign, obscure. But the difference here is not really between two different kinds of things, but between two different states of our own mind. Things which are now clear to us are things we have already understood. An act of understanding has occurred in regard to them. Once the act has occurred, what was formerly puzzling, foreign, obscure now makes sense. We can even explain it to others and wonder why they have trouble grasping it. Between the earlier state of our mind and the later state, there has occurred the act of catching on, the flash of insight, the moment of seeing the light.

This act occurs at various levels and in different contexts. By an act of insight we grasp the solution of a problem, or get the meaning of a parable, or understand why a thing is the way it is, or see how something works, or what it is for. But by a related act of insight, we grasp the evidence that some event has occurred or that something is a fact or that some thesis is true. By another single insight, an artist, a novelist, an engineer may conceive in a moment some vast creative project that could be undertaken. By another, I can suddenly come to an awareness of what my present situation calls for, what here and now I ought to do. Finally, insight occurs in the context of existential decision, when an encounter, a challenge, an experience of loss, gives me a glimpse of myself as I really am—or as I could be—and calls for a decision about myself.

THE SECOND STEP: FINDING THE GAP

II. Once we have identified the act clearly in our own consciousness, *the second step* is to notice that the act is not the same as what results from the act. The act is in a moment, often an unguarded, unexpected moment. The act is not wholly under our control; often it seems just to strike us from nowhere. But the results of the act can be lasting and are under our control.

Moreover, there is a gap between the act and the possession of the results. There is a period of fumbling—sometimes only a split-second long, sometimes much longer. During the gap, we are sure we have seen the point, but we fumble, trying to express the point to ourselves, trying to put into a sentence or into a sketch or an outline exactly what it is we have seen. If we do not deliberately express it to ourselves—do not try to formulate the rule by which the thing works, to outline the project, to jot down the insight or at least put it into words—the insight itself tends to slip away like a dream and may be lost. But by pausing for a moment, deliberately adverting to what we have just understood, pulling it together, putting it into words, we can make it a permanent possession. Now it can be called up anytime. And soon it will seem so familiar and obvious to us that we can hardly imagine our earlier feeling that its object was difficult.

A gap occurs similarly in the other contexts and levels at which insights occur. There is a gap between grasping the evidence for a fact and actually affirming on our own responsibility, because of the evidence we have grasped, that this thing is indeed a fact. We have reviewed the evidence, by insight something has clicked so that we truly grasp the sufficiency of the evidence. But the same moment we are aware that we can now say, "Yes, this is true," we are also aware that we can check over the evidence again just to be sure and can perhaps raise still further questions before affirming anything. Hesitant people put off making the judgment of truth as long as possible, no matter how clear their grasp of the evidence. Rash people or people under the influence of strong emotion may plunge into making affirmations too quickly. But in every case there is a gap between the insight and the affirmation.

Another way of verifying the existence of the gap is to recall times we may have learned a definition by heart and repeated it by rote without any act of understanding ever intervening. In this case, we seem to have the results of understanding, but we hold them purely as an object of memory. Such a definition can be easily forgotten; it is not really our own possession. If we have to use it in a new situation, we hardly dare change a single word. But how different this is from a situation where we have actually understood something and therefore know why it is defined the way it is. Now there is no danger of forgetting how to define it. Because of the understanding, we can reconstruct the definition when we need it, adapt it to different situations, illustrate it with different examples, perhaps even improve upon it.

Finally, we are surely familiar with situations of being quite aware that we ought to do something, but not wanting to face squarely up to what we know we know; or of facing it, but flatly deciding not to act in accordance with what we know to be right. There is a familiar gap between seeing the good to be done and actually deciding to do it. So too with our own self-image. We could courageously face up to and accept the reality of who we are and how different that reality is from what we might be. But most of us don't. Most people don't; most people hide from something that hovers threateningly in their consciousness, and refuse to choose in accordance with their knowledge. When they do make the genuine, honest, existential decision in accordance with their perceptions, then they are sharply conscious of moving over the tremendous gap between realizing "I ought" and saying "I will."

THE THIRD STEP: UNDERSTANDING THE ANALOGY IN ELEVEN POINTS

III. The third step is to see that the analogy to the Persons of the Trinity is in what lies on the two sides of the gap we have been sketching. What lies on the one side issues from what lies on the other: the permanently possessed concept or definition from the insight; the judgment of fact from the grasp of the evidence; the decision from the awareness of what we ought to do. The way it issues is analogous to the way the Persons of the Trinity may be conceived to issue forth from one another. We can sum this up in eleven points.

A. *First,* there is a real issuing. The awareness we have of the gap makes us equally aware that something (concept, judgment, decision) has come out from something else (act of understanding, grasp of the evidence, judgment of value). What lies on the one side of the gap is not identical with what lies on the other side. I can refrain from making the judgment in accordance with the evidence I perceive to be sufficient; I can refuse the decision I perceive to be right, good and consistent with my knowledge. My consciousness will be very different, depending on whether I do or do not go ahead to it. But my act of understanding remains the same. B. *Second,* the issuing takes place in one consciousness. I consciously move from understanding to expressing my understanding to myself, from seeing the evidence to making the judgment, from judging the value to deciding, choosing, loving, without in any way moving outside my own consciousness. Moreover, the movement is strictly a movement of consciousness itself. It involves no motion in space, not even the stirring of a single muscle. C. *Third,* the issuing does not add to the reality, fullness or completeness of that from which it issues. All the perfection of what comes forth—all its content, determination and value— is already in that from which it issues. [Technically phrased, the issuing is not from potency to act, but from act to act.] The act of understanding is not merely an incomplete concept; perceiving the evidence, I know as much as I know when I make the judgment based on that perception; a judgment of value is as determinate as the choice which reflects it. D. *Fourth,* whatever perfection, reality, determination, fullness or act is found on the originating side of the gap is found also on the other side. For that which issues forth not only gets its whole reality from that other out of which it issues, but its whole being is precisely to express that other. The being of a concept is to express perfectly and exactly and comprehensively the insight. The whole being of a judgment is to be an expression of the grasp of the sufficiency of the evidence; the point of a decision is to embrace exactly that which was judged to be of value. E. *Fifth,* what issues forth—though really distinct from what was on the other side of the gap (cf. A. First, above)—still has absolutely the same content, but the content is in a different relative situation. F. *Sixth,* what issues forth is dependent on that from which it issues. Without the act of understanding, there could be no concept; without the grasp of the evidence, there could be no judgment; without a judgment of value, no decision. Everything in the issuing term is from that term from which it issued. G. *Seventh,* the originating term nevertheless does not cause the term which issues from it. No action of causing, making, producing is involved. The act of understanding simply is itself, and because it is, the concept can be. But the act does not create the concept; grasping the evidence does not produce the judgment. We are perfectly conscious that even while having grasped the sufficiency of the evidence, we can hold back from making the judgment; just as seeing the good to be done, we can abide there and never proceed to the appropriate decision or choice. H. *Eighth,* the acts of insight from which concept and judgment issue are both insights into our conscious experience. But the judgments of value from which decision, choice or love issue forth are always based not only on our conscious experience, but also on the judgments of truth or fact we have already made. *I. Ninth,* our consciousness is not divided by the issuing but actually made more one. Proceeding to concept, judgment and choice do not divide consciousness, but integrate it. *J. Tenth,* the more perfectly the issuing forth takes place, the greater the identity of the terms on either side of the gap, and the more the gap itself tends to disappear. That is, a brighter, more intelligent person would more quickly, more competently and more thoroughly incorporate into concepts the content of an act of understanding than would a duller person. A more thoroughly moral person would more rapidly move from seeing what ought to be done to deciding to do it, and would more easily and naturally incorporate the entire judgment of value into the final decision, leaving out nothing whatever. A person with a well-trained mind and good intellectual discipline would move with greater ease and security from evidence grasped to a firm, true, self-committing judgment.

Progressing up the scale of possibilities toward envisioning greater and greater intelligence, goodness, perfection, we see how the two terms of the conscious process come closer and closer toward perfect unity. Thus, the more perfectly the issuing of the concept takes place, the more the concept and the act of understanding are one. The more perfectly the concept is itself, the more it presents absolutely all that is in the act of understanding.

Thus in an infinite intelligence of absolute perfection and goodness, all would be instantaneous. The most thoroughgoing, perfect issuing forth of perfectly expressed understanding and flawless choosing would be absolutely one with the act of understanding itself and the true judgment of value. "That which proceeds within by intelligible emanation does not have to be separate; in fact, the more perfectly it proceeds, the more it is one with that from which it proceeds" (Sum. theol. I, 27, 1 ad 2m). *K. Eleventh,* the more perfectly the issuing forth takes place, the more perfect the resulting unity of the consciousness. The consciousness which has proceeded to accurate self-expression in concepts which embody its understanding, in judgments which conform to its own grasp of the evidence, in choices, decisions and loving embrace of what it honestly believes to be of value, is a consciousness which is one, whole and at peace with itself.

So that is the analogue. There is no other like it in the world of human experience. Its essential success depends on certain ways in which the operations of the human mind are different from the operations of all the material reality in human experience.

Thus the human mind in operation parallels many aspects of the Church's teaching on the Trinity. For *A* (cf. point A above, and so through all eleven) the Persons of the Trinity really do issue forth from one another, the Son from the Father and the Spirit from the Father and the Son. The Person who comes forth is not identical with the one from whom he comes; the Son is not the Father; the Spirit is not the Father and Son.

B. The Persons come forth from one another in one God, without movement, without going outside of God. *C.* The processions in God are not from imperfect to perfect, but from perfection to perfection. The Father is perfect God; the Son is perfect God; the Spirit is perfect God. *D.* The whole reality of the Son is from the Father; the whole reality of the Spirit is from the Father and the Son. *E.* Each of them has exactly the same divine nature; they differ only in being Originator and Originated, to or from one another. *F.* The persons who issue are dependent on the ones from whom they issue, yet *G.* the Father does not cause the Son, the Father and Son do not make the Spirit. *H.* The procession of the Spirit is distinct from the procession of the Son, since it presupposes a different origin, just as human deciding, choosing and loving is distinct from the concept or the judgment.

I. The procession of the Persons does not conflict with the perfect unity of God, but rather is a confirmation and perfection of unity. *J.* The perfect issuing forth of Son and of Spirit in God is one of perfect identity in all things except their mutual relationships: the one who proceeds is always distinct from the one from whom he proceeds. Otherwise all is identical. Moreover, in God the proceeding would take place with such infinite perfection that there would not be any gaps. There would be only the reality of the Three, related to one another in various ways as origins and/or originateds. *K.* Thus there would be three Persons in one God, really distinct, really having their origins from one another, yet God would be absolutely, perfectly, transcendently One.

THE FOURTH STEP: IS IT MERELY ANALOGY?

IV. The final step is to apply the analogy seriously. That is, the above steps have indicated no more than that human consciousness provides a very good comparison, helping us find in our own experience items which seemed utterly strange and baffling when we heard them proposed only as doctrines about God. But to apply the analogy with full seriousness, to make it the key to a systematic account of the Trinity, is to go on to the further possibility that this analogy might be more than just a helpful example. It might in some real way be true of God.

For other analogies, such a suggestion would be nonsense. No one thinks God is a shamrock or a quantity of water, steam or ice, no matter how enlightening those comparisons might prove. No teacher means to suggest either that God is a fountain or a lamp. But in sober reality philosophers do hold that God knows and God wills. In sober reality, God is supreme intelligence and perfect understanding. Now perfect understanding is obviously something very different from what any of us mortals do. But perfect understanding is still truly understanding.

Because our understanding is imperfect, it always has to be on the move. It goes through steps and stages. There could be no steps or stages in God.

Moreover, we need to express our understanding to ourselves because we do not really possess the thing which we understand. It is not a part of our mind. But God does possess all God understands. Nothing is outside God's mind. God already is all the perfection of being.

But granted all that, and granted that infinite intelligence would not have to leap over gaps of any kind, cannot God's infinite act of understanding still truly express itself to itself? Cannot God's choosing issue from the understanding he so expresses? We do not know. But if it is so in God, then infinite expression proceeds from the infinite act of understanding, distinct from it, but with no gaps between them, and so perfectly that the infinite expression contains all the infinite perfection of the act of understanding itself, which is God himself. The expression of the infinite act of understanding would be an infinite expression, like the act itself in everything except that it would not be the act, but an expression of the act. And the loving choice of the Idea of Being (content of the infinite act of understanding) would be an infinite embracing of infinite truth as value, just as it is, and yet the choice would be, as choice, distinct from that which is chosen. Without gap, without motion or change or growth, in one divine consciousness, expression would issue from understanding and approving choice issue from both—eternally.

Since what has been described could be looked on as God's making of himself, the closest analogy to it among all human acts of insight and decision lies in the moments when we existentially face the question of who we are and, by our existential decision, determine and implement the answer as to who we shall be.[10]

Such a proceeding of understanding from understanding and love from both could then reasonably be thought of as occurring in God. Whether the proceedings do occur or not, however, reason has no way of knowing. Still, there may be indications from revelation that this is a fact. The use of the term "the Word" for the second Person in the New Testament and in tradition, as well as the linking of the Spirit with Love in the same sources, may be such indications.

If it is a fact, then all the doctrines on the Trinity can be understood as a unified whole. Then infinite intelligent consciousness, the understanding of everything about everything, expresses that understanding (= itself) to itself in an infinite Word. That consciousness as *expressing* the understanding is not the consciousness as *doing* the understanding; the expressed is not the expresser. Yet both are one consciousness, perfectly self-possessed. Each is infinite intelligent actuality, reality, being. But infinite intelligent being is a person. Moreover, consciousness, having understood and expressed reality to itself, chooses and loves in accordance with the reality perceived, again in an infinite act of intelligent self-consciousness. But that which proceeds, as proceeding, is not that from which it proceeds. Yet the proceeding love, as infinite and perfect, matches—has all the content of—that from which it proceeds and is its equal in every way.

There can be only two such processions, for there can be only one infinite act of understanding everything about everything and only one infinite act of approving that understanding.[11] Two processions can terminate in only two who proceed; so God is a Trinity, not a quaternity or more.

By this analogy, moreover, it is clear why only the Son is said to be begotten.[12] Being generated or begotten means being brought into the same nature as the one who is begetting. But the ultimate definition of God's nature, insofar as our philosophy can achieve one, is that God is the unrestricted act of understanding (*Insight* 677). Therefore his formulating his understanding to himself is aimed at the existence of what is of the same nature as himself, whereas his embracing of that knowledge in love aims not at understanding but at being.

Finally, this account is not a rationalism which would demonstrate the Trinity from human reason, because this is all pure hypothesis.[13] Its reality depends on whether or not God truly has a "dynamic consciousness,"[14] that is, whether God somehow experiences an exigence to express his knowledge in a Word. God certainly cannot be proved to need a concept or a word as we need one. All the reasons we need one are rooted in imperfections in our way of knowing. Potency is the root of our dynamism, in the sense that potency always means there is room for more. But in God there is no potency and never any room for more.

Does God have a dynamic consciousness? We do not know. Faith only tells us there is a Trinity of Persons; and the analogy of our dynamic consciousness is very helpful in our conceiving for ourselves what that could possibly be like and possibly mean. For those concerned about the understanding of the faith, that is enough for the day.

THE TRINITY AND THE FUNCTIONAL SPECIALTIES

The foregoing simply exemplify briefly some of Lonergan's contributions to the theology of the Trinity. The writings in which he made those contributions can be seen as living examples of the "functional specialties" of his later work, *Method in Theology*. His systematic treatise, aimed exclusively at understanding, is "Systematics." His "dogmatic" treatise, insofar as it is over-all an effort to specify exactly what the doctrines are to which he feels obliged and committed as a Catholic, is the functional specialty of "Doctrines."

The choice of doctrines is made from the sweep of possibilities reviewed in "Dialectic" (cf. *Method*). He practices the dialectic in his survey of the other positions within the *Pars Analytica* some of which was translated into English as *The Way to Nicaea*. Here he both satisfied himself as to why so many other opinions have prevailed as to the proper expression of the doctrine and has set the direction of his own basic choice.[15]

The "Foundations" step is made when he reviews the fundamental choice he made in committing himself to this thinking part of this faith community. That step is performed in *Insight*. There Lonergan sets up the expectation that a religion will present revealed mysteries to be believed. He specifies the role that such mysteries will play in the psychological, moral and intellectual development of an intelligent human being. Thus he lays down for himself the norms by which he will make his choice, by applying these Foundations, among the possibilities revealed in Dialectic. Here too, in the foundational work of *Insight*, he specifies the reality which is to be attributed to the religious and dogmatic affirmations of any treatise on such a mystery.

What of the first three functional specialties? Research, interpretation, history, besides being the general background of his works, are found directly and as his own work exclusively only in the treatise on the Verbum in St. Thomas.[16] There he sets out to establish a single point of interpretation: What is the point of the Trinitarian psychological analogy for Aquinas? This requires reconstructing the intellectual history of a certain question in a certain period, and so he does the research and the history as well as the interpretation.

Finally, he practiced the specialty of Communications by writing, editing and publishing the books.

NOTES

[1]*De Deo Trino II. Pars Systematica*, Caput I Sectiones 3–4, esp. pp. 24f.
[2]The book is *De Deo Trino I. Pars Dogmatica*.
[3]*De Deo Trino I. Pars Dogmatica*.
[4]*DDT II, Pars Systematica*, Caput VI, De divinis missionibus.
[5]*DDT II*, Quaestio XI, Quo sensu Deus sit Persona.
[6]*DDT II*, Quaestiones XXIX–XXXII.
[7]*DDT II*, p. 11.
[8]A footnote on the first page of the first of the Verbum articles was a very

helpful orientation to the main point of the project. The note illustrated the common misunderstanding of Thomas' analogy with a citation from Billot: "et omnino simile est in sensibus." In spite of the fact that this position is supported by "Scotus, Scotistae, et non pauci alii qui tamen se S.Thomam sequi credant" (DDT II, p. 69), "re vera omittitur id ipsum secundum quod invenitur similitudo inter Deum trinum et intellectum humanum; quo omisso, multum quidem laboratur, multum disputatur, at nihil clarum concluditur" (*ibid.*). ("By Scotus, the Scotists, and even by very many who sincerely believe they are following St. Thomas," "in fact it leaves out the very point where the resemblance between the human intellect and the triune God is to be found; and once that is left out, no matter how hard one works, no matter how long one argues, no clear conclusion can ever be reached." The note is unfortunately omitted in the book *Verbum*.

[9]For the first three steps, cf. DDT II., pp. 68–92.

[10]*DDT II*, pp. 90–91.

[11]*DDT II*, Assertum II.

[12]*DDT II*, Assertum III.

[13]For the fourth step, cf. *DDT II*, Quaestio II. Utrum naturali rationis lumine demonstrari possit in Deo esse Verbum, and the next note (14).

[14]*DDT II*, pp. 28, 82, 84–5, 104–107.

[15]*The Way to Nicaea*, translated by Conn O'Donovan from the First Part of *De Deo Trino* (1964) Philadelphia: Westminster, 1977

[16]*Verbum: Word and Idea in Aquinas*, ed. David Burrell (London: Darton, Longman and Todd, 1960).

Quentin Quesnell

IX. Grace

"The love of God is poured forth in our hearts by the Holy Spirit who is given to us" (Rom 5:5). This is the key to all of Lonergan's writings on grace. In this phrase he recognizes the transformation of human living of which not only Paul but the rest of the New Testament speaks with such enthusiasm.

Here is the ground of every human experience of "falling in love with God," which Lonergan so eloquently describes in *Method in Theology*. Here is the core of conversion, the study of which is to be the center of all significant theology in the future.

Lonergan's best known treatment of this is in the numerous scattered references and asides in *Method*. There, although he is not focusing on an integrated account of grace, but exclusively on the notion of method itself, he nevertheless drops frequent intriguing hints about this central religious reality. He speaks of the added factor in human experience which makes theology a distinct science; of the mystical specialization of consciousness and the meaning of prayer; of conversion and falling in love with God. Comparing this reality to its Christian technical expression gives him his most prominent example of "basic special categories" and "derived special categories."

But it would be a mistake to suppose that the unintegrated exposition of *Method* indicates a "later Lonergan" slowly breaking his way through from sterile intellectualism to an awareness of this important topic. Lonergan has been writing about this all through his life, and he has treated it in a fully integrated way in three places: the "Gratia Operans" articles, *Insight* and the Latin notes "De Ente Supernaturali."

THE GRATIA OPERANS ARTICLES

"St. Thomas on Gratia Operans" was the title of a series of articles in *Theological Studies,* based on Lonergan's own doctoral dissertation for the Gregorian University. "Gratia Operans" is merely the technical term in

Scholastic theology for the phenomenon we have been discussing: it is grace operating to transform a sinner into a friend of God. This is what the Church understands by God's promise in Ezekiel to "take away your heart of stone and give you instead a heart of flesh" (Ez 36:26). This is the phenomenon which Aquinas describes as "the greatest work of God," "greater than creation itself" (Summa Theologiae I-II, 113, 9).

In the "Gratia Operans" articles, Lonergan focused on this phenomenon. His main concern there was to show that his own doctrine concerning it was identical with the doctrine of St. Thomas. That required a careful historical study of the situation in which Thomas wrote on grace. But the most important confirmation of Lonergan's interpretation lay not in merely piling up proof texts from Aquinas' works, but in showing, in instance after instance, how, using Lonergan's interpretation, Thomas' solutions to most of the classical problems of theology made better sense and fitted together into a more integrated whole than they did following any other interpretation. The articles demonstrate this in regard to the classical questions of grace and free will, divine foreknowledge and predestination, sufficient and efficacious grace, habitual and actual grace, and the numerous other subdivisions of actual grace usually listed by theologians, as well as all the questions centering on how God influences human actions (various kinds of premotion, middle knowledge, etc.).

It is impossible to summarize all that accurately here, but the general pattern can be sketched. As in *Insight* Lonergan had shown that the key to all knowledge lay in understanding what it is to understand, so in these articles he demonstrates that a thorough grasp of this one transforming reality of "operating grace," the phenomenon called "justification" or "the infusion of sanctifying grace" or "God's love poured forth in our hearts," contains the answer to all the questions on grace that have vexed theologians through the centuries. The pattern of the individual answers typically involves application of the method sketched in *Insight* (387–390; 524–525) and *Method in Theology* (343–344). Theological affirmations are tested for what they imply on being, truth and objectivity. Then wielding the two-edged sword of position/counter-position, where the content of a true judgment "is determined by intelligent grasp and reasonable affirmation and, after affirmation, by nothing else" (*Insight* 560), he distinguishes pseudo questions from real questions, makes the structural transpositions into concrete propositions and explanatory formulations required for metaphysical equivalence (*Insight* 502–507) and lets the faith-propositions themselves stand forth in new clarity and simplicity.

The actual presentation of the details is metaphysical and very technical, using the thought-patterns and the objective language of Scholasticism. It has to be passed over here. For a short summary of Lonergan's answers to several of the main issues in philosophical terms, the interested reader may consult pp. 661–664 of *Insight* ("in the eighteenth place" with its corollaries, and "in the twenty-first place").

THE TREATMENT OF INSIGHT

The second principal organized treatment of this central religious reality is in *Insight*. *Insight* contains so many things, so fully treated, that readers occasionally forget the clear words of the Introduction, that "the aim of the book is to issue an invitation to a personal, decisive act" (xix). "Up to that decisive achievement, all leads. From it, all follows" (xviii). That decisive act is "the appropriation of one's own rational self-consciousness" (xxviii).

The Introduction deliberately does not state clearly, however, that "rational self-consciousness" is only Lonergan's term for "moral self-consciousness," that is, for the state of mind in which one wonders, What ought I to do? What ought I to make of myself? (599–600). It is the state of mind of one aware that in every deliberate action, "each of us is engaged in publishing the one and only edition of ourselves."[1]

The book *Insight* then is aimed at bringing the reader to a full, personal awareness of oneself as an existential person, in one's own existential situation, fully aware of the problem of one's own moral deficiencies and confronted with the question of how fully to embrace the religious solution which alone can solve that problem. Through many prior stages, the book labors to help the reader appropriate all the other levels of consciousness which moral decision presupposes. But the end always remains to make the reader vividly aware that full self-appropriation "demands the transformation of self-reliant intelligence into an intelligence searching for faith (intellectus quaerens fidem)" (731).

The theologically alert reader knows this is the realm of grace. In the theological Epilogue to *Insight* Lonergan implicitly confesses that chapter 20 was written with the theological doctrine of grace in mind (744). Yet the word "grace" never occurs in the body of *Insight*.[2]

Grace cannot be described philosophically. But a philosophy firmly grounded in human consciousness can describe the anguish of a consciousness always and necessarily in movement toward a goal beyond its attainment. And such a philosophy can describe the bewilderment of an existence in which sensitive awareness, intellectual awareness and moral awareness are combined in a single self-questioning consciousness.

Such a philosophy can clearly chart the path of human development. It can make clear the inner need we have to be true to ourselves, maintain integrity, achieve authenticity. It can show that just as this inner need drives us to understand in accordance with the data and to judge in accordance with the evidence, so too it constrains us to choose, decide and act in accordance with that which we have actually judged to be the intelligent and reasonable and right course of action.

The same inner drive which makes us want to understand our experiences and makes us want to check out whether our insights were correct eventually reveals itself as a moral obligation when we move to questions of deciding and doing. For we cannot live at peace with ourselves if we do not choose and act in accordance with what we know to be true. When our minds have formed the honest judgment that this action or that is the intelligent and reasonable thing to do in this situation, then we cannot do the opposite without damage to our inner integrity—a damage of which we are fully aware.

Thus disjointed consciousness becomes bad conscience. That consists in knowing that this is what we really ought to be doing—not because some law says so or some superior has ordered it, but because we see that this is exactly what the situation calls for—and then refusing to do it.

But such a disjointed consciousness is familiar to us all. It is the human situation. "I see the better, and choose the worse." "The evil that I would not, that I do" (Rom 7:19). It is in theological terms the need for grace; but Lonergan's philosophy can describe it as the well-known human phenomenon it is.

Lonergan's philosophy can even account more precisely for why this is such a common human experience. For this he turns to the process of development itself. Our knowing is always in development. But making the right moral choices presupposes that development completed. Right moral choices are made by balanced individuals who accurately understand themselves and the world about them. But none of us begins life as an individual of that sort. We do not begin in possession of the development which only living itself can furnish us with. We begin as a self which is the center of its own universe and only gradually do we come to perceive another self which we could—and know we should—become (473–474).

Another way of accounting for the gap between human knowing and human moral performance is through an analysis of the process of willing and choosing itself. Besides the act of willing, there is in each of us the habitual state of consciousness behind the act, the state called "willingness." There are many things each of us is perfectly capable of doing, but which it would never enter our heads to do. Our education, our surrounding culture and environment, our personal tastes and past experience have simply left some doors closed to us. Those things, while not physically impossible, are beyond the range of our personal "antecedent willingness," and because they are beyond that range, we are simply not ready to do them.

Now the range of human intelligence extends to all that could possibly be known. So it is quite possible that our understanding and judgment will make clear that something ought to be done, but the something we have envisioned with our minds will be so out of the range of our personal "antecedent willingness" that we will turn away from any possibility of acting in accordance with what we have seen.

Are examples needed? Let us draw them from the safe realm of the past. Surely some eighteenth century Spanish gentlemen, challenged publicly to defend their honor in a duel, had the intelligence to see the disproportion between a spoken insult and the loss of one—perhaps two—human lives. Almost certainly some one or other slave-owner, in the long history of human slavery, must have perceived the unreasonable nature of buying and selling fellow human beings. Such insights and judgments, however, could not result in proportionate decisions and actions so long as lack of antecedent willingness made them seem no more than idle fantasies.

The fully successful human life requires an habitual antecedent willingness which leaves us actually open and ready to embrace the good wherever it may reveal itself. Lonergan calls this "universal antecedent willingness" and says it must be as broad and as deep as the range of the pure desire to know. That means it must leave us ready for anything. Moreover, if it is to be effective, it must be combined as well with a sensitivity and intersubjectivity which are disciplined enough to enable us to move firmly, joyously toward the good revealed in true judgments.

Where is such perfect willingness to come from? It does not demand any revelation to show that such a state of mind is not a common human possession. Lonergan's philosophy has as one of its basic principles the intelligibility of the universe. But a world where "horses act like horses, fish act like fish, but men act like damfools" is not fully intelligible. Something is lacking. There are loose ends here, which can be tied together only by looking to another higher integration, comparable to the way biology is a higher integration of loose ends of chemistry and physics, intelligence as a higher integration ties together the loose ends of sensitive experience, and judgment, as a higher integration, ties together the loose ends of spontaneous insights.

Is there a higher integration beyond human knowing and willing? Is there an explanation of why, in spite of the weaknesses just discussed, some human beings do seem to live lives which actually are examples of sustained development, even though the odds are against it? Must not philosophy wonder then why some human beings seem to choose and love all the right objects of virtue long before they could possibly have reasoned themselves into the correct theoretical positions to justify their choice? (As a matter of fact, often while intellectually clinging quite tenaciously to some of Lonergan's dreaded "counterpositions".)

Again, we are at the edge of the realm of grace. Philosophy cannot say directly why individuals occasionally seem to escape the "moral impotence" which is the human lot. But it can sketch the sort of "higher integration" which would meet the problem, and which therefore one might expect an intelligently ordered universe to provide.

Lonergan does such a sketch in chapter 20 of *Insight*. There solving the problem would require that God introduce new habits into the individual's intellect, will and sensitivity, habits which would arise, not as "the result of accumulated insights, for such accumulation takes time, and the problem arises because man has to live during the interval in which insights are being accumulated" (697).

Such habits, freely given by God, without the preceding labor of understanding and judgment, will provide the higher integration which a consciousness in development needs. That higher integration will touch on all which needs healing in the individual's mind and sensitivity. But its essential and central element will be the universal antecedent willingness which makes us ready to embrace whatever action is called for in the actual universe. This is a willingness ready to embrace all of being. And Lonergan has no trouble showing that in fact such willingness is identical with the love of God above all things and all other things for the sake of God (698–699).

Thus, God's gift, solving the individual's problem of moral impotence, is a gift of a habit of universal love. In fact, in an imperfect universe where there is already a rule of sin, this habit will dispose those who receive it to "love all men with a self-sacrificing love," ready "to love their enemies," and "to return good for evil" (699).

Finally, can one say that *Insight* is describing grace? No, it is describing only certain observable human needs, and it is speculating on how an intelligent, loving and all-powerful God might be expected to alleviate them. The solution Lonergan envisages will, he thinks, be "universally accessible" (696) but will be provided to human beings individually only "through their apprehension and with their consent" (697), according to the standard pattern, by which higher integrations do not violate underlying patterns of operation (451f). How many persons in fact do apprehend the solution and consent to it so as to receive its benefits? Reason alone can affirm only that men and women will do this "in accord with the probabilities" (698).

DE ENTE SUPERNATURALI

For a direct treatment of the reality Lonergan has been pointing toward in these most general terms, we must leave the attitude and the language of philosophy alone and move to a theological viewpoint. But a theological viewpoint is always the viewpoint of some specific religion and phrased in the terminology of some specific religion. In Christian terms, then, the reality behind the account of *Insight* is grace. Grace, in the Christian tradition, provides and achieves everything called for in chapter 20 of *Insight*, and more. The chapter in fact ended with a philosophic speculation that the reality might be more—much more—than had been described. "In the thirty-first place" Lonergan clarifies that an actual solution which provided the needed higher integration and nothing more would be only a minimum. Such a solution "would not offer to charity more than the perfection of a total self-sacrificing love in a creature for his or her creator" (725). But the actual solution could be more and do more. What that more would be remains beyond the power of philosophical reason even to guess.

In *De Ente Supernaturali*, then, Lonergan proceeds to speak of this reality, the solution offered, in purely Christian language. It is a solution that does provide the higher integration called for in chapter 20 of *Insight*, but which also provides much more, far exceeding the minimum human needs. The Christian language Lonergan uses here is explicitly that of the Roman Catholic tradition. Systematic theology is the attempt to state exactly what the doctrines of a given religious tradition mean. It would make no sense to try to do that without using the language of the tradition itself.

Here the doctrine, the revealed mystery of faith to be understood, is stated in *the first thesis*. "There exists a created communication of the divine nature, by which in created beings there occur actions which attain God as he is in himself." Such a created communication or sharing of the divine nature is found, as faith teaches, in Christ, who is God incarnate, and in the Beatific Vision, the perfect union of the blessed with God in heaven, where "we shall be like him, for we shall see him as he is" (I Jn 3:2). But Lonergan's concern here is with the actions by which in this life ordinary human beings actually "attain God as he is in himself"—that is, above all with the Christian virtue of charity.

Charity in Catholic teaching is the habit of loving God above all things and loving all things because one loves God. By it one loves God as he is in himself and loves one neighbor as oneself. Why does that imply a created communication of the divine nature? Ultimately, because "God is love" (I Jn 4:16). Therefore, "whoever abides in love, abides in God and God in him" (*ibid.*). Love is the heart and soul of the transformed life which is called "sharing the divine nature" in 2 Peter 1:4. "The love of God, poured forth in our hearts by the Holy Spirit" (Rom 5:5) is the identical love which unites us with God in the next life, according to the Catholic understanding of I Corinthians 13:8–13, where "love never fails" though other gifts "pass away," "cease," "lose their meaning," "come to an end."[3]

The second thesis places this datum of faith into the perspective of "the theorem of the supernatural" (cf. *Insight* 742; *Grace and Freedom*, p. 16).

This is the suggestion that such a created communication of the divine nature, making it possible to love God as he is in himself, exceeds the powers not only of human nature, but of any conceivable created nature. It is "absolutely supernatural." This theorem, he says, is "the rule and source" of all else in the treatise. It is the principle around which a treatise on grace can be systematically organized. Like similar theorems in other treatises (*Insight* 742) it is not itself a datum of faith, any more than the theorems organizing empirical sciences are data of experience. It is an insight, expressed in a definition: "Let us mean by supernatural that which . . . " It can then be used to clarify and put order into the available (revealed or empirical) facts.

The theorem of the supernatural was worked out in the early 13th century. It was a breakthrough in theology, which finally made it possible to escape innumerable logical squabbles over grace and freedom. For centuries theologians had worried over the question: How could one be bound to do something that was not within one's power? Either the love of God above all things was in one's power—and then there was no need for grace (= the Pelagian heresy)—or the love of God was not in one's power, and then it could hardly be the criterion of one's being saved or lost.

With the notion of the absolutely supernatural, it became possible to say that perfect charity could be needed to live a good human life, even though it was beyond nature's power. Something beyond nature's power and expectation could be provided by God freely, as a gift from friend to friend. "One is free to do not only what lies within one's own personal power, but also all that one can accomplish through the kindness of friends. Now God makes himself our friend, and makes available to us the gift of his love. Therefore we are free—with his help—to love him as we ought. And since his help will always be given to those who ask it, there is nothing repugnant about our being obliged to such love."

Here, in this notion of a gift beyond the reach of any created nature, also lies the "extra" which God's actual solution grants over and above the minimum necessary which *Insight* 20 described. The details of what that extra provides, however (divine friendship, divine fatherhood, divine indwelling, the seal of the Spirit, the union of the Body of Christ, the face to face vision of God, etc.) can be known only from revelation. They cannot be concluded by reason, not even theological reason. Therefore Lonergan considers it an abuse of the theorem of the supernatural that it was gradually extended to imply the existence of a new and invisible world of otherwise unknowable entities: a world of the "merely entitatively supernatural," where human beings in grace acted pretty much the way everyone else does and even for the same motives, but where their acts, because performed in grace, have about them some new wonderful quality perceptible to God alone (or to God and his recording angel), making them worthy of eternal life.

Lonergan himself uses the theorem of the supernatural to account for divine love in human experience and to explain the relation of that love to other conscious, deliberately chosen, morally good actions. He rejects the traditional, almost universal, extension of it to a world of unknowable (unconscious) human spiritual realities. "It is hard to admit some quality within our own acts of knowing and willing which is unknowable to us except by divine revelation. Knowing and willing by their nature are knowable and known to the one who is knowing and willing." "To postulate such an unknown quality is really to do damage to the faith. For it is to claim that Christ died in order to put this unknown, invisible quality into our acts; to claim that God will give eternal life, not because our actions are good, but because they are decorated with this unknowable extra quality." "Those who defend such a position with the cry of 'mystery' are in fact appealing to a mystery which was never revealed by God but concocted by speculating theologians" (Third thesis, second scholion).

This point becomes the central issue in *the third thesis*. This thesis explains that if a conscious, deliberate, morally good action is done for the end of possessing God as he is in himself (in belief that such an end is possible and with hope of attaining it), then that action is absolutely supernatural, just as truly as charity itself is. The reason is that all conscious, deliberate acts are done for some end or goal, and that a consciousness oriented toward God as last end (= in love with God) is also moving toward God in all its choices of intermediate goals. That ultimate orientation to God, and not any mysterious extra quality or unconscious "elevation," is what makes all such conscious acts absolutely supernatural. The difference is in the intelligent, known, deliberate over-all orientation of one's life. There is a significant and experiential difference between a life which places God as the highest value and one that places anything else there. It is with that difference that the Christian theology of grace is concerned.

At this point it might be well to take account of an objection sometimes heard from readers of *Method in Theology*. Many claim that they have no personal experience of "being in love with God," that here Lonergan seems to slip away from the concrete world in which he usually moves so surely. The objection would probably arise in regard to this thesis too. Where and when does this conscious, deliberate orientation to God above all and in all actually occur in normal living?

Two observations have to be made. First, the love of which he speaks, though conscious, does not have to be formulated in Christian, personal terms in order to solve the problems of human moral weakness. In the minimum form, demanded by the sketch in *Insight*, it is a love of God as "the unrestricted act of understanding," the active intelligibility of the universe. The person consciously and deliberately oriented toward knowing the truth and living up to it as fully as possible is already in love with God under another name (683–84; 698–99). The problem of "salvation outside the Church" is not a relevant issue here.

The second observation is one that Lonergan makes elsewhere while writing about the indwelling of the Holy Spirit: "A power or a habit is known through the concrete acts that flow from it, and to know the real extent of a power, one starts by examining the greatest and best of those acts. Thus, although new-born infants are truly human beings and so are people who are sleeping and people who are sick or insane or about to die, still they are not the ones we normally go to first when we want to investigate what human nature is capable of. In the same way, while it is true that infants can be in the state of grace and so can people who are asleep and people who regularly deliberately commit venial sins and even people who are just on the verge of mortal sin, still it is not reasonable to try to get a sense of the divine indwelling by going only or chiefly to people like those. What the divine indwelling is can be better seen in each person the more that person is one who lives not for self but for Christ, who lives in Christ, who is 'in the spirit,' etc." (*De Deo Trino, Pars Systematica (II)*, Assertum xviii).

In other words, the logical place to look for concrete examples of being in love with God is at the lives of persons generally recognized as outstanding examples of such love: the saints of the past and saintly people of the present who give the world pause by instances of self-sacrificing love. The place to look in our own lives is not when we are busy, distracted, worried, excited, bored, but at times of special recollection, when, deliberately pondering questions of what life is all about, we set goals for ourselves in time and perhaps for eternity. The time too is in moments of special crisis, when we are forced to a judgment and a personal articulation of our own values. For instance, when we reject some opportunity because to take it would conflict seriously with our moral values, or when we undertake some long and difficult project at considerable cost to ourselves, because we hope it will benefit others, many of whom we may never have met.

It is at such moments of fully deliberate existential self-determination that questions about one's ultimate objective are pertinent and possible. And it is from the direction we give ourselves at such times of coolly deliberate choice that our ultimate love must be judged.

Clearly the fire of God's love will burn higher in some than in others. But by examining notable instances it will be easier to say whether or not it is there in our own lives at all. As *Method in Theology* describes it,[4] it is quite to be expected that in the ordinary life this love is present more as a quiet undertow than as a raging fire; and that one may discover it perhaps only after many years to have been the ultimate governing reality in one's existence, behind all one's thoughts and choices. This would be particularly true of persons not raised within a religious tradition that can help them speak ("basic special categories": *Method* 281–292) of their own deepest hunger and that can give them a name ("derived special categories": *ibid.*) for the object of that hunger (cf. *Insight* 683–84; 665–66).

At any rate, Lonergan's point in thesis three is that the love and other good actions which count are realities of consciousness, not magical, invisible, unknowable; not only entitatively supernatural.

Thesis four argues that the actions of intellect and will of which we have been speaking—acts of the love of God above all and acts which direct us to other ends because God makes them lovable—are realities which can be produced in us by God alone. We cannot orientate ourselves to God as he is in himself. An act of love that does so orientate us to him and that then colors all our other acts and choices is a love that is produced in us by him. Any absolutely supernatural action we do is God's action in us.

In thesis four, especially Scholion Two, this doctrine is defended as an inevitable conclusion from the datum of faith and from the notion of the supernatural, once that notion is formulated. All the efforts of theologians to create intermediaries whereby the actions can instead be produced by *us* with God's *help* (first and second pre-motions, intrinsically efficacious grace, elevation, etc.) are shown to be implausible metaphysical double-talk. The flat admission that certain actions are produced in us by God is "the elegant and very simple solution taught by St. Thomas and overlooked by theologians ever since Scotus" (Scholion 2, #99).

The final orientation of will produced in us by God is the gift of God's love "poured forth in our hearts by the Holy Spirit who is given to us" (Rom 5:5). With that gift come other infused habits which make it easy and natural to produce other acts of other virtues. Finally a series of scholia to thesis 4 examine its relation to "the natural desire for the vision of God" (which Lonergan defends in the same way Thomas Aquinas does) and the general metaphysics of how divine and human operations interrelate.

Thesis 5 proposes that all deliberate, conscious actions of a person who has chosen God as end are so influenced by that basic decision (produced in us by God) that those actions themselves fulfill all the traditional descriptions of "actual grace." That is, actual graces are not mysterious, invisible extra beings sent out from God to help us (how?) do good actions. The actual graces are our own intellectual and volitional acts, insofar as these stand under the influence of the last end we have chosen. Both the orientation to the end and the individual acts are absolutely supernatural, God's gift, though in different ways. Charity reveals God's grace possessed as a habit; the resulting individual actions are grace-in-act, which is what "actual grace" really means.

The fifth is the last thesis. Thus Lonergan has substituted five short, clear, systematic theses for the elaborate structure of the typical Scholastic course on grace.

Part of the shortening has been by intense concentration on the systematic question to the exclusion of all others. If he were to follow the pattern of what he did in the Trinity course, he would still have to supplement this systematic treatise with an account focused on "Doctrines," that is, a justification of his own way of formulating the basic doctrine held on faith alone. It would also require a "Dialectic" showing how the other theologies which have appeared through the centuries are errors to the left or the right of the "positional" development, that is, are "counter-positions," to be explained in terms of excessive influence from one side or another of "the polymorphic consciousness of man" (*Insight* 427).

Here Lonergan has focused on the heart of the matter: the existence of a divine gift of being able to love God above all things and all other things because we love God. That love is a divine gift, beyond our powers, which changes all the rest of life. It is a pre-disposition to acts of love which can embrace the universe that actually exists. This makes it possible to embrace the good wherever it reveals itself, without being trapped by selfish concerns over profit to oneself.

This pre-disposition—the infused habit of charity—is granted to all adults who are not in the state of mortal sin. But it works itself out in manifest actions "in accord with the probabilities" (*Insight* 698). There are the saints; there are high moments of even ordinary lives, where the orientation will be the conscious center of attention. But then there is also the rest of life as well, where its presence will be only that of a general, remote orientation, not adverted to so much as taken for granted. Then it will govern the rest of life the way the final destination of a trip along a highway remains the whole point and purpose of the trip without keeping the traveler from attending to many other things along the way.

The Christian life is a succession of acts trying to carry through that high orientation given us by God. Those acts by which we live the Christian life are themselves what Christian tradition has been referring to as "actual graces."

Lonergan has transposed the center of attention of the treatise on grace, turning it into a question of psychological reality. It concerns the making of existential decisions about oneself and one's orientation in life, rather than quibbles over myths and possible worlds. The unity of his theology is revealed in the fact that making such self-constituting existential reflections and decisions provides the basic analogy to the processions of the Son and the Spirit in his treatise on the Trinity (*De Deo Trino*, II. *Pars Systematica*, pp. 90–91).

RELATION OF THE THREE MAJOR EXPOSITIONS
IN TERMS OF METHOD IN THEOLOGY

The treatise *De Ente Supernaturali* is an example of the functional specialty of "Systematics," aimed exclusively at understanding the meaning of a doctrine that a given religious tradition holds as true and revealed. An important aspect of this understanding is ordering the material around a central theme and clarifying its relation to other faith doctrines. The language used in such an exposition is the language of the individual faith tradition: what *Method* calls "basic and derived special categories" (281–292). Here references to the infused habit of charity and the details of the Christian life are "basic special categories." References to sanctifying grace, the Holy Spirit, God to be loved and possessed as he is in himself, the beatific vision, the hypostatic union, are "derived special categories."

The "Gratia Operans" articles are an exercise in "Interpretation," trying to pin down the meaning of the text of Thomas on a given issue. This requires, as often, a background of work in "History," trying to analyze exactly the development of Christian thought in the periods before and after Thomas, as well as an accompanying "Dialectic" with at least the most prominent counter-positions on grace. The categories used are both "special"—proper to theology alone—and "general"—common to theology and philosophy.

Insight is where Lonergan does the work of "Foundations." This is the work of the converted thinker, fully aware of all the levels of consciousness, and open to whatever further reality is implied in his experienced orientation beyond the realm of proportionate being. Such a person tries to spell out exactly what concrete intelligibilities any proposed theological reality must possess. By sketching a "heuristic structure" of transcendent being, he offers himself "a set of alternative answers; and then through an appeal to the facts it becomes possible to settle which of the alternatives is correct" (*Insight* 696). Thus the same thinker will be able in Doctrines to select from the range of Dialectic on the basis of these Foundations (*Method* 282).

Insight is written in "general theological categories," that is, in philosophical and psychological language which can be used in laying down a general anticipatory sketch of theological reality as well. As Foundations, *Insight* does not specify what categories to use for any final answers, but only determines the degree of validity which may be assigned such categories (*Method* 298).

Very briefly, then, *Insight* sketches a question and the general nature of an answer in philosophic terms. *Method in Theology* gives the answer in general religious terms, intended to be applicable to any religious tradition. *De Ente Supernaturali* gives the answer in Christian belief terms; and "the

Gratia Operans" articles show that Lonergan's answer is the best interpretation of Aquinas' doctrine and the only solution to many classic theological problems. The theme of all four is the one from which we began: "The love of God is poured forth in our hearts by the Holy Spirit who is given to us" (Rom 5:5).

NOTES

[1]The Subject," in *A Second Collection,* p. 83.

[2]Except for the purely historical reference on p. 527.

[3]Those familiar with Scholastic theology will wonder whether Lonergan simply identifies sanctifying grace with the infused habit of charity. He touches the question directly only in an aside in paragraph 14 of Thesis I, saying it "does not touch the substance of the teaching, but only the way of ordering the material in a treatise on grace."

In fact, Thesis I does argue that God's giving us a love directed to himself implies so changing us as persons that his love can be in us. Thus he does conclude logically to a "principium remotum quo"—a basic principle in us by which such loving is possible: "just as if a cow actually understood something and made choices based on the understanding, you would not conclude simply, 'This cow understands and wills'; you would conclude, 'This cow has a mind,' and even 'Here is a cow's body informed with a rational soul' " (Thesis I, Quid sit creata communicatio, #12). Technically, sanctifying grace would be the change in us as persons (principium quo creatum, proportionatum et remotum); charity would be the habitual love. In this treatise, Lonergan leaves it at that.

For a further discussion of how actual loving implies that first we be changed into friends of God and of how that change in us is the external *terminus* which gives historical reality to the sending of the Spirit, one must consult the treatise on the Trinity (*II. Pars Systematica,* 234–35; 239–40; 256).

[4]P. 113.

X. Jesus, the Son of God

A CONTEXT:
RECOVERING THE FULL HUMANITY OF JESUS

The year 1951 marked the fifteen hundredth anniversary of the Council of Chalcedon. The spate of scholarly activity generated by that occasion has proved, in retrospect, to be the beginning of a sea-change being undergone by contemporary Roman Catholic Christology. What became clear first of all was the existence of a gap between the Christology of the then-current Latin seminary manuals and the teaching of the council whose doctrine they intended to systematize. If Chalcedon affirmed the full humanity as well as divinity of Jesus, the textbook tradition seemed to have favored the latter at the expense of the former. On the level of popular piety this imbalance fostered what Karl Rahner has called a crypto-monophysitism in which people imagined Jesus as a divine being in human garb. Hence there began, under Chalcedon's tutelage, a movement of recovering the full humanity of Jesus.

In its first phase, through the decades of the 1950's and 1960's, that movement operated on two fronts. On the first of these one made use of philosophical resources. Rahner, for example, employed a philosophical anthropology in an effort to develop the intelligibility of the doctrine of Chalcedon. Attempting to dispel any crudely mythological notion of a divine being intruding upon an otherwise indifferent world of human experience, he presented the hypostatic union as the point at which God's self-communication and human self-transcendence meet in uniquely perfect correspondence. Meanwhile, on the biblical front, New Testament scholars were highlighting the human features of the Gospel portrait of Christ—weariness, sorrow, ignorance, and the like—which the Christology of the manuals had tended to downplay and even explain away.

A second phase of the current retrieval of Jesus' full humanity began when Roman Catholic exegetes and systematic theologians absorbed and extended the results of the so-called "New Quest of the Historical Jesus" which had originated in 1953 among German Protestant students of Rudolf Bultmann. The liberation of Roman Catholic biblical scholars is a saga in itself.

Begun with Pius XII's hesitant approval of the historical critical method in 1943, and culminating in an Instruction of the Pontifical Biblical Commission in 1964, it released an enormous and fruitful wave of scholarship. Catholic biblical scholars were no longer bound to defend fundamentalist positions on the authorship and composition of biblical literature, nor were they any longer subject to strictures imposed by uncomprehending dogmatic theologians. Freed to probe the New Testament documents as expressions of the religious significance of Jesus rather than as factual biographies, they quickly immersed themselves in the methods of their discipline, form and redaction criticism and the like.

Besides advancing our grasp of the theologies and Christologies of the various New Testament documents as well as of the complex tradition process from which those documents emerged, this development also pointed scholars back to the origin of that process, to the one whose religious significance the growing tradition was attempting to articulate and communicate. Roman Catholics joined forces with others who were attempting, by means of historical-critical methods, a reconstruction of at least the main features of Jesus' ministry.

Two books, both of which appeared in their original languages in 1974, and both of which have become quite widely known, exemplify this phase of Roman Catholic Christology. In a work of astonishing erudition Edward Schillebeeckx set out to reenact the process which led from Jesus' ministry and the impact it made on the first disciples to the writing of the earliest Gospel, Mark. If the "New Quest" produced its first classic in 1956 with the appearance of Guenther Bornkamm's *Jesus of Nazareth*, Schillebeeckx' *Jesus. An Experiment in Christology* is surely the second. And if Bornkamm's work is a slender summary of results, Schillebeeckx invites his reader to work with him from data to results in a work of massive proportions.

1974 also saw the appearance of Hans Küng's *On Being A Christian*, notable for our purposes for the boldness with which it makes the historical Jesus the primary norm for Christian faith. There is, of course, an ambiguity in this move, for it seems to ignore the distinction between the actual figure who lived two thousand years ago and any historical reconstruction, the latter being always in principle subject to revision. Be this as it may, Küng's work certainly represents a climax of a sort to the movement we have been reviewing, from the crypto-monophysitism engendered by an ahistorical repetition of the language of Chalcedon to the recovery of the full humanity affirmed by that council, first in either philosophical terms or on the basis of the New Testament portrait of Christ and then on the basis of historical efforts to reconstruct the figure to whose religious significance the Gospel portrait attests.

One might wish to conclude this review of the recovery of the full humanity of Jesus in contemporary Roman Catholic Christology by suggesting the emergence of a third phase. Historians focus on the past, of course, but their own commitments and values play a significant role in how they interpret that past, and it is well to make the latter element of the historical enterprise explicit. Quite recently, then, there has occurred in various contexts an awakening to contemporary experiences of suffering, injustice, and oppression, experiences which have led theologians to articulate a self-criticism of the Christian tradition as well as to discover, precisely in reconstructions of the historical Jesus, resources for creative advance. In this respect the emergence of feminist Christologies and those of Latin American liberation theologians marks a third phase in which the recovery of Jesus' full humanity draws its impetus from a quest for a redemptively integral Christian praxis.

LONERGAN'S CHRISTOLOGICAL WORKS

The Writings. Fr. Lonergan first taught the prescribed seminary course on Christology in 1948 at Regis College, Toronto. He picked it up again in 1952 and, having moved to Rome the following year, repeated it biannually at the Gregorian University until 1965. Some years later, in 1971, Lonergan occupied a chair at Harvard, and while there he chose Christology as the topic of one of his two courses. From the Roman years we have three published works devoted to our topic. There is the major textbook, *De Verbo Incarnato,* running to just under six hundred pages. Much shorter is its companion piece, a monograph entitled *De constitutione Christi ontologica et psychologica.* The latter evoked criticism which Lonergan deemed worthy of a public response, and so there appeared an article, "Christ as Subject: A Reply." A decade later, after his return from Rome, Lonergan devoted a further article to "Christology Today: Methodological Reflections." These four publications comprise the chief data on Lonergan's direct contribution to contemporary Christology.

New Wine, Old Skins. The nineteenth century Jesuit professor and later cardinal J. B. Franzelin, composed a treatise which provided the basic model for subsequent Latin seminary manuals in Christology, and this is the genre which dictates the format of Lonergan's *De Verbo Incarnato.* He covers his material in seventeen theses; in each he states the thesis, defines its terms, determines its theological note (i.e., the degree to which the content of the thesis demands the assent of Catholics), lists its adversaries, and proposes his argument. The first ten theses focus on the dogma of the hypostatic union, first as contained in the New Testament, then as defined by the patristic councils, and finally as systematically interpreted in a predominantly metaphysical context. Four more theses develop the impact of the hypostatic union on the human nature involved in terms of the various gifts of grace with which Christ as human was fittingly endowed, the kinds of human knowledge, both special and ordinary, which he exercised, his sinlessness and freedom. A final three theses treat Christ's redemptive work.

As this outline indicates, Lonergan's textbook conforms to the requirements of the dogmatic manual of its day. The reader quickly discovers, however, that the content of Lonergan's course strains that format to the limit. Just a few examples can illustrate this point. Lonergan's first thesis, on the New Testament, offers a conventional initial list of adversaries ranging from Gnostics to Monophysites, but when he turns to consider more recent adversaries, his list expands into a discussion of the possibility of dogma as such, expatiates on the development of modern critical history out of its existential and narrative antecedents, and concludes that the radical problem posed by such figures as R. Bultmann and F. Buri lies not in the practice of history or exegesis but at the level of philosophy and method.

Lonergan's third thesis, on the unity of Christ's person, requires only two pages to prove its dogmatic point, but this is preceded by twenty-seven pages of pre-notes tracing the development of the question in patristic thought up to the Council of Chalcedon. A similar disproportion swells the material of the next thesis, on Christ's two natures, and when Lonergan turns from conciliar teaching to its theological systematization, he inserts a common preface to his three theses on the metaphysics of the hypostatic union. In this preface he devotes seventeen pages to clarifying the key metaphysical terms to be employed and another half-dozen pages on the range of understandings of the notion of person entertained from Peter Lombard to contemporary Scholastic theologians.

As we shall see, Lonergan's tenth thesis, on the consciousness of Christ, breaks through the conventional metaphysical context altogether, and when he later takes up the traditional doctrine on the various kinds of human knowledge in Christ (beatific vision, special infused and ordinary experiential knowledge), he treats his reader to a chain of sixty-eight direct quotations from authors beginning with Irenaeus and extending to Peter Lombard. One last example: the proof of the thesis devoted to Christ's human freedom requires only two pages, but Lonergan appends another eighteen pages in order to define and master the real problem involved in the matter.

If these examples suggest that Lonergan was laboring mightily to cram alien material into the neo-Scholastic tract, the reason for this lies in the fact that his own aims were at cross-purposes with those which governed the genre within which he had to work. The Scholastic manual comprised a set of theses to be demonstrated, an operation geared to attaining certitude in the possession of truth. For Lonergan, however, the chief aim of systematic theology was not certitude but understanding of what one knew by faith to be true. Again, the neo-Scholastic manual derived from a cultural context in which one attributed the permanence of truth to what were, in fact, historically-conditioned expressions or formulae, and so Lonergan typically prefaced his brief dogmatic demonstrations that the councils had defined what they had defined with lengthy pre-notes reintroducing those definitions into their original historical context. Lastly, the manuals assumed the possession of a perennially valid philosophy, and yet that philosophy was in concrete fact diverse, variously understood and misunderstood by the major figures in the Scholastic tradition. Hence Lonergan wielded the metaphysics derived in *Insight* from his intentionality analysis like Ockham's razor, slicing through the obscurities on which many a traditional dispute on matters like the definition of person often rested.

In several ways, then, in his effort to recall theology to its proper goal of understanding, in his endeavor to open theology up to modern historical scholarship, in his attempt to purify and revitalize the metaphysical context in which theology was conducted, Lonergan was attempting to pour new wine into old skins. The entire situation was, as he himself remarked not too much later, hopelessly behind the times, and its demands on the theologian were impossible.

No one could have foreseen how quickly the whole edifice of neo-Scholasticism was to collapse, and yet the past two decades have witnessed its virtual disappearance. In the article responding to the criticism evoked by his position on the psychology of Christ, Lonergan had found it obvious to remark that a new notion like that of the subject could not become useful for theology until it had been transposed into classical Scholastic categories. Today the opposite is the case, as progressively fewer theologians find themselves at home with those categories and the tradition from which they issued. If today Lonergan's Latin texts lie buried amid the rubble of neo-Scholasticism, many a valuable insight lies buried with them. To give but one example: the history of the period following upon Chalcedon is notoriously complex, and Lonergan was able to make sense out of its conflicts as moments in a process of groping for the analogous notion of a "real, minor distinction" between the two natures of Christ. But since the Scholastic doctrine of distinctions no longer occupies a place in the *lingua franca* of theologians, an illuminating insight like this will be helpful to very few.

Given the disappearance of the neo-Scholastic context, what remains of Lonergan's work during his years in Rome? Furthermore, since the moving viewpoint of *Insight* continued to develop, so that one can speak of earlier and later phases in Lonergan's thought, what further Christological advances did he make? To address these questions we may take our bearings from the most recent of his Christological writings, the article entitled "Christology

Today." From this perspective we shall first examine the more recent use he makes of the transposition of Chalcedon originally worked out in the tenth thesis of the Latin textbook and in the accompanying monograph. If this transposition develops the meaning of Chalcedon, we may, second, look into the methodological suggestions Lonergan offers as a route to the question of the truth of that meaning. Finally, we may determine where Lonergan stands within the general movement of contemporary Christology with which we began, the movement of recovering the full humanity of Jesus.

CHALCEDON TRANSPOSED

The Difficulty. Numerous voices in contemporary Western culture urge us to become full and authentic persons. This focus on becoming is a modern development; it was quite absent from medieval philosophy. The latter set forth a metaphysical analysis of our humanity which, in its doctrine of the soul and its powers, took the form of a faculty psychology. That doctrine simply prescinded from consciousness and thus from the dimension in which human becoming occurs. In modern times, however, German idealists took consciousness as the central category in constructing their various theogonies or systems of divine becoming, and existentialists followed through by focusing squarely on the process of free self-creation in which human beings find themselves ineluctably involved. Some psychologists, too, once the autonomy of their discipline was won, have taken a humanistic turn to propose the ideal of releasing one's affective and interpersonal potential in order to become a full, authentic person.

These developments have their shadow side. Insofar as contemporary culture also harbors forces which foster the formation of narcissistic, alienated individuals, a market has been created in which personhood can be rationalized as a commodity and a profit turned on the techniques which promise its attainment. Even this distortion bears witness to the fact that personhood is a value which has come into its own. A new context, phenomenological and psychological, has emerged in which being human is understood in terms of entering into interpersonal relations and developing in interaction with the humanly constructed world in which one finds oneself. Thus one becomes a human person.

The patristic councils promulgated the dogma that in Christ there was one divine person made known in two complete natures, one divine and the other human. The systematization of the dogma which became classical derives from Leontius of Byzantium, who drew the conclusion that while Christ possessed a complete human nature, that nature was of itself impersonal; there was in Christ no human person. Today, however, this statement can appear contradictory and implausible. Is it possible to affirm, with Chalcedon, that Christ lived a fully human life without being a human person?

The Latin Works. The issue had already begun to exercise Catholic theologians in the first half of the twentieth century, beginning perhaps with the Franciscan Déodat de Basly. As might be expected, the attempt to assimilate a novel issue into the neo-Scholastic context called forth a process of trial and error marked at first by no little befuddlement. Inept questions were posed, unclear concepts wielded, extreme positions reached, and obscure compromises suggested. By the 1950's the process had already evoked a papal encyclical recalling the parameters of orthodoxy in the matter.

At the time Lonergan came on the scene the issue was crystallized around the question of Christ's human knowledge. How could Christ on the one hand enjoy both the beatific vision and the special, infused knowledge attributed to him by the tradition and, on the other, possess a human consciousness historically conditioned and open to development like any other?

In that context Lonergan's approach was to pick up from the teaching of the Third Council of Constantinople. That council, following out the logic of Chalcedon's two natures, taught that in Christ there existed two wills and two natural operations. It followed, for Lonergan, that there likewise existed in Christ two consciousnesses.

How was this to be understood? Lonergan stressed the difference between the self-presence of the subject as subject and the intentional presence of objects, identifying these as two distinct, if inseparable, aspects of consciousness. He then invoked the metaphysical principle that the operations of a person belong to the person from its nature. Since these operations include conscious operations, it followed that there was to be found in Christ the fully human self-presence of the divine Son. And since, finally, such self-presence is a matter of experience rather than of understanding or judgment, since self-presence is a different matter from reflective self-knowledge, that human self-presence was compatible with the characteristics of openness and development emphasized by modern views of human consciousness. In this instance Lonergan's approach to the question of Christ's human self-knowledge proved quite similar to that of Karl Rahner, in that both, by distinguishing consciousness as experience from reflective knowledge, established room for a fully human consciousness of the divine person.

More Recently. In his Latin works Lonergan aimed to meet the demands of the modern turn to the subject by expanding the traditional theology of the hypostatic union. That theology had to be transposed from a strictly metaphysical context, in which the role of consciousness was neglected, to a psychological context. The project was, however, complicated by the necessity of articulating in the language of the Scholastic tradition the terms and relations proper to the new, psychological context. In the article on "Christology Today," however, Lonergan is able to take a simpler, more direct approach.

Fidelity to Chalcedon commits him to the position that since the person of Christ is divine, and since the divine person assumed a complete human nature, it is indeed possible for Christ to have lived a genuinely human life without being a human person. Fidelity to Chalcedon today, however, makes a further demand. The position must be made intelligible by showing how what it asserts is possible, by laying out what it means for a person who is, as person, divine and not human, to nonetheless lead a genuinely human life.

To meet this demand Lonergan develops the following statement: "The person of Christ is an identity that eternally is subject of divine consciousness and in time became subject of a human consciousness" ("Christology Today," p. 61). What is immediately obvious about Lonergan's statement is that while its meaning may be that of the conciliar dogmas, at least the language is just as clearly not. Lonergan has transposed the conciliar meaning into a context in which one speaks, not of substance, nature, will, and operation, but of identity, subject, and consciousness. What characterizes the latter set of terms, as opposed to the metaphysical concepts which comprise the first set, is that their meaning can be articulated by reflecting on our common experience of ourselves.

What does it mean to be a person? For Lonergan being a person involves first of all identity. Identity itself means, in some sense, oneness, and Lonergan renders that sense technically precise, employing his analysis of the components of human knowing to do so.

At the level of experience one encounters the oneness of a datum, of an instance of something, but what that something is remains to be grasped by understanding. Understanding in turn yields the oneness of an intelligible unity, but again there is a further step. Only critical reflection grasps the correlation of that understanding with the datum of experience, issuing in the judgment which posits the intelligible unity as real, as in fact itself and nothing else. It is, in Chalcedon's phrase, "one and the same," and to be such is its identity. Identity, then, designates the concrete existence of an actual individual, distinct from all others.

Being a person, then, means being an identity, but not every identity is a person. Furthermore, our experience of ourselves is an experience of change and difference as much as it is an experience of identity. We experience the obvious change that our biological advance from infancy through youth and beyond entails. The biological cycle in turn undergirds a far more crucial arena of development and difference, for as we master the conscious operations by which we move into the world mediated by meaning, the human world of the adult, we experience as well the intellectual, moral, and religious imperatives which call us to cognitive and real self-transcendence, and each of us forges a unique life's story out of our mix of fidelity and infidelity to those imperatives.

In our experience of ourselves we can locate the element of identity, for it is we ourselves and no other who undergo the changes wrought by the biological life-cycle and who forge ourselves by responding in varying degree to the imperatives of self-transcendence. Our identity as persons is that of the subject of the conscious operations by which our life's story is forged. And insofar as those conscious operations do in fact constitute a life's story, a story of real change and difference and yet a single story, they comprise the unique subjectivity of each of us.

This distinction between the subject and its subjectivity, derived from our self-experience, proves crucial to Lonergan's transposition of conciliar dogma. Once he has reached the distinction, it allows him to affirm without intrinsic contradiction that while Christ's identity is divine, that of the second person of the Trinity, the divine person became subject of a fully human subjectivity which, as Chalcedon would have it, was in no way confused or intermingled with the divine consciousness of which he was from all eternity subject. Given that fully human subjectivity, Christ as man possesses everything that the modern turn to the subject demands for a human being and possesses it in a fashion compatible with his identity as divine, not human, person.

METHOD AND THE TRUTH OF DOCTRINES

Modern Western culture has made the turn to the subject, an advance which brings with it a new set of conditions for the intelligibility of religious doctrines. It is this exigence for a development of intelligibility that Lonergan meets by transposing Chalcedon from an older, metaphysical context to a psychological one. At the present time, when personhood has emerged as a prominent cultural value, it seems initially to make no sense to affirm that one can be fully human without being a human person. Lonergan's careful, technically precise analysis demonstrates that, contrary to the commonsense impression one may initially glean, there is no contradiction or paradox involved in making such an assertion about Christ. Given Lonergan's transposition, the doctrine satisfies contemporary requirements for coherent meaning.

This achievement does not, of course, restore to the doctrine the plausibility it has lost in various quarters under the eroding influence of modern developments. Lonergan's transposition provides an instance of the sixth among the functional specialties which comprise his program for theological method, the specialty he calls doctrines. The work of that functional specialty corresponds to the cognitional level of judgment; it involves selecting those doctrines from the past which one deems true and articulating them in terms proper to the differentiation, beyond common sense and theory, of the realm of interiority. But the path to doctrines, and hence to the truth of Chalcedon, is long. In Lonergan's vision of theological method, it passes first from research through foundations.

What assistance does Lonergan offer one wishing to traverse that path in order to raise the question of the truth of the Chalcedonian doctrine? What light does he shed on theological method as it becomes specifically Christological? In answer to these questions we can note what Lonergan has to say, first, about the genesis of the Christological question, and then about the components of contemporary Christological method.

Beginning from Praxis. Christians recognize the New Testament as God's word, the outer word that gives shape and expression to the inner word of grace uttered in their hearts. As an outer word the New Testament thematizes a call to religious conversion. Hence it makes its appeal to the existential subject operating on the level of consciousness on which real, and not merely cognitive, self-transcendence is at stake.

The New Testament makes this appeal in a specific fashion. Surrender to what is transcendent in lovableness, to the holy mystery toward which the word, God, points, becomes a matter of discipleship. Surrender to the Father becomes a matter of following Christ. Thus the central concern of the New Testament is a radical, simple, personal, and above all practical message; Christ's call to follow him.

In the decision for discipleship one begins to surrender to transcendent love and to undergo the awakening to and transformation of all other values which authentic response to that love entails. But this primary, practical response engenders further response. Exegetes have traced the process by which simple acclamations like "Jesus is Lord" gave rise to further confessions, lengthier formulae, and eventually, to provide a context for them all, to the composition of the Gospels. This process exhibits the genesis of the Christological question from Christian religious praxis. If the primary message is a call to discipleship, a call to follow Christ, that call quickly begets the further question: Who is this Jesus?

Negotiating Historical Consciousness. The Gospels were called into being to answer the Christological question as it takes rise, on a personal and religious level, from the praxis of Christian discipleship. Their various answers in turn gave rise to further questions, and so the Christological process continued into the patristic era and, in the context of that era, generated the classical conciliar dogmas. These found systematic elaboration in medieval Scholasticism, and that synthesis remained a stable achievement until the Enlightenment. Today, however, the continuity of the Christological tradition has been interrupted, and so an older path to answering the Christological question has been barred.

As Lonergan puts it, stating the general case, "Scholarship builds an impenetrable wall between systematic theology and its historical religious sources . . . " (*Method in Theology*, p. 276). An earlier age could assume that the Gospels offered a straightforward account of the way things were; they recorded trustworthy first-hand or at most second-hand accounts of what Jesus had said on various occasions and what he did. When, more recently, that assumption began to be challenged, the line of defense lay in mounting arguments for the credibility of the biblical witnesses. Meanwhile, however, the discipline of history was undergoing a development which would leave that defensive stratagem high and dry, useless. For since the nineteenth century history has become critical. Instead of assessing the credibility of witnesses to determine whose account of the past is to be believed, historians have come to regard all remains of the past as evidence, data to be rendered intelligible by the historian's constructive, inventive hypotheses.

In this perspective the New Testament serves directly as evidence on the beliefs of the early Christian movement, while the actual sayings and deeds of Jesus become a matter of a complex and delicate process of inference. Thus, as one result of the shift to a critical stance, the nineteenth century has bequeathed to us the problems associated with the distinction between the "historical Jesus" and the "Christ of faith."

This development may be uncomfortable for the traditional self-understanding of Christian faith, nourished as this was by the first naiveté of a precritical view of history. Yet to resist this development today means a retreat into fundamentalism. Lonergan represents a different approach. Not only has the discipline of history taken a critical turn; it has also continued to develop. Most notably, historians since the nineteenth century have become critical not only of their sources but also of their own operations. Thus Lonergan can point out that the operations of historians may be determined by a variety of goals, leading to results which are both diverse and yet mutually compatible. The New Testament, for example, can provide data for both the textual critic and the exegete. It can also provide data for the historian who takes as his goal that declared by von Ranke, the father of critical history, namely, to discover the facts of the past as they actually occurred.

The latter pursuit has given us the "historical Jesus" in diverse forms ranging from the liberal lives of Jesus of the nineteenth century to the various products of the "New Quest" of the past three decades. What characterizes them all, however, is the element of discontinuity between the figure of Jesus as historically reconstructed and the Christ figure(s) of the New Testament. Crudely put, it appears initially that the New Testament presents Jesus as saying things he never said and doing things he never did. Hence, if one invokes factual veracity as one's criterion for the truth of the New Testament, modern historical scholarship will generate a hermeneutic of suspicion—"It says in the Bible . . . but it ain't necessarily so," as Sporting Life has it in *Porgy and Bess.*

The path to recovery lies in recognizing the New Testament for what it is, not factual history but *Heilsgeschichte,* the telling of Jesus' story from the viewpoint of the religious significance discovered in him by Christian faith. In this case one recognizes in the New Testament first-hand evidence, not on a factual biography of Jesus, but on the beliefs of the early Christian communities. Those beliefs, formulated in diverse literary modes, express the judgments of fact and value which inform a way of living, the way of Christian discipleship. As such they mediate religious conversion in a Christian context, so that the criteria for grasping their truth lie, not in the canons of any positivistically conceived historical method, but in faith understood as the cognitive aspect of the transformation effected by the gift of God's love. Even as there is no such thing as a brute fact, so also there is no such thing as a value-free, presuppositionless history. The horizon of the historian plays a decisive role in the selection and assessment of the data on the past, and so religious conversion will enter into determining whether an historian will prove capable of rendering those judgments of fact involved in discerning the Christ of faith.

If modern scholarship opens a gap between the "historical Jesus" and the "Christ of faith," Lonergan suggests that a contemporary Christology will take its data first of all from the New Testament as first-hand evidence, not on the life of Jesus, but on the beliefs of the early Christian movement, on the judgments of fact and value which inform Christian praxis. Such evidence remains, of course, simply that, data. As both the further history of Christianity and the ongoing enterprise of contemporary exegesis testify, the meaning of the expressions of belief found in the New Testament remains a further question.

THE HEURISTIC STRUCTURE OF CHRISTOLOGY

Lonergan's transposition of the doctrine of Chalcedon opened onto the question of the truth of that doctrine. To pick up on that topic, and to indicate as well how theological method becomes specifically Christological, we can turn next to a sample Lonergan offers to illustrate the heuristic structure of Christological method.

Heuristic Structure. A heuristic in general arises from the conjunction of data on the side of the object with the operations of the self-transcendent subject and the norms or criteria immanent to those operations. So, to cite an example favored by Lonergan, fire has long intrigued human curiosity. We seek to understand what fire is, and our answers have been diverse. The ancient Greeks counted it among the four basic elements, later thinkers posited a volatile substance called phlogiston, and Lavoisier's notion of oxidation now holds the field.

Each answer differs significantly from the others, but the path toward reaching them has remained constant. On the side of the data there have been the sensible data of flames and heat, and these have met, on the side of the subject, the spirit of inquiry manifest in the desire to know what would be known when the data were understood, leading one to accept explanations so long as these appear to account for all the data, but with a readiness to reject them should further investigation prove them inadequate and to embrace revised or even radically different explanations if these offer a more adequate account.

The point of the example is to illustrate the identity of science. That identity does not rest on any permanent body of knowledge, on some set of unchanging scientific truths. But science does remain itself as a method, as a heuristic structure of discovery arising from the conjunction of data to be understood with the eros of the human mind and with the norms immanent to the process of cognitive self-transcendence.

Christology, like science, is an enterprise of human inquiry, and so it exhibits in at least a formal sense the same heuristic structure. Christologies have been diverse down through the centuries, but each results from the conjunction of data with the operations of the self-transcendent subject and the norms immanent to those operations. As theological, however, Christology also differs from science. What that difference is and how it affects the heuristic structure of Christology will become clear when we examine Lonergan's sample of the latter.

A Selection of Data. Christian praxis, the way of living engendered in response to the call to discipleship which mediates religious conversion and renders it Christian, gives rise to the Christological question: Who is this Jesus? In response to that question the Gospels were composed, and from them an ongoing Christological process has emerged. That process continues today, animated by the same question of Jesus' identity. What approach to the question does Lonergan suggest?

On the side of the data he singles out three points: ("Christology Today," p. 58):

1) that Jesus is named time and again from different viewpoints and in different contexts the Son of God;

2) that we through faith are sons of God and by baptism are one in Christ (Gal 3, 26–28), that God has sent his only Son that we

might acquire the status of sons as is proved to us by the sending of the Spirit of Christ crying in our hearts "Abba! Father!" (Gal 4, 3–7; Rom 8, 14–17); and

3) that the Spirit we have received from God knows all and has been given us that we may know all that God of his own grace gives us (I Cor 2, 10–16; Jn 14, 16.17.26).

Clearly some principle of selection is operative here. Of the myriad titles conferred on Jesus in the Christian tradition, Lonergan concentrates on but one, Son of God. To that datum on Jesus' identity he adds others which link it to descriptions and explanations of Christian religious conversion and, further, to the cognitive dynamic set in motion by that conversion. On the one hand, then, Lonergan's selection of data is strikingly narrow, a single Christological title. On the other hand, the further data he adds to that title point to a context which is at once soteriological, pneumatological, trinitarian, and ecclesiological.

A Multiple Question. That nest of data gives rise to the Christological question in a specific form. How are we today to understand Jesus as Son of God? Further, placed in the context of contemporary scholarship, the question presents itself as a set of options. Lonergan discerns four possible answers, and if the manner in which he arranged the data relevant to the question suggested that some principle of selection was at work, that impression grows stronger as he lays out the components of the multiple form in which the question presents itself today.

First, if one concentrates on the title alone, one may proceed to determine its meaning by establishing a context in antecedent Jewish usage. Hence, against the background of the literature of the ancient Near East, including the Old Testament, one may ask whether the title Son of God carries a mythic or merely honorific sense, as it did in the context of the institution of ancient monarchies.

Second, if one moves from the first point of Lonergan's selection of data to draw from the second point the idea of divine sending, a further possibility stands forth. Does the title Son of God serve to indicate Jesus' messianic function, and only that, with no connotation of divinity?

Third, a fuller move into the second selection of data would link the title more firmly to expressions of Christian self-understanding. The New Testament speaks of believers as sons of God through Christ and in the Spirit. Does this mean that, as Christians experience God in themselves as Spirit, so also they call Jesus Son of God to express their experience of God's presence to them in Jesus as Word?

Finally, in addition to the honorific, messianic, and "functional" meanings of the title, Christian tradition presents one more possibility to be reckoned with: "Or does the Sonship of Jesus mean, as the Church for centuries has understood it, that Jesus was truly a man leading a human life, but his identity was the identity of the eternal Son of God consubstantial with the Father?" ("Christology Today," p. 58).

The Role of Foundations. The conjunction of data with the effort of the Christian believer to understand them constitutes a heuristic structure which generates a question. In the context of contemporary scholarship, that question assumes a multiple form. We may observe that the order in which Lonergan ranges the possible answers reveals a strategy. The answers ascend in comprehensiveness, so that each after the first is capable of sublating those which precede it, while to claim any prior to the last as definitive would exclude those which come after it; in that case, the possible answers present themselves as dialectically opposed.

The question persists: Which of the available options expresses the true meaning of Jesus' divine sonship? But the heuristic structure of Christology does more than raise a question. As the pattern of operations by which the subject achieves self-transcendence, that structure also contains, immanent to itself, the norms governing a response to the question.

At this point the difference between the Christological question and the question about the nature of fire, between theology and science, comes into play. For science is a matter of cognitive self-transcendence for which the relevant norms lie in the attentiveness, intelligence, and reasonableness of the scientific inquirer. Theology, however, as the effort to mediate between a religious tradition and a cultural matrix, rests in its second, mediated phase on the religious, as well as intellectual and moral, authenticity of the theologian.

Hence, before arriving at a judgment among the competing meanings of Christ's divine sonship presented by contemporary scholarship, it is necessary for purposes of theological discourse to render public the religious, intellectual, and moral authenticity which will govern that judgment. Between dialectic and doctrines there intervenes foundations, whose task is to objectify conversion, to generate the general and special theological categories with which to articulate the horizon within which the converted subject meets the competing claims laid out in dialectic. Foundations will thus formulate the criteria by which one will judge the truth of doctrines received from the past, the criteria immanent in the operations of the converted subject.

From Foundations to Doctrines. Faced with the question of the meaning of expressions which attribute to Jesus the title Son of God, in the multiple form in which the question presents itself today, what criteria are relevant to making the judgment which it is the business of the functional specialty, doctrines, to make? Lonergan suggests two, and they clarify how, implicitly, his foundations have been operative both in selecting the data relevant to the question and in ordering its components.

A first criterion, he suggests, lies in our own experience of sonship. This criterion allows one to account for the first two points among the data he has selected as relevant, namely, data on Jesus as Son of God and on Christian believers' understanding of themselves as sons of God through Christ and in the Spirit. By this criterion the third possibility among the four which comprise the multiple form of the question finds validation and cancels out reductionistic versions of the first two, "for if the Spirit in us is God, surely God was in Jesus too" ("Christology Today," p. 58). On this criterion, to call Jesus Son of God is more than to assign him a merely honorific title or to acknowledge his messianic mission; it is to claim that God is present in Jesus as Word.

Presence, however, is an ambiguous term requiring clarification. What is the relationship between Jesus and the divine Word? Does he differ significantly from the prophets of Israel? Is he merely one more human being, outstanding perhaps for his fidelity to God and rewarded for his obedience with a plenitude of God's presence to him? Historically these were some of the questions which animated the development of Christological doctrine beyond the New Testament into the patristic era.

The criterion which Lonergan finds relevant to answering them corresponds to the third point of the data he has selected. It consists in a recognition that the development of doctrine is a matter of clarifying Christian experience by progressively discerning the cognitive implications of that experience, and that such discernment draws its light from the gift of God's Spirit at the heart of Christian experience. Through that process of discernment the Christian Church moved from its experience of God present in the man Jesus as Word to confess Jesus' identity as divine. Lonergan is suggesting, then, that if anyone has discovered in the Christian community the tradition which mediates his or her religious conversion, so that that person can therefore acknowledge in the community the guiding presence of the Spirit, that same person also possesses the foundational reality which provides the criterion for judging the truth of Chalcedon. On the basis of that reality one can move from foundations, as Lonergan has done, to acknowledge the truth of the Chalcedonian doctrine and to transpose its intelligibility to meet the requirements of the contemporary stage of meaning.

CONCLUSION: LONERGAN IN CONTEXT

Our overview of Lonergan's contribution to Christology has moved through two stages. We began by examining how he transposes the intelligibility of the Chalcedonian dogma beyond the Scholastic metaphysical analysis in order to meet the demands of the modern turn to the subject. We moved next to consider how Lonergan elaborates a new context for that transposition within his overall programme for theological method. If the transposition of Chalcedon provides an exercise in the functional specialty, doctrines, he also sketches the components of Christology as a heuristic structure of discovery; that structure comprises, in condensed fashion, each of the other specialties as well. In the sample Lonergan offers, concentrated on the meaning of Jesus as Son of God, the interplay among dialectics, foundations, and doctrines became especially evident.

Christology supplies us with one area in which Lonergan has moved beyond the stance of the methodologist to implement the method in practice. Our exposition of his performance has been by no means exhaustive. We have left aside, for instance, his tantalizing suggestion that our own experience of development proceeding "downward" as a result of the transformation effected by the gift of God's love offers an analogy for understanding one dimension of Jesus' human consciousness. Furthermore, Lonergan's sample is highly condensed. It would be a lengthy constructive project to work out the grounding in foundations of the criteria he brings to bear on judging the truth of Chalcedon.

It would likewise require a further article to trace out the relations between Lonergan's contribution and the other currents in contemporary Christology. Perhaps the following brief comments will serve for the present.

First, the recovery of Jesus' full humanity began as a corrective movement in recent Christology. The transposition of Chalcedon worked out in the tenth thesis of *De Verbo Incarnato* and in the accompanying monograph can be located as a moment in the first phase of the movement. In that phase, under Chalcedon's tutelage, philosophical resources were employed to render an account of Jesus' fully human consciousness.

Second, Catholics have plunged zestfully into the "New Quest for the Historical Jesus." Lonergan's response to this phenomenon is by no means Bultmannian. He acknowledges fully the legitimacy of the emergence of critical history and its application to the New Testament. On the other hand, he sounds a note of caution. Any historical reconstruction of Jesus' earthly career will reflect the presuppositions of the historian so that, given as well the nature of the data, such reconstructions are liable to be both diverse and highly hypothetical. Hence, Lonergan insists, such reconstructions are unsuitable to constitute the starting point of Christology; that starting point lies in the New Testament as the earliest direct evidence available on Christian beliefs about Jesus.

Third, Lonergan would likewise insist, along with feminist and liberation theologians, that Christian praxis, the life of discipleship, sets both the foundations and the goal of theology in its second, mediated phase. He might also, however, urge a more differentiated view of the theological task, one recognizing the distinction and relative autonomy of the various functional specialties.

Lastly, the recovery of Jesus' full humanity may have begun as a corrective movement; it has, however, inaugurated a revolution. Begun under the tutelage of Chalcedon, the movement has left its mentor behind; the Chalcedonian dogma no longer provides the starting point and framework for Christology but has been relativized as but one moment in the Christological process. This revolution has been most effective on the level of the popular Christian imagination. If the "high, descending" approach of traditional Christology tended to produce Rahner's crypto-monophysitism, people today are being taught to think of Jesus first of all as a human being subsequently confessed as divine.

But in an age both historically minded and distrustful of metaphysics, developments in Christology beyond the New Testament may find themselves effectively disregarded. Nicea may be written off to Hellenization, Chalcedon reduced to just another model. The effect is to render the Christian confession of the divinity of Christ vague and obscure.

Lonergan, at least, would respond with a perhaps solitary challenge. As he sees it, current conditions foster a regression to an ante-Nicene stage in Christology in which theologians are content to speak at most of God's presence in the man Jesus. Such a mode of speech may be catechetically appropriate, but Lonergan would insist that there is more to theology than communications. More specifically, he would urge that the truth is not reducible to the imaginable. If the symbolic discourse of the New Testament possesses a cognitive dimension, patristic conciliar dogmas marked an advance in clarifying the element of meaning implicit in the Christian praxis set in motion by that discourse. In that case the path forward for theology lies, not in a simple return to the maternal womb of the religious imagination, nor in truncating the achievements of the tradition, but in appropriating fully the religious, moral, and intellectual foundations of authentic Christian praxis.

FOR FURTHER READING

Bernard Lonergan, "Christ as Subject: A Reply," in *Collection: Papers by Bernard Lonergan, S.J.* (New York: Herder and Herder), pp. 164–197.
————, "Christology Today: Methodological Reflections," in R. Laflamme and M. Gervais, eds., *Le Christ Hier, Aujourd'hui et Demain* (Quebec: Les presses de l'université Laval, 1976), pp. 45–65. Also in F. Crowe,

ed., *A Third Collection* (New York/Mahwah: Paulist Press, 1985), pp. 79–99.

Frederick M. Crowe, "Eschaton and Worldly Mission in the Mind and Heart of Jesus," in J. Papin, ed., *The Eschaton: A Community of Love* (Villanova University Press, 1974), pp. 105–144.

————, "The Mind of Jesus," *Communio* 1 (1974), pp. 365–384. Also in Laflamme and Gervais, *op. cit.*, pp. 143–156.

————, "Son and Spirit: Tension in the Divine Missions?" in *Science et Esprit* 35 (1983), pp. 153–169.

Charles C. Hefling, Jr., "Redemption and Intellectual Conversion: Notes on Lonergan's 'Christology Today,' " in F. Lawrence, ed., *Lonergan Workshop* Vol. 5 (Chico, CA: Scholars Press, 1985), pp. 219–261.

XI. Redemption

Lonergan argues in *Insight* that any religion which is to provide a solution to the problem of evil will present a set of basic beliefs (721). Principal among those beliefs will be "an announcement and an account of the solution" which God has provided (ibid.).

In the Christian religion, that solution to the problem of evil is the redemption. The announcement and account of the solution is the proclamation of the paschal mystery, the kerygma: "Christ suffered and died and rose from the dead, and this is our salvation." This is the good news, the Gospel, "the solution to man's problem of evil" in Christian terms.

In *Insight*, further, Lonergan describes in some detail, though always in general terms, how an announcement and account of the solution will work on those who hear it. But under the general terms, it is not hard to see that Lonergan has in mind the specific model of the Christian proclamation of the death and resurrection of Christ.

He explains that the solution cannot be presented "in the bloodless ballet of metaphysical categories" (547). It must "penetrate to the sensitive level and envelop it" (723). It cannot be a mere explanation of God's mind, for "explanation does not give man a home" (547). God's truth must be "embodied in images that release feeling and emotion and flow spontaneously into deeds" (547). It is supposed to change human lives, motivating us to "the perfection of a total and self-sacrificing love" (722; 698–700). Therefore it must be something which "holds our sensitive integrations open to transforming change" (546). It must be something which "captures men's sensitivity and intersubjectivity" (723); that is, it must provide something to see, hear, touch but ideally that something must be a someone, a fellow human, to make possible that special sympathy and mutuality which is "the primordial basis of human community," the fellow-feeling which produces spontaneous effects the mind cannot explain, but which can only be felt (523). The solution must come in what *Method in Theology* calls "an incarnate meaning" (73).

How truly the story of Jesus does all that is obvious. Even Lonergan's choice of the word "mystery" to describe this sensitive embodiment of the solution points deliberately, he reveals, to the "centuries in which the sayings and deeds of Jesus were the object of preaching and reverent contemplation" (547).

Most evidently dominated by the thought of the Christian fulfillment are the two paragraphs of "in the 27th place" (723–724). There he explains that the sensible embodiment of God's solution to the problem of evil must, in any religion, perform three functions. First, it must perform the function of a *sign*, that is, must at one level have a fixed interpretation and meaning (533). Here Christ crucified, as the sensible reality, clearly has the fixed interpretation and meaning of the Church's doctrines of resurrection, redemption, and salvation.

Second, the solution must also be a *symbol*, that is, a sensible reality linked to a meaningful content which cannot yet be specified, which therefore simply points beyond all specific content to "the known unknown," the beyond, the ever more, to which human knowing and loving implicitly aspire (533). In Christianity this is the endless value of the cross as an object of contemplation. It points to *all* of God's love, giving itself to the ultimate limits. "God so loved the world that he gave his only Son. . . . " "He loved me and delivered himself for me. . . . " It contains the whole horror of sin, the mystery of evil doing its very worst, etc.

Third, the solution must show itself a *psychic force*, that is, on the level of sense and of intersubjectivity—of fellow-feeling—produce effects which can be felt even though they cannot be captured in words or concepts. In Christianity the crucifix has this effect on any sensitive person, and artists have loved to portray the scene again and again over the centuries. Artists and poets may, of course, be drawn to it as their way to make their own contribution to proclaiming the message of salvation; but certainly an equally powerful reason has been simply the profound emotional force which emanates from the scene on Calvary. It is one of those "images so charged with affects that they succeed both in guiding and in propelling action" (723).

And so, in summary, Lonergan describes the embodiment of God's solution to man's problem of evil as "a mystery that is at once symbol of the uncomprehended, and sign of what is grasped and psychic force that sweeps living human bodies, linked in charity, to the joyful, courageous, whole-hearted, yet intelligently controlled performance of the tasks set by a world order in which the problem of evil is not suppressed but transcended" (723–24). Such mystery "is a permanent need of man's sensitivity and intersubjectivity . . . " (724). Wherever presented, but certainly and above all in Christianity, it produces its effect insofar as it is "not fiction but fact, not a story but history" (724). That is what the kerygma is, an account of what really happened to a real man. As such, it works on every hearer to "command his attention, nourish his imagination, stimulate his intelligence and will, release his affectivity, control his aggressivity and, as central features of the world of sense, intimate its finality, its yearning for God" (724).

There is no doubt that the Christian mystery of Christ's suffering and death fulfills, as an object for sensitivity and intersubjectivity, all that might be hoped for from a central religious mystery. As a part of a major world religion, it works, and works well. In *Insight*, Lonergan is purportedly describing only the characteristics of religion in general, or of any religion which might claim to provide God's solution to man's problem of evil. Therefore, he can simply stop with the general description we have just given and leave it to the reader to identify where in history concretely such a solution exists (696; 721; 724; 729). In particular the reader is left to make up his or her own mind as to which of the religious answers available in the modern world represents "the full realization of the solution" and which is only an "emergent trend" (724; 729; 698; 720).

But when Lonergan writes as a Christian theologian, he has to do more. The description of *Insight* justifies Christianity as a religion; but the theologian must reflect on religion, and indeed on a specific religion. He has to devote himself to "grasping and clarifying and expressing the significance, the implications, and the applications of the truths of faith" (722). He has the profound task of "conceiving and expressing the solution in terms of the universal viewpoint" (722); that is, in terms of a philosophy which is solidly rooted in the activities of human consciousness. He has to take the same Christian account of the redemption which works so well on a sensitive and intersubjective level, tie it in with the accepted interpretations of the Christian tradition and still make sense of it in language that can be checked against each person's conscious experience.

This is not so easy. The entire story of redemption bristles with difficulties as soon as one ceases merely to treat it as a story and tries to give a reasonable account of what it was, why it was necessary, how it worked, what makes it effective. Many of the difficulties occur to even the small child beginning the study of catechism. Why was God so angry? Why should the whole world be held guilty for the sin of Adam and Eve? Why should God be appeased only by someone suffering and being killed in punishment for this sin? Why should the killing of someone who has *not* sinned help to take away the guilt of someone else who has? Buddhist and other non-Christians are impressed, unfavorably, with "the Christian bloodthirsty God," this "monster of absolute justice." If Christ did pay the penalty for all, why does God's punishment continue (for all human beings still must die, and if they die in mortal sin, they are punished in hell)?

So many things about the story seem so blatantly illogical that the theologian's task is no easy one. To complicate the issue still further, there are practically no Church dogmas on the subject. There is a "universal teaching and preaching," Lonergan finds, but no succinct conciliar definitions. Still, it was largely with the redemption in mind, to maintain the full reality of the redemption, that the series of Christological councils were held and that the numerous definitions of early councils on the nature of the Incarnate Word were made. They argued that Christ must be fully divine and fully human, for they were convinced that "what [of human nature] he has not taken up, has not been redeemed."

So the truth in the background of all that is to be said here is the truth with which the treatise on the Trinity ended: that the person about whom we are talking here is Christ, the Lord, the Incarnate Word of God, that is, the one sent by the Father for redemption. The meaning of his being sent was clarified under Trinity, and further specified in the treatise on the Incarnate Word. When we make the traditional statements about redemption—he redeemed, gave his life for sinners, offered a sacrifice in his blood, and so on—these are statements about God the Word, co-eternal with the Father. He is the subject; not the Father or the Spirit or a fourth person, as if Jesus of Nazareth were someone else besides the second person of the Blessed Trinity, the Word Incarnate. The Catholic faith is that there are three persons in God, and one of them died for us.

Lonergan takes all this up in his dogmatic treatise *De Verbo Incarnato*, theses 15–17. The first two of these theses try to specify what exactly he takes to be the Catholic doctrine of which an understanding must be sought and why he takes it. (This is what Lonergan later calls "Doctrines.") In the first thesis (#15) he analyzes the New Testament texts commonly used by the Church in teaching the redemption. He looks for the basic, minimal content of these texts—that which they must at least be saying and to which therefore a Catholic theologian would direct his or her efforts at "understanding the faith." In the second thesis (#16) he takes up directly the theory which has dominated Church tradition on the redemption since at least the twelfth century—the satisfaction theory linked with the name of Anselm—and shows that it can be and has been understood in many different ways, and specifies the way in which he can accept it seriously as something to be integrated into his own theology. The third thesis (#17) gives Lonergan's own account of the essence, the intelligibility, of the redemption. (This is "Systematics" among the later Functional Specialties, aimed purely at understanding the meaning of a given mystery.) We will take these three theses in order.

THESIS 15: THE NEW TESTAMENT WITNESS

Lonergan's systematic treatise begins as always with an attempt to specify exactly what is the truth of faith which is here to be understood. Since there are no defined dogmas on this topic he turns to the tradition, which itself focuses on the Scriptures. The doctrine, he says, is "clearly contained in the Scriptures and heard in the preaching of the Church across the world."

The thesis lists the phrases in which Church teaching normally speaks about redemption, shows their origins in New Testament statements, and then concludes in regard to each statement what its definitive content, its faith content, actually is, that is, what these texts are calling on Catholics to believe.

He is not doing historical research into what the Scripture phrases once implied, nothing comparable to Aulen's *Christus Victor* or Bousset's *Kurios Christos*, which uncover scriptural categories that have not played a part in Church teaching since the very earliest period.

The thesis asks about redemption in the sense of the process of redeeming, not the final state, that is, what Christ did for us, not what we eventually gained or may gain. (The final state, "what we gained," "salvation" in its many senses, is covered in other parts of theology: Church, original sin, moral impotence, grace and virtues, sacraments, last things.) Lonergan picks out seven of the most common images and expressions which are different ways of saying what Christ did:

1. Christ paid a price (with all the variations of Mk 10:45; Mt 20:28; 1 Tim 2:5–6; 1 Pet 1:18; 1 Cor 6:15–20; Gal 3:13; 4:5; 2 Pet 2:1; Rev 5:9; 14:3–4; etc.).

2. Christ's suffering and death were vicarious: were done "on account of sins and for sinners" (*propter peccata et pro peccatoribus*), with reference to all Scripture passages saying "for all, for each, for sinners, for us, for our sins, for the many," as well as those on "propitiation," "bearing our sins" (1 Pet 2:24), "made sin for us" (2 Cor 5:21).

3. Christ's death was a sacrifice by him as high priest in his own blood, following the account of Hebrews.

4. His death was an act of obedience, as in Jn 10:17f; Mk 14:36; Phil 2:8, and Heb 10:5–7.

5. Christ intercedes for us as eternal priest (Heb 7:25; Rom 8:34; 1 Jn 2:1),

"rose for our justification" (Rom 4:25); prays for us and sanctifies himself for us (Heb 8:1f; Jn 17).

There is no space here to analyze the details of Lonergan's treatment of each of these. In general, especially on the expressions that cause most trouble theologically (those under #1 and 2 above), he refers the reader frequently to the many exegetical studies of Stanislaus Lyonnet of the Pontifical Biblical Institute, whom the Vatican had suspended from teaching shortly before the opening of the Second Vatican Council because his work on redemption in the New Testament was considered too dangerous.

Lonergan's treatment of the texts here aims at finding the doctrine which is "clearly contained in the Scriptures and heard in the universal preaching of the Church" (Nota Theseos, 395). Naturally, this requires seriously reviewing disputed points, but also carefully avoiding them in one's final conclusions.

In general, Lonergan's conclusion is that no one of the images he examines needs to be taken as more than another way of saying Christ's suffering and death were "some kind of mediation," a mediation which took the form it did "because sins had been committed and because men were sinners." That is, he reads the texts as saying that the suffering, death and resurrection of Christ had some connection with human salvation, but without specifying exactly what the connection was. There is something there in what Christ did and suffered for which we should be grateful, for his having done it is related to the spiritual good we have attained or can ever hope to attain. Moreover, Christ did what he did because sins had been committed, because men are sinners: "propter peccata et pro peccatoribus." But more than this is left simply in figures and images in the New Testament, and therefore is left open to the diverse understandings of different individuals. In other words, the conclusion of the first thesis, as an exercise in "Doctrines," is that the records of Scripture leave the theologian with great liberty in formulating what contribution exactly Christ made to our salvation, or why what he did has had an effect on us. The Church merely passes on the string of metaphors, which are not even mutually reconcilable in specific detail. The thesis also leaves salvation itself undefined except in scriptural imagery.

THESIS 16: THE THEORY OF SATISFACTION

But in theology the Scriptures are not the whole story. There is also tradition to consider. This brings us to the theory of "satisfaction." The theory of satisfaction is a theological attempt to supply the answer which the Scriptures do not supply: what exactly was the connection between our salvation and the events of Christ's life? It does this by tying together the whole complex of scriptural material around the notion of sin as an offense against God. The result is that Christ's contribution to redemption, what Christ did for us, was to satisfy God's offended honor, to put back in balance the terrible disorder which the offense against God created.

The Scriptures, as we saw in the previous thesis, present only the scattered metaphors. Before the eleventh century, no one thought of pulling them together around the idea of God's offended honor and explaining Christ's fate as a matter of returning satisfaction to God for that offended honor. It was Anselm's invention, and a powerful one it has turned out to be. Since then, it has found its way into many Church documents, as at least the presupposition of their teachings. It is the standard presentation in school catechisms around the world, as it is the staple of most theological presentations.

A typical explanation of this theory would be as follows: Adam's sin was an offense against God, and because Adam was the head of the human race, the offense was held to the account of the entire race. Now the gravity of an offense is measured by the dignity of the person offended. So Adam's sin, which offended the infinite God, was really an infinite offense. It required infinite satisfaction (compensation, reparation). But an act of satisfaction is measured by the dignity of the person who does the act. Therefore no act of Adam or even of all finite human beings together could ever satisfy for the original offense. Moreover, since infinite satisfaction would be required to restore the balance of justice, God could not simply forgive the sin and freely cancel the debt without violating his own infinite justice. The case would have been hopeless if it were not for the Incarnation. Jesus Christ could offer adequate satisfaction. Because he was truly a man he was identified with the sinful race of Adam, and so could pay the debt for sin and sinners. But because he was also truly God, his acts of satisfaction would be of infinite value, equal to the offense. Christ therefore, as representative of the whole human race, offered satisfaction for us all ("vicarious satisfaction").

To millions of people, including many theologians, Christ's vicarious satisfaction, as just explained here, is the very heart of the Christian faith. Yet, as was said above, it causes serious problems for many if not most people.

Lonergan is keenly aware of the difficulties. He describes certain popular accounts as "perversions of the notion," even when found among "Catholic theologians who seem to think their notion is nothing other than true and genuine Catholic doctrine" (Thesis 16, sententiae, #9). Others, he says, present a notion of God's justice that is "immoral or at least amoral" (Sententiae #19), and to make such presuppositions about God "cannot easily be distinguished from blasphemy" (Praenot. X #14).

But the basic notion of satisfaction he finds too deeply embedded in the tradition to be merely ignored. He also feels that "on the level of images and feelings, there is perhaps no other way to come to grips with the suffering and death of Christ except as a substitution for us sinners and a making up for our sins." As a matter of images and feelings, however, this is only "symbolic apprehension." On the same level of images and feelings, a balance is maintained "by other elements of doctrine, devotion and practical living." But when such notions are turned into "categories of logical apprehensions for supposed explanation," as they frequently are, they have to be corrected and drastically purified. That is what he sets out to do in this thesis.

He notes that the usual difficulties with satisfaction stem from the fact that satisfaction is viewed in strictly legal terms, of quid pro quo justice. He then proposes that the legal image of satisfaction is not, either historically, sociologically, or in ordinary good sense, a term which is drawn from the law courts and it should not make people think of the law courts, the world where strictly measured punishments are legally meted out for crimes. The image of satisfaction actually comes from the world of personal relationships, of love and of friendship. Guilty "offenders" in law may, when sentenced, be said to "satisfy" for their crimes when they have spent the ten years in prison to which they were condemned. But it is much more common to speak of "offending" another person by an unkind remark, by a show of ingratitude, by protracted neglect; in this context, "satisfaction" is not a matter of undergoing some punishment. It is simply a matter of doing something which expresses one's sorrow and regret—sorrow for having offended the other and which shows one still loves and esteems that person as before, in spite of the impression one's "offense" may have made. In normal life we make up for an offense with a gift, a note of apology, an effort to be especially helpful, to do something that we know pleases the other very much. It is because we do such things that the person we have offended is normally "satisfied."

The act or the gift, moreover, is a way of asking forgiveness. When one does them, or even offers them, one is asking and hoping that the offended person will forgive. This is worlds removed from the law court attitude. "The condemned person going off to jail does not hope that on completion of the ten-year sentence the judge will grant forgiveness. After paying the penalty, nothing is left to be forgiven" (De Verbo, 489). The "medicine has been taken," the "debt to society paid." During the original trial, forgiveness may have been sought by the accused or the accused's lawyer, but supposedly it was denied: sentence was passed, the prescribed punishment had to be endured. From then on, undergoing the punishment, paying the debt, was not a step toward being forgiven. It was paying off what was owed, just like sending a check to pay off any other bill, though even less pleasant.

Thus, in the social context of offending and satisfying, actions are lovingly done or gifts are lovingly given to show affection and esteem for the person along with sorrow over the past offense, and they are done with the hope of attaining forgiveness. In the legal context, on the other hand, forgiveness is ruled out, while penalties are imposed and paid, no matter with what disposition of soul.

Thus there are two different world-contexts in which we can speak of satisfaction. One context involves a crime and the enduring of a certain quantity of punishment, assigned as proportionate to the crime. It is in this thought-world that "satisfaction" to God involves so many difficulties. When satisfaction to God is proposed in this context, people cannot help wondering why this legalistic God cannot simply practice what the Gospels preach and forgive his enemies, love those who wrong him. In this context people cannot help asking why, after the satisfaction offered by Christ, this God should still have any right to punish sinners, for Christ has borne all sins, paid the entire debt.

But this criminal, legal context is not the right one in which to think about the Christian God. Far from demanding proportionate punishment and waiting to be placated or appeased, God "first loved us and sent his Son as propitiation for our sins" (1 Jn 4:10.19) and "God was in Christ reconciling the world to himself, not counting our sins against us" (2 Cor 5:19) and "God, who is rich in mercy, because of the exceeding love wherewith he loved us, even when we were dead in sins, brought us to life together with Christ" (Eph 2:4–5); and "God commends his love toward us, because while we were still sinners, in the proper time Christ died for us" (Rom 5:8) [all texts cited by Lonergan, p. 478]. And far from our handing God a bill of account which Christ has stamped "Paid," we daily ask God's forgiveness for ourselves for our sins, because of Christ (p. 498).

The other thought world, in contrast, involves personal relationships, love, sorrow for the offense and an effort to do something which will show that sorrow, something which will please the person offended, and please him or her, if possible, more than the offense may have hurt them, and to do this as a way of asking their forgiveness, and with the hope that they will indeed forgive. This other thought-world and context, with due allowance for imperfect metaphors, can be analogously but seriously applied to the Christian view of the God-humanity relationship.

The thought-world of satisfaction, thus rightly, personalistically understood, can be illustrated from a common Catholic practice—namely, confession. In confession one tells one's sins and is assigned a "penance." The penance—usually a couple of easy prayers—can hardly be said to be a proportionate punishment for the sins. It is not intended to be. It is a demonstration of love and good will on the part of the penitent. True, the priest, in the name of the Church, does make performing the penance a condition of forgiveness. But the forgiveness is still a gift; it is not earned by the penance.

The penance, moreover, cannot be performed sullenly, begrudgingly. It has to be performed in love. It is a way of doing something to express one's regret and an effort to do something pleasing to the God one has offended. No one cares on the other hand whether the person in jail is undergoing his or her punishment in a spirit of love or not. It is the punishment itself which matters there. But in sacramental satisfaction, as in cases of personal offenses being forgiven, the disposition is everything.

So far we have not said anything about "vicarious satisfaction." In the world of law-courts vicarious satisfaction would mean that another and innocent person would undergo the assigned punishment in place of a condemned, guilty criminal. Here, strictly speaking, even the legal notion of satisfaction breaks down. No decent person finds truly tolerable the idea that a condemned, guilty criminal should roam the streets while his or her husband or wife, brother or sister or friend spends years behind bars in his or her place. In truly criminal matters, even the legal system will not deliberately punish the innocent in place of the guilty. People today find the very suggestion repugnant. That repugnance carries over to the standard accounts of Christ's satisfaction as usually explained.

There is one legal context in which vicarious satisfaction is quite conceivable, namely, in matters of money or property. It makes little difference to the court who pays a debt which a person owes. Someone else can easily step in and offer to pay one's bills, put up bail, even pay a fine in one's place. The court's attention in such matters is on the object at issue—on the material and the proper quantity of the material owed. It does not matter who does the paying. Hence, Anselm's emphasis on the measuring of the quantity of satisfaction needed to repay an offense against God (comparing the dignity of the one offended with that of the person offending) may have easily occasioned slipping over into a legal context he never intended.

But in the world of personal relationships, it is not like that. There the attention is not at all on the things, but completely on the persons. The satisfaction called for is that the offending party show love and esteem for the offended along with sorrow over the offense. These cannot be measured quantitatively. They are judged by the disposition of the person doing them. A precious gift or a generous or difficult act may symbolize the disposition of the penitent, but they are not the satisfaction itself. They are at most a material part of it.

Can someone else substitute for us in this personal, social context? Can someone else, in our name, reconstitute a friendship we have caused to be broken? There is no fixed punishment waiting for us which they can undergo in our name. Their offering a gift, doing a noble action in our name, would hardly suffice in itself. But it does seem possible, if certain special conditions of love and friendship would be met. If they are to approach another in our name and make a gesture of good will which supposedly shows our esteem, our sorrow, our love, they must be persons known to be very, very close to us, as well as persons highly esteemed, cared for, by the person with whom they will have to deal. There must be some plausible way that we and they can truly be regarded as one. The good will in us has to be somehow recognized too and perhaps even implied by our closeness to the party who is going to "offer satisfaction" in our name.

Whether such a thing does happen in modern social relations is another question. But at least it is not utterly implausible or distasteful. At any rate, the real point is that if one puts satisfaction and even vicarious satisfaction into that context, it can be applied to what Christ did for us.

In this way of looking at what Christ did, his passion and death were "a supreme expression of detestation of sin and of supreme pain over the offense against God" (476). It was a supreme act, above all, of love (475) and of obedience to God (487–488). "This expression of detestation of sin and grieving over sin were his satisfaction" (502). Placating God had no role whatsoever to play in this (478). That idea is pure perversion. So is any suggestion that Christ (the innocent) was punished for our sins, sins he did not commit. That suggestion is immoral (484). Even worse is any suggestion that he assumed any guilt whatsoever. To say he "bore our sins" in the sense of "becoming sinful" is heretical.

But a human act of infinite love and sorrow over sin and submission to God was appropriate in a world full of sin, hatred and rebellion, and he provided that act. It was a supreme act, above all, of love (475) and of obedience to God (477–478). He performed, by his self-gift, an act of perfect love such as we could never have done for ourselves (476). To love like that was appropriate to his divine nature. But we love like that only insofar as God gives us a share in his own way of loving. So this act of Christ, the God-man, can be the grounds of all human-divine friendship. We can be lovable insofar as we can reasonably be regarded as close to him and one with him in self-offering.

Thus it is true that Christ did what he did "because men had sinned and because they were sinners," i.e., not to "take away" sins we had committed, but to keep us from committing new ones (498), and to enable us to work out the overcoming of the consequences of the sins we had committed. "On account of sins" does not mean in order to take sins away. It means that this fact of sin is the reason why, in divine justice, Christ had to suffer and die. "For sinners" does not mean to bring sinners to some good end, but that the fact of their being sinners is the motive why he did what he did (all this on

p. 486). Also notice on p. 499: "It comes down to the same . . . " and on p. 500: "It is all here: he suffered and died because he detested sins and was grieved over our sins."

So again, in summary (502): "Satisfaction is the suffering and death of Christ as expression of detestation of sin and of grieving over sin. From this, all the traditional statements about the redemption can be concluded and explained: that it can be considered vicarious suffering for sin; that it was an operation for the restoring of God's honor; that it pleased God more than sin had displeased God; that it was a gaining of merit; that it was taking the penalty and obtaining pardon."

What about the need to restore God's order of justice? God's order of justice, Lonergan insists, is not our notion of quid pro quo, restoring balance, making things even. The order of God's justice is the order God approved of in bringing this world into existence, just as it is. There are no after-thoughts with God. God directly wills all the good in the world; he indirectly wills physical evils (i.e., where one thing is destroyed for the sake of others); and he does not in any way will moral evils, sins, but only permits them insofar as he wills that free, intellectual creatures should exist. God's justice is present in the actual ordering of world events—an order in which people do sin and in which also the sinner can be redeemed and be justified. This is the order referred to in the Easter Vigil: "O certe necessarium Adae peccatum . . . O felix culpa" (465). God always sees and wills the entire process. There is no need for the elaborate structure of proportionate repayment which grew up to explain the theory of satisfaction. [The order of God's justice is treated in Praenotamina VII and VIII, pp. 463–470.]

This then is Lonergan's notion of satisfaction. Is it an adequate presentation of Christian tradition? He says, "Because this is theology, we have to weigh the different opinions, their origin, developments and conflicts before we can make a judgment whether our own short and simple statement of ideas is in conformity with Catholic tradition" (*Sensus Theseos* #7). So, in a short exercise in Dialectic (pp. 436 to 447), he shows in the history of theology how others have erred in regard to this right idea of satisfaction. No other except Thomas Aquinas is found able to be interpreted in a way completely compatible with what Lonergan holds. He does claim that it can be shown historically that Anselm's idea of satisfaction grew out of the liturgical context he himself uses as an example (confession—as above), and he is able to explain why Anselm's conception was distorted by being put into a context it did not require and did not fit (p. 471). Like any other individual theologian, Lonergan can do no more than present his evidence and draw what seem to him the appropriate conclusions.

THESIS 17

In order to align himself solidly with the tradition, Lonergan clarified in great detail his stand on the theological doctrine of satisfaction in Thesis 16. He purified the notion, and indicated that he subscribed to the notion in that purified sense; in any less pure sense, he did not subscribe to it. His purified sense of satisfaction was what Anselm originally intended it to be: a theological intelligibility, enabling theologians to pull together the scriptural data on what Christ had done for us.

But, after discussing the tradition, Lonergan personally has another and better theological understanding of the redemption to offer. He devotes Thesis 17 to that.

Lonergan's suggested understanding of the redemption is also, of course, drawn from the tradition. But it is not drawn from the technical, scientifically expressed, central theological tradition. What he works from here has to be sought in the lived tradition of the Church, in the tradition of worship, of spirituality, and of devout reading of Scripture. That these are central traditional realities, no one would dare doubt. And one of the reasons why formal conciliar definitions of the redemption have never been made is that the lived, spiritual, scriptural tradition has always been so strong that no need has been felt for technical definition.

At any rate, the intelligibility on which Lonergan focuses does not appear in Scholastic textbooks and is not taught in catechism. When it does appear in the most well-known central piece of medieval theology, the *Summa Theologiae* of St. Thomas, it appears there in a category which scientific theologians frequently pass over with disdain. It is among the "fitting reasons" [*rationes convenientiae*] (*S. Th.* III, 1,2). Lonergan does not disdain it. He insists that it is the heart of the matter. To understand why, he includes in this thesis a short lesson on the importance of "fitting reasons" in theology.

EXPLANATIONS BY FITTING REASONS IN THEOLOGY

Most scientific theologians prefer necessary reasons. Lonergan maintains here, as he always has, that very little of reality can be explained by necessary reasons. Modern science, he points out, made a great step forward when it gave up the Aristotelian dream of finding necessary reasons and settled for accurately recording and correlating the way things are, simple matters of fact. Scientists soon found that an important, though imperfect, intelligibility could be reached that way.

In theology there are even better grounds for not insisting on necessary reasons. For God is never necessitated. God's acts are always free. We know God has understood and chosen a certain world because we see that this world exists. We are in it. This is the world God made, so this is the world God chose and loves. Therefore this world must be a choice worthy of God's infinite wisdom and goodness. But why God chose it we do not know. Nor do we know whether it is in fact better than other possible worlds of which we have no concrete knowledge.

Therefore Lonergan holds that in theology "fitting reasons" often get one as far into the heart of things as a human mind can go. One looks for the intelligibility of things as they are in this universe, but without imagining that things had to be this way. One does not have to imagine that these are the reasons for which God acted. They are the reasons which appear *in* things as they are, the good which one can see in what in fact happens to exist. This intelligibility and this good are—to use the scientific comparison again— mere correlations among facts which we experience and know, correlations which we can make and do make in the light of what we have been given by the Christian revelation in which we believe.

Such reasoning has only one value—that it offers intelligibility. But that is what systematic theology is all about (Cf. *Method in Theology*, Chapter 13, "Systematics"). It does not give certitude, and always has to be adjusted, modified in the light of new evidence, data, if such come to light (just as in science). Therefore conclusions from "fitting reasons" have the lowest possible theological note, because they are low in certainty. But they can be as high in intelligibility as the human mind can attain.

Theologians who insist on necessary reasons confine themselves either to truisms or to constructing hypotheses about other possible arrangements of the universe based on definitions and essences. About all this, Lonergan says with St. Thomas, "In supernatural matters, where no revelation is given, no conclusion can be drawn" (513). He holds that "one begins to approach an understanding of the faith only when one asks not what would follow from such and such a hypothesis, but whether and how it is fitting that God has chosen this actual order and not some other. In other words, one's understanding of faith about the redemption increases only to the extent that one perceives why in fact God willed us to be saved by Christ in the way we actually are" (512).

FINDING FITTING REASONS FOR CHRIST'S REDEMPTION

So that is what Lonergan says he is going to look for and offer, and no more: that which Thomas looked for and offered in *S. Th.* III, 1, 2, namely, fitting reasons for the fact that Christ suffered and died and rose from the dead and this is our salvation.

The argument from "fitting reasons" provides intelligible correlations of facts. Therefore one has to start with facts.

I. THE FACTS, FROM SCRIPTURE AND TRADITION

Facts in theology come from revelation, witnessed to by Scripture and tradition. So as a first step toward his argument, Lonergan reviews the facts as found in the traditional reading of the New Testament.

In five pages (519–524) he presents the New Testament message of the death and resurrection of Christ as the key to every aspect of human life. He sums up his finding from Scripture, tradition and life in a three-step formula. He says the Scriptures present those three steps as reality in Christ and as a pattern of salvation for all the rest of us. The steps are: 1. sin produces its own evil effects in human life; 2. those evils, resulting from sin, can be transformed into something beautiful and good; 3. God blesses that transformation. Lonergan calls that three-step process "the law of the cross." In Christ himself the process appeared as 1. his suffering and death (the results of sin); 2. his acceptance of that suffering and death out of obedience and love, thus transforming the evils into something morally good; 3. God's raising him from the dead.

Thus redemption happens by undergoing the evils resulting from sin, and by God's grace and good will transforming them into goods (506). Moreover, "what happened to Christ becomes a general law for the members of Christ's mystical body: 'Whom he foreknew, he also predestined to be made conformed to the image of his Son' (Rom 8:29); 'if however we suffer with him so that we may also be glorified with him' (Rom 8:17)."

In the New Testament, "the law of the cross is inculcated in both precepts and examples across the whole range of human activity, so that [step 1] every evil in human and voluntary affairs is seen as somehow the result of sin (*S. Th.* I, 48, 5); [step 2] each one then daily takes up his cross (Mt 16:24) and fulfills what is wanting of the sufferings of Christ (Col 1:24); [step 3] and then to those who love God, all things work together unto good (Rom 8:28)." This pattern is applied in the New Testament to the basic content of the sacraments (Rom 6:4). It is laid down as the principle governing Christian morality (Rom 6:11) and asceticism, or growth in spirituality (Rom 8:13). But it is also a message about physical reality: our bodily death will be succeeded by resurrection and eternal life (Phil 3:20f).

II. HOW AND WHY SUCH A PATTERN
OF SALVATION IS FITTING

Now, granted that the fact of a Christian pattern of salvation is, in Scripture and religious tradition, such as he described, the remaining task is to look for the fittingness of that pattern as the way of salvation for sinful men, to draw the correlations. Lonergan does this on pages 524–536. Here he first reflects on the nature of this "law of the cross." The law of the cross is not absolutely necessary, but merely the factual way that this universe happens to be set up. Moreover, the law of the cross does not operate with the universality of a physical law. Many can look at life and not see that this *is* its law; they can hear the Christian explanation of the law of the cross and still reject it as "religion of slaves" (Nietzsche) or as "opium of the people" (Marx). It is a law for all, but the "all" refers to human beings who are free. Therefore the law will be followed by those who have heard it, understood it, accepted it, not by others. But it will work for those who will let it work. "It is commanded by our Lord and by his apostles in the scriptures; it is inculcated not only by words but by examples, and those of the greatest; and it was so perfectly lived out in the head, in Christ, that . . . the rest of us have only to ask and we shall receive" (526).

The fittingness of human redemption in the pattern of the law of the cross can be considered from the human side or from the divine. The human side is the one Aquinas emphasized. Aquinas stressed how this specific way of redemption was the way most calculated to move humanity away from evil and toward good. He showed how Christ's incarnation, death and resurrection promote faith, hope, charity, repentance. He concentrated on the changes such a redemption could work in human beings because he took it as obvious that the redemption was not designed to change God. God needed no soothing, no placating. His disposition is perfect and loving and always has been. The redemption happened to change us, and we are changed by what we come to know and value and choose.

Lonergan develops his fitting reasons from the human side by stressing that "this actual way of redemption befits sinners; namely, that they not merely be converted by God (passively), but that they also by their own efforts turn themselves to God; that all men together should share in the wages of one another's sins, individual and social alike, and by sharing them willingly transform them into the occasion of greater virtue with Christ, as the Apostle ordered: 'Do not be overcome by evil, but overcome evil with good' (Rom 12:21)."

Once men have sinned, "there is no way of perfection open to them except that which is laboriously attained by removing the evil in life and converting self to good" (529), and so true is this that at first glance one might say that the law of the cross is more a law for us than it is for Christ" (529).

But when Lonergan turns to listing fitting reasons from the divine side, he reminds us at once that according to the Christian faith, Christ, the eternal Son, "for us men and for our salvation came down from heaven . . . and suffered under Pontius Pilate" (creed). He made this law of the cross thoroughly his own. " 'The cross of Christ' is a common expression. For the cross is properly Christ's, first because he bravely and perfectly undertook it; and because through him and through the perfection of his deed . . . there are now connected to the cross both the grace of God in bearing it and the glory for the sake of which it is borne" (529). "The Christian faith is, in fact, that Christ chose for himself that way of perfection which he knew was most necessary to us" (528), the way of enduring the evils sin has caused in order that through the loving and obedient enduring we may transform them into the virtue which saves.

A more detailed analysis of fitting reasons from the divine side would consist, Lonergan says, in trying to relate the law of the cross to divine wisdom and to divine goodness and love. He takes divine love first.

DIVINE LOVE

How does Christ's death-resurrection pattern of salvation befit divine love? Love tends to similarity and to union. Christian faith is that the eternal Word of God wanted to be like us. "Though in the form of God" (Phil 2:6), "the Word became flesh" (Jn 1:14), took flesh of a woman, of the seed of David, of the Israelites, "took the form of a slave" (Phil 2:7), and "the likeness of the sinful flesh" (Rom 8:3). He put himself "under the dominion of death" (Gal 4:4), under the law, that he might undergo the curse of the law. He wanted to share flesh and blood (Heb 2:14), in all things made like his brethren (Heb 2:17), tempted in all save sin (Heb 4:15); he had to be perfected by sufferings (Heb 2:10) and from sufferings learned obedience (Heb 5:8), obtaining salvation with a loud cry (Heb 5:7) and finding eternal redemption (Heb 9:12) (531).

Made like us, he offered himself out of love, as he himself testified: "Greater love than this no one has, that he lay down his life for his friends" (Jn 5:13). The intimacy and tenderness of this powerful love are compared to the love of a man for his wife, and of a man for his own flesh (Eph 5:25–30). Christ felt this love in himself and showed it externally. He knew that we were "foolish and slow of heart to believe" (Lk 4:25); but he also knew that "I, if I am lifted up from the earth, will draw all things to myself" (Jn 12:32) (531).

"From his making himself like us and from his great love it results that we carry our own crosses now not alone, not left to ourselves, but in association with Christ, conformed to Christ, joined to Christ. We do not merely suffer in order to reach glory; rather we suffer with Christ in order to be glorified with Christ (Rom 8:17). From this results the paradox proper to Christians: to rejoice in sufferings. 'The disciples rejoiced that they were held worthy to suffer contempt for the name of Jesus' (Acts 5:41). Paul rejoiced in his suffering for the Colossians and filled up in his body what was wanting to the sufferings of Christ (Col 1:24). All Christians who share in Christ's suffering now indeed rejoice that in the revelation of his glory they may exult (1 Pet 4:13)" (532).

"And this love of the Son reveals and commends the love of God to us" (532). The Father "first loved us" (1 Jn 4:10) "when we were dead in sin, on account of the exceeding love with which he loved us, rich in mercy" (Eph 2:4–5); "God was in Christ reconciling the world to himself" (2 Cor 5:19); and "God commends his love in us, because when we were sinners still, at the proper time Christ died for us" (Rom 5:8).

DIVINE WISDOM

If the redemption we have received correlates perfectly with the infinite divine love, then it befits divine wisdom as well; for the excellence of love flows from the excellence of wisdom. God chooses what is truly worth choosing.

But besides that, the law of the cross is specifically described in the New Testament as a manifestation of divine wisdom. That divine wisdom is proclaimed to be a mystery, God's secret counsel, opposed to worldly wisdom (1 Cor 1:23ff) and revealed through the Holy Spirit (1 Cor 2:10–16).

Lonergan cites St. Augustine's efforts to express this wisdom (534). "The all good, all powerful God would not ever allow anything evil in his works unless he was so good and so omnipotent that he could turn evil into good" (*Enchiridion* c. XI). And again: "God judged it better to make good out of evil than to refuse to allow any evil at all" (*Enchiridion*, XXVI).

Lonergan comments: "What could be said more profoundly than that? God could create a world in which there were no evils, but 'God judged it better to turn evil into good than to refuse to allow any evil at all.' But this 'turn evil into good' is precisely the law of the cross. Therefore, we can say, God preferred the law of the cross over refusing to permit evil. In fact, God so preferred the law of the cross that 'he did not spare his only Son, but delivered him up for us all' (Rom 8:32)."

Lonergan concludes that "the mystery of divine wisdom and the mystery of divine love are one" (535). Moreover, "the severity and the more abundant divine mercy which gave his Son ('and with him all else' [Rom 8:32]) are also one" (535).

A final aspect of divine wisdom appears in the way the limitations of nature are transcended. For "a good tree cannot make bad fruit, nor a bad tree good fruit" (Mt 7:18) (535). "Nothing can move itself from potency to act, and much less from obediential potency to supernatural act. How then is it possible that fallen and sinful nature by good will should overcome evil and come to share the glory of God?" (535).

It is not possible. God alone is the Agent able to focus human living on the supernatural end, which is God himself. God alone could do it. Moreover, God could have done it alone. By a simple act of his power, he could have transformed sinners and saved us all. But God chose to transform us through a mediator, through Christ.[1]

Here we must reflect back on Lonergan's conclusion in Thesis 15 that the Scriptures leave the details of Christ's mediation unspecified. They do not state clearly and unambiguously without metaphor what it is Christ did for us. Lonergan's theory does make it possible to specify the mediation. What Christ did for us was to accept the role of being mediator. That means, accept that the law of the cross be so worked out in him that we might find in him the pattern of our redemption. He was willing to do first that which we, as sinners, most needed to do. He freely permitted his life and death to be the promulgation of this law, thus providing the highest and most inspiring example of its working, and thereby commending the love of God to us, so that we could say, "As he has loved us, let us love one another . . . lay down our lives for one another."

All this is summed up in the wording of Thesis 17: "The reason for the suffering, death and resurrection of Christ is this: God wisely decided and lovingly chose to take away the evils of the human race not by an act of power but by transforming those evils into a supreme good through the working of a just and mysterious law of the cross."

We have already seen all the elements of that thesis in our discussion. Specifically: "the evils of the human race" refers to all the consequences of sin in the bodies and souls of individuals and of society. Lonergan's note explicitly refers to the fuller treatment of *Insight,* Chapters 7, 18 and 20.

"Transforming those evils into a supreme good" has already been discussed, as well as the meaning of "the law of the cross." A more detailed analysis of that "supreme good" describes it as "the whole Christ, head and members, both in this life and in the world to come" (503–504).[2]

When the thesis says, "God chose to take away the evils of the human race not by an act of power" the reference is to the fact already discussed that God could have made a world without moral evil or could have abolished evil from this world by a single stroke, a miraculous intervention. But he preferred "the law of the cross." "He chose" sums up our discussion of divine wisdom and love.

The law of the cross is called "just" because it expresses what is naturally incumbent upon human beings who have sinned or even been born into a sinful world: bearing the inevitable consequences of human sin in a distorted human society. The law of the cross is called "mysterious" because it involves "the mystery of divine choice itself, always beyond human comprehension, and because it touches on what is traditionally spoken of as 'the mystery of evil.'" But the law of the cross is especially called 'mysterious' because it relates to what Christian spiritual tradition calls "the mysteries of the life, suffering and death of Christ," that is, to the events, concrete and sensible, of Christ's life taken as the object of pious contemplation. "By such contemplation we can, with human sensibility and feeling, consider the relation of divine wisdom and goodness to the mystery of human evil" (507).

Here Lonergan's exposition is clearly of a piece with his treatment in *Insight* 20, pp. 723–724, the text from which we began this study of the redemption. Christ crucified and risen is "the solution as sensible," the "mystery that is at once symbol of the uncomprehended and sign of what is grasped and psychic force that sweeps living human bodies, linked in charity, to the joyful, courageous, whole-hearted, yet intelligently controlled performance of the tasks set by a world order in which the problem of evil is not suppressed but transcended."

There in *Insight* he laid it down that "the solution as sensible must be not fiction but fact, not a story but history." Here in *De Verbo*, Thesis 17, he writes, "The law of the cross is the intrinsic intelligibility of the redemption." And he adds that because the Son of God became man, suffered, died and rose, "we find that this intrinsic intelligibility is not mere possibility or idle speculation. In Christ our head, we find it is a fact" (527).

NOTES

[1]This is the difference to which Lonergan points between his theory and that of Abelard. Abelard wrote "before the theorem of two orders, the natural and supernatural, had been worked out, and before theological method could be clearly distinguished from philosophical." Therefore, when Abelard presented the essence of the redemption as "Christ manifested divine love to us, whence we, aroused to love in return, attain forgiveness of our sins,"

this seemed to omit the fact that justification is not to be achieved by human efforts but is the work of God alone. Lonergan characterizes this as a "gravior simplificatio" and takes care to avoid making the same mistake.

[2]"The form of the whole Christ" is the phrase Lonergan uses to include all the ways the human race can share in God's riches: the incarnation, grace, the life of faith and charity on earth and of vision and love in heaven (516–517). This form is to be produced in the whole human race, "and that can be done only by removing evil and advancing in good. But since human beings are intelligent creatures, this form can be fittingly produced in them only by the law of the cross, that is, in such a way that the evils which result from sin not be taken away miraculously by the power of God but be patiently tolerated and so transformed into the occasion of greater good with the help of God" (517).

Joseph A. Komonchak

XII. The Church

When we were studying theology in Rome, David Tracy and I would occasionally go to see Fr. Lonergan and pester him with questions. He always received us graciously and was kind enough to take our questions seriously, although more than once the quality of his responses shamed our questions. In one of these conversations I asked him about redemption, phrasing my question, as I recall it, in terms of Aristotle's four causes. In reply, Fr. Lonergan suggested that redemption was one of those realities that could not adequately be dealt with in Aristotelian categories, that it required a theory of history and historical categories. I confess that at the time I was more intrigued than illumined by the remark.

Some years later, as I was beginning to teach ecclesiology, I reread the "Epilogue" to *Insight*, which contains one of the most important statements on the Church in Lonergan's writings. It is introduced by a distinction in a theological treatise between the material element—the data to be taken into account—and the formal element—the pattern of terms and relations, or of categories—through which a coherent understanding of the data is achieved. His application to the Church read: "Now while the Scriptural, patristic, and dogmatic materials for a treatise on the Mystical Body have been assembled, I would incline to the opinion that its formal element remains incomplete as long as it fails to draw upon a theory of history." (*Insight*, p. 742)

Suddenly I saw the connection between this passage and his earlier remark on redemption. Redemption had to be dealt with as an historical phenomenon, in a treatise "on the concrete universal that is mankind in the concrete and cumulative consequences of the acceptance or rejection of the Gospel." And that is also the context of a treatise on the Church. The governing, synthetic categories of ecclesiology had to be a theory of history, "a theory of development that can envisage not only natural and intelligent progress but also sinful decline, and not only progress and decline but also supernatural recovery." (*Insight*, p. 743)

I write this as preface to an essay on a topic which some readers may

222

find it surprising to find in this volume. For Lonergan has, as far as I know, never taught a course on the Church and certainly he has never published a book or major article on what usually passes for a topic in ecclesiology. Perhaps this is at least in part because he has never considered the usual categories in which ecclesiology is discussed to be adequate to the phenomenon meant by the Church. But, if one takes seriously his remarks at the end of *Insight,* then one can say that important elements for an adequate theological interpretation and explanation of the Church are to be found in his work. They are not, it is true, worked out in full in any single place; and perhaps more than with regard to many other themes in theology, they require a certain measure of interpretation and extrapolation. They are, nonetheless, important, and even as sketched in *Insight,* prove to be remarkably prophetic of many of the methodological shifts which we have only since come to term "the political turn" in theology.

This essay, then, will be devoted to a discussion of the context and categories of ecclesiology and of how they enable one to conceive of the genesis of the Church.

HISTORY AS THE CONTEXT OF ECCLESIOLOGY

Both in *Insight* and in *Method,* Lonergan has sketched a theory of human history which especially attempts to identify and to describe its generating principles. While three principles are identified and described separately, they co-exist, and so actual human history is what results from their simultaneous operation. Human history is the story of progress, decline and recovery, and its principles are intelligence, sin and grace.

Progress. The first principle of human history is the exercise of intelligence and freedom. Within given situations human beings ask questions, achieve some measure of insight, verify their ideas, and then act upon them, thus altering the original situation and themselves. The new situation thus produced in turn provokes new questions, new insights, new judgments, new decisions and new actions, thus producing another new situation, which in turn provokes new questions, etc., etc. The exercise of intelligence at once fulfills the person and generates historical progress, and were intelligence always in act and freedom always faithful to the demands of intelligence, human history would be the story of a gradual and cumulative progress.

Lonergan's description of progress and its principle serves two purposes. First, it points to a real dimension of human history. If it has known its disasters, tragedies and crimes, history has also known achievements and triumphs, and "in the aftermath of economic and political upheavals, amidst the fears of worse evils to come, the thesis of progress needs to be affirmed again" (*Insight,* p. 688) Second, an important part of any effort to avoid in the future the mistakes and tragedies of the past must be an understanding of the dynamism and structure of an intelligent, reasonable and responsible historical subject. When evidence abounds of the decline of reason and of the banalization of progress, it is more important than ever to be reminded of an authentic human ideal.

Decline. Surely no one needs to be persuaded that the circle of human progress turns smoothly and moves on cumulatively. Individuals, societies or cultures do not advance in straight lines; development is always precarious and achievement fragile. Decline is as much a fact of human history as is progress.

Lonergan traces the root of decline to the deflection of human consciousness from its intrinsic and ideal norms: intelligence, reason and responsibility. He calls this negative principle "bias"; the Christian theological term for it is "sin."

Bias appears in three forms in Lonergan's analysis. *Individual bias* is a person's subordination of the demands of intelligence, reason and responsibility to selfish needs and interests. Consciousness is made to serve egoistic purposes, and its self-transcending thrust is blunted. *Group bias* is a sort of collective selfishness by which the needs and interests of a group within the larger society constitute the primary criterion for its actions. Intelligence, reason and responsibility here are deflected from their service of the common good of the whole society to serve local and particular interests. Finally, there is a *general bias,* a culture-wide surrender of transcendent exigencies to the tyranny of "common sense." It is the surrender of criticism, resignation to the habitual, the rationalization of the "real."

While Lonergan has his own terms for these instances of decline and his own explanation of them, what he is analyzing is not unfamiliar. Individual bias is what Christians normally mean by sin or crime. Group bias has parallels with what lately has come to be known as "social sin." General bias is perhaps less well-known, but it is not unfamiliar especially to cultural critics, whether they draw on classical sources or on later, critical social theory.

A few remarks are in order. First, the analysis of decline presupposes the analysis of progress. All criticism presumes an ideal of personal and social human integrity. This gives a further value to the description of how human consciousness would unfold itself, both in individuals and in societies and cultures, were it not deflected from its ideal and normative goals. Second, the relationship between the three levels of bias itself needs analysis. For individuals are born and reared within groups and cultures, and much of the challenge they face in their own tasks of self-constitution and much of the resources with which they may face them derive from the meanings and values realized in groups and cherished in cultures. On the other hand, groups and cultures are achievements of individuals, whose distinct and personal existence embody the group and cultural ethos or gradually begin to alter and even to transform it. This relationship will be particularly important in our consideration of the role of the Church.

Recovery. The Christian faith rests on and centers in the conviction that God has not left the human race to its own devices, but that he has intervened to repair the evil we have done, to reverse its momentum, and to restore its creative powers. In other words, in the only world that concretely exists, it is not enough to speak of the opposed principles of intelligence and bias; there is a further component, God's grace and revelation, a redemptive principle of human history.

On the Catholic understanding, redemption is the healing of the human mind and heart and the restoration of the basic human potentiality for intelligent and responsible action through its sublation into a supernatural life in imitation of, obedience to and union with Jesus Christ. To our tendency to lose faith in the powers of our minds to reach the truth (cultural bias) comes the faith which receives the unfailing Word of God. To our tendency to surrender in despair to the endless cycle of power and weakness (group bias) comes the hope that rests on the assurance of Christ's victory over even death and on his promise of the Spirit and eventual triumph. And to that egoism that puts our own interests and good above all others (individual bias) comes the love which finds its highest exemplar in the forgiving and absorbing love of Christ for those who did him evil.

Where minds have been clarified by the revelation of God, where spirits have been fortified by his promise, and where hearts have been liberated by his love, there exist in and among human societies people who can be the agents or subjects of historical action which breaks the reign of sin and permits the recovery of the native powers of the human soul. The doctrine of redemption is the articulation of this possibility within human history. In its full range, soteriology is a theology of history. And as concretely articulated, soteriology requires a theology of the Church as an event within the endless struggle of the three historic principles of progress, decline and redemptive recovery.

CATEGORIES FOR A THEOLOGY OF THE CHURCH

The outline given above of a theology of history is not the context of ecclesiology in the sense of a starting-point which one may articulate and then leave behind. It is the context in the sense that it must always inform one's attempts to make sense of the Church as an historical achievement, as a community brought to be among the variety of other human communities and as a moment in the historical self-realization of mankind.

To the degree that the genesis of the Church is a constitutive element in the divine response to the problem of human evil, ecclesiology must always include and try to make coherent sense of the strictly theological dimensions of the Church, i.e., those elements which only faith can receive and which describe the unique and transcendent character of the Church as the People of God, the Body of Christ and the Temple of the Spirit. Ecclesiology has, therefore, rightly always been suspicious of various kinds of sociological reductionism. The life which Christians live and the intersubjectivity which they enjoy in the Church are "supernatural," beyond our merits and even our ambitions, a reality whose very existence and whose deepest characteristics we can know only through God's revelation. Only faith can know the final truth about the Church.

But not only do such unique and transcendent claims not exhaust the reality of the Church, they are not even adequately dealt with theologically if they are not related to the historic mission of the Church as a sign and agent of God's redemptive purpose in history. Here again one must remember what Lonergan and several other theologians restored to Catholic consciousness in the two decades before Vatican II: that the "supernatural" does not refer to an otherworldly, abstract reality. It refers to this concrete world, where it describes the incredible claim that what we think to be natural and reasonable does not exhaust the range of the possible and the real, but that, by God's favor, there is possible to us an historical existence that shatters the probability-schedules of sin and elevates us to a life and action beyond our merits and dreams. The transcendent, supernatural dimensions of the Church do not elevate it out of the range of concrete historicity; they declare the real meaning of human historicity and contribute to its realization. Participation in the supernatural life of the Mystical Body, for example, is not a retreat from historical responsibility into sectarian escapism; it is itself a response to the divine intervention and an exercise of that historical responsibility by which history is freed from its false to its true self. The Church is the community in which history can come to full consciousness of itself, where the *communio peccatorum* can be healed and transformed into a *communio sanctorum*, revealing and serving the redemptive recovery of human history.

In other words, if ecclesiology must avoid the danger of sociological reductionism, it must be no less careful of avoiding the opposite, a theological reductionism that articulates the inner dimensions of the Church in a way that neglects the redemptive role of the Church within human history and alongside other human communities. A sect might be content with such a vision of the Christian Church; but because redemption is not liberation from the world into a safe because separate world but a liberation that enables us to be the redeemed and redemptive subjects of the world's self-realization, a Church cannot but understand even its most distinctive features in terms of what is fundamentally at stake in the drama of human history.

In discussing theological categories, Lonergan suggests a twofold division into "general" and "special" categories. "Special" theological categories refer to objects proper to theology. In relation to the Church, I take these to refer to dimensions of the Church which are not knowable by reason alone, but only by revelation, and which thus escape the competence of the human sciences. Examples are the biblical notions of People of God, Body of Christ, Temple of the Spirit, etc. Only theology would make use of these categories in order to make sense of the Church. "General" theological categories refer to objects that are studied by other disciplines as well as by theology—in other words, dimensions of the Church that the human sciences can also interpret and explain. Among these I would include such categories as "community," "institution," "society," "history," etc.

Both sorts of categories appear in Lonergan's brief description of the Church in *Method in Theology:* "The Christian church is the community that results from the outer communication of Christ's message and from the inner gift of God's love," and when later he suggests that the Church be conceived of as "a process of self-constitution, a *Selbstvollzug.*" (*Method,* pp. 361, 363) The genesis of the Church by the Word of Christ and the grace of the Spirit includes elements of the Church that only a theology living by faith can study. But these transcendent principles produce within this world a human community among other communities, a process of self-constitution alongside other such processes. In these respects and in these dimensions the Church is studied not only by theologians but also by sociologists, students of religion, historians, political theorists, etc.

To understand what Lonergan means by the general theological categories of "community" and "self-constitution," we must turn to some important notions which he develops in the course of his discussion of meaning. Human beings are born not only into a natural world, physical, chemical and biological, but also into a human world of families, communities, societies, economies, polities, cultures, etc. The difference between the human world or worlds and the natural world is that, while the latter is not created by human beings, the human world is. Both of the worlds can be considered to be "objective," in the sense that they stand over and against the newborn individual as a pre-given world within whose massive reality he must work out his own destiny. But, as much as human beings may master nature and as much as the transformations of nature may fundamentally condition the way in which they live their lives, nature is not a human product, and society is.

To describe the distinctively human world Lonergan uses the phrase "the world constituted by meaning." Social realities (to use a shorthand phrase) are brought about by the conscious operations of groups of human beings. They express and embody shared ways of understanding and evaluating the world and the relationships among people. They are expressions of the efforts of past and present generations to make sense of the world and to live in it intelligently, reasonably and responsibly. They are realities which cannot be understood without understanding what their creators have meant and valued. In this they differ from purely "natural" realities as a wink differs from a facial tic, an arrowhead from a piece of flint, and a city from a beehive.

A community is an example of a world constituted by meaning. For Lonergan, community is an achievement on four levels. It is made possible by some measure of common experience, a common history which the members can think and talk about together. Community is given form and reality through common understandings and common judgments, an agreement as to the meaning of the common experience. And community becomes effective through common commitments for the sake of common values. Communities, then, are not primarily to be defined spatially; they begin and end where a community of experience, understanding, judgment and decision begins and ends.

A second, related notion must be introduced at this point, that of "the world mediated by meaning." This world Lonergan distinguishes from the world given immediately either to sense or to internal consciousness. This latter world is a narrow world, restricted to the range of one's own personal experience. But no human being lives in so narrow a world. We all live in a world, which we would vigorously insist is also "the real world," which is known to us at least originally and in good part only because it has been mediated to us by others. Through their communications to us we come to know of past and distant things, persons and events which we will never personally experience. Our own efforts at understanding this far larger world are greatly assisted by hearing what others have understood of it. We sort out what is true and false about it not only by our own efforts and by reference to our own experience but also by testing various claims against the vast number of things we already hold to be true in part because of the testimony of others. And when we try to distinguish good and evil, we do so in dependence on and in dialogue with the evaluations of the world we have learned from others. Thus, by far the greater part of the world we inhabit, both natural and human, is mediated to us by the acts of meaning of predecessors and contemporaries.

With these two notions of the worlds constituted and mediated by meaning and value, we have two basic elements in an attempt to locate the place and role of the Church. For they describe the concrete social context within which we as individuals and as a group attempt to live out our lives. As personal as is the project of existential self-realization which each of us must assume, it is never an isolated or merely private effort. It occurs within an objective matrix, partly natural and partly social or historical. We had no choice over the world into which we were born and within which important moments of our socialization took place. And that pre-given world in large measure determines the concrete range of historical possibilities over which we will be able to exercise our freedom.

But it is not only that we must work within and deal with the objective world, as already constituted by the meanings and values of predecessors and successors; the concrete selves which we become are also profoundly affected and conditioned by the worlds constituted and mediated by meaning and value. The world constituted by meaning and value is a social world created by others and so embodies in its language and symbols, roles and institutions, economic and political development, a certain understanding and appreciation of human life. It is on this culture that others draw when they mediate its richness to us. The language with which they speak to us already interprets and orders the world. The symbols they use promote affective and cognitive responses appropriate to that world. The roles and institutions channel our freedom into expected and rewarded kinds of life and activity. The stages of economic and political development provide an outer limit of what we are likely to be able to do with our own energies. Through the mediation of others, what is commonly called socialization, we are raised to be persons who can be at home in the world those others have made and sustained. And, should there come a time when we take conscious control of our own lives, we always do so as persons who have grown up in such a world and become the persons we are in good part because of it.

This account so far is simply one version of what today is often called "historicity." Human existence is historical, concretely located in time, space and culture. Each generation has to try to live intelligently, reasonably and responsibly at its time, in its place, and with the resources of its culture. Each new generation's historic responsibility begins where another's has left off.

But the real drama of each succeeding generation's responsibility is seen in its full concreteness only when it is recalled that history is no straight-line or ever ascending progression. That there has been progress cannot be doubted, and much of what anyone of us can do today we owe to the labors of past generations. But besides progress, there is also sinful decline. And among the creations of past generations, embodied in the world constituted by meaning and mediated to us by those who have socialized us into that world, there also are the historical and cultural effects of past and present generations' failures to act intelligently, reasonably and responsibly. The world we have entered by birth and by socialization is a confused mixture of intelligence and folly, of reason and irrationality, of responsibility and irresponsibility. In our families, communities, societies, economies, polities, and cultures, we have encountered individual and group bias and the surrender of critical reason to the demands of practicality. Not only that, there is a good chance that we have ourselves assimilated as the obvious way of living our lives a similarly confused view of the world and sense of values. We do not begin our lives as did Adam and Eve, innocents in an innocent world; we are born somewhere east of Eden, and we are ourselves, unfortunately, all too much at home in our exile.

But for Christian faith, there is not only progress and decline; there is also the gift and hope of redemptive recovery. In the message of Christ, there is given God's own interpretation of our condition and of a way to overcome it. In the person of Christ himself there is given a personal incarnation of a human life that can undo the effects of sin in a forgiving love and surpass the fear of death in the power of resurrection. In the grace of the Spirit there is given the possibility of a personal conversion that can prevent sin from bringing us under the reign of egoism and resigned irresponsibility. Christ has brought us a truth that can set us free, and where the Spirit of the Lord is, there is freedom.

At the core of this redemptive possibility stands the individual person, given the possibility of free and authentic life before God in imitation of Christ and in the power of the Spirit. But concretely this redemptive possibility works itself out historically, and this means in accordance with the general laws of concrete existence outlined above. A new community, defined by new experiences, new insights and judgments, new values and commitments, came to be in response to the life, teachings, death and resurrection of Jesus Christ. That community, which we call the Church, was and is the concrete social and historic difference he has made. It is the enduring sign of his life and work because it is their effect. A new community of meaning and value has been constituted in this natural world of ours: a new intersubjectivity in grace, with its own language and symbols, its own roles and institutions, its own interpretative and evaluative culture. Among the many worlds constituted by meaning and value there exists one which defines itself by reference to Jesus Christ and lives by the grace of his Spirit.

And because this community of meaning and value exists, there is the concrete possibility that when successive generations have the world mediated to it, that world will be the world of God's creation, Christ's redemption, and the Spirit's power. The language and symbols a person learns now speak of God as well as of man, of both sin and forgiveness, of resurrection as well as of death, of freedom and not merely of constraint. Personal examples will be not only of selfishness and alienation but of generosity and reconciling love. Roles and institutions will direct people toward authentic living. The community that is the sign and effect of Christ thus becomes the instrument of his enduring redemptive efficacy. The Church continues to be the concrete difference Christ makes in human history and society.

As Christ's message and life is the outer communication and interpretation of the inner gift of the Spirit by which God calls all human beings to salvation, so the Church is the social and historical articulation of the redemptive meanings incarnate in Christ and of the redeemed subjectivity made possible by the Spirit. It is, on a first view, the redeemed community brought about by Christ and the Spirit, an intersubjectivity transformed by grace, the fellowship of the Spirit, which embodies in fellow-feeling and mutual service, forgiveness and reconciliation, gesture and rite, common beliefs and values the gathering of individuals out of their particularity and alienation into one body under one God and in one Spirit. The daily re-gathering of this people is itself already an occurrence of salvation, the triumph of Christ's word and grace over sin and the realization of redemptive communion.

On a second view, the Church so gathered is also the historical instrument of the redemptive work of Christ and the Spirit. In its fellowship, witness and service, the Church gives visible social expression to the interpretation and evaluation of human life which are summed up in Christian faith, hope and love. For its members the Church becomes the matrix by which we are sustained in our way of understanding reality, in our hope that we can escape the determinisms to which we are so often tempted to surrender, in our efforts to love as Christ has loved. For others the Church, as the embodied communal bearer of Christian meanings and values, determines the concrete probability that they will take the Gospel seriously and ask for themselves whether this might not be what human life could possibly be like. A sociologist might speak of the Church in this respect as a "plausibility-structure" for the Christian interpretation of existence. If that description does not necessarily warm our hearts, we might give thought to the process by which we have each come to appreciate the world in the light of Christ or been en-couraged to try to live in imitation of him, and then ask whether in fact it has not been the Church which at almost every crucial point has supplied us with words for our groping efforts, with examples to demonstrate its value, and with prayers and rites to strengthen and illumine our resolve.

THE CONCRETE GENESIS OF THE CHURCH

When Lonergan speaks of the Church as "a process of self-constitution," he alludes to a central feature of the Church's existence. For, like other human communities, the Church is also something which is made to come to be, under grace, by the conscious operations of its members. This is not at all to deny the divine initiative in the genesis of the Church; but it is to specify how that initiative is effective in the world. The Venerable Bede put it metaphorically: "Every day," he said, "the Church gives birth to the Church." With a little help from social theorists, the theologian might say that every day the Church reproduces itself by reproducing its constitutive acts of Christian meaning and value, by everyday believing, hoping and loving again. The day that the Church ceases to believe, hope and love is the day that the Church dies.

There are two inseparable moments in this daily genesis of the Church, an objective moment and a subjective. The objective moment involves reference to the founding and perennially constitutive meanings that center around the life, teachings, death and resurrection of Jesus Christ. These meanings are the insights, judgments and values that give form, act and effect to the community of the Church. The Church finds these meanings objectively represented in the Scriptures, in the tradition, in dogmas, in the liturgy, in the examples of holy lives, past and present, etc. These stand over and against each generation of Christians as the criterion of their fidelity to Christ's word. They are the objective principle of the unity of the Church across generations and across cultures. And without these meanings it would be something other than the Church that is realized.

But the objective meanings that make the Church a distinctive community do not effect the Church except insofar as they are received and appropriated by each successive generation of Christians. They are of themselves only potential principles of unity; they become effective principles of a single communion amidst historical and cultural diversity only when they are affirmed and embraced in acts of historical self-responsibility. Faith comes from hearing, St. Paul said, but he also said that no one can say that Jesus is Lord except in the Holy Spirit. And it is the act of personal and communal appropriation of the Gospel that is the second, subjective moment in the Church's daily genesis.

This perhaps helps to explain why Lonergan's most extensive discussion of the Church in *Method in Theology* occurs in a chapter on "Communications." For the Church is the effect of God's self-communication in word and grace; its fundamental existence is that of communion in meaning and value; it continues in existence as a process of communal self-constitution; and it fulfills its role in history by communicating the word and grace by which it lives. "Communications," then, refers not only to an activity of the Church outward, but to the very process by which it continues to exist at all.

When the subjective moment in the genesis of the Church receives attention, the focus necessarily shifts to the particular situations in which its constitutive meanings and values are communicated and received. And with this focus the role of the Church as an instrument of the redemptive recovery of history comes immediately to the fore. For the Gospel is always preached to individuals and groups living in specific historical moments, in communities and societies shaped by human progress and marred by human sin. The call to Christian hope is always a challenge to withstand the temptations to be content with the horizons in which local varieties of sin are comfortable. The invitation to Christian love is always a call to overcome quite specific temptations to selfishness and alienation. If, on a rather formal and abstract level, there is a general and universal Christian meaning and value, the Gospel only liberates in the concrete, as a word and grace which makes people free in the ever different here and now.

There is not, then, a first moment in which the Church comes to be through its constitutive faith, hope and love and then a second moment in which it looks around at the world to see what it might bring to it. The preaching of the Word of Christ is already an act within and with reference to the historical moment, and the decision to believe is itself an act of free response within and in terms of that moment. Preaching the Word and receiving it in faith are acts which interpret the world not only in general but also in its particular and specific character here and now and which constitute first the preacher and then the believer as historical agents. In other words, the communication and reception of the central Christian faith is a process constitutive of redemptive recovery. And the same holds true of the acts of hope and love. In that sense, the basic process by which the Church constitutes itself in response to Christ's word and the Spirit's grace is already a "political" act, that is, an act that decides for and/or against specific options about the character of human society and the direction of human history. It is the process by which God's redemptive intervention in man's making of man becomes historically and socially visible and effective.

For all these reasons, the interplay between faith and culture is a crucial question. There is, on the one hand, the constitutive faith which derives from and interprets the life, teaching, death and resurrection of Jesus Christ and which is objectively represented in the Scriptures, tradition, dogma, liturgy, etc. On the other hand, there is the mandate to preach this Gospel to all nations so that all peoples and cultures may be saved by receiving, appropriating and living out the Gospel. Throughout the two millennia of its existence, the Church has always been engaged in this process of cultural communication. It began even within the New Testament, where the tension between Jewish and Hellenistic culture is already visible, as, for example, when Paul and Peter must try to settle how much of Judaism is necessary when the Gospel is preached to and lived by non-Jews. The process continued when the Church moved out into the various cultures of the ancient world, when it attempted to convert the "barbarian" tribes, when it became the religious center of medieval Christendom, and when it undertook the vast missionary activity of the modern era.

For Lonergan this process of transforming contemporary culture represents the key challenge of the contemporary Church. At the Second Vatican Council the Church entered upon a grand effort of self-assessment and reform. The twentieth century Church was the heir of those previous efforts to make Christian faith the directing force of Western culture and of the transformations of Christianity which those efforts had effected. But for Pope John XXIII to have called the Council under the banner of *aggiornamento* was to admit that the Church had not yet adapted itself to the specific challenges of contemporary culture and history. It was still too dependent on decisions made in other historical circumstances and with the resources of a culture long past. The near-explosion of familiar "Roman Catholicism" after the Council, Lonergan argues, is less a crisis of faith than of culture. It is the crisis entailed in the new appropriation of the faith required for the Church to be an active and effective force in changed historical circumstances and by using new cultural resources.

This is the context in which to make sense of Lonergan's distinction between "classical" and "historical" consciousness. He offers a description of the culture that until fairly recently was still dominant in the Church:

> . . . it was named simply culture. It was conceived absolutely, as the opposite of barbarism. It was a matter of acquiring and assimilating the tastes and skills, the ideals, virtues, and ideas, that were pressed upon one in a good home and through a curriculum in the liberal arts. This notion, of course, had a very ancient lineage. It stemmed out of Greek *paideia* and Roman *doctrinae studium atque humanitatis,* out of the exuberance of the Renaissance and its pruning in the Counter-reformation schools of the Jesuits. Essentially it was a normative rather than an empirical notion of culture, a matter of models to be imitated, or ideal characters to be emulated, of eternal verities and universally valid laws. (*Second Collection,* p. 101)

The problem with this notion of culture is twofold. First, it failed to perceive its own particularity and relativity, and, second, it has disappeared, apparently forever. Because of the first defect, the Church found itself bound to a cultural form and to historical decisions and policies which might have been appropriate in one set of cultural circumstances and in one historical moment but which were quite inadequate to different circumstances and moments. The Church could not effectively be present and active in a world which had abandoned the normative and universalistic presuppositions of classical culture. And if, secondly, this abandonment appears to be irreversible, the Church is faced with the tremendous challenge of articulating its central faith and of structuring its own redemptive activity within and for a culture whose emergence it had often vigorously resisted.

This challenge itself has two dimensions. First, in areas long since evangelized, it requires the Church to deal with the distinctively modern culture which has replaced the classical culture, and, second, in other cultures it requires it to undertake a task of evangelization without the normative and universalizing presuppositions of that now obsolete cultural ideal. The difficulties of this twofold challenge should not be underestimated. The Church begins this task, inevitably, as the historical subject which has become what it is through that vast project of cultural interaction outlined above, whose most recent form was the assimilation of a notion of culture which did not admit of the need for change. In this situation, it is very difficult to sort out the Gospel from the way in which the Gospel has developed in that historical and cultural interaction. Inevitably there will be disagreements as to what may or may not be reformed or even discarded as simply culturally specific forms of the Christian faith or life. This has made the task of an appropriate and effective historical and cultural self-constitution of the Church in the new culture of the West and in the varied cultures of the world a much more difficult task than it might have been conceived to be when earlier cultural self-constitutions were regarded as permanently fixed, normative and universalizable.

With this analysis of the modern cultural crisis for the Church, Lonergan offers a way of understanding the chief challenges the Church faces both in Western European cultures and as it strives now to permit the Gospel to become, in non-European culture, "not disruptive of the culture, not an alien patch superimposed upon it, but a line of development within the culture." (*Method*, p. 362) And what is at stake here is not simply whether there shall be a Church tomorrow, but whether, by entering into, transforming and being transformed by the variety of cultures, the Church shall be what it is supposed to be, the historical and social bearer of God's intervention for the redemption of human history and culture.

CONCLUSION

One should not turn to Bernard Lonergan's writings for a complete and systematic theology of the Church nor even for discussions of most particular ecclesiological topics. But in his thought one can find extremely interesting and fruitful foundations for the effort to situate the Church as one of the actors in the drama of human history. The result of such an effort may be not only to gain new insights into the reality of the Church, but also to assist the Church to become "a fully conscious process of self-constitution," ready and able critically and confidently to undertake its role as an instrument of the redemptive recovery of human history.

SUGGESTED READINGS

Insight, chapters 7, 18 and 20.
Method in Theology, chapters 2, 3, 4, and 14.
"Theology in Its New Context," in Second Collection, pp. 55–67.
"The Absence of God in Modern Culture," in Second Collection, pp. 101–116.
"Healing and Creating in History," in Bernard Lonergan: 3 Lectures, pp. 55–68.

Stephen Happel

XIII. The Sacraments: Symbols That Redirect Our Desires

> The need of teaching and preaching, of rituals and common wor-
> ship, is the need to be members of one another, to share with one
> another what is deepest in ourselves, to be recalled from our way-
> wardness, to be encouraged in our good intentions. (Bernard Lo-
> nergan, "The Future of Christianity," *Collection* II, 157.)

The themes of Lonergan's thoughts on the sacraments are encapsulated in
the epigraph: religious friendship, an ability to participate in the common
pursuit of God, an affective education which gives us hope in our struggles,
and the willingness to be corrected when we stray in our life's journeys.
Though Lonergan has treated the sacraments rarely in any explicit manner
in his career, sacramental life has entered his discussions in many areas of
theology and its method.[1] The work which follows, like the preceding chapter
on ecclesiology, weaves together partial strands of thought and incomplete
patterns of ideas which Lonergan himself only intimates. But, insofar as it is
faithful to his own positions, it presents the way in which the sacraments perform, sometimes perhaps unconsciously, as part of his theological method.
Since coherent notions about the sacraments do emerge from Lonergan's
work and his thought does illumine contemporary discussions in this area, an
exposition such as this helps validate the method for which he argues.

We will pay attention to the way in which Lonergan himself has integrated specifically Christian theological forms into his thinking. In what follows, I shall look first (I) at the fundamental role that images and symbols
play in our experience, then (II) point out how these symbols lead us toward
divine Mystery or away from it, (III) note how these symbols redirect and
reconstruct our social experience, and (IV) conclude with some comments
about the ways in which Lonergan's perspectives contribute to a contemporary theology of the sacraments.

I. IMAGES IN COGNITION, EMOTION AND ART

Images are necessary at all levels of human consciousness. Images can be the sensible content (through sight, smell, sound, kinesthetic sense, etc.) of our perceptual flow, a signal which abstracts some particular item for understanding, or a symbol which helps us discern what we do not yet know. "Some sensitive awareness and response, symbolic of the known unknown, must be regarded as a generally and permanently recurring feature of human living."[2] In other words, without images, we would not know anything at all. They always provide potential for insight, the material imagination from which insight takes its particulars. Insights single out some of the things we know through our perceptual images; but images are the operation of our consciousness at its primary level, a level we never entirely discard. Lonergan's sense of the embodied character of human knowing is important to his thoughts on the sacraments.

Besides being formative of our cognitive experience, images also function as part of our affective life. In the drama of life, our imaginative consciousness already charges certain patterns with emotional and ethical value. The images of our daytime development can draw us or repel us well beyond their cognitive content. Images in our dreams can express to our sleeping consciousness feelings we would prefer to bury. We may attribute the added charge of feeling to childhood experience, to an archetypical collective unconscious or to social traditions; but in every case, we recognize that "the materials that emerge in consciousness are already patterned, and the pattern is already charged emotionally and conatively."[3] Psychic health involves the differentiation and integration of our neural demands and our psychic determinations with reflective understanding and judgments of value. The symbols of our psyche, therefore, can (and usually do) reflect both the skewed patterns of our human problems and our developments toward mental health.

Human sensibility can also be differentiated in such a way that it becomes the spontaneous, self-justifying joy of art. Artistic images are symbolic of a twofold human freedom: on the one hand, they liberate us from the weight of biological self-preservation; on the other, they free the mind from the constraints of science. Art attempts to bring the human subject into participation with, or into an enactment of, the reality described. It strains for truth and value without defining them in scientific terms; rather it discloses the reality to be experienced in "deep-set wonder." In a sense, art sets the tone, the style in which human questions arise. Because human beings are questions to themselves, art invites us to explore possibilities beyond simple fact and anticipates the answers we dread or those for which we hope. "The work of art is an invitation to participate, to try it, to see for oneself."[4] Through the formed feeling of artistic truth, we learn to live in a richer world.

The images described here are all patterned carriers of meaning. It is true that we experience random noise, confused pigmentation, befuddled touch; but we know each because they are set off against patterns in the concrete. Knowing something, loving someone, imagining a poem are all human events; as such, they intend to objectify the subject who knows, loves and imagines. The arc which exists between the one who intends to love and the one who is loved is meaning.[5] Understanding something of what is intended by the term "meaning" is crucial to Lonergan's notions of the role of the sacraments in ecclesial life.

Meaning is always embodied. There is the spontaneous, vital identification that occurs when two people share common feelings about a topic. Although this "we" is important, we attend to it while it is occurring, rather than before an event. A parent catches a child when he or she slides out of the high chair—without deliberation, without prior decision. This intersubjectivity is the matrix of all human meaning. Beyond this common feeling, however, there are intersubjective communications of meaning, found in gestures and speech. Our physical perceptions are a patterned set of variable movements; they mean something to us. If we smile at someone, there is understood a natural, spontaneous meaning. It may have many intentions (recognition, irony, contentment, enigma), even simultaneously, but they are not inferred, propositional meanings. They reveal or conceal immediately to another what is at stake for us.

In this context of intersubjective meaning, Lonergan discusses the role of art, symbols, language, and finally incarnate meaning. Incarnate meaning can contain all the others, so we can begin there. This carrier of human meaning identifies a person or a group by an entire style of gestures, words, attitudes and symbols. It can be seen more in a way of life or in a collection of deeds than in a single idea. We experience incarnate meaning when we say that someone in our society has charisma, panache, verve. We know it in brilliant diplomats as well as in demagogues. We see it in the dull, boring and empty vacancy of some lives.

Interpersonal incarnate meaning stylizes itself through art when individuals or groups pattern their experiences in colors, tones, volumes, and movements. Painting, music, sculpture and dance organize our various perceptions to concentrate and heighten our ordinary experience.[6] Art's patterns avoid "using" the art object for extrinsic purposes; the beauty which appears in ordered passion may teach a lesson, but not by intrusion of a moral. The artifact is there for fascination, wonder, courageous viewing of a new and different world.

Symbols, as has been noted, communicate our psychic health or illness; as we shall see in the next section, they contribute to our ongoing discovery of truth and love. In an important sense, we are the symbols through which our minds, bodies, and hearts communicate. Symbols speak the patterned feelings of our lives; they precede our usual sense of logic and collaborate with reflective awareness to give it weight and depth.

Speech, however, provides incarnate intersubjective meaning with its "greatest liberation,"[7] according to Lonergan. Our conscious intentionality is molded by our native tongue. The already embedded traditions of speech lead us, display a world's conscious order and orientation. Tenses, moods, voices of activity and passivity, and grammar itself structure our world and enable us to distinguish the foreground from the background, the figure against the horizons.

Lonergan distinguishes ordinary, technical and literary linguistic meaning. Ordinary speech collaborates in the day-to-day pursuit of the common good. It vanishes through its usefulness, expressing elliptically what is required to get a task accomplished or an agreement made. But eventually it becomes necessary to differentiate labors, tools and tasks; from the languages of common sense, there arise technical terms and definitions, the jargon necessary to focus specialized work. Skills develop further into systems and theories, where inquiry is often pursued for its own sake, formulating the logic and methods required to establish ever more complex specialties. Literary language has the benefit of permanence; it aims at a fuller statement to make up for the fact that its audience may not be present, its author dead, its logic incomplete. Floating between science and symbol, literary language uses figures of speech to convince and persuade.

Lonergan maintains that meanings function in our experience in a number of ways. The meanings can function cognitively in moving us toward what is meant, efficiently in that we can work in collaboration on farms, cities, industries and legal or diplomatic negotiations. Meaning can function constitutively when it forms the components of social institutions and human cultures; it becomes communicative when it is passed on in traditions of training and education.

We have expended some energy in this section trying to outline the ways in which images operate in human experience. This has been necessary because patterned images as they operate in intersubjective gestures, cognition, artistic behavior, symbolic expression, and language provide the foundation for the way in which sacramental actions carry Christian meaning. The sacraments exist as the activities of embodied meaning-intending individuals and communities. The sacraments are cognitive, affective, even artistic symbols which enable us to be touched by and to touch the God present to us in Jesus Christ. To understand, however, how the sacraments contribute to our religious life, we must turn to other aspects of human experience which mark Lonergan's interpretation: the blockages of bias, the social surd and the need for conversion. Christian sacraments face these problems directly. They are not simply symbols of an unalloyed, naively innocent creation.

II. SYMBOLS ON THE WAY TOWARD MYSTERY

Images can contribute either to myth or to mystery. There is no middle ground. By myth, Lonergan does not mean the sophisticated positions of either anthropologists or historians of religion; rather, he uses the pejorative notion of common sense which believes that some interpretations mystify rather than clarify. Myth (in his more technical revision of ordinary language) is the opposite of explanation, objects of investigation as they are related to each other. Myth describes things as related to us; it reflects the untutored desire to formulate the nature of reality. "As we feel the gravitational field to be directed from above to below, so a man at the antipodes would have to move about like a fly walking on the ceiling of a room."[8] Mythic consciousness experiences and imagines, understands and judges, but it does not differentiate these human operations. Through a mythic use of our images, we can uncritically mistake our way of relating to the world with the world's way of relating to itself and us. We never recognize the relative independence of others.

But there is also mystery, because there are always further questions. We desire to know what is the case about all of reality, without restricting the scope or nature of our investigations and we cannot eliminate the constantly receding horizon from human life. Even beyond the most elaborate poetic proclamations, after the most rigorous scientific investigations, there will remain some further question. Mystery is the use of images on the way toward self-integration and knowledge about reality. Where myth makes use of images in a non-exploratory fashion, as an end-product of human knowledge, images operating in mystery anticipate the ultimate experience of understanding and love. Images become the symbols of God's presence. Just as the imagination operates within human cognition, affect and art to provide the heuristic content for knowledge, so image as symbol performs an exploratory function to determine the goals of the unrestricted desire to know and to love. As we advance in self-knowledge and the ability to differentiate the intentions of our conscious life, so we also become more effective in the choice of dynamic images to symbolize our thrust toward mystery.[9]

We are never, however, without either idols or symbols, myths or mysteries. Since we seek a union of intellectual and sensitive experience in symbolic activity, we sometimes substitute end-products for heuristic images.

The origination of this problem is to be found in bias, described in earlier chapters of this book. The self-deceptive egoism of individual bias refuses to allow completely free play to inquiry; instead, fears constrict our intellectual vision and refuse to ask questions which might require us to change. This blindness blocks human development at the individual and the group level and establishes cycles of social decline.

The reversal of these confusions, the slow achievement of progress in human affairs needs to be accomplished on the level of the disease. It requires a cure from within. If the sin is egoism, the remedy must be an altruism which liberates the individual within community. If the expression of failure is in myth, the solution must be through images opening into mystery: human "sensitivity needs symbols that unlock its transforming dynamism and bring it into harmony with the vast but impalpable pressures of the pure desire, of hope, and of self-sacrificing charity."[10] This process takes place in the experience of religious conversion and its expression in prayer and sacrament.

Conversion is the ultimate experience of being in love. It involves self-surrender to the heart of mystery, to an uncomprehended "who," given in a mystical way. The shift in our attention from all finite loves and hates, whether interpersonal, familial or philanthropic to concern for the Transcendent Other, available in the unmediated experience of love and awe, occurs first in that incarnate meaning that we are. We discover that by God's gracious love, we are a meaningful word already spoken, a beloved whose very being is the expression of God's turning toward us. In essence, our conversion toward God is the created effect of divine love. We could not pray if God had not already invested himself in our hearts and minds.

Religious conversion is therefore always an embodied experience. It involves the developing expressions of our own incarnate interiority. Like human love, it requires expression for visibility. Our first articulation occurs within the symbolic body we inhabit as part of our personal identity. Spontaneous prayer, a pure intending of God, is the first expression of our religious love. Prayer is our loving attention to God; sacraments are the public prayer of a community founded upon the life, death and resurrection of Jesus of Nazareth.

Here we can see how converted Christians become religious artists. Their lives have a style of incarnate meaning which identifies with the story of Christ. The loving prayer of Christ for his Father articulates the fundamental "we" which spontaneously marks human community. Speaking to one another and to God, they communicate their sense of the religious interconnections which bind them together. Through religious art, ritual symbols, preaching, poetry and theology, they identify themselves as Christians in our world. Just as expressing our own incarnate meaning makes us more ourselves, so understanding that meaning makes us more free. Just as artists are "emergent, ecstatic, originating freedom,"[11] so religious creators meet their own Christian identity in the self-expressions of incarnate meaning. Without them, Christians would not know who they were.

Although the language just used is derived from the more recent writings of Lonergan, it has a subterranean history deeper than might be supposed. In the early 1940's, when Lonergan was teaching in Montreal, he was asked to give a course on the sacraments and later on the Eucharist. There and in subsequent work on marriage, Christology, redemption and prayer, he was able to outline the interconnections among interior religious change, symbolic expression and sacramental effectiveness. During the twenty-five to thirty years that this thought germinated, it appeared primarily in Latin notes published for the immediate needs of students and in a Scholastic framework demanded by the educational style of the times. Careful attention, however, to vocabulary, references, and the shape of arguments reveals a slowly emergent organic development which flowers in *Method in Theology*. The carefully pruned language of *Method* has deep roots.

The three themes which focus Lonergan's pre-*Method* concerns on the sacraments are both philosophical and theological: friendship as self-sacrificing love, mutual self-mediation, and symbolic mentality. Let us begin with the notion of symbol.

In 1940–43, Lonergan analyzed sacramental efficacy not as a blind spontaneity, but as an intentional power, as a matter of choice. The Holy Spirit is the cause of God's grace through the sacraments; strictly speaking, we cannot say that sacramental actions "cause" God's appearance. Thus, when trying to interrelate Christ's sacrifice on the cross, the final supper with the disciples and our celebration of Eucharist, Lonergan appeals to the notion of symbol. Christ symbolized his own sacrificial spirit through the final supper.

Symbol means the expression of affective life, a combination of intellect and will which can occur in a single act or word. Symbol discloses a previously unknown interior reality. Appropriate symbolization occurs if there is a natural aptitude, a law or convention, and/or finally an intrinsic, dynamic proportion between the symbol and the symbolized. Lonergan's goal is to clarify the kind of participation that exists between Christ and his action and the Church and its action. The common denominator is the Eucharistic symbol of sacrifice. "Common to all sacrifices is that they are outward signs, acts more charged with meaning than the outward acts of themselves possess. Behind the sacrifice, effecting it, giving it its excess of meaning, there is the sacrificial spirit."[12] Just as for Christ the supper was a real, proper symbol of his sacrificial affect, so for the Christian congregation the Eucharist, though as gift from Christ not by necessity or nature, is the proper symbol of our suffering for one another. What is true of Christ in principle, as origin of loving sacrifice, becomes true in us by our willing reception of his grace.

The notion of self-sacrificing love and its symbolic expression returns in Lonergan's thinking on Christ as Savior. In thinking through what it means to say that Christ died for our sins, Lonergan maintains that the proper analogy for understanding the classic vocabulary is not commercial business (satisfaction for debts owed), but interpersonal love (friendship). The heart of his reading of the Scholastic tradition is a passage from Thomas Aquinas' *Summa Contra Gentiles* (III, Q. 158, 7) in which Aquinas speaks of the voluntary acceptance of another's suffering as the height of friendship. To suffer for someone that one loves, to lay down one's life for one's friend, to carry another's burdens is to experience the graced reversal of the biases of competition, hatred, anger and inflicted malice. Lovers unite their wills with their beloved, no matter what the cost to themselves. Christ bore our pain, despite the fact that we had created it and that he was innocent.

This gift of self-sacrifice is symbolized especially in two sacraments: penance and marriage. In reconciliation, we "satisfy" by our penances for certain aspects of our sins. The ascetic willingness to suffer for another provides the psychic and religious base expressed outwardly in prayer, alms, and self-denial. But where Christ satisfied for others, thereby providing a way for us, we can only recall our own sins, and by participation share in the sufferings of Christ. By our freely-chosen self-sacrifice, we unite ourselves with the offered love of Christ.

In remarks about the sacrament of marriage, Lonergan explicates these notions of love at some length. The generous gift of one person to another in marriage is a transcendent act which faces human selfishness directly. By loving the other faithfully, two people effectively realize "another self in Christ," thereby providing a symbol of the way in which "all members of the mystical body are known and loved as other selves."[13] This achievement of a common life by two people must be dynamically active, lived out day by day. In this way, it becomes the "focal point in the stream of history for the fostering of growth in the mind and heart of Christ."[14] The replacement of egoism by altruism is the essence of sacramental symbols. Just as Christ healed human existence by his love in the face of wrath, just as "suffering did not impair His balanced grip of truth, nor injustice close His heart," so the sacraments of Eucharist, penance and marriage enact the Christian assembly's share in this virtuous remedy. They are not "things," but ongoing symbolic events in the life of the community.

The religious language of mutual self-sacrifice is reinforced by two more philosophical notions: mutual self-mediation and symbolic expression. In a lecture of 1963, Lonergan describes what it means for the Christian to pray to and in Christ.[15] After lengthy opening remarks, he describes the kind of presence he means to apply to our prayer life. The examples he chooses are significant: the love of friendship, the education of children, and marriage. In each case, we become ourselves through another. We reach a sense of self-originating love through the gift of someone else. Prayer is like that. We do not just direct our attention to Christ as an object to be known or loved; but we meet that other as one who has become himself precisely through taking upon himself our experience, especially suffering and death.

In fact, Christ's entire identity, his mediation of himself, his discovery in his own journey, occurred precisely through his gift of himself to those who did not "deserve" his love. We could, perhaps, attain some measure of perfection through suffering according to abstract principles, but instead of an abstraction, we encounter a person who "chose to perfect himself, to become the perfect man, by his own autonomous choices . . . because of us, and thinking of us and thinking of what we needed to attain our own self-mediation." Insofar as we pray, we make this activity conscious, present in some symbolic fashion.

Symbols are necessary, therefore, in religious experience as in all of life. They are required because we are sensitive beings and because we require social communication. Just as we cannot love one another without some expression through sense in our social world, so too in our life with God, we need external symbols to make our experience known and loved. Christian symbols, therefore, make evident what is true of the "normal artistry of everyday life,"[16] by intensifying and condensing that experience into patterns and rituals. At the same time, a certain psychic distance permits us to reenact our existence in other dimensions. Since we live at the artistic and symbolic level, we cannot do without religious symbols any more than we can ignore them in other realms of our lives. "Symbols remain necessary and constant in human experience whether [we] attend to them or not."[17] They become peculiarly apt carriers of meaning for religious experience because they always announce, even impose upon the viewer or hearer a "plus," the splendor or majesty that reveals itself in things. In the often silent speech of artistic symbols, there emerges a "presence that cannot be defined or got hold of."[18]

Religious symbols work, not by conceptual logic, but by the laws of the imagination and affect. They do not make involved distinctions; they use representative figures (the "New Adam"), focus experience polysemantically without the use of the principle of contradiction (like a mustard seed, a merchant in search of a pearl, a father who had two sons, and so on), operate by repetitions, contrasts, ornamental variations, and intensify themes by condensing multiples into unity. Prayer and the sacraments, therefore, will be our symbolic mode of entering into life with Christ, our way of articulating that innermost union of wills by which God awakens our love for him. When written into permanent form, they will operate "somewhere in between logic and symbol," to provide normative styles by which symbolic actions should be performed.

It is not surprising that the sacraments function as the prescriptive symbolic expression of Christian meaning. Not only do they tell us the truth, they constitute our horizon as believers and effectively determine the way we become Christians in the world. The common meanings that they enact symbolically become the anticipations of the goal of Christian life. Indeed, if the Latin tract on the Trinity is correct, the self-sacrificing love which the sacraments re-present shares in the loving relationship of the three persons in God.[19] Divine other-directed love is symbolized in the earthly anticipations of the kingdom that Christians call the sacraments.

III. THE REDIRECTION OF OUR SOCIAL DESIRES

Christian sacraments are a virtuous remedy, not for private suffering and personal pain, but for the social decline created by human sins. Self-sacrificing love requires the public expression which overcomes the longer and shorter cycles of community-destruction. Just as images function in Lonergan's cognitional theory to guide us toward mystery out of the wilds of myth, so Christian sacraments as the symbols of the community redirect our social desires. The basic problem, says Lonergan, is "to discover the dynamic images that both correspond to intellectual contents, orientations and determinations yet also possess in the sensitive field the power to issue forth not only in words but also in deeds."[20] Such cultural images will not be a matter of force or propaganda; they will offer possible appropriation of the truth, refusing to allow us to forget human failures. They will be related to art and literature, theater and broadcasting, journalism and history, academy and university, and a breadth of public opinion.[21]

The Christian sacraments are the symbols which announce and effect the community's transformation. Not only do they invite us to conversion, they effect the measure of religious transcendence which we permit them. Insofar as we allow ourselves to hear God's voice within the interchanges of sacramental activity, so much do we allow our cultural biases to be reshaped. Our positive tendencies are supported; our negative choices are overcome. Through the mutual self-mediation which occurs in these religious symbols, Christians become at once more themselves and more temples of God's spirit. By their passage through the narrative heard, Christians assume more fully the story of the One who addresses them. The narrative structure of the Eucharist, for example, drawing us from initiating welcome through collective memory to ethical dismissal, encourages our participation in the willing acceptance of others' suffering. The shape of the wedding rite focuses the faithful promise which assumes responsibility for a single other. The confession of guilt, the acceptance of an ascetical satisfaction, and the celebration of forgiveness anticipate a community in which such mercy is a habit, rather than a single instance. Through the sacraments, the reign of the social surd is incrementally, symbolically broken. The sacraments become a norm for society's future as well as a judgment upon its past. Through bodily participation, the worshiper explores the communal images which record the subversive memory of Jesus as well as the transformations enacted by earlier communities of believers. Participants in the sacraments achieve a union with a tradition of converting experience which, in turn, transforms their own thoughts and desires.

The images that function in the sacraments are the fulfillment of the cognitive, affective and artistic desires which define human experience. Just as images provide us with the potential for insight and help orient the questions of our experience, so sacraments operate as part of our religious sensibility to direct us cognitively toward the Unknown Mystery we call God. In the same way that dreams can dominate our sleep and symbols can affectively control our unconscious life, so the sacraments can express the love which is willing to sacrifice itself for someone else. And just as artistic images express feeling in patterns and colors, shapes and volumes, tones and gestures,[22] so sacraments share the complex historical meanings which show that they reflect the styles of human self-constitution.

At each level the sacraments reorient the biases which can operate to miscue us to the nature of our world. In opposition to deceit, lies and half-truths, the sacraments record the story of one who told the truth despite its death-dealing consequences. Contrary to the egoism which so easily occupies our world's patterns of diplomacy and statecraft, the sacraments oppose an affective response which chooses to suffer the pain of enemies rather than to destroy them. In place of images which demonstrate the fragmentation of our world or exploit that breakage for purposes of self-aggrandizement, the sacraments propose images which heal. Insofar as communities attempt to enact these symbolic activities, to recite these symbolic words, they will be transformed by the love of God which has chosen to use them.

Sacraments, in other words, structure the common meanings of communities. They provide an incipient common experience to which groups can attend and by which they can identify membership. They encourage complementary ways of understanding which establish trust. They determine common judgments so that people live in the same world; and most importantly, they invite people into common values and promote similar decisions. As the common activity of the Christian churches, sacraments educate people into the religious conversion which may in turn mediate moral and intellectual change. They are the primary process by which the Church constitutes itself as social carrier of religious values. Through the message they enact, "the self-sacrificing love that is Christian charity reconciles alienated [human beings] to [their] true being, and undoes the mischief initiated by alienation and consolidated by ideology."[23] In doing this, the Church will recognize that it need not ask people to renounce their own culture, but proceed "from within their culture and . . . would seek ways and means for making it into a vehicle for communicating the Christian message."[24] The Christian sacraments will find their way within the cultures in which they are inserted, transforming the language, customs and life they encounter. Working with the various disciplines of a given culture, preachers, liturgists and theologians will assist the Church in becoming more fully itself. The dialogue will take place in such a fashion that the Christian gestures and words will assist the images of the local culture (whether cognitive, affective, or artistic) to find their own authentic meaning. And insofar as images and symbols precede reflective solutions to human problems, the sacraments will begin to determine the ways in which societies see themselves.

IV. LONERGAN AND THE THEOLOGY OF THE SACRAMENTS

The contributions of Bernard Lonergan to the theology of the sacraments are not to be found in the ongoing recovery of historical data about Catholic and Protestant worship nor in answers to specific neo-Scholastic questions concerning sacramental activity. His assistance to contemporary theology of the sacraments is much more far-reaching. It permits us to rethink the way in which we envision the role that the sacraments play in our lives.

By voicing the public role that symbols play in human social development, Lonergan removes the sacraments from a narrowly Catholic confessionalism to the world stage. The self-sacrificing love symbolized in the Eucharist affects the way in which nations are formed, diplomacy is undertaken and business is conducted. The mercy and forgiveness enacted in the sacrament of reconciliation is the ritual call to, and anticipation of, an end to competitively destructive economies. The perverse rituals of political totalitarianism are to be overcome not through the leveling of political forms into uniformity, or the egalitarian tolerance of all social expressions, but through their gradual transformation by authentic symbols. Lonergan helpfully interprets the way in which symbolic activity operates in the emergent probabilities of human affairs. In this, the sacraments remain remedies not just for private difficulties, but for the inhumanities wrought socially and politically.

The Christian sacraments are the symbolic expression of religious conversion. By focusing the redemptive meaning of prayer and public worship within the experience of being-in-love with God, Lonergan shows that sacraments function at the highest level of human operation, that of values. They overturn incorrect, unethical and irreligious values and supplant them with truths, good actions, and authentic values. The ultimate religious value is the self-sacrificing love which Christ expresses through his death for his friends. This founding value of Christian experience continues within ongoing sacramental praxis. Individual change is worked out within the communal life defined by the sacraments.

Lonergan's earliest contribution to sacramental theology was his awareness that symbolic activity operates more by way of affective life and artistry than through the logic of metaphysics. The sacraments were not about objects, but actions and events; they were not about things to be manipulated, but symbols which emerged from affect. The self-sacrifice of Jesus symbolically articulated himself in the final supper with his disciples; Catholics share the identical affective generosity through their celebration of the Eucharist. The language of mutual self-mediation which Lonergan uses to speak of Christ's presence to the prayerful believer is an extension of this earlier analysis. Lonergan was aware, much earlier than most theologians, that sacramental activity was in the realm of human self-making—and that this did not necessarily prohibit its ontological status or later metaphysical analysis. Historical meanings, whether those created by Christ or those formed by Christians, could be thought through and appropriated within the theological tradition.

The language of symbol was also given a status interdependent with that of conceptual analysis. Sacraments do not have to function in the same way that doctrines did. As symbolic activity, they are polyvalent, affective, tensive, disclosing what logic often wishes to eliminate. They focus upon representative figures rather than universal concepts, do not prove by syllogistic mediation but by convergence of multiple images. Rarely linear in their movement, they condense into a unity for the sake of intensified experience.

To discuss symbol, Lonergan borrows the language of two thinkers: Pitirim Sorokin and Suzanne Langer. Sorokin, briefly noted in the early work on sacrament, provided the sociologist's validation of the social function of symbol in the formation and deformation of cultures. Moreover, the metaphysical definition of symbol which Lonergan uses at this stage ("objective manifestation in which a superior perfection is reproduced or expressed in a lower order") formalizes Sorokin's notion of idealizing symbols into ontological categories. Where Sorokin understands religious cultures as thoroughly symbolic, "immersed in the contemplation of the superempirical" through a language which can have no internal relationship to "unchangeable Being," Lonergan describes an internal dynamic conjunction between the symbol and the symbolized.[25]

When Lonergan later utilizes Langer on art, he focuses upon the patterned affect which is communicated within the artistic symbol through the internal relations of colors, tones, volumes and movements. Moreover, artists become themselves through the production of works of art. Liberated from biological necessities, from being a "replaceable part adjusted to a ready-made world," artists unfold their meaning within the artwork itself, inviting others to participate, to try out their world.

The combination of conversion toward the mysterious Other, symbols in culture, and artistic expression is a powerful restorative for sacramental theology. It permits the theologian to articulate the intersubjective character of sacraments, both as the interchange of believers and as their conversation with God in Christ. It allows a more public and social dimension to emerge in sacramental activity and encourages liturgists and believers to think of the sacraments as the primary expression of their ecstatic artistic religious self-making.

Ultimately, Lonergan's thinking on the sacraments permits contemporary theologians to combine literary-critical and social-scientific interpretations of the sacraments (such as philosophy of authorship, transmission and reception; psychology of catharsis; anthropology of ritual development; and sociology of historical status-formation) with the classical concern for instrumental causality and ontological change. In essence, he demonstrates, at least in the one instance, the way in which classical metaphysics can be integrated into contemporary concerns for interiority and history. The sacraments clearly work, for Lonergan, as symbolic structures of consciousness; but this does not vitiate their ontological, constitutive import. Such symbolic patterns make us what we are individually and socially. The sacraments are human events, but by that token they are not necessarily excluded from being divine events as well. What Lonergan has accomplished in principle is a recovery of the instrumentality of sacraments precisely as human instruments. They make present divine grace through the human properties of interiority and intersubjectivity.

To extend Lonergan's understanding of the sacraments, while locating it in the framework of human activity, is not difficult.[26] It becomes possible to see the sacramental life of the community within rituals in general. Ritualized symbols: actions, visual presentations, words, sounds, and so on express all aspects of our experience. Broadly speaking, we can distinguish four basic types: (see Figure 1) ritualization which patterns our bodily self-expressions, decorum which focuses our socialized manners, ceremony determining political affiliations, and liturgical expression which expresses our

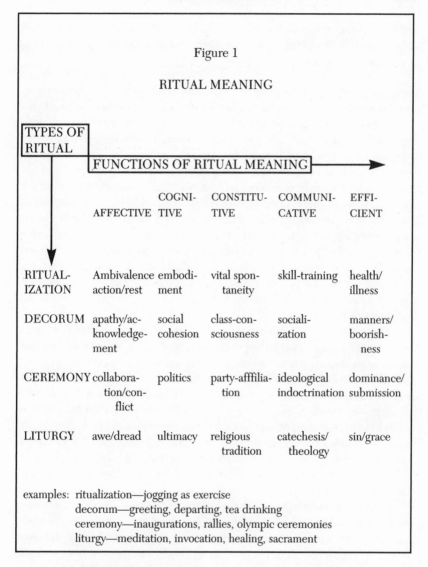

Figure 1

RITUAL MEANING

TYPES OF RITUAL	FUNCTIONS OF RITUAL MEANING				
	AFFECTIVE	COGNITIVE	CONSTITUTIVE	COMMUNICATIVE	EFFICIENT
RITUALIZATION	Ambivalence action/rest	embodiment	vital spontaneity	skill-training	health/illness
DECORUM	apathy/acknowledgement	social cohesion	class-consciousness	socialization	manners/boorishness
CEREMONY	collaboration/conflict	politics	party-afffiliation	idelogical indoctrination	dominance/submission
LITURGY	awe/dread	ultimacy	religious tradition	catechesis/theology	sin/grace

examples: ritualization—jogging as exercise
decorum—greeting, departing, tea drinking
ceremony—inaugurations, rallies, olympic ceremonies
liturgy—meditation, invocation, healing, sacrament

religious and Christian commitments. Each has an aspect which is determined by desire, knowledge, socio-cultural community, the transmission of traditions, and the need for results.

To take one category, decorum is a ritual in our ordinary life which sorts out our feelings of disinterest or interest in someone, establishes social cohesion, constitutes class-consciousness, socializes us into what the society thinks are either good manners or boorishness. Ceremonies deal with the public political realm and worship with the transcendent. In progressively ascending order, worship includes the lower affective, cognitive, constitutive, communicative and effective functions of ritual.

Christian liturgy does not replace other rituals (celebrating Eucharist does not satisfy one's need for exercise), but it includes their concerns in its own while raising them to another level. So, for example, the ritual patterns which might achieve health or illness (being rubbed with oil) may become part of a Christian ritual having to do with religious well-being. Symbolic rituals hold their place between the routines which facilitate experience (such as brushing one's teeth in the same way every day) and obsessions which cripple our lives (such as the rigid compulsion to wipe the telephone mouthpiece after someone calls us). Moreover, ritualizations, decorous greetings, ceremonious rallies, even liturgical invocations can be used either for myth or for mystery, as magical idols through which one may hope to procure favor (whether physical, social, cultural or religious) or as symbolic artistry which allows individuals and communities to transcend themselves toward divine love. Through ritual patterns, people become themselves; through Christian rituals, individuals put on the mind and heart of Christ.

The pattern for Christian sacramental experience is the central sacrament, Christ Jesus. In him, the gracious word of God's love was always disclosed in public, symbolic fashion from the incarnate, non-verbal meaning of his body through the healing gestures which comforted sinners to the most articulate words which came from his lips. As he developed in his autonomous choice of suffering for us, he more surely symbolized the manifest love of God for us. His turning to the Father was the constant conversion of his humanity to the One who loved him; the Father's continual care for Christ was disclosed in the ecstatic joy of the resurrection. Here one life's journey was the perfectly artful symbol of both divine love and human self-expression.

Christ's conversion to the Father becomes our conversion when we assume responsibility for the events which extend his gestures and words through the tradition of believers. Prayer to and through Christ is the only adequate symbol or sacrament for Christian self-discovery. When we walk the road of the sacraments, we take up the cross with all its attendant burdens of others' sufferings. When we bear the cross ritually, we find that there is one who has borne it before us and entered glory through suffering. We discover that the actions we perform disclose the presence of a God who loves our world more than we can ever dream to love ourselves. Through our own actions, we share in the life of God.

NOTES

[1]To my knowledge, Lonergan's explicit unpublished work on sacraments consists of the following: "De Materia Confirmationis" and "De Sacramentis in Genere" (Montreal, 1940–41); "De Notione Sacrificii" (Montreal, 1943–44) and the "Mediation of Christ in Prayer" (Lecture at The Thomas More Institute, Montreal, 24 September 1963). All are available through the Lonergan Research Center, Regis College, Toronto, Canada. Published work will be cited in the usual fashion.

[2]Bernard Lonergan, *Insight: A Study of Human Understanding* (New York: Philosophical Library, 1967), pp. 440, 458, 533; idem, *Understanding and Being: An Introduction and Companion to Insight*, ed. Elizabeth A. Morelli and Mark D. Morelli (New York: Edwin Mellen Press, 1980), p. 180; idem, *Method in Theology* (London: Darton, Longman and Todd, 1972), p. 86.

[3]*Insight*, p. 189.

[4]*Method in Theology*, pp. 61–64; see also "The Philosophy of Education: Lectures (1959)," eds. James and John Quinn (Toronto: Regis College, 1980), pp. 280–315, where Lonergan uses Suzanne Langer's observations to describe the nature and role of art in culture, while inserting and correcting her neo-Kantian epistemological basis into his own critically realist cognitional theory. Often, as in the sentence quoted in this text (p. 297), observations from this material appear word for word in *Method in Theology* (p. 64).

[5]For the remarks which follow, see *Method*, pp. 57–84.

[6]Lonergan stresses the way in which art concentrates the experience of common sense in the "Lectures on Education," pp. 284–293. Almost identical comments are to be found in *Method*, pp. 61–64.

[7]*Method*, p. 70.

[8]*Insight*, p. 539.

[9]Signs, therefore, or images as symbol, have a certain causative nature. This clearly becomes a link within the way in which sacraments, both signs and causes, and sign *as* cause, gain a cognitive and ontological grounding in Lonergan's cognitional theory. See, on the contrary, the position of Xavier Marquart, "La causalité des signes: réflexions sur la valeur philosophique d'une explication théologique," *Revue Thomiste*, 32, n.s. 10(1927)40–60.

[10]*Insight*, p. 723; see also "Philosophy of Education," pp. 344–347, on the way in which the style of a culture will be transformed not only by conceptual criticism, but also by the elemental meanings of art as borne in culture, history and religion.

[11]*Method*, p. 63.

[12]Bernard Lonergan, "The Mass and Man," *The Catholic Mind* 45 (Sep-

tember 1947), 574. Note the similar thoughts of Karl Rahner in "The Eucharist and Suffering," *Theological Investigations*, trans. Karl-H. and Boniface Krüger (Baltimore: Helicon, 1967), III, 161–170.

[13]Bernard Lonergan, "Finality, Love, Marriage" (originally published in *Theological Studies* 4 [1943], pp. 477–510) in *Collection*, ed. F.E. Crowe (New York: Herder, 1967), p. 33. Karl Rahner makes a similar point about the nature of the sacramentality of marriage as the "willing of salvation for the other" in "Marriage as a Sacrament," *Theological Investigations*, trans. David Bourke (New York: Herder, 1973) X, 199–222.

[14]"Finality, Love, Marriage," p. 37.

[15]"The Mediation of Christ in Prayer," Lonergan Research Center; now available in *Method: Journal of Lonergan Studies* 2. (March 1984) 1, 1–21.

[16]"Philosophy of Education," p. 298.

[17]*Ibid.*, p. 299.

[18]*Ibid.*, p. 300.

[19]Bernard Lonergan, *De Deo Trino, II. Pars Systematica* (Rome: Gregorian University, 1964), pp. 186–208.

[20]*Insight*, p. 561.

[21]*Ibid.*, pp. 236–41.

[22]See "Philosophy of Education," pp. 297–299.

[23]*Method in Theology*, p. 364.

[24]*Ibid.*, p. 363.

[25]See, for example, Pitirim A. Sorokin, *Social and Cultural Dynamics: Fluctuation of Forms of Art* (New York: American Book Company, 1937), I, 247–250; II: *Fluctuation of Systems of Truth, Ethics, and Law* (New York: American Book Company, 1937), p. 91; and *The Crisis of Our Age: The Social and Cultural Outlook* (New York: Dutton, 1941), pp. 30–32, 36–52. References by Lonergan to Suzanne Langer's works may be found in *Insight*, pp. 184, 544; "Philosophy of Education," pp. 280–315; and *Method in Theology*, pp. 61, 64.

[26]The problem of studying ritual is manifold, fundamentally interdisciplinary. Ronald L. Grimes, in *Beginnings in Ritual Studies* (Lanham, Md.: University Press of America, 1982), esp. pp. 1–51, establishes a "non-normative" typology. I have adapted his terms, advancing the discussion by clarifying the rather "mixed" focus of his progression (from ritualization, through decorum, ceremony, liturgy, and magic to celebration) which sees celebration as the ideal ritual form. Recognizing that magic and celebration are actually negative and positive forms of self-transcendence (myth and mystery), I then reorder his ritual types, using Lonergan's notion of meaning and the functions of meaning in an explanatory fashion. This paradigm provides a hint toward how Lonergan's genuinely interpretive framework can contribute to the study of the sacraments.

Matthew L. Lamb

XIV. The Social and Political Dimensions of Lonergan's Theology

It may seem puzzling to close this introduction to Bernard Lonergan's theology with a discussion of its social and political dimensions. He wrote about ethics, but did he ever develop a social ethics? He wrote about the human good and praxis, but did he ever develop a political theory? The very way of posing these questions, however, runs the risk of missing the very real social and political significance of Lonergan's work. For it would be a mistake to conceive of Lonergan's contributions to theology in terms of specific treatises within specific disciplines. Rather, he envisages new ways of doing theology, ways which have yet to be fully explored and appropriated. This is especially apropos of the social and political dimensions of his theology.

If the function of theology is to mediate the significance and role of religion within a cultural matrix, and if the foundations of such an enterprise are conversions, then theology has inescapable social and political consequences insofar as any culture has social and political dimensions. By referring to a "cultural *matrix*," Lonergan was indicating the generative and transformative relations between religion, culture, and theology.[1]

In conversations he would comment on the importance of theology in the process of practically transforming scientific cultures and technological societies away from evil and toward life. This is stated pointedly in the Epilogue of *Insight* where Lonergan indicates how even fully developed empirical human sciences would need theology in order to meet adequately the issue of evil and the mystery of God's transformation of evil into good:

> In a word, empirical human science can become practical only through theology, and the relentless modern drift to social engineering and totalitarian controls is the fruit of man's effort to make human science practical though he prescinds from God and from the solution God provides for man's problem.[2]

Empirical human science becomes practical through theology. This would strike most psychologists or sociologists as strange, if not outright absurd. Lonergan is hardly a fundamentalist, ready to wave the Bible at any and all social problems. Nor is he a dogmatist, eager to deduce a course of action from the premise of some Church dogma. He goes on to state emphatically that theology can in no way substitute for the human sciences.[3] What, then, does he mean?

This introduction to the social and political significance of Lonergan's theology will attempt an answer to this question in the three following sections. Consistent with the theme of this introduction to his thought, the first will outline how Lonergan moves from desire to community, while the second will sketch the presence of community within societies with their technologies, economies, and polities. It is important to understand this basic orientation in the social and political dimensions of Lonergan's theology, for it calls into question many modern presuppositions. The final section will then outline his understanding of modernity as caught within a longer cycle of decline, and how a genuinely humanist ethics and praxis is open to religion and theology if it is to deal adequately with suffering and evil. In the terms of Lonergan's transposition of Hegelian categories, the first two sections will deal with the *thesis* of the heuristic of genuine human social development. Once one understands how Lonergan understood that thesis, it is easier to grasp how he understood the *antithesis* of social decline and the *synthesis* of a higher viewpoint with a redemptive reversal of decline.[4]

FROM DESIRE TO COMMUNITY

In order to understand how Lonergan approaches society and polity it is important to remember that he is primarily interested in fostering in the readers an attention to what they are doing while they are correctly understanding what is read. The first five chapters of *Insight* are particularly difficult since many readers most probably do not have sufficient background knowledge of physics and mathematics. Even those who do have such a background knowledge can often miss the point by simply attending to the theories Lonergan is discussing without understanding how he is functionally relating those theories to the recurrent occurrences of insights.

In chapters six and seven of *Insight* Lonergan is engaged in a similar effort, only now he is functionally relating a much more diverse and heterogenous quest for insight, not in mathematics or in physics, but in everyday life. These chapters on Common Sense are crucial to understanding how Lonergan approaches social and political issues. He has remarked that he considered them, along with the chapters on judgment, as especially significant.

In several very important ways these chapters forge critical correctives to much of modern social theory and practice.

Chapter six sets out the terms and relations constitutive of "common sense and its subject." Each and every human being who grows beyond infancy is such a subject. No one has to go to a school or get a diploma in order to develop some degree of common sense. Each and every human being to some degree experiences a spontaneous self-correcting process of learning in which ranges of activities are learned and perfected, from learning to walk and to talk into unlimited ranges of skills as varied as each and every human life.[5] In later writings Lonergan referred to the work of Jean Piaget as exemplifying the earliest infant manifestations of this spontaneous self-correcting process of learning. What is important for Lonergan is not this or that proverb exemplifying common sense, nor the many theories on common sense and ordinary language which philosophers have spun, but how we humans spontaneously inform our concrete experiences with meaning and value.[6]

Prior to such skills, however, are the manifold of desires which motivate us to acquire skills. The desire to know truthfully, or the desire for authenticity, or the desire for God, touches the innermost core of all human desiring. Yet it usually takes a great deal of intellectual, moral, or religious development before those desires are even named, let alone cultivated. More obvious and accepted are the needs for nourishment, shelter, and offspring. These needs for intussusception and reproduction are humanly experienced as desires, not—as with other animals—as instinct. Where other animals respond instinctually to needs for food and sex, humans experience these as desires eliciting intentional responses.[7] Because they are intentional, there is an almost endless variety of skills which humans invent and learn to fulfill these desires. Feeding and mating skills vary from culture to culture and over time, but such variations in common sense skills all *function* relative to feeding and mating. Lonergan calls attention to these functional activities and relations.

What is desired are very concrete and particular goods: food, drink, clothes, home, intimacy, children. These particular goods and the desires humans have for them are to be found in all cultures, times, and places. What is found, however, are the *dynamic functional relations* between desires and their fulfillment. How these functional relations are concretely lived are open to unlimited differences from culture to culture, time to time. Lonergan designates the functions as transcultural. In attending to these functions, he is not indulging in some idle idealist speculation cut off from the very real needs and desires humans have for particular material goods. "What is good, always is concrete."[8]

The development of common sense indicates how insights and the process of learning are hardly esoteric activities confined to ivory towers or scientific laboratories. By showing how common sense is intellectual when it develops the practical skills needed for attaining concretely particular goods, Lonergan effectively counters the tendency since the Renaissance to contrast the supposed skepticism of empirical science with the naiveté of common sense.[9] In both empirical science and common sense, self-correcting processes of learning are functioning. True, they function very differently in each. But it is simply wrong to set the two in conflict and opposition, as though common sense were rife with ignorant superstitions eventually to be overcome by the clear and clean concepts of science, or as though science was intrinsically skeptical and to be controlled by an omnicompetent common sense.[10]

While discussing the intellectual aspects of common sense, then, Lonergan does so only to set the record straight on the intrinsically *practical* orientation of common sense toward the realization of desired particular goods. To mistake Lonergan's concern for consciousness as "idealism" is to fall into the modern dichotomies between consciousness and life, mind and body, science and common sense, which misses the very practical import of his entire project. Both idealism and materialism result from an oversight of insight, as does the false dualism between body and mind.[11] At the end of his Preface to *Insight* Lonergan called attention to the very practical aspect of his project:

> There remains the question, What practical good can come of this book? The answer is more forthright than might be expected. For insight is the source not only of theoretical knowledge but also of all its practical applications and, indeed, of all intelligent activity. Insight into insight, then, will reveal what activity is intelligent, and insight into oversights will reveal what activity is unintelligent. But to be practical is to do the intelligent thing and to be unpractical is to keep blundering about. It follows that insight into both insight and oversight *is the very key to practicality.*[12]

Practicality is not just one type of experience or activity. It is as varied as are the desires which give rise to skills. Common sense practicality is always concretely specialized: a good hunter is not thereby a good farmer, a good teacher is not thereby a good business person, and so on. From the perspective of consciousness and desires, one can distinguish a variety of streams or patterns in which experience flows. Immanent within experience and desire is "a factor variously named conation, interest, attention, purpose."[13]

Depending upon our interests or purposes, our experiences are dynamically patterned. In *Insight* Lonergan mentions at least seven patterns (biological, aesthetic, artistic, dramatic, practical, intellectual, and mystical) and analyzes four (biological, aesthetic, intellectual, dramatic).[14] In *Method in Theology* these patterns of experience are mentioned within a discussion of differentiations of consciousness and are listed as biological, aesthetic, intellectual, dramatic, practical, and worshipful.[15]

The point is not the number, but how Lonergan derives them in terms of interests or purposes. Needs generate desires and desires generate interests. In biological patterns of experience all conscious activities and desires are directed toward fulfilling the biological needs of intussusception, reproduction, or—when our lives are threatened—self-preservation. Extroversion is a central characteristic of consciousness within this pattern, that is, the real is the "already-out-there-now-real." Hunger and thirst can hardly be sated by even the most realistic photos of food and drink. The extroversion of consciousness is a striking affirmation of the embeddedness of human awareness in physical, organic and animal environments. In terms of emergent probability, biological patterns of experience are the basic schemes of recurrence which condition (contrary to all forms of idealism), but do not determine (contrary to all forms of materialism), all other human schemes of recurrence.[16]

Aesthetic patterns of experience are those in which human experience begins to be experienced for its own sake, slipping "beyond the confines of serious-minded biological purpose" into the "liberation and self-justifying joy" of play, music, dance, and the endless variations of symbolic activity. Like the other patterns of experience, here too it is not a question of "formal" aesthetics. Spontaneously our experience slips into such aesthetic patterns; this is why Lonergan can distinguish aesthetic from artful patterns, where in the latter further differentiation occurs toward what we know as more formal art.[17] Similarly, the intellectual pattern of experience, though less common than the aesthetic, spontaneously arises to the degree that the pure and unrestricted desire to know empowers us to wonder and question. The self-correcting process of learning, present in all the patterns, is here given free reign. Yet, as Lonergan observes, "to learn thoroughly is a vast undertaking that calls for relentless perseverance."[18] The same could be said of the worshipful or mystical patterns of experience.[19]

No one lives exclusively in any one pattern of experience. Human experience is "polymorphic": the stream of conscious living flows in many different patterns and many blends of patterns. The primordial work of art any of us performs is our own daily living, how we experience and live out patterns and blends of patterns. This everyday living Lonergan terms the dramatic pattern of experience. As dramatic subjects we are by no means isolated. There is the embeddedness in biological, genetic, neurological, and psychic sets of schemes of recurrence relating us unconsciously and consciously to others. No matter how good we are at directing the drama of our lives, we are never fully in control. Not only do we not choose our relatives, we don't choose when or where we enter onto the stage of world history.

Our embeddedness in nature and history is not merely extrinsic to how we act in the drama of living. Between the neural processes we biologically inherit and the patterns of experience we historically inherit, there functions what Freud termed the psychic censor. Lonergan transforms the context of Freud's work rather remarkably, and this correlates with similar transformations in social theory. Freud tended to describe the psychic censor as a force at odds with the force of wish or desire. Political analogies are used to describe how the psychic censor is like a "jealous ruler" or "autocrat" seeking to enforce control over impulses and desires. Similarly, as Paul Ricoeur remarks, for Freud human being is to-be-threatened, with the ego seeking to dominate and dreams disguised fulfillments of suppressed or repressed desires. Freud tended toward the tragic affirmation of a never ending conflict between desire and death, *Eros* and *Thanatos*.[20]

Lonergan provides a framework for integrating Freud's discoveries without their reductionist, dominative, and tragic connotations. The psychic censorship is normally *not* in conflict with the self-correcting process of learning. It is not dominative and repressive but cooperative and *constructive*, selecting the materials which form the matrix of insight and understanding, as it mediates between neural demands and the psyche. Yet this preconscious process is often derailed by what Lonergan terms "bias." This term does not mean simply "an inclination of temperament." Rather he gives bias a precise meaning: aberrations of human understanding which exclude and repress insights, along with the further relevant questions they would have engendered.

Bias distorts and inhibits conscious performance in the drama of everyday living by blocking or blinding understanding. It also distorts the pre-conscious censorship, inhibiting images and affects conducive to insights. Thus bias for Lonergan has a dual aspect: (1) aberrations of the psychic censorship prior to conscious attention whereby it becomes *repressive* rather than constructive; (2) the inhibited and alienated conscious performance conditioned by the repression of the constructive and cooperative functions of the censorship. The first Lonergan terms dramatic bias, the second individual bias. There is no primordial conflict between desire and the unconscious. Primordially pre-conscious censorship is cooperative, constructively promoting images and affects conducive to insights and practical understanding of how to fulfill the desires. Conflict arises from the repression brought about by dramatic bias.[21]

So also in our social living, Lonergan sees the primordial stance as one of cooperation rather than conflict. Desires for the basic goods of food, shelter, and intimacy are recurrent, and so is the cooperative labor which seeks to fulfill them. The practical intelligence which generates labor is itself recurrent. Desires for particular goods need to be met, not just once or twice, but in a recurrent fashion. As the individual develops skills, so practical intelligence informing communal labor engenders cooperative roles and tasks, thereby institutionalizing the recurrent production of particular goods into what Lonergan terms a good of order. Rather than individuals fulfilling their desires for nourishment and shelter on their own, there emerge the vast networks of cooperation and specialized tasks, institutionalized as farming, fishing, food processing, markets, grocery retailing, builders, architects, furniture factories and retailers, etc.[22]

Just as recurrent desires are good, so recurrent labor institutionalized in cooperative roles and tasks is good. Analogous to Freud's censor, Marx tended to view social cooperation and the division of labor as inevitably resulting from domination and conflict. Typical of modern thinkers, Marx understood human beings as having conflictive relations with nature and among themselves.[23] Paul Ricoeur calls Freud and Marx "masters of suspicion" because they suspected that unconscious or unknown conflicts tend to dominate everyday living. They suspected that the whole of consciousness is "false consciousness." In the metaphor of a drama, although the actors think they are in control of their roles on stage, in fact their performance is determined by hidden directors, whether it be Freud's unconscious or Marx's capital.[24]

Lonergan does not contest that these factors can and do influence or condition the drama. In the framework of emergent probability, the works of Freud and Marx call attention to personal and social underlying schemes of recurrence which can, and often do, condition the drama of life in the negative and alienating ways they analyzed. Yet Lonergan calls our attention to the intellectual performance of Freud and Marx in concretely transcending the inhibitions and alienation through their insights and commitments to the values of reflective understanding.[25] If Freud attended to the recurrent schemes of desires and Marx to the recurrent schemes of labor, then Lonergan attends to the recurrence of intelligence with its non-dominative desires and practical insights. Just as images are the matrix and conditions for the emergence of insights, so recurrent desires and recurrent labor provide matrices and conditions for ongoing recurrences of practical intelligence. This enables Lonergan to attend to the dynamic orientation of consciousness which is capable of transcending any and all false consciousness. If by the "whole of consciousness" one included this dynamic orientation to raise ever further relevant questions, then, of course, no one could ever discover that it even was "false." There are self-correcting processes of learning whereby, for example, anyone who learns, even though the context of the learning is dominative, can by his or her learning begin to question and criticize the dominative context.[26]

Relative to Freud and the recurrence of desire, Lonergan points out how the conditional character of underlying manifolds do not dominate or rigidly determine the higher schemes of recurrence. There are in the lower manifolds of psyche potentialities for gentleness and understanding, creativity and goodness, as well as potentialities for parricide and cannibalism, incest and suicide. These latter possibilities, while they are actualized in some instances, much more commonly are rejected as irrational and immoral. Desire is not repressed but liberated and refined as we reject dominative evil and do good. Desire flourishes in genuine conscience. Cultural reductionism ignores these very positive and constructive aspects of psychic censorship collaborating with conscience. Domination and conflict are so identified with "reality" that even the positive and constructive are reduced to repression. Such a reductionism becomes a cultural pessimism, asserting "that under the disguise of a phenomenal consciousness there lurks a monster that is the reality of each of us and the effective master of our lives."[27]

COMMUNITY GENERATES SOCIETY

The development from desire to intersubjective communities of family and clan is hardly the end of desire. Lonergan indicates how recurrent patterns of cooperation in productive labor can, and often are, fruits of practical intelligence. Recurrent desires generate labor, and recurrent labor, when informed with human cooperation, recurrently generates practical intelligence. Ever more efficient tools and technologies develop. These technologies in turn evoke economies, with ever more complex patterns of production, capital formation, and consumption. Even with relatively simple technologies and economies, as practical intelligence increases, so does the need for attention to human cooperation itself, for the problem of generating effective agreement becomes recurrent. This is, for Lonergan, the function of politics. The political specialization of common sense is meant to promote agreement, consensus, in the service of practical and intelligent cooperation.[28]

Against idealists, Lonergan's analysis indicates how technological schemes of recurrence condition economic schemes of recurrence, which, in turn, condition polities and politics. Against materialists, his analysis indicates how the emergence of practical intelligence and patterns of cooperation cannot simply be reduced to the underlying technological and economic conditions. Indeed, a presupposition of such reductionism, evident in the materialism of capitalism and communism, is a failure to understand practical intelligence informing patterns of cooperation and how that intelligence is non-dominative. This is why Lonergan can write that the materialist, whether Behaviorist or Marxist, "is condemned by his own principles to be no more than a manipulator."[29]

The interlocking schemes of recurrence making up technologies, economies, polities are what Lonergan terms "a good of order." By this he does not mean some automatic functioning that is good simply because it is there—as in "law and order." The good of order is concretely a good only to the extent that the cooperation ensures "the recurrence of all effectively desired instances of the particular good," and that the interdependence of effective desires and cooperation is "understood and accepted."[30] Lonergan resolutely refuses to reify social processes into automatic and inhuman mechanisms. Human intelligence and commitment can never be dispensed with:

> The same economic set-up is compatible with prosperity and with recession. The same constitutional and legal arrangements admit wide differences in political life and the administration of justice. Similar rules for marriage and the family in one case generate domestic bliss and in another misery.[31]

Lonergan did not succumb to the temptation Gandhi saw as a plague of modernity: to think humans could create systems so good that humans themselves need not be good.

The social good of order is utterly concrete for Lonergan. He insists that it is "not some design for utopia, some theoretic ideal, some set of ethical precepts, some code of laws, or some super-institution."[32] To understand the good of order concretely is to avoid reifying institutions. All the great institutions of history are fundamentally, for Lonergan, manners in which humans develop skills, roles, and tasks in cooperation with one another. Institutions make up a good of order to the degree that such cooperative skills, roles, and tasks are understood and accepted.[33] We reify institutions to the extent that we do not advert to how they are expressions or products of human cooperation. We believe that institutions have a life of their own, independent of human agency; they are likened to machines which run by themselves. This attitude of reification confuses institutions with material products of human agency. We can live in buildings and enjoy skyscrapers without adverting to the many human beings who cooperated in their building. But institutions are made up neither of bricks nor of concrete, but of living human beings. Social institutions are more like languages than they are like material objects; they are not fixed and immutable entities, but change as the ways in which the human cooperation constituting them change.[34]

The good of order is intrinsically oriented toward freedom. Freedom itself is not merely an extrinsic option relative to the proper functioning of social institutions, once one understands that these are constituted by human cooperation. Initially, this means that all institutions are for the sake of human beings, not human beings for the sake of institutions. The centrality of human cooperation means that the good of order is intrinsically oriented toward values. Human cooperation is alive with the desires and feelings which are intentional responses to values. Feelings respond to values in accord with scales of preference.[35]

Lonergan distinguishes vital, social, cultural, personal, and religious values. Vital values are those associated with acquiring, maintaining, and restoring human physical health and well-being. Social values are those involved in the cooperative technological, economic, and political good of order which condition the vital values of the whole society. Cultural values are those which discover, express, validate, criticize, correct, develop, and improve the meanings and values of human living. Personal values are persons originating the values of attentiveness, intelligence, reasonableness, responsibility, love. Religious values are "at the heart" of human living insofar as the question of God is implicit in all human questing and questioning.[36]

Lonergan's understanding of freedom is intrinsic to the related and recurrent operations of consciousness. The operations do not force us to be attentive, intelligent, reasonable, responsible. The transcendental imperatives are the gentle invitations of conscience, not the loud commands of a dictator. More often than not we discover how inattentive, stupid, unreasonable, and irresponsible we individually and collectively have been. Similarly, the scale of preference indicates how vital and social values condition cultural, personal, and religious values (against any form of idealism), while cultural, personal, and religious values are neither negated nor reduced to vital and social values (against any form of materialism).

It is within this context of freedom and value that Lonergan finds the social correlative to the structures of consciousness: community. Communities occur where "people are joined by common experience, by common or complementary insights, by similar judgments of fact and of value, by parallel orientations in life."[37] Just as consciousness is a complex movement of desire through feelings and images, insights and judgments, to decisions and actions, so community is the cooperative quest arising from common experiences, seeking common meanings, truths, and values. Spontaneously intersubjective communities of families, kin, and clan evoke over time more intentional civil communities. Similar to conscious intentionality, community is a concrete transcendental for Lonergan. The personal and the communal are intrinsically related. Community is generative, not only of feeling and desire, but also of intelligence and goodness. All of the concretely existing social institutions, insofar as they embody attentively intelligent and reasonably responsible cooperation, are generated by communities. Thus Lonergan sees community as the ideal basis of society: "Without a large measure of community, human society and sovereign states cannot function."[38]

Community, like consciousness itself, is no guarantee of intelligence, goodness, or holiness. Lonergan did not indulge in romantic idealizations of community over against the cold mechanisms of bureaucratic, industrialized societies. This does *not* mean that consciousness and community are simply neutral playing fields, indifferent to truth or falsity, goodness or evil. The drama of conscious living can be marked by great inattentive, stupid, unreasonable, and irresponsible actions. Still, an uneasy conscience can witness to the native orientation of desire toward genuineness.[39]

Similarly, human intersubjectivity is oriented toward cooperative intimacy and labor, cooperative quests for common and complementary meaning and value, common orientations toward genuineness. Very often, however, such communal cooperation is lacking:

> Community is not just an aggregate of individuals within a frontier, for that overlooks its formal constituent, which is common meaning. Such common meaning calls for a common field of experience and, when that is lacking, people get out of touch. It calls for common or complementary ways of understanding and, when they are lacking, people begin to misunderstand, to distrust, to suspect, to fear, to resort to violence. It calls for common judgments and, when they are lacking, people reside in different worlds. It calls for common values, goals, policies and, when they are lacking, people operate at cross-purposes.[40]

What are the grounds, in Lonergan's analysis, for this breakdown of community and the resulting alienation?

The reasons are as diverse as each of the concrete situations wherein communities break down. Lonergan is attempting to elaborate heuristic relations or functions operative in manifolds of different instances. There are many psychological analyses which will often be relevant for understanding why recurrent desires are denied or repressed. Lonergan indicates how sexual repression and oppression distort both conscious living and psychic censorship, forcing neural demand functions into incongruous paths, and destroying intelligent and responsible relationships.[41] The variations on this "common problem" (as Lonergan understates it) range over the multitude of sexual pathologies, including such gender related pathologies as the misogyny to which feminists now call our attention. Class oppression in countless forms has profoundly distorted labor, technologies, economies, and polities.

Racism, and other forms of oppression, have ravaged the lives and cultures of millions.

One could go on listing the many types of critical analysis of why human communities break down. Many of them are complementary, some contradictory, but all can only be adequately judged in reference to the concrete situations they attempt to analyze. The significance of Lonergan's analysis of common sense in this regard is twofold.

First, there is no way that a genuinely concrete analysis can do away with the concreteness of common sense judgments, evaluations, and decisions. Theories, no matter how critical and comprehensive, simply cannot cover all of the variables operative within concrete historical situations. Grand theories of history and humanity can become oppressive and dominative unless they acknowledge the fundamental significance of intelligence operative in the myriad concrete situations where men and women live. Common sense is not a concession to some incompleteness in our theories, sooner or later to be subsumed, as Hegel hoped, in a complete and coherent theory. Common sense, analogous to statistical methods, can never be totally subsumed into explanatory theories.[42]

Second, Lonergan has succeeded in indicating how intelligence is constitutive of common sense, in terms of incomplete sets of insights and judgments ever to be completed by more insights and judgments in each and every concrete situation. Now, what is central in all of the analyses of the breakdown of community is obviously analysis—that is, intelligence attempting to understand correctly how and why human cooperation and community fails. Lonergan's analysis is not meant to supplant analyses of classism, racism, sexism, militarism—any more than his analysis of space and time is meant to supplant geometry or quantum mechanics. Rather, by showing how intelligence is operative in common sense and in community, Lonergan provides a framework within which to correct any obscurantism in such analyses, whether they be of empiricist/materialist or conceptualist/idealist varieties.

Ironically, first victims of such obscurantism are all those who either never knew the analysis in question, or understood it poorly. The past is relegated to "pre-history," and ever more diverse schools or tendencies develop within the social theories. In one way or another, light and brilliance is attributed to the favorite theory; what cannot fit is dismissed as darkness. Common sense is dismissed as unintelligent chaos, to be controlled and manipulated by those who possess the correct theory.[43]

Yet, it is intelligence in act, it is men and women correctly understanding and responsibly acting, which is decisive. If no theory can completely express human intelligence, so also can no community genuinely claim to be the repository of all knowledge and wisdom. This applies, not only to social analysis, but as well to social order. If desires generate the practical intelligence embodied in tools, in economies, and in polities, if recurrent desires generate intersubjectivity and community, still both desires and intelligence are manifolds incapable of complete and coherent expression. Conscious intentionality is not the same as knowledge. While the practical intelligence operative within a community is varied and manifold as each working member, still no one individual knows explicitly the totality of that common practical intelligence.

Desire, as Lonergan reminds us, "is not to be confused either with animal impulse or with egoistic scheming."[44] We have seen how desires for particular recurrent goods generate the good of a communal or social order in which those particular goods can be more or less regularly met, and how such good of order is oriented toward human freedom. Human desires evoke the dramatic artistry of everyday living with the many practical ways in which communities and individuals pursue vital, social, cultural, personal, or religious values. Vital values generally concern particular goods, social values regard goods of order, while cultural, personal, and religious values involve more directly the free orientations of persons choosing genuine values.[45]

In seeking to attain any of these values, individuals and communities experience radical tensions between intersubjective spontaneity and intelligently devised social order or practical common sense. For Lonergan "tension" has no pejorative connotations. All development involves tension between the limitations of present achievements and going beyond those limitations to new achievements. Within emergent probability there is always tension between underlying manifolds and the higher integrations realizing the potentialities of those manifolds. In human development, genuineness requires that the tension be acknowledged, and such genuine acknowledgement is the basis for harmonious cooperation.[46]

Thus, it would be a mistake to read Lonergan's discussion of the tension between intersubjective spontaneity and intelligently devised social order as though it were a variation on the theme, so common in modern social theories, of opposing the emotive routines of "primitive" intersubjectivity and the rational demands of advanced industrial society. Lonergan is not simply taking over the concepts of *Gemeinschaft* versus *Gesellschaft*, of community versus society, with which the social theorist Ferdinand Tönnies initiated what in later social theorists would become lists of supposed antagonisms between human spontaneity and social conformity:

(1) Max Weber's contrasting ideal types of affective value-orientations, with traditional or charismatic authoritarianism, and instrumentalist rationality, with bureaucratic authoritarianism;

(2) Emile Durkheim's contrasts between mechanical solidarity and organic solidarity;

(3) Talcott Parsons' framing of the basic problem of social order as how

to control individuals locked in a Hobbesian "war of all against all," with a consequent extrinsicism endemic to his functionalist methods;

(4) Jürgen Habermas' contrasts between life-world and technical, economic systems, as well as Anthony Giddens' concessions to domination and constraint in social structure.[47]

While it would far exceed the scope of this introduction to spell out in sufficient detail these social theories, they are mentioned here only to alert the reader to possible misunderstandings. The tension between spontaneous intersubjectivity and practical intelligence is by no means an ultimate dualistic antagonism or conflict, in which social authorities must impose rules and control the chaos or anarchy ascribed to spontaneous intersubjectivity. Instead, the radical tension of community is a very positive dynamism natural to human life, wherein practical intelligence comes up with new possibilities, new skills, new insights, new tools, new ways of cooperating to attain the human good. The realization of those new ways of living or acting stands in tension with the old routines and established patterns. No matter how complex and specialized social institutions become, they always remain the products of human communal cooperation, whether for good or ill.[48]

The breakdown of community, the barbarism which the analyses of class oppression, racism, sexism, and militarism record so painfully, is rooted, not in the tension of community, but in what Lonergan terms "the dialectic of community." This is, of course, a very unusual perspective for those who accept those modern social theories which claim that industrialization, urbanization, and an inexorable bureaucratization mean that community is increasingly impossible. For Lonergan, however, community is the social correlative to conscious intentionality. Just as it is impossible to so alienate and repress human conscious intentionality so that the alienated and repressed would have no experiences, insights, judgments, so there is no way that alienation, repression, and social oppression can completely extinguish community. Stated more positively, just as Lonergan envisages a positive constructive function within the psychic censorship whereby it fosters the images conducive to insight and understanding, so he envisages a positive, constructive function within the radical tension of community whereby creativity and community progress.

Similarly, just as the psychic censorship conditions but does not rigidly determine our consciousness, so the radical tension between spontaneous intersubjectivity and developing practical intelligence conditions, but in no way determines, how communities develop or fail to develop. Just as the censor can become repressive, blocking unwanted insights, so the tension can become repressive, alienating intersubjectivity and thwarting practical intelligence. Rather than a creative tension, there emerges the dialectic of community.

If the tension between spontaneous intersubjectivity and practical intelligence were always characterized by attentiveness, intelligence, reasonableness, and responsibility, then there would be progressive authenticity and an expanding series of related communities among peoples. Such, obviously, is not a description of the course of human history on this planet. Quite the contrary! The concrete and dynamic orientations of individuals and groups are neither cooperative nor complementary, but conflictive and contradictory. Just as image and concept are severed from one another and clash unless mediated by insight and understanding, so intersubjectivity and practical intelligence are severed and clash when not mediated by community.

Lonergan's notion of community breaks with the naive realism of those who would see physical force as the source, and forcing others to obey one's commands as the carrier, of social power. Genuinely human social power—rather than reified and alienated phantoms—has its source in intersubjective cooperation, and its carrier is community. Just as genuine social power expands responsibility and freedom, so genuine authority resides in such communal cooperation.[49] Contrary to much of modern social theory, "it would seem to be a mistake to conceive the sociological as simply a matter of external constraint."[50] Indeed, force, constraint, militarism reveal a failure, a terrible blindness and fear, at the core of all societies which depend on them for their social cohesion.[51] The difference between genuine social power and authority, on the one hand, and dominative power and authoritarianism, on the other, is similar to the differences between love and rape. Social theories tend to reflect, rather than correct, the underlying alienations in modern societies.

MODERNITY, DECLINE, AND REDEMPTIVE PRAXIS

In September of 1942 Lonergan reviewed a book by a Polish academic with the provocative title *Is Modern Culture Doomed?* The question was very much a part of his work on economics and, later, *Insight*. In the review he acknowledged how modernity is marked by materialism:

> . . . eighteenth century capitalism, nineteenth century communism and twentieth century nazism. Such is the great materialist trinity: communism is a collectivist reaction against capitalist individualism; nazism is a nationalist reaction against the international character of finance and world revolution. Despite their differences and oppositions, all three agree in their dedication of man, soul and body, to the goods of this world. None of them acknowledges . . . a higher end. . . . Their consequences are not a matter of abstract

deduction. The experiment has been performed and still is being performed on the quivering body of humanity. The results are not pleasant.[52]

The quivering body of humanity states well the fact of how each and every human being is genetically, psychically, socially, and spiritually related to others, not in some extrinsic fashion, but intrinsically. Emergent probability within both nature and history criticizes the extrinsicism in both monadic individualism and forced collectivism. Massive human suffering witnesses to "a single dialectic of community" embracing both an endless series of individual dramas and the entire history of humankind.[53]

If the key to genuinely human progress is attentive, intelligent, reasonable, and responsible cooperation in ever expanding and complementary networks of community, the key to decline is a repression of such cooperation and community. Lonergan's notion of dialectic does not apply to nature, whether physical or human, but only to the repression of nature. Specifically, Lonergan sees in the repression of the desire to know, to raise ever further relevant questions in order to understand correctly, a major factor in the dialectics of the dramatic subject. The censor is blocked in its constructive function and becomes repressive. Similarly, when the tension of community, with its dynamic cooperation between intersubjectivity and practical intelligence, is disrupted by the repression of one or the other, then the tension is no longer creative but destructive.[54]

This process of repression Lonergan terms "bias." His concern is with a blocking or blinding of understanding which is conscious but not necessarily known as such. The connotation of bias as pre-dispositional and prejudicial conveys this. In dealing with dramatic, individual, group, and general bias, Lonergan offers the framework within which he could attempt to situate the discoveries and concerns of Freud, Marx, and all those seeking to understand the pathologies afflicting the human condition and interested in transforming that condition.

Lonergan's emphasis on the constructive and creative orientations of psyche and of community was not an optimist's romantic utopianism. What concerned him was the failure of modern analysts of repression, alienation, and domination to attend to their own intelligent performance of probing, questioning analysis. He fully agreed that there was a cancerous flight from understanding and human solidarity in history, but he objected to the modern tendency to so totalize the negation—whether it be repression, inhibition, alienation, or domination—that one would overlook or minimize how in the very analysis of those negations is the empowerment toward transformation. Psyche, conscious intentionality, community, and human history are not "locked into" decline, domination, and destruction. Pre-dispositions and prejudices can be corrected.

Lonergan gives bias his own meaning as repression of unwanted insights and further relevant questions. Since, for him, recurrent intelligence is the operative principle of expanding effective human freedom and progressive transformations of human society, one expects that he also locates the basic pathology as a block to such recurrent intelligence. It is intelligent to be attentive to neural demand functions and the patterned rhythms of psyche. Repression and inhibition bias and block that attention. This does not mean that such repression and inhibition is fully deliberate and chosen. As with all the biases, Lonergan sees the social and historical contexts as primary. Thus the dialectic of community conditions manifolds of individuals in how their endopsychic censorship functions with regard to neural demands:

> In this relationship, the dialectic of community holds the dominant position, for it gives rise to the situations that stimulate neural demands and it molds the orientation of intelligence that preconsciously exercises the censorship.[55]

Individual bias differs from dramatic bias insofar as it is more intentionally egoistic and self-scheming. The repression and inhibition of the dramatically biased person can sometimes lead to much too weak an ego-development and too inordinate a submersion in the intersubjective affects of the family or group. Individual bias is the incomplete development of intelligence which fails to acknowledge how the dynamic orientation of intelligence is toward a good which is common to all. The individually biased person can be very skillful in intelligently advancing his or her own interests; yet intelligence is ruled out of court when it begins to question the limitations and distortions of those interests. What especially concerns Lonergan is how such individuals block the development of practical common sense and, at times, distort their experience into an instrument of individualism.[56] Just as psychology and psychiatry are most developed in the fields of such dramatic and individual pathologies, so also it is not surprising, given Lonergan's analysis, that capitalist cultures, with their excessive individualism, would be most advanced in exploring both the illnesses and possible therapies.

Group bias results from extended failures to adapt communal living to the changes required by practical understanding. In society and history, as in nature, situations and events call forth ongoing processes of change and adaptation. Indeed, change is even more operative in the human realm since intelligence is an active source of endless new questions, insights, meanings and values, technologies, economies, and polities. There are social groupings defined implicitly by the patterned relations of a social order. While the tension of community leads to whole sets of interrelated groups cooperating by contributing their specialized expertise toward the common good, that co-operative complementarity disappears when group differences are not defined by intelligent social function, but by the group egoism of wealth, race, or ethnic origin—"while intelligence heads for change, group spontaneity does not regard all changes in the same cold light of the general good of society." Just as the individualist tends to reject insights when they challenge his egoism, "so also the group is prone to have a blind spot for the insights that reveal its well-being to be excessive or its usefulness at an end."[57]

Technological, economic, and political development becomes distorted as the new insights and more reasonable policies are rejected and repressed. Authority becomes authoritarian as it has recourse to domination and oppression to preserve class, race, ethnic, or other forms of group dominance. The aberrations which group bias cause invite, however, their own reversals. Hegel's dialectic of master and slave, as well as Marx's class analysis, exemplifies how the dialectic of community heads toward reversal. Whether the dominant groups are reactionary or revolutionary, there are always possibilities that the group conflicts and struggles will bring the oppressed groups, with their insights and policies, into dominance. While this succession of dominance and oppression seems an accurate description of so much of human history, it also indicates the serious limitations and distortions of understanding the dialectical process as ultimately one of domination. If group against group were all that was operative, then it would seem that there would be a continual succession of domination and oppression, of new masters oppressing new slaves, who, in turn, etc.[58]

Individual and group biases result from individuals and groups repressing the further relevant questions and insights which would lead them to understand how their particular desires, fears, and interests are not ultimate criteria for what is intelligent and responsibly good. Constructive and creative tension degenerates into repression and conflict. Mention was made of Paul Ricoeur's reference to Freud and Marx as masters of suspicion, and how Lonergan could take up their concerns while rejecting any notion that the whole of consciousness could be false. Freud's concern with pathological distortions in our recurrent desires is taken up in Lonergan's notions of dramatic and individual biases. Marx's concern with the alienation in the recurrent processes of labor is taken up in Lonergan's notion of group bias.

Now Lonergan's own concern for the recurrent stifling and repression of intelligence led to his notion of general bias. Becoming resigned that the cycles of dramatic, individual, and group biases cannot be broken, that conflict and contradiction are ultimately endemic to the human condition in a universe and a history shot through with chaos and absurdity, is symptomatic of what Lonergan terms general bias. There is a deep-seated tendency in common sense to resist those questions, insights, and ideas which would radically transform all present achievements. As Lonergan writes:

> Every specialist runs the risk of turning his specialty into a bias by failing to recognize and appreciate the significance of other fields. Common sense almost invariably makes that mistake; for it is incapable of analyzing itself, incapable of making the discovery that it too is a specialized development of human knowledge, incapable of coming to grasp that its peculiar danger is to extend its legitimate concern for the concrete and the immediately practical into disregard of larger issues and indifference to long-term results.[59]

General bias affects all cultures, groups, individuals as a resistance of present achievements against further developments of intelligence. Common sense with its intelligently devised social orders is especially prone to this general bias insofar as its immersion in the concrete and immediately practical all too easily encourages a repression of those questions and insights which concern larger issues and long-term results. Thus common sense tends to get stuck in a recurrent tendency to dismiss such questions and insights as no more than the interests of "another group." Human history becomes no more than a cyclic recurrence of one group dominating, to be overthrown by the oppressed whose liberation is the prologue to their dominating others.

Besides Freud and Marx, Ricoeur mentions a third "master of suspicion" whose work is relevant here, Friedrich Nietzsche. For him the cyclic recurrence of domination and oppression was unbreakable. The will to power of heroic individuals and groups—his "Uebermenschen" are literally "superhumans"—leads them to overcome the resentments characteristic of the oppressed. Heroic self-assertion in the face of terror and ultimate nihilism is the fate of those who would struggle successfully within the cycles of domination and oppression. "Within" is the operative word, for in the horizon described by Nietzsche's superhuman there is no overcoming of an eternal cyclic recurrence of domination.[60]

This describes well the distorted dialectic of community, and it is far more painful than philosophers, including Nietzsche, imagine. For general bias traps societies and histories in what Lonergan terms "the longer cycle of decline." The dismissal of intelligence, the continued and extensive flight from understanding, are justified by hard-headed appeals to "reality." But the social reality is less and less informed with human attentiveness, intelligence, reasonableness, and responsibility insofar as the communities generating the societies fail to live up to those dynamic orientations. History becomes overloaded with what Lonergan calls "false facts" as the actual existence of what should not be. On the international scale, the actual existence of what should not be is the ground of *Realpolitik:* "We have to defend the nation; everything would be fine if the other people did what they ought to do, but they don't, and so we can't."[61]

Indeed, it is Lonergan's view that history is compelling us toward a fateful realization of just how destructive our complacent acceptance of general bias has become.

The longer cycle of decline is what grounds the false facts which are piling up, as it were, toward the end of the twentieth century. Intelligence seems to have less and less relevance as the social and political "realities" are informed with the false facts of superpower political rivalries, short-sighted economic and industrial policies, and weapons races of enormous proportions. The quiet voice of reason seems foolish nonsense amid the noise of solemn assemblies caught in the longer cycle of decline:

> The false fact leads to a grasp, an insight, that is not so much an inverse insight as a perverse insight. . . . There is the mounting irrelevance of intellect and reason, initially in particular cases with regard to particular things, but it gradually builds up. If, for example, a philosopher were to tell the members of the United Nations that what we have to do is achieve self-appropriation and follow reason, they would know he was a fool.[62]

The building up of the false facts is what Lonergan terms "the social surd." Intelligence is no longer genuinely critical, since it is in no position to distinguish between social achievements and social surds, between progress and decline. Instead of following the pure and unrestricted desire to know, intelligence surrenders to the non-intelligibility of the false social facts named "reality":

> Reality is the economic development, the military equipment, and the political dominance of the all-inclusive State. Its ends justify all means. Its means include not merely every technique of indoctrination and propaganda, every tactic of economic and diplomatic pressure, every device for breaking down the moral conscience and exploiting the secret affects of civilized man, but also the terrorism of a political police, of prisons and torture, of concentration camps, of transported and extirpated minorities, and of total war.[63]

The painful experiments which Lonergan described as being carried out on the quivering body of humankind over the past two centuries by capitalist individualism, communist collectivism, and fascist nationalism decline, as our century winds down, toward the social surd of massive militarism and "the unbroken tension of a prolonged emergency" in which the "realistic" alternatives are total nuclear destruction or totalitarian world empire.[64] The nuclear arms race challenges humankind to make a momentous step in enlightenment and understanding. Violence and domination intrinsically imply each other in such a way that violence is inadequate even as a tool of liberation and progress. The fundamental issue of the historical process is not force or power but community and understanding. Practicality will end up destroying itself, doing away with humankind, unless such a shift toward intelligence is made.[65]

We have seen that the tension of community generates reversals of individual and group biases insofar as other individuals or groups take up the questions, insights, and issues repressed by the dominant individual or group. But general bias, with its longer cycle of decline, is not susceptible of such shorter cycle reversals. The tension of community generates reversal of general bias "only by confronting human intelligence with the alternative of adopting a higher viewpoint or perishing."[66]

Surds confront intelligence with an immanent need and desire for higher viewpoints. The higher viewpoint does not make the surd intelligible; rather out of the non-intelligibility of the surd intelligence seeks a higher integration wherein the surd is transcended. Lonergan indicates how fruitful this process is in mathematics and the natural sciences.[67] The social surd of the longer cycle of decline only intensifies an awareness of the limits of practical common sense and the need to attend to those dimensions of human living which transcend immediate practicality such as "delight and suffering, laughter and tears, joy and sorrow." Culture is this human capacity to raise the questions and reflect, feel and act in ways which satisfy both human intelligence and the human heart.[68]

Culture will reverse the longer cycle of decline to the extent that it promotes the expansion of effective freedom, enabling and empowering human beings to be the attentive, intelligent, reasonable, and responsibly loving subjects of their own personal and communal histories.[69] The challenge to culture is to develop what, in *Insight*, Lonergan termed cosmopolis. Cosmopolis is the flowering of the tension of community into free and critical cooperation among communities on a world scale.[70]

Lonergan's dialectic of community relative to group and general bias exposes the limitation of nationalism. His concern with community as intrinsically oriented toward intelligence and social institutions addresses a basic issue in the pathological distortion of nationalism to legitimate domination, as in all types of fascism. The last decade of his life was devoted to understanding the dynamic correlations of terms and relations constitutive of complex, large economies. Both capitalism and communism are armed to the hilt with nuclear weapons, yet neither system represents truly intelligent and responsible economies. A genuine global revolution of justice and peace demands a deeper understanding of just how both capitalism and communism dysfunction as economic systems. Lonergan's work in macroeconomics is not a half-hearted attempt to find some "middle" ground between capitalism and communism; it is a cogent and sustained effort to articulate an explanatory understanding of complex exchange economies.[71]

In later writings such as *Method in Theology* the term cosmopolis is not used. Cosmopolis and culture are unable to meet the further questions that arise in the light of the immense and massive histories of suffering which have bloodied the pages of history, making, in the words of Walter Benjamin, monuments of culture monuments of barbarism as well. The surd of massive suffering, domination, and oppression resists the higher viewpoints which human consciousness and community alone can give. We can grieve for the dead and the innocent victims; we can erect monuments in their memory and overthrow the dominative structures which oppressed them, but that is not full justice. There are limits to liberation, both personal and cultural, which manifest the impotence of intellectual and moral horizons alone—no matter how high the viewpoint within those horizons—to humanize and transform human history.[72] Even a moment's reflection upon the billions and billions of dead victims over the course of history, even of those histories of revolutions for justice, makes a mockery of any pretense to human self-sufficiency. A genuinely redemptive praxis requires more than we humans can accomplish on our own.

In the chapter on grace the reader has been introduced into how the classical theorem of the supernatural was just that, a theorem. It is a solution, and a solution to very real and concrete problems of human history and the alienation and massive histories of suffering which stain every paragraph and page of human history on this planet. Lonergan transposes the classical distinction into the modern contexts by carefully articulating some of the main elements in a critical theory of human history. There is not a complete intelligibility in that history, far from it.

By understanding social and political events within shorter and longer cycles of decline, Lonergan names the suffering and evil of domination and alienation as surds. So the higher viewpoint of self-appropriating cultures is immanently oriented toward religious faith and the free gifted revelation of God's enduring love for us. Grace does not make sin and evil intelligible, any more than higher mathematical operations with irrational numbers make the numbers any less irrational, or any more than ongoing discoveries in physics remove the lack of intelligibility in constant velocity.[73]

As the chapter on redemption indicated, Lonergan's theology of redemption is one in which the law of the cross is the immanently transcendent intelligibility of human history. Christ's passion, death, and resurrection do not make the massive histories of suffering intelligible or meaningful in themselves. Quite the contrary. Rather, the paschal mysteries transform the dialectic of community by, if I may use the expression, intensifying the tension of community, heightening human "intersubjective awareness of the sufferings and needs of mankind."[74] The massive wounds afflicting human sensitivity and intersubjectivity can be creatively healed only by *living* a faith, hope, and love attentive to the mysterious presence of God calling each and every human being into a Triune Community of Infinite Intelligence generating Infinite Understanding spirating Infinite Love. Such a gifted call makes possible a transformative communion or community, not only among present generations, but also with all the generations of humankind. Eternity, after all, is not the unending extension of time many philosophers and theologians have imagined.[75]

The call to Triune Community is a higher integration *of* all the concrete human communities constituting human history. The chapters on the Church and sacraments introduced how human sensitivity and intersubjectivity can be healed in the new psychic and social integrations embodied in Christian communities of worship, prayer, and socially transformative action.[76] When Lonergan speaks of the law of the cross as the immanently transcendent intelligibility of human history, he is at the very least trying to communicate to theologians the need for much more work "on the concrete universal that is mankind in the concrete and cumulative consequences of the acceptance or rejection of the message of the Gospel."[77] More than that, he is indicating how, as he used to repeat in lectures, the Church has the mission to transform the world in the light of Christ's preaching and practice. Much too often in history the Church ends up compromising that preaching and practice by conforming to the deformations of the world.[78]

Redemptive praxis is the mission and task of the Church, understood as aspiring to become a creatively transformative and healing presence down the centuries of history. Evil, sin, domination—these massive surds in human history are incapable of being explained, let alone explained away. The redemptive praxis informed by faith, hope, and love is required since the absolutely supernatural solution to the problem of evil is primarily a solution to be practiced and lived, and only through that living understood. This is why Lonergan later would speak of the primacy of praxis as a movement from above downward, from existential commitment and action through understanding to the transformation of ourselves and our world.[79]

Religious conversion is not a merely extrinsic process which may or may not occur with little or no difference to human histories. Religious conversion is intrinsically related to intellectual and moral conversions. Intelligence, goodness, and holiness are integral with each other, not in terms of some classical ideal but in the ongoing practice of striving for ever fuller attentiveness, intelligence, reasonableness, responsibility, love. The fully humanist position, if it gives full scope to the eros of intelligence and the desires of the human heart, "loses its primacy, not by some extrinsicist invasion, but by submitting to its own immanent necessities."[80] If the human sciences are going to become genuinely practical, expanding effective human freedom, then a methodologically transformed theology has to become a creative collaborator in this project.

The social and political dimensions of Lonergan's theology are hardly some ethical afterthoughts tacked onto positions already developed. They are intrinsic to the very doing of any theology involved in faith seeking understanding and understanding seeking faith. *Insight,* as he said, is a prolegomenon to *Method in Theology,* for if theology is to enter intelligently and responsibly into reversing the longer cycle of decline, with the latter's overwhelming threat of planetary omnicide, then theologians must overcome not only their own biases but also the danger of any specialist to ignore the long-term results and deeper issues beyond his or her own specialty. Any specialization of intelligence, not only the myriad specializations of common sense, is infected by general bias.

What is more, by articulating the related and recurrent operations of human conscious intentionality, Lonergan has provided a non-dominative basis for communal, regional, national, and international collaboration toward peace and justice. He does not offer a theory to be imposed from without. Rather he presents an invitation to a self-appropriation which cognitively, morally, and religiously respects and seeks to promote the effective freedom of all human communities. The truth of the higher viewpoint offered by religion and faith is not a truth to be imposed, for such imposition and dominative use of religion has always been a sign, not of a profound faith, but of precisely those biased flights from understanding which genuine faith and religion heal.

As Lonergan pointedly indicated in his Roman lectures on the Incarnate Word: Divine wisdom and goodness saves humankind, not through forceful removal of evil, but the mystery of compassionate suffering whereby evil is transformed into good. Ecumenical dialogues within Christianity, as well as the dialogues among the world religions, point the way toward non-dominative affirmations of truth, each religious tradition affirming its truth and seeking, out of a deepened appropriation of that truth, to dialogue with others. If the modern age began in revulsion against the wars of religion, it is closing with a much stronger revulsion against the wars of nations. Ecumenism points the way toward dialectics and dialogue without force and domination.[81]

This has been no more than a brief introduction to the social and political dimensions of Bernard Lonergan's theology. I hope that it indicates in some small way how his invitation to "creative collaboration" is an intellectual praxis which is eminently practical and political. Surveying the technological, economic, and political contradictions causing so much suffering in the modern world, Lonergan's orientation and method are uniquely capable of removing the tumors of the many flights from insight and understanding without recourse to the violence, force, and domination which have been the hallmarks of empires and superpowers. If humankind on this planet has a future, then theology and religious institutions will have to collaborate in promoting communities of prayer, understanding, and redemptive praxis.

NOTES

[1]Cf. his *Method in Theology* (New York: Crossroad-Seabury, 1972), p. xi.

[2]Lonergan, *Insight: A Study of Human Understanding* (New York: Philosophical Library, 1958), p. 745.

[3]*Ibid.* p. 746.

[4]Cf. *Insight* pp. 372–74, 421–24. *Method in Theology* pp. 52–54, 241.

[5]Cf. *Insight* pp. 173ff.

[6]Cf. *Method in Theology* pp. 27–30. Note how Lonergan concentrates on the functional relations in the process of learning in terms of experiences, direct and reflective insights, decisions and actions, further experiences, etc. Thus Lonergan can write that *any* skill "can be analyzed as a group of combinations of differentiated operations."

[7]Cf. *Method in Theology* pp. 30–31.

[8]*Method in Theology* p. 27.

[9]Cf. *Insight* p. 294. This contrast also gave rise to the Cartesian contradiction between a supposedly "critical consciousness" and an "incredulous common sense"; cf. *Insight* pp. 84–86, 130–39, 289–99, 386ff.

[10]Cf. *Insight* pp. 411–21; also Lonergan's *Understanding and Being,* edited by Elizabeth and Mark Morelli (New York: The Edwin Mellen Press, 1980), pp. 113–19.

[11]Cf. *Insight* pp. 401–30, 514ff. This misreading of Lonergan is evident, from two very different perspectives, in Richard Roach's "Lonergan and Praxis" in *Communio* and Charles Davis' "Lonergan on Praxis" in *Science Religieuse.*

[12]*Ibid.* pp. xiii–xiv, emphasis mine. Lonergan himself recalled this in his Halifax Lectures; cf. *Understanding and Being* p. 101–19.

[13]*Insight* p. 182.

[14]*Ibid.* pp. 181–206; 385.

[15]*Ibid.* pp. 29 and 286.

[16] On emergent probability, cf. Charles Hefling's essay in this volume and references. Extroversion and concerns for physical needs are proper to this pattern of experience, cf. *Insight* pp. 182–84.

[17]Cf. *Insight* pp. 184f; *Method in Theology* pp. 61–64.

[18]*Insight* p. 186.

[19]Cf. *Method in Theology* pp. 105–07; *A Third Collection*, edited by Frederick Crowe (New York: Paulist Press, 1985) pp. 119–27.

[20]Cf. Sigmund Freud, *The Interpretation of Dreams* (New York: Avon Books, 1965) pp. 175–78, 193–95, 626–60. Paul Ricoeur, *Freud and Philosophy: An Essay in Interpretation* (New Haven: Yale University Press, 1970) pp. 180–86. On the tragic in Freud, as well as the misunderstandings of Freud due to translation, cf. Bruno Bettelheim, *Freud & Man's Soul* (New York: Knopf, 1983), especially pp. 91–112. In the final chapter of *Civilization and Its Discontents* Freud indicated how censorship is related to aggression and death.

[21]Cf. *Insight* pp. 187–206. For Lonergan the psychic, with its censorship functions, mediates between the organic and the intellectual schemes of recurrence in human living. On the unconscious and pre-conscious in Lonergan, cf. *ibid.* pp. 455–87. Also cf. the work of Robert Doran, especially *Subject and Psyche* (Washington, DC: University Press of America, 1977).

[22]Cf. *Insight* pp. 207–11; *Method in Theology* pp. 47–51.

[23]Cf. Karl Marx, *Capital* (New York: International Publishers, 1973) volume I, pp. 322–35. Domination and conflict with nature and with other humans are primordial for Marx and inform his understanding of cooperation as dominative. Thus, Marx holds that Linguet is probably correct in declaring "hunting to be the first form of cooperation, and man-hunting (war) one of the earliest forms of hunting" (p. 334). Genuine freedom for Marx could only begin, even under communism, only *after* labor had procured the particular goods or basic necessities; cf. *Capital* volume III, pp. 819–21.

[24]Cf. Paul Ricoeur, *Freud and Philosophy: An Essay on Interpretation*, translated by Denis Savage (New Haven: Yale University Press, 1970) pp. 32–36. Ricoeur has a third master of suspicion, Friedrich Nietzsche, who will be mentioned later in regard to general bias. Also Lonergan's *A Third Collection* pp. 157, 160; and Charles Reagan and David Stewart, eds., *The Philosophy of Paul Ricoeur: An Anthology of His Work* (Boston: Beacon Press, 1978) pp. 213–19.

[25]Cf. *Insight* pp. 198–99, 233, 238, 241, 625.

[26]Cf. Hefling on emergent probability and schemes of recurrence. On the self-correcting process of learning, cf. *Insight* pp. 174–75, 286–303, 706, 713–18.

[27]*Insight* p. 206.

[28]Cf. *Insight* pp. 207–09, 235.

[29]Cf. *A Third Collection* p. 107. This, of course, does not mean that everyone who espouses the principles of materialism is a manipulator. Lonergan clearly differentiates between theoretical inferences and those who espouse the theories, cf. *Insight* p. 625.

[30]*Method in Theology* p. 49; *Insight* pp. 213–14.

[31]*Method in Theology* p. 49.

[32]*Ibid.*

[33]Cf. *Insight* pp. 213–14.

[34]Cf. *Method in Theology* pp. 79–81.

[35]This orientation of the good of order toward freedom and interpersonal relations was omitted by Michael Novak in his false presentation of Lonergan's understanding of the human good in *The Spirit of Democratic Capitalism* (New York: American Enterprise Institute, 1982) pp. 71–80.

[36]Cf. *Method in Theology* pp. 30–32, 50, 104–05.

[37]*Method in Theology* pp. 50–51.

[38]Cf. *Insight* pp. 211–14; *Method in Theology* pp. 50–52, 79–81, 356–61.

[39]Cf. Walter Conn, *Christian Conversion* (New York: Paulist Press, 1986).

[40]*Method in Theology* pp. 356–57, also 268–69.

[41]Cf. *Insight* pp. 196–99.

[42]*Insight* pp. xxiv–xxvi, 91–102, 421–23.

[43]Cf. *Method in Theology* pp. 20ff, 181–96.

[44]*Insight* p. 212.

[45]*Method in Theology* pp. 47–52.

[46]*Insight* pp. 442ff, 473: "Now the tension that is inherent in the finality of all proportionate being becomes in man a conscious tension. . . . Present desires and fears have to be transmuted and the transmutation is not desirable to present desire but fearful to present fear. Moreover, as has been noted, the organism reaches its highest differentiation under the psychic integration of the animal, and the psyche reaches its highest differentiation under the intellectual integration in man. Because psychic development is so much more extensive and intricate in man than in other animals, it is involved in a more prolonged tension and it is open to more acute and diversified crises." Also pp. 477–78.

[47]For a general introduction to these contrasts, cf. Gregory Baum, *Religion and Alienation* (New York: Paulist Press, 1975) esp. pp. 41–61, 162–92. Jürgen Habermas, *The Theory of Communicative Action* (Boston: Beacon Press, 1984–86); Anthony Giddens, *Central Problems in Social Theory* (Berkeley: University of California Press, 1979) and his *The Constitution of Society* (Berkeley: University of California Press, 1984).

[48]Cf. *Insight* pp. 477–78, 627–29.

[49]Cf. "Dialectic of Authority" in Lonergan's *Third Collection.*

[50]*Insight* p. 215.

[51]Cf. *Insight* p. 238.

[52]*Is Modern Culture Doomed?* by Andrew J. Krzensinski (New York: Devin-Adair, 1942) reviewed by Bernard Lonergan in *The Canadian Register* September 19, 1949, p. 8.

[53]*Insight* p. 218; also his *De Verbo Incarnato* (Rome: Gregorian University Press, 1964) pp. 552ff. and his review of C. Houselander's *This War Is the Passion* in *The Canadian Register* April 11, 1942, p. 5 (Quebec edition).

[54]On Lonergan's notion of dialectic, cf. the exchange with Glenn Hughes in *Method: A Journal of Lonergan Studies* 1983 pp. 60–73; also *Insight* pp. 206, 422.

[55]*Insight* p. 218.

[56]*Ibid.* pp. 218–22. On pathological, as distinct from healthy, instrumentality of experience, cf. Lonergan's *Philosophy of Education,* chapter 9, to be published in the forthcoming *Collected Works* by the University of Toronto Press.

[57]*Insight* p. 223.

[58]Cf. *Insight* pp. 224–25, 235, 630ff.

[59]*Insight* p. 226.

[60]Cf. Paul Ricoeur, *Freud and Philosophy* pp. 32–36. Lonergan addresses these themes in *Insight* pp. 228–34, 627ff; *Method in Theology* pp. 33–34; *Collection* pp. 246ff.

[61]*Understanding and Being* pp. 290–91.

[62]Lonergan, *Understanding and Being,* p. 291. The Halifax Lectures of 1958 indicate, in regard to this issue, a move by Lonergan to a more differentiated attention to the fourth level of values in his later work.

[63]*Insight* p. 232.

[64]For a comprehensive introduction to these alternatives in the longer cycle of decline, cf. Peter Paret, ed., *Makers of Modern Strategy: From Machiavelli to the Nuclear Age* (Princeton: Princeton University Press, 1986). Note Lonergan's dark description of our situation in *Insight* p. 232: "What is the subsequent course of the longer cycle generated by the general bias of common sense? In so far as the bias remains effective, there would seem to be only one answer. The totalitarian has uncovered a secret of power. To defeat him is not to eliminate a permanent temptation to try once more his methods. Those not subjected to the temptation by their ambitions or their needs, will be subjected to it by their fears of danger and by their insistence on self-protection. So in an uneasy peace, in the unbroken tension of a prolonged emergency, one totalitarianism calls forth another. On an earth made small by a vast human population, by limited natural resources, by rapid and

easy communications, by extraordinary powers of destruction, there will arise sooner or later the moment when the unstable equilibrium will seem threatened and the gamble of war will appear the lesser risk to some of the parties involved. If the war is indecisive, the basic situation is unchanged. If it is totally destructive, the longer cycle has come to its end. If there results a single world empire, then it inherits both the objective stagnation of the social surd and the warped mentality of totalitarian practicality; but it cannot whip up the feverish energy of fear or of ambition; it has no enemy to fight; it has no intelligible goal to attain."

[65]Cf. *Insight* pp. 238–39.

[66]*Ibid.* p. 235. Throughout the sections of *Insight* dealing with the longer cycle of decline, Lonergan uses many expressions to convey the evil it wreaks on humanity: "total war," "world empire," "complete disintegration and decay," "ultimate nihilism," "the destruction of all that has been achieved"; cf. pp. 232–35.

[67]Cf. *Insight* pp. 15–25.

[68]*Ibid.* p. 236.

[69]Cf. *Method in Theology* pp. 52–55, 93–99. On effective freedom, cf. *Insight* pp. 607–33. Note how Lonergan's notion of freedom is one of effective empowerment, one which transposes the classical notion of virtue into the context of intentionality analysis. When one is inattentive, stupid, irrational, or irresponsible, one is not expanding one's freedom. Quite the contrary, it is being constricted and jeopardized.

[70]*Ibid.* pp. 238–42.

[71]Lonergan's economics manuscript will be published within the next two years as a volume in his *Collected Works* by the University of Toronto Press. Among the very few professional economists who have read it in manuscript form there are interesting reactions. Those within Western capitalist cultures tend to remark how Lonergan seems to have a good, but unexceptional, understanding of the accelerator functions in exchange economies. Those within Eastern communist countries tend to remark how the manuscript has a good, but unexceptional, understanding of the basic distributive functions. The present generation of economists in both cultures would require rather profound reorientations to appreciate how Lonergan's work revisions exchange economies.

[72]Cf. *Insight* pp. 619–33.

[73]Cf. *Insight* pp. 24–25, 687–730.

[74]*Insight* p. 741.

[75]Cf. chapters on Trinity and Philosophy of God. To my knowledge only Lonergan was able adequately to recover Aquinas' understanding of eternity as Infinite Presence transcendent to all spatiotemporal events. All the "acts"

of God are eternally God; thus creation did not occur "back at the beginning" "before" redemption. All these are imaginative constructions totally inadequate to an analogous understanding of God's Eternal Presence.

[76]Cf. the chapters by Joseph Komonchak and Stephen Happel.

[77]*Insight* p. 743. Also his "Creating and Healing in History" in *A Third Collection*.

[78]Cf. *Insight* pp. 742–48 and *Method in Theology* pp. 326–27 on "the shabby shell of Catholicism."

[79]Cf. *Insight* pp. 723–48; *Method in Theology* pp. 267–71; "Healing and Creating in History" and "Dialectic of Authority" and several other essays in *A Third Collection* pp. 5–34, 100–65. There are also a series of lectures on the pastoral mission of the Church which have not yet been published.

[80]*Insight* p. 728.

[81]Cf. *A Third Collection* pp. 55–73, 100–09, 202–250; also Vernon Gregson, *Lonergan, Spirituality, and the Meeting of Religions* (New York: University Press of America, 1985).

Selected Readings

General

ARTICLES BY LONERGAN

Lonergan, Bernard. "Cognitional Structure." *Collection.* Frederick E. Crowe (editor). (New York: Herder and Herder, 1967), pp. 221–239.

———. "Dimensions of Meaning." *Collection,* pp. 252–267.

———. "Existenz and Aggiornamento." *Collection,* pp. 240–251.

———. "*Insight* Revisited." *A Second Collection.* William F.J. Ryan and Bernard J. Tyrrell (editors). (Philadelphia: The Westminster Press, 1974), pp. 263–278.

———. "The Subject." *A Second Collection,* pp. 69–86.

———. "Theology in its New Context." *A Second Collection,* pp. 55–68.

ARTICLES BY OTHERS

Byrne, Patrick. "The Fabric of Lonergan's Thought." *Lonergan Workshop VI* (Scholars Press, 1986), pp. 1–84.

Crowe, Frederick E. "Bernard Lonergan." *The Encyclopedia of Religion. Mircea Eliade* (editor in chief). (New York: Macmillan Publishing Company, 1987), Vol. 9, pp. 19–20.

———. "Bernard Lonergan's Thought on Ultimate Reality and Meaning." *Ultimate Reality and Meaning,* 4: 1 (1981), pp. 58–89.

———. "Early Jottings on Bernard Lonergan's *Method in Theology,*" *Science et Esprit,* XXV: I, pp. 121–138.

———. "The Origin and Scope of Bernard Lonergan's *Insight.*" *Sciences Ecclesiastiques,* Vol. 9 (1957), pp. 263–295.

Gregson, Vernon. "The Dialogue of Religions and the Religious-Secular

Dialogue: The Foundational Perspective of Bernard Lonergan." *Journal of Ecumenical Studies,* 18: 4 (Fall 1981), pp. 537–560.
Shea, William M. "Horizons on Bernard Lonergan." *Horizons: Journal of the College Theology Society.* 15: 1 (1988), pp. 77–107.

BOOKS BY LONERGAN

Lonergan, Bernard. *A Third Collection.* Frederick E. Crowe (editor). New York: Paulist Press, 1985.

BOOKS BY OTHERS

Crowe, Frederick E. *Appropriating the Lonergan Idea.* Michael Vertin (editor). Catholic University of America, 1988.
———. *The Lonergan Enterprise.* Cambridge, Mass.: Cowley Publications, 1980.
Dunne, Tad. *Lonergan and Spirituality: Towards a Spiritual Integration.* Loyola University Press, 1985.
Fallon, Timothy and Riley, Philip (editors). *Religion in Context.* Lanham, MD: University Press of America, 1988.
Gregson, Vernon. *Lonergan, Spirituality, and the Meeting of Religions.* The College Theology Society: Studies in Religion 2. Lanham, MD: University Press of America, 1985.

Chapter I

ARTICLES BY LONERGAN

Lonergan, Bernard. "Cognitional Structure." *Collection,* Frederick E. Crowe (editor). (New York: Herder and Herder, 1967), pp. 221–239.
———. "Dimensions of Meaning," *Collection,* pp. 252–267.

ARTICLES BY OTHERS

Budenholzer, Frank. "Science and Religion: Seeking a Common Horizon." *Zygon: Journal of Religion and Science* 19 (1984), pp. 351–368.

Flanagan, Joseph. "Lonergan's Epistemology." *The Thomist* 36 (1972), pp. 75–97.

Gregson, Vernon. "The Dialogue of Religions and the Religious-Secular Dialogue: The Foundational Perspective of Bernard Lonergan." *Journal of Ecumenical Studies,* 18: 4 (Fall 1981), pp. 537–560.

Kroger, J. "Polanyi and Lonergan on Scientific Method." *Philosophy Today* 21 (1977), pp. 2–20.

MacKinnon, Edward M. "Cognitional Analysis and the Philosophy of Science." *Spirit as Inquiry: Studies in Honor of Bernard Lonergan, S. J. Continuum* 2 (1964), pp. 343–368.

Meynell, Hugo. "Lonergan's Theory of Knowledge and the Social Sciences." *New Blackfriars* 56 (1975), pp. 388–398.

Reck, Andrew J. "Insight and the Eros of the Mind." *The Review of Metaphysics* 12 (1958–59), pp. 97–107.

BOOKS BY LONERGAN

Lonergan, Bernard. *Insight: A Study of Human Understanding.* See esp. chs. 1–11. New York: Philosophical Library, 1958.

———. *Method in Theology.* See esp. ch. 1: Method. New York: Herder and Herder, 1972.

BOOKS BY OTHERS

Barden, Garrett and McShane, Philip. *Towards Self-Meaning: Exercises in Personal Knowledge.* New York: Herder and Herder, 1969.

Crowe, Frederick E. *The Lonergan Enterprise.* Cambridge, Mass.: Cowley Publications, 1980.

Haught, John. *Religion and Self-Acceptance.* New York: Paulist Press, 1976.

Novak, Michael. *Ascent of the Mountain, Flight of the Dove.* New York: Harper and Row, 1971.

Tracy, David. *The Achievement of Bernard Lonergan.* New York: Herder and Herder, 1970.

Chapter II

ARTICLES BY LONERGAN

Lonergan, Bernard. "Existenz and Aggiornamento." *Collection.* Frederick E. Crowe (editor). (New York: Herder and Herder, 1967), pp. 240–251.

————. "The Subject." *A Second Collection.* William F.J. Ryan and Bernard J. Tyrrell (editors). (Philadelphia: The Westminster Press, 1974), pp. 69–86.

————. "Religious Commitment." *The Pilgrim People: A Vision with Hope.* Joseph Papin (editor). (Villanova: Villanova University Press, 1970), pp. 45–69.

ARTICLES BY OTHERS

Conn, Walter E. "Passionate Commitment: The Dynamics of Affective Conversion." *Cross Currents* 34: 3 (Fall 1984), pp. 329–336.

————. "The Ontogenetic Ground of Value." *Theological Studies* 39: 2 (1976), pp. 313–335.

Crowe, Frederick E. "An Expansion of Lonergan's Notion of Value." *Lonergan Workshop VII* (Scholars Press, 1988), pp. 35–57.

Tyrrell, Bernard J. "Feelings as Apprehensive-Intentional Responses to Values." *Lonergan Workshop VII* (Scholars Press, 1988), pp. 331–360.

BOOKS BY LONERGAN

Lonergan, Bernard. *Insight: A Study of Human Understanding.* See esp. ch. 18: The Possibility of Ethics. New York: Philosophical Library, 1958.

————. *Method in Theology.* See esp. ch. 2: The Human Good. New York: Herder and Herder, 1972.

————. *Understanding and Being: An Introduction and Companion to Insight.* Elizabeth A. Morelli and Mark D. Morelli (editors). New York: Edwin Mellen Press, 1980.

BOOKS BY OTHERS

Carmody, John. *Reexamining Conscience.* New York: Seabury, 1982.

Conn, Walter E. (editor). *Conversion: Perspectives on Personal and Social Transformation.* New York: Alba House, 1978.

————. *Conscience: Development and Self-Transcendence.* Birmingham, AL: Religious Education Press, 1981.

————. *Christian Conversion: A Developmental Interpretation of Autonomy and Surrender.* New York: Paulist Press, 1986.

Gilligan, Carol. *In a Different Voice: Psychological Theory and Women's Development.* Cambridge: Harvard University Press, 1982.

Haughton, Rosemary. *The Transformation of Man: Conversion and Community.* New York: Paulist, 1967.

Kegan, Robert. *The Evolving Self: Problems and Process in Human Development.* Cambridge: Harvard University Press, 1982.

Kohlberg, Lawrence. *The Psychology of Moral Development.* San Francisco: Harper and Row, 1984.

Nelson, C. Ellis (editor). *Conscience: Theological and Psychological Perspectives.* New York: Paulist/Newman, 1973.

Chapter III

ARTICLES BY LONERGAN

Lonergan, Bernard. "Prolegomena to the Study of the Emerging Religious Consciousness of Our Time." *A Third Collection.* Frederick E. Crowe (editor). (New York: Paulist Press, 1985), pp. 55–73.

———. "Healing and Creating in History." *A Third Collection,* pp. 100–109.

ARTICLES BY OTHERS

Carmody, Denise L. "Lonergan's Religious Person." *Religion in Life.* 44: 2 (Summer 1975), pp. 222–231.

Crowe, Frederick E. "Complacency and Concern in the Thought of St. Thomas." *Theological Studies* 20 (1959), pp. 1–39, 198–230, 343–395.

Doran, Robert. "Jungian Psychology and Christian Spirituality." *Review for Religious* 38 (1979), pp. 497–510, 742–752, 857–866.

Price, James. "The Objectivity of Mystical Truth Claims." *The Thomist* 49 (1985), pp. 81–98.

———. "Lonergan and the Foundation of a Contemporary Mystical Theology." *Lonergan Workshop V* (Scholars Press, 1985), pp. 163–195.

BOOKS BY LONERGAN

Lonergan, Bernard. *Method in Theology.* See esp. ch. 4: Religion. New York: Herder and Herder, 1972, pp. 101–120.

———. *Philosophy of God, and Theology.* Philadelphia: Westminster, 1973.

———. *A Third Collection.* Frederick E. Crowe (editor). New York: Paulist Press, 1985.

BOOKS BY OTHERS

Conn, Walter E. (editor). *Conversion: Perspectives on Personal and Social Transformation.* New York: Alba House, 1978.

Dunne, Tad. *Lonergan and Spirituality: Towards a Spiritual Integration.* Chicago: Loyola University Press, 1987.

Fallon, Timothy and Riley, Philip (editors). *Religion and Culture: Essays in Honor of Bernard Lonergan.* Albany, NY: State University of New York Press, 1987.

Gregson, Vernon. *Lonergan, Spirituality, and the Meeting of Religions.* The College Theology Society: Studies in Religion 2. Lanham, MD: University Press of America, 1985.

Meynell, Hugo. *The Theology of Bernard Lonergan. AAR Studies in Religion* 42, Atlanta: Scholars Press, 1986.

Shea, William M. *The Naturalists and the Supernatural: Studies in Horizon and an American Philosophy of Religion.* Macon, Georgia: Mercer University Press, 1984.

Chapters IV & V

ARTICLES BY LONERGAN

Lonergan, Bernard. "Aquinas Today." *A Third Collection.* Frederick E. Crowe (editor). (New York: Paulist Press, 1985), pp. 35–54.

————. "The Future of Thomism." *A Second Collection.* William F.J. Ryan and Bernard J. Tyrrell (editors). (Philadelphia: The Westminster Press, 1974), pp. 43–54.

————. "Lectures on Religious Studies and Theology." *A Third Collection,* pp. 113–165.

————. "Theology in its New Context." *A Second Collection,* pp. 55–68.

————. "The Transition from a Classicist World-View to Historical-Mindedness." *A Second Collection,* pp. 1–10.

ARTICLES BY OTHERS

Crowe, Frederick E. "Development of Doctrine and the Ecumenical Problem." *Theological Studies* 23 (1962), pp. 27–46.

————. "Doctrines and Historicity in the Context of Lonergan's Method." *Theological Studies* 38 (1977), pp. 115–124.

————. "Dogma versus the Self-Correcting Process of Learning." *Foundations of Theology*. Philip McShane (editor). (Dublin: Gill and MacMillan, Ltd., 1971), pp. 22–40.

Gregson, Vernon. "On Learning from an Error." *Method: Journal of Lonergan Studies*, Vol. 1: 2 (October 1983), pp. 223–232.

————. "The Historian of Religions and the Theologian." *Creativity and Method: Essays in Honor of Bernard Lonergan, S.J.* Matthew Lamb (editor). (Milwaukee: Marquette University Press, 1981), pp. 141–152.

Helminiak, Daniel A. "Lonergan and Systematic Spiritual Theology." *New Blackfriars* 67 (1986), pp. 78–92.

Kelly, Anthony. "Is Lonergan's Method Adequate to Christian Mystery?" *The Thomist* 39 (1975), pp. 437–470.

Loewe, William. "Toward a Responsible Contemporary Soteriology." *Creativity and Method*, pp. 213–228.

McKinney, Ronald. "Lonergan's Notion of Dialectic." *The Thomist* 46 (1982), pp. 221–244.

Meynell, Hugo. "Lonergan's Method: Its Nature and Uses." *Scottish Journal of Theology* 27 (1974), pp. 162–180.

————. "Lonergan's Theory of Knowledge and the Social Sciences." *New Blackfriars* 56 (1975), pp. 388–398.

O'Callaghan, Michael. "Rahner and Lonergan on Foundational Theology." *Creativity and Method*, pp. 123–140.

Orsy, Ladislas. "Lonergan's Cognitional Theory and Foundational Issues in Canon Law." *Studia Canonica* 13 (1979), pp. 177–243.

Rahner, Karl. "Some Critical Thoughts on 'Functional Specialties in Theology.'" *Foundations of Theology*. (Dublin: Gill and Macmillan, Ltd., 1971), pp. 194–196.

Rende, Michael L. "The Development and the Unity of Lonergan's Notion of Conversion." *Method: Journal of Lonergan Studies* 1 (1983), pp. 158–173.

Riley, Philip. "History and Doctrine: The Foundational Character of Bernard Lonergan's 'Christian Philosophy.'" *Religious Studies and Theology* 5 (1985), pp. 79–96.

————. "Theology and/or Religious Studies: Bernard Lonergan's Option." *Lonergan Workshop IV* (Scholars Press, 1983), pp. 115–140.

Tekippe, Terry J. "On Learning from an Error: A Response to Vernon Gregson." *Method: Journal of Lonergan Studies*, 2: 1 (1984), pp. 41–48.

Tracy, David. "Lonergan's Foundational Theology: An Interpretation and a Critique." *Foundations of Theology*, pp. 197–222.

————. "Theological Models: An Exercise in Dialectics." *Lonergan Workshop II* (Scholars Press, 1980), pp. 83–108.
Vass, G. and Mathews, W. "Lonergan's Method: Two Views." *The Heythrop Journal*, 13 (1972), pp. 415–435.

BOOKS BY LONERGAN

Lonergan, Bernard. *Method in Theology*. See chs. 5–14. New York: Herder and Herder, 1972.
————. *Philosophy of God, and Theology*. Philadelphia: Westminster, 1973.
————. *The Way to Nicea: The Dialectical Development of Trinitarian Theology* (trans. Conn O'Donovan). Philadelphia: The Westminster Press, 1976.

BOOKS BY OTHERS

Crowe, Frederick E. *Son of God, Holy Spirit, and World Religions. The Contribution of Bernard Lonergan to the Wider Ecumenism*. Toronto: Regis College Press, 1985.
Doran, Robert. *Psychic Conversion and Theological Foundations: Toward a Reorientation of the Human Sciences*. AAR Studies in Religion 25, Scholars Press, 1981.
————. *Subject and Psyche: Ricoeur, Jung and the Search for Foundations*. Washington D.C.: University Press of America, 1977.
Gelpi, Donald. *Experiencing God: A Theology of Human Emergence*. New York: Paulist Press, 1978.
Hefling, Charles C. *Why Doctrines?* Cambridge, MA: Cowley Press, 1984.
Moore, Sebastian. *The Crucified Jesus Is No Stranger*. New York: Seabury, 1977.
————. *The Fire and the Rose Are One*. New York: Seabury, 1980.
O'Callaghan, Michael. *Unity in Theology: Lonergan's Framework for Theology in its New Context*. Lanham, MD: The University Press of America, 1980.

Chapter VI

ARTICLES BY LONERGAN

Lonergan, Bernard. "The Absence of God in Modern Culture." *A Second Collection*. William F.J. Ryan and Bernard J. Tyrrell (editors). (Philadelphia: The Westminster Press, 1974), pp. 101–116.

———. "Finality, Love, Marriage." *Collection.* Frederick E. Crowe (editor). (New York: Herder and Herder, 1967), pp. 16–53; see esp. pp. 18–22.

———. "Mission and the Spirit." *A Third Collection.* Frederick E. Crowe (editor). (New York: Paulist Press, 1985), pp. 23–34.

———. "The Natural Desire to See God." *Collection*, pp. 84–95.

———. "Natural Knowledge of God." *A Second Collection*, pp. 117–133.

———. "On God and Secondary Causes." *Collection*, pp. 54–67.

ARTICLES BY OTHERS

Byrne, Patrick H. "God and the Statistical Universe." *Zygon* 16 (1981), pp. 345–363.

———. "Relativity and Determinism." *Foundations of Physics* 11 (1981), pp. 913–932.

Hefling, Charles C. "Science and Religion." In *The New Dictionary of Theology.* Joseph A. Komonchak, Mary A. Collins, and Dermot A. Lane (editors). (Wilmington, DE: Michael Glazier, Inc., 1987), pp. 938–945.

Lawrence, Fred. "Method and Theology as Hermeneutical." *Creativity and Method: Essays in Honor of Bernard Lonergan, S.J.,* Matthew Lamb (editor). (Milwaukee: Marquette University Press, 1981), pp. 79–104; see esp. pp. 94–96.

McShane, Philip. "Insight and the Strategy of Biology." *Lonergan's Challenge to the University and the Economy.* (Washington, DC: University Press of America, 1980), pp. 42–59 and 164–168.

Melchin, Kenneth R. "History, Ethics, and Emergent Probability." *Lonergan Workshop VII* (Scholars Press, 1988), pp. 269–294.

Nilson, Jon. "Transcendent Knowledge in *Insight:* A Closer Look." *The Thomist* 37 (1973), pp. 366–377.

O'Donovan, Leo. "Emergent Probability and the Method of an Evolutionary World View." *The Personalist* 54: 3 (Summer 1973), pp. 250–273.

BOOKS BY LONERGAN

Lonergan, Bernard. *Philosophy of God, and Theology.* Philadelphia: Westminster, 1973.

———. *Understanding and Being: An Introduction and Companion to "Insight."* See esp. ch. 10, pp. 292–304. Elizabeth A. Morelli and Mark D. Morelli (editors). New York: Edwin Mellen Press, 1980.

BOOKS BY OTHERS

McShane, Philip. *Randomness, Statistics and Emergence.* Notre Dame: University of Notre Dame Press, 1970.

Melchin, Kenneth R. *History, Ethics and Emergent Probability.* See esp. pp. 59–121. Lanham, MD: University Press of America, 1987.

Meynell, Hugo. *The Intelligible Universe: A Cosmological Argument.* London: Macmillan, 1982.

Tyrrell, Bernard. *Bernard Lonergan's Philosophy of God.* Notre Dame: University of Notre Dame Press, 1974.

Chapters VII & VIII

ARTICLES BY LONERGAN

Lonergan, Bernard. "The Dehellenization of Dogma." *A Second Collection.* William F.J. Ryan and Bernard J. Tyrrell (editors). (Philadelphia: The Westminster Press, 1974), pp. 11–32.

ARTICLES BY OTHERS

Dunne, Tad. "Trinity and History." *Theological Studies* 45 (1984), pp. 139–152.

Meynell, Hugo. "Bernard Lonergan." *One God in Trinity.* Peter Toon and James Spiceland (editors). (Westchester, IL: Cornerstone Books: 1980), pp. 95–110.

Thomas Aquinas. *Summa Theologiae,* I, qq. 29–45.

BOOKS BY LONERGAN

Lonergan, Bernard. *De Deo Trino: Pars Dogmatica.* 2nd ed., Rome: Gregorian University Press, 1964.

———. *De Deo Trino: Pars Systematica.* 3rd ed., Rome: Gregorian University Press, 1964.

———. *Verbum: Word and Idea in Aquinas.* David B. Burrell (editor). Notre Dame: University of Notre Dame Press, 1967.

———. *The Way to Nicea: The Dialectical Development of Trinitarian The-*

ology (trans. Conn O'Donovan). Philadelphia: The Westminster Press, 1976.

BOOKS BY OTHERS

Meynell, Hugo. *The Theology of Bernard Lonergan. AAR Studies in Religion* 42, Atlanta: Scholars Press, 1986.
Murray, John Courtney. *The Problem of God Yesterday and Today.* New Haven: Yale University Press, 1964.

Chapter IX

ARTICLES BY LONERGAN

Lonergan, Bernard. "De Ente Supernaturali" (available through Lonergan Research Institute, Regis College, Toronto, Ontario).
———. "Mission and the Spirit." *A Third Collection.* Frederick E. Crowe (editor). (New York: Paulist Press, 1985), pp. 23–34.
———. "The Natural Desire to See God." *Collection.* Frederick E. Crowe (editor). (New York: Herder and Herder, 1967), pp. 252–267.
———. "Natural Knowledge of God." *A Second Collection.* William F.J. Ryan and Bernard J. Tyrrell (editors). (Philadelphia: The Westminster Press, 1974), pp. 117–133.
———. "Religious Experience." *A Third Collection,* pp. 113–128.
———. "St. Thomas' Thought on Gratia Operans." *Theological Studies* 2 (1941), pp. 289–324; 3 (1942), pp. 375–578.

ARTICLES BY OTHERS

Price, James. "Conversion and the Doctrine of Grace in Bernard Lonergan and John Climacus." *Anglican Theological Review* LXII: 4, pp. 338–362.
Quesnell, Quentin. "Grace." *The New Dictionary of Theology.* Joseph A. Komonchak, Mary A. Collins, and Dermot A. Lane (editors). (Wilmington, DE: Michael Glazier, Inc., 1987), pp. 437–450.

BOOKS BY LONERGAN

Lonergan, Bernard. *Grace and Freedom.* J. Patout Burns (editor). New York: Herder and Herder, 1971.

————. *Insight: A Study of Human Understanding.* See esp. ch. 20: Special Transcendent Knowledge. New York: Philosophical Library, 1958.

BOOKS BY OTHERS

Meynell, Hugo. *The Theology of Bernard Lonergan. AAR Studies in Religion* 42, Atlanta: Scholars Press, 1986.

Chapter X

ARTICLES BY LONERGAN

Lonergan, Bernard. "Christ as Subject: A Reply." *Collection.* Frederick E. Crowe (editor). (New York: Herder and Herder, 1967), pp. 164–197.
————. "Christology Today: Methodological Reflections." *A Third Collection.* Frederick E. Crowe (editor). (New York: Paulist Press, 1985), pp. 74–99.

ARTICLES BY OTHERS

Crowe, Frederick E. "Eschaton and Worldly Mission in the Mind and Heart of Jesus." *The Eschaton: A Community of Love.* J. Papin (editor). (Villanova: Villanova University Press, 1974), pp. 105–144.
————. "The Mind of Jesus." *Communio* 1, (1974), pp. 365–384.
————. "Son and Spirit: Tension in the Divine Missions?" *Science et Esprit* 35, (1983), pp. 153–169.
Hefling, Charles C. "Redemption and Intellectual Conversion: Notes on Lonergan's Christology Today." *Lonergan Workshop V* (Scholars Press, 1985), pp. 219–261.
Kereszty, Roch. "Psychological Subject and Consciousness in Christ." *Communio* 11 (1984), pp. 258–277.
Loewe, William. "Jesus Christ." *The New Dictionary of Theology.* Joseph A. Komonchak, Mary Collins, and Dermot A. Lane (editors). (Wilmington, DE: Michael Glazier, 1987), pp. 533–543.
Moloney, Raymond. "The Mind of Christ in Transcendental Theology: Rahner, Lonergan, and Crowe." *The Heythrop Journal* 25, (1984), pp. 288–300.

BOOKS BY LONERGAN

Lonergan, Bernard. *De Verbo Incarnato.* Rome: Gregorian University, 1964.

BOOKS BY OTHERS

Meynell, Hugo. *The Theology of Bernard Lonergan.* Chico, CA: Scholars Press, 1986.

Moore, Sebastian. *The Fire and the Rose Are One.* New York: Seabury, 1980.

Chapter XI

ARTICLES BY LONERGAN

Lonergan, Bernard. "The Redemption." *Three Lectures.* (Montreal: Thomas More Institute Papers, 1975), pp. 1–28.

ARTICLES BY OTHERS

Gregson, Vernon. "The Faces of Evil and Our Response: Ricoeur, Lonergan, Moore." *Religion in Context.* Timothy Fallon and Philip Riley (editors). (Lanham, MD: University Press of America, 1988).

Loewe, William. "Encountering the Crucified God: The Soteriology of Sebastian Moore." *Horizons* 9 (1982), pp. 216–236.

———. "Lonergan and the Law of the Cross: A Universalist View of Salvation." *Anglican Theological Review* 59 (1977), pp. 162–174.

———. "Toward a Responsible Contemporary Soteriology." *Creativity and Method: Essays in Honor of Bernard Lonergan, S.J.* Matthew Lamb (editor). (Milwaukee: Marquette University Press, 1981), pp. 213–228.

Ring, Nancy. "Sin and Transformation from a Systematic Perspective." *Chicago Studies* 23, (1984), pp. 303–319.

Vertin, Michael. "Philosophy of God, Theology, and the Problems of Evil." *Lonergan Workshop III* (Scholars Press, 1982), pp. 149–178.

BOOKS BY OTHERS

Gregson, Vernon. *Lonergan, Spirituality, and the Meeting of Religions.* See esp. ch. 4. The College Theology Society: Studies in Religion 2. Lanham, MD: University Press of America, 1985.

Moore, Sebastian. *The Crucified Jesus Is No Stranger.* New York: Seabury, 1977.

———. *The Fire and the Rose Are One.* New York: Seabury, 1980.

———. *The Inner Loneliness.* New York: Crossroad, 1982.

Chapter XII

ARTICLES BY LONERGAN

Lonergan, Bernard. "The Dialectic of Authority." *A Third Collection.* Frederick E. Crowe (editor). (New York: Paulist Press, 1985), pp. 5–12.

———. "Healing and Creating in History." *A Third Collection,* pp. 100–109.

ARTICLES BY OTHERS

Komonchak, Joseph A. "Ecclesiology and Social Theory: A Methodological Essay." *The Thomist* 45 (1981), pp. 262–283.

———. "History and Social Theory in Ecclesiology." *Lonergan Workshop II* (1981), pp. 1–53.

———. "Lonergan and the Tasks of Ecclesiology." *Creativity and Method: Essays in Honor of Bernard Lonergan, S.J.* Matthew Lamb (editor). (Milwaukee: Marquette University Press, 1981), pp. 265–273.

BOOKS BY LONERGAN

Lonergan, Bernard. *Method in Theology.* See esp. ch. 14: Communications. New York: Herder and Herder, 1972.

BOOKS BY OTHERS

Quesnell, Quentin. *The Authority for Authority.* Pere Marquette Theology Lecture. Milwaukee: Marquette University Press, 1973.

Chapter XIII

ARTICLES BY LONERGAN

Lonergan, Bernard. "Finality, Love, and Marriage." *Collection.* Frederick E. Crowe (editor). (New York: Herder and Herder, 1967), pp. 16–53.
———. "The Mass and Man." *The Catholic Mind,* 45 (September 1947), pp. 571–576.
———. "The Mediation of Christ in Prayer." *Method: Journal of Lonergan Studies,* 2 (March 1984) 1, pp. 1–26.

ARTICLES BY OTHERS

Hefling, Charles C. "Liturgy and Myth: A Theological Approach Based on the Methodology of Bernard Lonergan." *Anglican Theological Review,* 61, pp. 200–223.
Happel, Stephen. "Sacrament: Symbol of Conversion." *Creativity and Method: Essays in Honor of Bernard Lonergan, S.J.* Matthew Lamb (editor). (Milwaukee: Marquette University Press, 1981), pp. 275–290.
———. "Whether Sacraments Liberate Communities: Some Reflections upon Image as an Agent in Achieving Freedom." *Lonergan Workshop* V (Scholars Press, 1985), pp. 197–218.
———. "Prayer and Sacrament: A Role in Foundational Theology." *The Thomist,* 45 (1981), pp. 243–261.
Shea, William M. "Sacraments and Meaning." *The American Ecclesiastical Review,* 169: 6 (1975), pp. 403–416.

BOOKS BY OTHERS

Grimes, Ron L. *Beginnings in Ritual Studies.* Lanham, MD: University Press of America, 1982.

Chapter XIV

ARTICLES BY LONERGAN

Lonergan, Bernard. "Christ as Subject: A Reply." *Collection.* Frederick E. Crowe (editor). (New York: Herder and Herder, 1967), pp. 164–197.

————. "Christology Today: Methodological Reflections." *A Third Collection.* Frederick E. Crowe (editor). (New York: Paulist Press, 1985), pp. 74–99.

————. "Healing and Creating in History." *A Third Collection,* pp. 100–112.

————. "Mission and Spirit." *A Third Collection,* pp. 23–34.

————. "Pope John's Intention." *A Third Collection,* pp. 224–238.

————. "A Post-Hegelian Philosophy of Religion." *A Third Collection,* pp. 202–223.

————. "Prolegomena to the Study of the Emerging Religious Consciousness of Our Time." *A Third Collection,* pp. 55–73.

————. "Theology and Praxis." *A Third Collection,* pp. 184–200.

ARTICLES BY OTHERS

Byrne, Patrick. "Economic Transformations: The Role of Conversions and Culture in the Transformation of Economics." *Religion and Culture: Essays in Honor of Bernard Lonergan, S.J.* (Albany: State University of New York Press, 1987), pp. 327–348.

Copeland, M. Shawn. "The Interaction of Racism, Sexism and Classism in Women's Exploitation." *Concilium: Women, Work, and Poverty.* Anne Carr and Elisabeth Schüssler Fiorenza (editors). (Edinburgh: T. & T. Clark, 1987), pp. 19–27.

Crowe, Frederick E. "Eschaton and Worldly Mission in the Mind and Heart of Jesus." *The Eschaton: A Community of Love.* J. Papin (editor). (Villanova: Villanova University Press, 1974), pp. 105–144.

————. "The Mind of Jesus." *Communio* 1 (1974), pp. 365–384.

————. "Son and Spirit: Tension in the Divine Missions?" *Science et Esprit* 35 (1983), pp. 153–169.

Doran, Robert. "From Psychic Conversion to the Dialectic of Community." *Lonergan Workshop VI* (1986), pp. 85–107.

————. "Theological Grounds for a World-Cultural Humanity." *Creativity and Method: Essays in Honor of Bernard Lonergan, S.J.,* Matthew Lamb (editor). (Milwaukee: Marquette University Press, 1981), pp. 105–122.

————. "Suffering Servanthood and the Scale of Values." *Lonergan Workshop IV* (1983), pp. 41–67.

Hefling, Charles C. "Redemption and Intellectual Conversion: Notes on Lonergan's Christology Today." *Lonergan Workshop V* (Scholars Press, 1985), pp. 219–261.

Lawrence, Fred. "Basic Christian Community: An Issue of 'Mind and the

Mystery of Christ.' " *Lonergan Workshop V* (Scholars Press, 1985), pp. 263–287.

————. "Method and Theology as Hermeneutical." *Creativity and Method,* pp. 79–104.

Melchin, Kenneth R. "History, Ethics, and Emergent Probability." *Lonergan Workshop VII* (Scholars Press, 1988), pp. 269–294.

Tracy, David. "Theologies of Praxis." *Creativity and Method,* pp. 35–52.

BOOKS BY LONERGAN

Lonergan, Bernard. *Insight: A Study in Human Understanding.* See esp. pp. ix–xxx, 173–244, New York: Philosophical Library, 1958.

BOOKS BY OTHERS

Conn, Walter E. *Conscience: Development and Self-Transcendence.* Birmingham: Religious Education Press, 1981.

Lamb, Matthew L. *Solidarity with Victims: Toward a Theology of Social Transformation.* New York: Crossroad, 1982.

Melchin, Kenneth R. *History, Ethics and Emergent Probability.* Lanham, MD: University Press of America, 1987.

Contributors

DENISE LARDNER CARMODY, PH.D., is university professor and chair of the Faculty of Religion at the University of Tulsa. She is also Director of the Warren Center for Catholic Studies. Her most recent publications are *Biblical Woman; Women and World Religion, 2nd ed.; The Story of World Religions;* and *Exploring the Hebrew Bible.*

WALTER E. CONN, PH.D., is professor of religious studies at Villanova University. He is also the editor of *Horizons: Journal of the College Theology Society.* He is the author of *Conscience: Development and Self-Transcendence* and *Christian Conversion: A Developmental Interpretation of Autonomy and Surrender.*

ROBERT M. DORAN, PH.D., is associate professor of theology at Regis College, Toronto School of Theology, and assistant director of Lonergan Research Institute, Toronto. With Frederick E. Crowe, he is a general editor of *The Collected Works of Bernard Lonergan* (University of Toronto Press). He is author of *Subject and Psyche, Psychic Conversion and Theological Foundations,* and *Dialectic in History* (forthcoming).

VERNON J. GREGSON, PH.D., is associate professor of religious studies at Loyola University, New Orleans and former chair of the department. He is the author of *Lonergan, Spirituality and the Meeting of Religions.* His essays have appeared in the *Journal of Ecumenical Studies, Horizons, Creativity and Method,* and *Religion in Context.*

CHARLES C. HEFLING, JR., PH.D., TH.D., is associate professor of theology at Boston College, where he also oversees the Lonergan Center. He is a priest of the Episcopal Church and the author of *Jacob's Ladder: Theology and Spirituality in the Thought of Austin Farrer* and *Why Doctrines?*

JEAN HIGGINS, PH.D., is professor of religion at Smith College. Her dissertation was on Bernard Lonergan: *Cultural Adaptation in a Revealed Re-*

ligion: An Analysis of the Transcultural Problem, Using the Categories of Bernard Lonergan, 1972. She has published articles in the *Journal of Biblical Literature*, the *Journal of The American Academy of Religion*, and *Cross Currents*. She is presently at work on a book on the Japanese novelist Shusaku Endo.

JOSEPH A. KOMOCHAK, PH.D., is associate professor of theology in the Department of Religion and Religious Education at the Catholic University of America, where he teaches courses on the church and on the history and theology of the Second Vatican Council. Co-editor of *The New Dictionary of Theology*, he has published articles in *Theological Studies The Thomist, The Jurist*, and *Concilium*.

MATTHEW L. LAMB, TH.D., is professor of theology at Boston College. He is the author of *History, Method, and Theology* and *Solidarity with Victims: Toward a Theology of Social Transformation*. His essays have appeared in *Creativity and Method, Language, Truth and Meaning*, and *La Pratique de la Theologie Politique*.

WILLIAM P. LOEWE, PH.D., is associate professor in the Department of Religion and Religious Education at the Catholic University of America. His articles have appeared in such journals as *Anglican Theological Review, Catholic Biblical Quarterly, Heythrop Journal, Horizons*, and *The Thomist*.

QUENTIN QUESNELL, S.S.D., is professor and chair of the Department of Religion and Biblical Literature at Smith College. He has published numerous studies on aspects of Lonergan's thought, and has most recently translated and edited the *De Deo Trino* for *The Collected Works of Bernard Lonergan*, to be published by the University of Toronto Press.

Index of Subjects and Authors